McGraw-Hill Reading

Wonders

Grade 4

W9-AWN-744

Your Turn
Practice Book

McGraw Hill Education

Bothell, WA • Chicago, IL • Columbus, OH • New York, NY

www.mheonline.com/readingwonders

C

The *McGraw-Hill* Companies

 Education

Copyright © The McGraw-Hill Companies, Inc.

All rights reserved. No part of this publication may be
reproduced or distributed in any form or by any means, or
stored in a database or retrieval system, without the prior
written consent of The McGraw-Hill Companies, Inc., including,
but not limited to, network storage or transmission, or
broadcast for distance learning.

Send all inquiries to:
McGraw-Hill Education
2 Penn Plaza
New York, NY 10121

Printed in the United States of America.

4 5 6 7 8 9 QMD 17 16 15 14 13

Contents

Unit 1 • Think It Through

Contents

Unit 2 • Amazing Animals

Contents

Unit 3 • That's the Spirit!

Contents

Unit 4 • Fact or Fiction?

Contents

Unit 5 • Figure It Out

Making It Happen

On the Move

Inventions

Zoom In

TIME For Kids

Contents

Unit 6 • Past, Present, and Future

Name _____

gracious	flattened	muttered	brainstorm
stale	frantically	official	original

Finish each sentence using the vocabulary word provided.

1. **(gracious)** The young girl _____

_____

2. **(stale)** After two days _____

_____

3. **(flattened)** He always fixed his hair _____

_____

4. **(frantically)** After we got separated _____

_____

5. **(muttered)** I could not hear _____

_____

6. **(official)** After she won the cooking contest, _____

_____

7. **(brainstorm)** We all decided to _____

_____

8. **(original)** The second book he wrote _____

_____

Name _____

Read the selection. Complete the sequence graphic organizer.

| **Character** |
| |
| **Setting** |
| |
| **Beginning** |
| |
| **Middle** |
| |
| **End** |
| |

Name _____

Read the passage. Use the make, confirm, or revise predictions strategy to predict what will happen in the story.

Coyote's Song

A boy was eating lunch in a field on his grandmother's farm.

12 | Her farm was large and he had explored and seen many things that
25 | morning. "Do not wander into the woods," Grandmother said. So he
36 | kept to the fields. As he ate his lunch, he heard the call of a blue jay.

53 | "I'll follow the sound of Blue Jay. I will find him and see his blue
68 | feathers and listen to his song. I will bring him bread."

79 | The afternoon sun was hot and there were many hills to climb,
91 | but the boy was determined to follow the call. He walked slowly and
104 | cautiously with care.

107 | Soon he ran into Coyote who was looking for lunch but not having
120 | any luck. He did not have a single crumb or morsel of food.

133 | "Hello," said Coyote. "I see you are enjoying an afternoon walk."

144 | "I've been exploring Grandmother's farm and now I'm looking for
154 | Blue Jay. I want to listen to his song, see his beautiful feathers, and
168 | give him bread."

171 | Coyote took one look at the bread and became hungrier. Quietly,
182 | he muttered to himself, "I will trick that boy, then he'll give me that
196 | bread."

197 | "I can sing a song and perform for you. Then you can give me your
212 | bread," Coyote said with a grin.

218 | "But howling and barking isn't a song, and you only have brown
230 | fur," said the boy. "I want to hear Blue Jay's song and admire his
244 | feathers, and I only have enough bread for him."

Name _____

Coyote's original plan didn't work, so he quickly thought of a new one. "Then I'll help you find Blue Jay," said Coyote. "I know where he sings. I can take you there through the woods."

The boy remembered Grandmother's warning. What was the harm, the boy thought to himself. "Then let's go," said the boy.

"We must run! Blue Jay will depart soon and then he'll be gone," said Coyote. Coyote began running through the woods calling out for the boy to run faster and faster.

The boy did not want to miss Blue Jay, yet the faster he ran the more he stumbled and tripped on tree roots. The woods became thicker and thicker, making it harder for the boy to run.

Accustomed to running in the woods, Coyote was used to jumping over the roots so he didn't fall. "Hurry! Blue Jay and his song and feathers will leave!" said Coyote.

"You could run faster if you were not slowed down and burdened by having to carry that bread. I can carry it for you, and then you can run faster," said Coyote.

"If you think that will help," said the boy, "here is the bread."

Coyote took the bread in his mouth and disappeared.

"Thank you for the meal!" Coyote howled as he ate the bread.

The boy had been tricked, and now he was lost in the woods. By evening he found his way back to Grandmother's home and explained to her what happened.

"You should know that leaving the right path to follow an easier one leads to trouble," she said. "Luckily, you only lost some old, stale bread."

Name _____

A. Reread the passage and answer the questions.

1. What are two events that happen after the boy hears Blue Jay?

_____

_____

_____

2. Why is the setting of the woods important to the story?

_____

_____

_____

3. Use the sequence of events to summarize the plot.

_____

_____

_____

_____

B. Work with a partner. Read the passage aloud. Pay attention to intonation. Stop after one minute. Fill out the chart.

	Words Read	–	Number of Errors	=	Words Correct Score
First Read		–		=	
Second Read		–		=	

Name _____

Before the Ball

I waved my wand. Light flashed, and in a puff of smoke, the pumpkin transformed into a beautiful horse and carriage! I turned to Cinderella and smiled. "Not bad. What do you think?" I asked.

"It's perfect!" Cinderella shouted. "How can I ever repay you for all you have done?"

"You can get into that carriage and get to the ball on time!" I said, and sent her on her way.

Finally, Cinderella was off to the ball. My work was done.

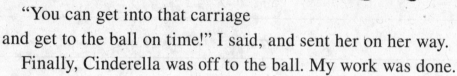

Answer the questions about the text.

1. How do you know this story is a fairy tale?

   _____

2. What events in the text identify it as a fairy tale?

   _____

3. What task does the main character have to complete? How does she complete it?

   _____

   _____

4. What other text feature does "Before the Ball" include? How does it show that the story is a fairy tale?

   _____

   _____

Read the sentences below. Circle the synonym clue in the sentence that helps you understand the meaning of each word in bold. Then, in your own words, write the meaning of the word in bold.

1. It can be fun to **explore** all the rooms of a museum. You can discover things you have never seen.

   _____

2. The pilot told us the plane would **depart** in five minutes. We were glad it would leave on time.

   _____

3. The camel moved slowly, **burdened** by all packages it carried. People who saw the camel thought it was too loaded down.

   _____

4. She **stumbled** into the room, tripping over the small step she had not seen in the doorway.

   _____

5. It was the **howling** that frightened the campers. Never before had they heard such a loud barking sound in the woods.

   _____

6. My cousin got **accustomed** to sleeping late during the summer. It was hard for her to get used to waking up early once school started.

   _____

7. When it came time to **perform** for the judge, the singer was not nervous. He had been singing in contests since he was a child.

   _____

Name _____

A. Read each sentence. Circle the word that has a short-vowel sound. Write the word on the line.

1. The strange bell always chimes so late! _____

2. My poor health was a good reason to stay home. _____

3. The tire was flat, so we needed to wait. _____

4. I could hear the crunch of the toy falling down the stairs. _____

5. She gave the team hints so they could find the clue. _____

B. Write the correct -ed, -s, and -ing forms for each verb.

Verb	+ ed	+ s	+ ing
1. float	_____	_____	_____
2. work	_____	_____	_____
3. start	_____	_____	_____
4. follow	_____	_____	_____
5. answer	_____	_____	_____

Name _____

Evidence is details and examples from a text that support a writer's ideas. The student who wrote the paragraph below cited evidence to show how the author used the story events to develop the character and plot.

Topic sentence →   In "Coyote's Song" the author uses a series of events to show what happens when a boy does not listen to his grandmother. At the beginning of the story, the boy's

Evidence →   grandmother warns him not to go into the woods. At first the boy listens, but then he meets Coyote. Through a series of events, Coyote convinces the boy to go into the woods. Then Coyote steals the boy's bread and leaves him in the woods. The boy makes it home, but he has learned a lesson.

Concluding statement →   The clear sequence of events makes it easy to understand how Coyote was able to trick the boy and steal his bread.

Write a paragraph about the text you have chosen. Cite evidence from the text that shows how the author used sequence of events to develop the plot. Remember to use evidence to support ideas and to use different sentence types.

Write a topic sentence: _____

_____

Cite evidence from the text: _____

_____

_____

_____

_____

_____

End with a concluding statement: _____

_____

Name _____

A. Read the draft model. Use the questions that follow the draft to help you think about what descriptive details you can add.

Draft Model

Once there was a princess who lived in a castle. She was tired of climbing stairs. She asked her father for a platform she could stand on that would carry her from floor to floor. Today we call it an elevator.

---

1. When and where does this story take place?

2. What descriptive details can be added to help the reader visualize the princess?

3. Why was the princess tired of climbing stairs?

4. What descriptive details could provide more information about the elevator?

B. Now revise the draft by adding descriptive details that create a clearer picture of the princess, her father, and the elevator.

_____

_____

_____

_____

_____

_____

_____

_____

Name _____

accountable	desperately	humiliated	self-esteem
advise	hesitated	inspiration	uncomfortably

Finish each sentence using the vocabulary word provided.

1. **(desperately)** Even though the girl was very tired, _____

   _____

2. **(self-esteem)** After the boy's team won a soccer game, _____

   _____

3. **(inspiration)** The girl's amazing science fair project _____

   _____

4. **(accountable)** The teacher told the students _____

   _____

5. **(advise)** I know the dentist will _____

   _____

6. **(uncomfortably)** During the summer, _____

   _____

7. **(hesitated)** The child walked to the edge of the pool but _____

   _____

8. **(humiliated)** At her dance performance, the girl _____

   _____

Name _____

Read the selection. Complete the problem and solution graphic organizer.

Character

Setting

Problem

Event

Event

Solution

Name _____

Read the passage. Use the make predictions strategy to check your understanding.

The Cyber Bully

15	Every time I got on the school bus, I felt sick and got butterflies in my stomach. I had recently moved to a new school, and no one on the
30	bus talked to me. I was certain I would never make any new friends.
44	Right off the bat, the very first week of school, I was in deep trouble.
59	It all started when my teacher, Mr. Evers, took us to the computer
72	lab to do an assignment. I was logging in when I noticed my
85	classmate, Corey, watching my fingers on the keyboard. He looked at
96	me and smirked. I could tell something was wrong.
105	"I know your password, Aaron," Corey said.
112	"Um…ok," I said.
116	Right away he logged into his computer using my password!
126	I thought about telling Mr. Evers, but I didn't want the other kids to
140	think I was a tattle-tale. After all, I was the new kid, and I didn't
155	want to get off on the wrong foot or make a bad impression. I decided
170	to just focus on my work.
176	A few minutes later I heard Mr. Evers say, "Aaron? Could you
188	come here for a second?"
193	Just as I was getting up, I got a message. "You better keep your
207	mouth shut," it said. I couldn't tell who it came from since it was
221	from my own account.
225	"What is the meaning of this e-mail you sent me?" said Mr. Evers.
238	I read it but couldn't believe my eyes!
246	"But I haven't been on e-mail at all!" I said. Then I realized that it
261	was Corey using my e-mail!

Name _____

"I...I..." I said. I felt like I was stuck between a rock and a hard place. I wanted desperately to tell the truth, but that would mean getting Corey into trouble. I worried about what the other students would think of me. I hesitated, thinking about what to do.

"I'm sorry," I said, deciding not to tell what happened.

"I'm giving you detention after school today," said Mr. Evers. He pulled out a pink detention slip and wrote my name on it. I felt humiliated as I walked back to my seat.

When the bell rang at the end of school, everyone got up from their desks to leave. I stayed behind to serve detention.

"Too bad," Corey laughed as he was leaving. Then it hit me. Corey would continue to bully me if I let him. I decided to be brave. I got up and walked over to Mr. Evers.

"Mr. Evers," I said. "I have something to tell you." I told him the whole truth about Corey stealing my password and using my account, and that I was sorry for not saying so earlier.

"I see," said Mr. Evers. "I would advise you to always tell the truth, Aaron, even if it means someone else might get in trouble. I will have a talk with Corey tomorrow."

I was still worried that the other students would be mad at me for telling Mr. Evers what Corey had done. But on the bus that afternoon a girl I recognized from my class sat next to me.

"I heard about what happened," she said softly. "You know you could have told us. No one should have to face a bully alone."

Another kid from my class turned around with a big grin on his face.

"Alana is right," the boy said. "We would have helped you. What are friends for? Hi, my name is Quentin."

Name _____

A. Reread the passage and answer the questions.

1. What problem does Aaron face?

_____

_____

_____

2. Why is Aaron worried about telling Mr. Evers the truth?

_____

_____

_____

3. What is the solution to Aaron's problem?

_____

_____

_____

B. Work with a partner. Read the passage aloud. Pay attention to expression and rate. Stop after one minute. Fill out the chart.

	Words Read	–	Number of Errors	=	Words Correct Score
First Read		–		=	
Second Read		–		=	

Name _____

Paul's Mix-Up

"You're going to be at the show next week, right, Paul?" Rosa asked as the students packed up their instruments.

"Of course I am!" Paul said. "We've been practicing for months!"

Luis looked at Paul with curiosity. "You said you might not be able to make it. What about the trip you're taking with your family?"

Paul froze. All week long he had been thinking about their show. He had forgotten about his family trip!

Answer the questions about the text.

1. How can you tell this story is realistic fiction?

_____

_____

2. What literary elements does the text include?

_____

_____

3. How does the dialogue make the story realistic?

_____

_____

4. What details about Paul make him a believable character?

_____

_____

Name _____

A. Read the idioms in the box. Find and underline an idiom in each sentence below. Then circle the context clues that help you understand the idiom.

butterflies in my stomach	between a rock and a hard place
right off the bat	get off on the wrong foot

1. Every time I got on the school bus, I felt sick, and got butterflies in my stomach. I had recently moved to a new school, and no one on the bus talked to me. I was certain I would never make any new friends.

2. Right off the bat, the very first week of school, I was in deep trouble.

3. I felt like I was stuck between a rock and a hard place. I wanted desperately to tell the truth, but that would mean getting Corey into trouble.

4. I didn't want to get off on the wrong foot or make a bad impression.

B. Read the sentences below. Underline each idiom. For each idiom, write a definition in your own words.

1. The test was a piece of cake because the questions were so easy.

   _____

   _____

2. He kept bothering me until I told him to cut it out.

   _____

   _____

Name _____

A. Circle the word with a long *a* vowel sound to complete each sentence. Then write it on the line to complete the sentence.

1. She had a big smile on her _____.

   face   hand   fan

2. The show will begin at _____ tonight.

   nine   five   eight

3. The drum _____ marched with the band.

   major   manner   jam

4. My feet _____ after walking so much!

   halt   ache   sleep

5. The cars stopped at the _____ crossing.

   cattle   railway   street

B. Circle the correct form of the verb in the right column. Then match the verb in the left column to its correct form.

Verb	Verb + *-ed* or *-ing*
1. dive	createing / creating
2. shake	carved / carveed
3. believe	diving / diveing
4. create	shacking / shaking
5. carve	believeed / believed

Name _____

Evidence is details and examples from a text that support a writer's opinion. The student who wrote the paragraph below cited evidence that supports his or her opinion about how well the author used realistic characters and events in the story.

Topic sentence →   In "The Cyber Bully," I think the author did a good job of making the characters and the events of the story seem realistic. Aaron is a new kid in school, and a bully picks

Evidence → on him. Like most kids, he worries about what the other students will think of him if he tells the teacher. Aaron solves the problem by talking to the teacher about the

Concluding statement → bully. I think Aaron did the right thing because I would have done the same thing. I thought the story was realistic because it was about a real problem that kids have to face in school. I liked the solution because it showed that telling a teacher about a bully is the right thing to do.

Write a paragraph about the text you have chosen. Cite evidence from the text to show how well the author used realistic characters and events. Remember to provide reasons that are supported by details.

Write a topic sentence: _____

_____

Cite evidence from the text: _____

_____

_____

_____

_____

End with a concluding statement: _____

_____

Name _____

A. Read the draft model. Use the questions that follow the draft to help you think about what details you can add about the central event.

Draft Model

Dan wanted to run for class president. He asked his friend to help him. He needed good ideas. "How about proposing a school-wide dance day?" his friend said, excitedly.

---

1. Why did Dan want to run for class president?

2. Why did he choose this friend to help him?

3. What does Dan think of the friend's idea?

4. What details would describe Dan's feelings and reactions?

B. Now revise the draft by adding details to help readers better understand and picture the event.

_____

_____

_____

_____

_____

_____

_____

_____

Name _____

| alter | collapse | destruction | severe |
| substantial | unpredictable | hazard | crisis |

Finish each sentence using the vocabulary word provided.

1. **(alter)** When she saw that it was going to rain, _____

_____

2. **(collapse)** The fort we made of sticks was so fragile, _____

_____

3. **(destruction)** When the tidal wave hit the trees on the beach, _____

_____

4. **(severe)** The show was interrupted _____

_____

5. **(substantial)** Having to rebuild after the storm _____

_____

6. **(unpredictable)** We tried to catch the firefly, _____

_____

7. **(hazard)** When our neighborhood flooded, _____

_____

8. **(crisis)** When all the lights went out in town, _____

_____

Name _____

Read the selection. Complete the compare and contrast graphic organizer.

Name _____

Read the passage. Use the reread strategy to check your understanding.

Rising Waters

Have you ever been in an earthquake or a tornado? These things
12 may never happen where you live. But flooding is something that can
24 happen in almost every part of the United States. Not all floods are
37 alike. Some floods happen over many days. A flash flood can happen
49 in minutes. Learning about floods can help you stay safe.

59 **Why Do Floods Happen?**

63 There are two types of floods. The first type happens when a river
76 has too much water. The water in a river rises over the river's banks.
90 This might happen because storms have caused too much rain to fall.
102 In rivers near mountains, melting snow can also cause floods. Warm
113 weather can quickly melt the snow. The water flows down to flood
125 the rivers.
127 The second type of flood happens when seawater is pushed onto
138 the land. This can happen during a hurricane. Strong winds blow
149 water onto the land. Earthquakes can also cause this kind of flooding.
161 The sudden movement of the ground can cause walls of water to rush
174 toward the shore.

Name _____

What Happens Next?

There can be many problems after a flood. If a farm floods, the water can drown the crops. This means that there will be less food for people to eat. Floods also cause damage to buildings and bridges. They can even wash away entire roads! This can make it hard for rescue workers to help people who are trapped by the water. But it is important to get food and drinking water to people during a flood. Everything they own may have been washed away. Or it might be covered in dirt. Sewers can overflow and make drinking water dirty. This makes it unsafe. Without clean food and water, people can get sick.

How Do People Avoid Floods?

All over the world, people work to avoid flooding. In many countries, people build walls to keep water away from the land. In one part of England, there is a large metal wall across a river. The wall is raised when the sea level gets too high. This keeps the river from flooding.

Photo by Lynn Betss, courtesy of USDA Natural Resources Conservation Service

In the United States, many towns have sold part of their land. The government used that land to create wetlands. These wetlands act like sponges that absorb water from floods. This helps stop the water from reaching towns and damaging them.

Floods can be scary, but flooding does not last forever. People are working to make floods less harmful to buildings, land, and themselves. Knowing how floods happen can help keep you safe. Being ready can help you stay safe too.

Name _____

A. Reread the passage and answer the questions.

1. **What are the two things being compared in the second and third paragraphs?**

   _____

   _____

   _____

2. **What do these two things have in common?**

   _____

   _____

   _____

3. **How are these two things different?**

   _____

   _____

   _____

B. Work with a partner. Read the passage aloud. Pay attention to accuracy. Stop after one minute. Fill out the chart.

	Words Read	–	Number of Errors	=	Words Correct Score
First Read		–		=	
Second Read		–		=	

Name _____

Forest Fires

Forest fires start and spread in different ways. The type of fire and the plants affect how it spreads. There are three types of forest fires. The first is a ground fire. It moves along the ground, sometimes below the leaf cover. Dead plant matter along the ground can burn for weeks and months. In a surface fire, low plants, twigs, and rotten logs catch fire. The flames can sometimes become tall and spread. The third type is a crown fire. It burns and spreads across the tops of trees and can be carried by the wind.

Answer the questions about the text.

1. **How do you know this is an expository text?**

_____

2. **What text features does the text include?**

_____

3. **What is the heading of this text? How could it be made more specific?**

_____

_____

4. **What does the diagram show? How does it add to the text?**

_____

_____

Name _____

Read each passage. Underline the context clues that help you figure out the meaning of each multiple-meaning word in bold. Then write the word's meaning on the line.

1. Have you ever been in an earthquake or a tornado? These things may never happen where you live. But flooding is something that can happen in almost every **part** of the United States.

_____

_____

2. Not all floods are alike. Some floods happen over many days. A **flash** flood can happen in minutes. Learning about floods can help you stay safe.

_____

_____

3. Floods also cause damage to buildings and bridges. They can even **wash** away entire roads! This can make it hard for rescue workers to help people who are trapped by the water.

_____

_____

4. The water in a river rises over the river's **banks**. This might happen because storms have caused too much rain to fall.

_____

_____

Name _____

A. Read the words in each row. Circle the word with the long e vowel sound. Then write the letters that make the long e sound on the line.

1. league   large   growl   _____

2. deck   sled   sleek   _____

3. scheme   shelf   sky   _____

4. marked   maybe   melted   _____

5. claim   dense   honey   _____

6. farming   family   laying   _____

B. Write the correct plural form of each noun. Use the plural ending -s, -es, or -ies.

Noun	Plural Form
1. kiss	_____
2. zebra	_____
3. buddy	_____
4. match	_____
5. stone	_____
6. box	_____

Name _____

> *Evidence* is details and examples from a text that support a writer's ideas. The student who wrote the paragraph below cited evidence that shows how the author compares and contrasts information in a text.

Topic sentence →   In "Forest Fires," the author includes an illustration that gives more details about the different types of forest fires. The author explains that there are three different

Evidence → types of forest fires. The first is a ground fire, the second is a surface fire, and the third type is a crown fire. The illustration shown adds more detail by showing what each type of fire looks like as it burns. The author uses

Concluding statement → the illustration to add more details that make it easier for the reader to understand how the fires are different.

Write a paragraph about the text you have chosen. Show how the author uses illustrations to add more details about the topic. Cite evidence from the text. Remember to include transitions that link ideas and use both simple and compound sentences.

Write a topic sentence: _____

_____

Cite evidence from the text: _____

_____

_____

_____

_____

_____

End with a concluding statement: _____

_____

Name _____

A. Read the draft model. Use the questions that follow the draft to help you think about what supporting details you can add.

Draft Model

   The park near my house is a great place to spend time. Many people enjoy hiking or walking in the park and looking at nature. The park has baseball fields.

---

1. Why is the park a great place?

2. What details would show what the park looks like?

3. What kinds of plants and animals might be in the park?

4. What do the baseball fields add to the park?

B. Now revise the draft by adding supporting details that help readers learn more about the park.

_____

_____

_____

_____

_____

_____

_____

_____

Name _____

| thrilling | capabilities | friction | gravity |
| accelerate | inquiry | identity | advantage |

Finish each sentence using the vocabulary word provided.

1. **(friction)** I use the brakes on my roller skates _____

_____

2. **(identity)** The policeman asked me _____

_____

3. **(thrilling)** At the amusement park, the roller coaster _____

_____

4. **(advantage)** The fact that the basketball player is very tall _____

_____

5. **(gravity)** The apple fell from the tree _____

_____

6. **(accelerate)** When traveling downhill, _____

_____

7. **(inquiry)** I used the Internet _____

_____

8. **(capabilities)** My friend is good at math and English _____

_____

Name _____

Read the selection. Complete the cause and effect graphic organizer.

Cause	➡️	Effect
	➡️	
	➡️	
	➡️	
	➡️	

Name _____

A. Reread the passage and answer the questions.

1. What is the cause in the following sentence from the passage?
   Charlie pushed the ball with his hand, and it rolled across the floor.

   _____

   _____

2. What is the effect in the following sentence from the passage?
   Charlie pushed the ball with his hand, and it rolled across the floor.

   _____

   _____

3. What is one example of an effect in the section "The Pull of Gravity"?
   What is the cause of this effect?

   _____

   _____

B. Work with a partner. Read the passage aloud. Pay attention to phrasing and rate. Stop after one minute. Fill out the chart.

	Words Read	–	Number of Errors	=	Words Correct Score
First Read		–		=	
Second Read		–		=	

Name _____

Science in a Soda Bottle

"You look bored. I know something fun you can make," Mom said.

"What?" I asked.

"I'll show you. You need an empty soft drink bottle and a catsup packet," Mom said as she got the supplies. "Put the packet in the bottle and fill the bottle all the way to the top with water. Then close the bottle."

When she picked up the bottle and squeezed it, the packet sank!

The water pressure squeezes the air in the packet, making it sink.

Answer the questions about the text.

1. How do you know this is narrative nonfiction?

_____

2. What text features does the text include?

_____

3. What is the heading? How could it be better?

_____

_____

4. What information do the illustration and speech bubble give you?

_____

_____

Name _____

Read each sentence below. Underline the context clues in the sentence that help you define each word in bold. Then, in your own words, write the definition of the word.

1. Charlie walked over to the **fire pole,** a metal pole which ran through a hole in the floor and connected the two levels of the firehouse.

   _____

2. **Inertia** means that an object at rest tends to stay at rest.

   _____

3. "A **force** is something that moves, stops, or changes the motion of an object," he said.

   _____

4. **Speed** is the distance an object moves in a certain amount of time.

   _____

5. **Gravity** is the force that pulls objects toward each other.

   _____

Name _____

A. Read each sentence. Underline the word with the long *i* vowel sound. Then sort the words by their long *i* spellings in the chart below.

1. Which of these is a prime number?

2. Make a slight turn at the next street.

3. She was minding the baby for you.

Long *i* spelled *i*	Long *i* spelled *i_e*	Long *i* spelled *igh*
4.	5.	6.

B. Write the correct -*es* and -*ed* forms for each verb ending in *y*.

Verb	+ es	+ ed
1. cry	_____	_____
2. fry	_____	_____
3. apply	_____	_____
4. deny	_____	_____
5. worry	_____	_____

Name _____

> *Evidence* is details and examples from a text that support a writer's ideas. The student who wrote the paragraph below cited evidence that shows how the author used headings to tell the reader what each section will be about.
>
> **Topic sentence** → In "A Firehouse Lesson," the author uses headings to explain what each section of each text will be about.
>
> **Evidence** → For example, the first heading in the text is "The Pull of Gravity." The heading lets the reader know that topic will be about gravity. The second heading is "A Ball in Motion." The heading tells the reader that this section will be about motion. The author's use of headings helps
>
> **Concluding statement** → the reader to know what to expect in each section of text.

Write a paragraph about the text you have chosen. Show how the author uses headings to tell the reader what each section is about. Cite evidence from the text. Remember to include a strong concluding statement and to use clauses correctly.

Write a topic sentence: _____

_____

Cite evidence from the text: _____

_____

_____

_____

_____

End with a concluding statement: _____

_____

Name _____

A. Read the draft model. Use the questions that follow the draft to help you think about how you can write an event sequence that unfolds naturally.

Draft Model

We went to a dairy farm. We saw a farmer milk a cow. He showed us how he turns milk into butter. We learned how cheese is made from milk.

---

1. When did the writer go to the dairy farm?

2. What did the writer do first?

3. What time-order word would tell when the farmer showed the writer how he turns milk into butter?

4. What time-order word would tell when the writer learned how cheese is made from milk?

B. Now revise the draft by adding time-order words that help readers better understand the writer's trip to the dairy farm.

_____

_____

_____

_____

_____

_____

_____

_____

Name _____

> process   routine   undertaking   compassionate
>
> funds   enterprise   exceptional   innovative

Use a word from the box to answer each question. Then use the word in a sentence.

1. What is another word for *a regular series of actions*? _____

_____

2. What is a sum of money set aside for something? _____

_____

3. What word might describe something that is out of the ordinary?

_____

4. What is another word for *something someone decides to do or start*?

_____

5. What word might describe someone who cares about other people?

_____

6. What is another word for *a difficult project*? _____

_____

7. What word might describe the steps you take to perform a task?

_____

8. What word might describe someone who is likely to introduce new ideas?

_____

Name _____

Read the selection. Complete the main idea and details graphic organizer.

Main Idea
Detail
Detail
Detail

Name _____

Read the passage. Use the reread strategy to help you understand the most important ideas in the passage.

A Helping Hand

	Do you like to help others? Helping out is an important part of
13	being in a community. There are many others who feel the same way.
26	Helping can truly make a difference in a lot of ways. It is something
40	you can do every day. Make a Difference Day is one day a year that
55	reminds us how great it is to help others.
64	We should all be active and make a difference to better our community.
77	There is always a way to make a difference. Sometimes it is giving food
91	to someone who needs a meal. Sometimes it is a cleaning a local park.
105	Make a Difference Day is a good time to get others involved. It is a
120	great time to get your friends to help you make a difference, too.
133	**Clean a Park**
136	Making a difference is about helping. It is also a good way to learn.
150	If you and your friends clean a park, you can study plant life there.
164	You might see animals you have studied. So while cleaning, you have
176	learned about plants and animals. You have also made the park a
188	cleaner place for them and for you.
195	**Meet New People**
198	It is helpful to clean your community. But it is also good to meet
212	the people who live there. You can easily learn about other people
224	who live near you. Just talking to someone can make a difference. You
237	and your classmates can visit a senior citizen center. Ask the people
249	there about their lives. They will gladly tell you what it was like when
263	they were your age. This makes a difference by showing you care. It
276	also helps you get to know other people in your community.

Name _____

Feed Someone in Need

Do you know how important a good meal is? Some people aren't able to have a good meal every day. Make a difference by collecting food for them. You and your friends can work as a team to collect food. Choose a food bank you would like to help. Work together to collect food donations from your friends and your community. Then give the food to the food bank. They will be grateful for your help. This is something you can do all year round. It not only helps people in need. It also helps you and your friends know what teamwork is.

Be Creative

Cleaning parks, meeting new people, and giving food are good. There is also something you can do with your creativity. You and your friends can make an activity book. How is this making a difference? There are children who might not have these books. Your teacher can make copies. Then your team can distribute them. Take them to places like clinics or hospitals.

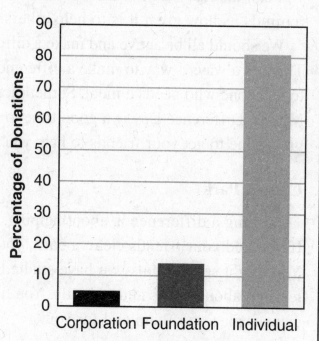

This graph shows where donations came from in North America in 2010. You can see that individuals like you give the most.

There are children there who would like these books. It is a book that you and your team created together. More importantly it is a book that made the day better for a child.

Making a difference is good. And Make a Difference Day is a good time to start. Making a difference can show you parts of your community you did not know about. You can meet new people and learn new things. Most of all, you can make a difference.

Name _____

A. Reread the passage and answer the questions.

1. What are three key details in paragraph 5?

_____

_____

_____

2. How are these details connected?

_____

_____

_____

3. What is the main idea of the whole passage?

_____

_____

_____

B. Work with a partner. Read the passage aloud. Pay attention to phrasing and rate. Stop after one minute. Fill out the chart.

	Words Read	–	Number of Errors	=	Words Correct Score
First Read		–		=	
Second Read		–		=	

Name _____

Donating to a Charity

Once your business starts making money, it's important to find a way to give back to the community. For instance, 9-year-old Jason O'Neill started a pencil topper business. After a few years of success, he decided to use some money to buy toys for a local children's hospital. In addition, he began holding an annual teddy bear drive so that others could help the hospital. Jason is a good example of a responsible businessperson.

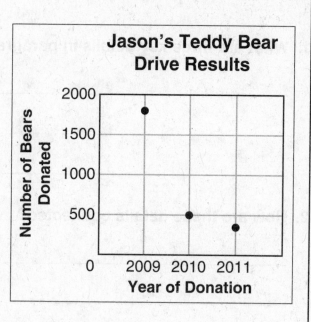

Jason's Teddy Bear Drive Results

Answer the questions about the text.

1. How do you know this text is a persuasive article?

_____

_____

2. What text feature is included? What information does it show?

_____

_____

3. What is the heading of this article?

_____

4. What does the author think about the article's subject?

_____

_____

Name _____

Read each sentence below. Underline the suffix of the word in bold and write the word's definition on the line. Then write your own sentence using the word in bold.

1. Helping can **truly** make a difference in a lot of ways.

_____

_____

_____

2. We should all be **active** and make a difference to better our community.

_____

_____

_____

3. They will **gladly** tell you what it was like when they were your age.

_____

_____

_____

4. They will be **grateful** for your help.

_____

_____

_____

Name _____

A. Read each sentence. Circle the word that has the long-vowel sound /ō/. Write the letter or letters that make the long-vowel sound /ō/ on the line.

1. Use the crane to lower the lumber to the ground. _____

2. The bolt of lightning shot across the sky. _____

3. The sad movie filled us all with woe. _____

4. My shadow stays behind me when I walk down the stairs. _____

5. Do you smell the chicken roasting in the oven? _____

6. My favorite quote is from that great author. _____

B. Read the words in the box. Mark the words that are not compound words with an X. Then list the compound words on the lines below.

workout	hunter	hands-on	childlike
catching	afternoon	half sister	weekend

1. _____   4. _____

2. _____   5. _____

3. _____   6. _____

Name _____

Evidence is details and examples from a text that support a writer's ideas. The student who wrote the paragraph below cited evidence that shows how the author uses key details to support the main idea.

Topic sentence → In "A Helping Hand," the author provides key details to support the main idea that everyone can help out in their community. **Evidence** → The author gives key details by providing examples of what people can do to help their community. Two of these examples are collecting donations for a food bank and cleaning up a local park. These details support the main idea. **Concluding statement** → The author's use of key details supports the main idea and gives the reader some good ideas of how to help others.

Write a paragraph about the text you have chosen. Show how the author uses key details to support the main idea. Cite evidence from the text. Remember to you precise language and to avoid run-on sentences.

Write a topic sentence: _____

_____

Cite evidence from the text: _____

_____

_____

_____

_____

End with a concluding statement: _____

_____

Name _____

A. Read the draft model. Use the questions that follow the draft to help you think about using sentences of different lengths to add interest and rhythm.

Draft Model

I think our community needs a frozen yogurt store. We have too many ice cream stores. Frozen yogurt is a healthy alternative to ice cream.

---

1. What sentences have related ideas that could be combined into a longer sentence?

2. What short sentences would you add to draw attention to the idea that frozen yogurt is a healthy alternative to ice cream?

3. What sentence would you add after the last sentence to help explain what it means? Would you make that sentence long or short to add rhythm?

B. Now revise the draft by using sentences of different lengths to add interest and rhythm.

_____

_____

_____

_____

_____

_____

_____

Name _____

| attracted | fabric | honest | soared |
| dazzling | greed | requested | trudged |

Use the context clues in each sentence to help you decide which vocabulary word fits best in the blank.

Flying high in the air, Eagle _____ over the forest. Something drew his attention in the forest below and he flew down to see it. It was something colorful that had _____ him. When Eagle landed on the forest floor, he saw a splendid piece of cloth with bright, _____ colors.

He knew that the cloth might belong to someone else, but he had always desired just such a scarf. _____ got the best of him, and he picked up the piece of _____. Just then, Big Bear appeared, walking slowly toward Eagle. Big Bear _____ up next to him.

"Can you help me find my scarf?" Big Bear _____. At first, Eagle thought about hiding the scarf. But instead of lying, he decided to be _____. "Oh, well," thought Eagle. He handed the scarf to Big Bear and flew away.

Name _____

Read the selection. Complete the theme graphic organizer.

```
┌──────────────────────────────────────────────┐
│                   Detail                     │
│                                              │
│                                              │
│                                              │
└──────────────────────────────────────────────┘

┌──────────────────────────────────────────────┐
│                   Detail                     │
│                                              │
│                                              │
│                                              │
└──────────────────────────────────────────────┘

┌──────────────────────────────────────────────┐
│                   Detail                     │
│                                              │
│                                              │
│                                              │
└──────────────────────────────────────────────┘

┌──────────────────────────────────────────────┐
│                   Theme                      │
│                                              │
│                                              │
│                                              │
└──────────────────────────────────────────────┘
```

Name _____

Read the passage. Use the ask and answer questions strategy to help you understand the folktale.

Anansi and His Children

	Anansi was a spider who had six children, each with his or her
13	own special ability. The first child was named See Trouble, because
24	he could perceive trouble from far away. The next was Road Builder,
36	followed by River Drinker, Game Skinner, and Stone Thrower. The
46	last child was named Cushion, because he was so very soft. They
58	were all good children who loved Anansi.
65	Anansi was curious about the world and liked nothing more than to
77	travel. He loved to explore places far from home, but one day Anansi
90	became lost! Back at home, See Trouble knew at once what had
102	happened.
103	"Brothers and sisters!" said See Trouble. "Come quickly. Father is
113	lost. We must help him find his way back home."
123	Road Builder stepped forward, strong and sure-handed. "I will
132	build a road that will lead us to our father," Road Builder said, and
146	he began to construct a road. The other five children followed Road
158	Builder down the road as he worked. They trudged on and on until
171	finally they came to a mighty river. But, hard as they tried, they could
185	not see their father.
189	"Brothers and sisters," See Trouble cried. "I know why we do not
201	see our father. He has been swallowed by Big Fish!"
211	"It's a good thing I'm so thirsty," said River Drinker as she walked
224	to the river's edge and put her lips to the water. With gulp after
238	enormous gulp, she drank every drop of water in the river. There in
251	the mud sat Big Fish. Now it was Game Skinner's turn to help. She cut
266	open Big Fish, and Anansi crawled out, free at last!

Name _____

But the danger was not over. Falcon swooped down from the sky, grabbed Anansi and soared into the clouds.

"Quickly, Stone Thrower!" yelled See Trouble. Taking careful aim, Stone Thrower hit Falcon with a stone. Anansi began to fall. Seeing this, Cushion ran to catch his father. Anansi landed on Cushion with a nice soft bounce, and Anansi was safe! The children cheered, happy to be with their father again.

On the way home, Anansi was attracted to something glowing in the woods. Always curious, he walked toward the glow and found something beautiful. It was a dazzling globe of light.

"Such a wonderful thing!" exclaimed Anansi. "I know just what I will do with it. I will give it to one of my children. But which one should I give it to?"

Seeking help, Anansi called to Nyame, who lived in the sky watching over all living things.

"I found this beautiful globe of light, Nyame. Will you hold it for me while I decide which child I should give it to?" Anansi asked.

"Gladly," said Nyame, and she reached down carefully to take the globe in hand. As she did so, a soft light fell on the forest.

Anansi went to his children and told them about the ball of light. All night long they argued over which one should receive the gift. Nyame watched from above as the argument went on and on.

It seemed they would never make a decision. So Nyame came to a decision of her own. Instead of giving the globe back to Anansi, Nyame placed it high above for every living thing to see. And that is the story of how the moon came to live in the sky.

Name _____

A. Reread the passage and answer the questions.

1. **Pick one of Anansi's children to write about. Write the name of the character and explain how he or she uses his or her ability to save Anansi.**

    _____

    _____

    _____

2. **What is the decision Nyame comes to at the end of the story?**

    _____

    _____

3. **What is one of the themes of this story?**

    _____

    _____

    _____

B. Work with a partner. Read the passage aloud. Pay attention to expression. Stop after one minute. Fill out the chart.

	Words Read	–	Number of Errors	=	Words Correct Score
First Read		–		=	
Second Read		–		=	

Name _____

The Tiger, the Brahmin, and the Jackal

The jackal said to the Brahmin, "I understand that you agreed to let the tiger free if the tiger agreed not to eat you." He turned to the tiger. "And I understand that as soon as you were free, you said you would eat the Brahmin anyway. But I still can't understand this cage here..."

The tiger snarled impatiently. "Foolish jackal! How many times do I have to explain it?" he said. He walked into the cage to demonstrate how it worked. As soon as he was inside, the jackal closed the door behind him and locked him in.

The jackal turned to the Brahmin. "I think you should leave this cage closed," he said.

Answer the questions about the text.

1. **How do you know this text is a folktale?**

_____

2. **What literary elements are included in a folktale?**

_____

3. **Choose a character. What quality do you think this character symbolizes?**

_____

_____

4. **What lesson do you think this folktale teaches?**

_____

_____

Name _____

Read each passage below. Write the root word and the definition of the word in bold.

1. Anansi was a spider who had six children, each with his or her own special **ability**.

   Root word: _____

   Definition: _____

2. "Such a **wonderful** thing!" exclaimed Anansi. "I know just what I will do with it. I will give it to one of my children. But which one should I give it to?"

   Root word: _____

   Definition: _____

3. "Gladly," said Nyame, and she reached down **carefully** to take the globe in hand.

   Root word: _____

   Definition: _____

4. Nyame watched from above as the **argument** went on and on.

   Root word: _____

   Definition: _____

Name _____

A. Read each sentence. Circle the words that have prefixes. Then write the words with prefixes on the line.

1. I had to relearn the lesson because my answers were incorrect.

_____

2. The imperfect lock made it difficult to unchain the bike.

_____

3. I did not understand how his room could be so unclean and in such disorder!

_____

4. The unhappy customer had to repeat that his meal was uncooked.

_____

5. The shirt was an irregular shape and caused discomfort.

_____

B. Write the correct -ed and -ing forms for each verb.

Verb	Verb + ed	Verb + ing
1. flap	_____	_____
2. drag	_____	_____
3. grin	_____	_____
4. scrub	_____	_____
5. admit	_____	_____

Name _____

> *Evidence* is details and examples from a text that support a writer's ideas. The student who wrote the paragraph below cited evidence to show how well the author used the characters' words and actions to communicate the message or theme of the story.
>
> **Topic sentence** → In "The Tiger, the Brahmin, and the Jackal," I think the author does a good job of communicating the message of the story. A Brahmin lets a tiger out of a cage because the tiger promises not to eat him. Once the tiger is free he says he will eat the Brahmin. A jackal tricks the tiger into walking back into the cage. The message of the story is to not trust your enemies. I think the author did a good job of communicating the message of the story because each character and event helped me to understand the theme.
>
> **Evidence** →
>
> **Concluding statement** →

Write a paragraph about the text you have chosen. Cite evidence from the text that shows how the author communicates the theme or message through the characters and events. Remember to include strong evidence that supports your opinion and to use correct capitalization and proper nouns.

Write a topic sentence: _____

_____

Cite evidence from the text: _____

_____

_____

_____

_____

End with a concluding statement: _____

_____

Name _____

A. Read the draft model. Use the questions that follow the draft to help you think about how you can create a strong opening by adding details.

Draft Model

A man met a fox. The fox asked the man for help. The man had to decide if he wanted to help the fox. Both the fox and the man waited while the man decided if he would help the fox.

---

1. Who is the man? Where does he meet the fox?

2. What is the problem that the fox has?

3. What details would explain how the man could help the fox?

4. Why is the man trying to decide if he will help the fox?

B. Now revise the draft by creating a strong opening by adding details.

_____
_____
_____
_____
_____
_____
_____
_____

Name _____

| cranky | frustrated | selfish | commotion |
| annoyed | specialty | attitude | familiar |

Finish each sentence using the vocabulary word provided.

1. **(specialty)** The bakery is known for _____

   _____ .

2. **(frustrated)** When I couldn't figure out the multiplication problem, _____

   _____ .

3. **(commotion)** We heard the two dogs barking loudly _____

   _____ .

4. **(annoyed)** The cat saw the bird on the other side of the window _____

   _____ .

5. **(attitude)** The boy is always ready to help _____

   _____ .

6. **(selfish)** When I have a secret, _____

   _____ .

7. **(familiar)** When I heard the song on the radio, _____

   _____ .

8. **(cranky)** When my baby sister is tired, _____

   _____ .

Name _____

Read the selection. Complete the theme graphic organizer.

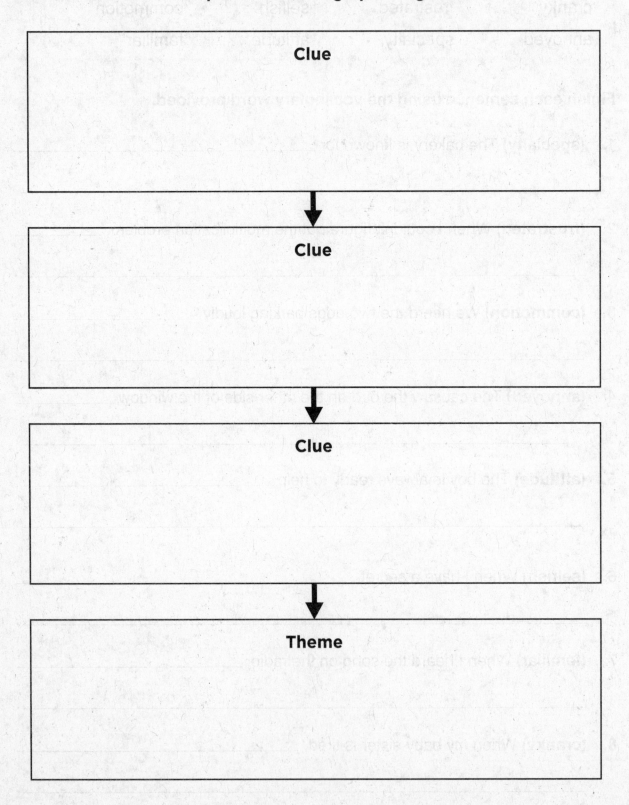

Clue

↓

Clue

↓

Clue

↓

Theme

Name _____

Read the passage. Use the ask and answer questions strategy to be sure you understand what you read.

Grant and the Flower Stem

List of Characters

3	Grant, an ant
6	Beatrice, a bee
9	Frank, a bee

12	**Setting**
13	A field in Kansas.
17	*Grant has wandered away from his work and has fallen asleep. The*
29	*next morning, he climbs to the top of a sunflower stem and finds a*
43	*small house made of beeswax. No one is home.*

52	**Grant:**	*(whispering)* What is this place? It looks like my house, but
64		everything is smooth and shiny! Everything in my house
73		is made of dirt and so rough. Oh man, I would love to live
87		here!
88		*(Beatrice walks in the door behind him.)*
95	**Beatrice:**	*(yelling)* Who are you? And, more importantly, what are you
106		doing here?
108	**Grant:**	I'm so sorry. My name is Grant. I just saw the stem to your
123		house and climbed up. I didn't know what I would find. But
135		your house is lovely! *(Cowering)* Please don't sting me!
144	**Beatrice:**	*(laughs)* It's nice to meet you. Stand up straight and tall. I
157		haven't stung anyone in years, not unless they deserved it.

Name _____

Grant:	That's a relief. I have heard stories about little ants that wander away and are stung by bees. I hear bees are very cranky.
Beatrice:	Goodness no. It takes a lot to get me irritated. Someone has to be very unpleasant to make me a grouch. I am usually very friendly. You should watch out for my husband, however; he is grumpier than I am.
Grant:	Is he going to sting me?
Beatrice:	My goodness, Grant, you are one nervous ant. You shouldn't worry so much. He won't sting you.
Frank:	*(Enters, but doesn't see Grant)* Good afternoon, Beatrice! Whose turn is it to make soup? *(Notices Grant)* Who are you, and what are you doing in my house?
Grant:	I'm sorry, sir. Your wife has been very generous to me. She offered me some tasty soup. Please don't sting me!
Frank:	*(to Beatrice)* Really, he thinks I'm going to sting him?
Beatrice:	He thinks all bees do is just see ants and sting them.
Grant:	All of the stories I've heard about bees are terrifying.
Frank:	Let me calm you down. Have you ever met a bee before?
Grant:	No, not before you two.
Beatrice:	I'll tell you what. We are going to feed you, and then Frank will fly you home. I'd like you to tell other ants about us, and let them know that we are not beasts. We are insects like everyone else. I'd also ask you to be more careful about believing all the stories you hear about other folks.
Grant:	I will. Thank you very much for not stinging me.
Frank and Beatrice:	*(sigh) (together)* You're welcome, Grant.

Name _____

A. Reread the passage and answer the questions.

1. What does Grant believe about all bees?

_____

_____

_____

2. Why does he believe this?

_____

_____

_____

3. What theme does Grant's interaction with the bees show?

_____

_____

_____

B. Work with a partner. Read the passage aloud. Pay attention to intonation. Stop after one minute. Fill out the chart.

	Words Read	–	Number of Errors	=	Words Correct Score
First Read		–		=	
Second Read		–		=	

Name _____

Goldilocks Returns

Act 1, Scene 2

[Setting: *The* THREE BEARS' *kitchen. The bears are standing around their kitchen table, explaining to the* POLICE DETECTIVES *what happened.*]

MAMA BEAR: [*Worried*] As soon as we had returned from our morning stroll, we knew something wasn't right.

PAPA BEAR: [*Angry*] Each of the bowls of porridge on the kitchen table had been tasted by someone!

BABY BEAR: [*Crying*] And whoever did it ate all of my porridge!

DETECTIVE #1: [*Looks at* DETECTIVE #2] This isn't the first time we've seen this, is it, boss?

DETECTIVE #2: [*Still studying the crime scene*] No sir. Call headquarters. Tell them Goldilocks is at it again.

[*End scene.*]

Answer the questions about the text.

1. **How can you tell the genre of this text is a drama?**

   _____

   _____

2. **How can you identify the dialogue in this text?**

   _____

3. **What do the stage directions explain?**

   _____

   _____

Name _____

Read each passage. Underline the antonyms that help you figure out the meaning of each word in bold. Then write the word's meaning on the line.

1. Grant: My name is Grant. I just saw the stem to your house and climbed up. . . . But your house is lovely! (*Cowering*) Please don't sting me!

Beatrice: (*laughs*) Grant. It's nice to meet you. Stand up straight and tall. I haven't stung anyone in years, not unless they deserved it.

_____

_____

2. Grant: That's a relief. I have heard stories about little ants that wander away and are stung by bees. I hear bees are very **cranky**.

Beatrice: Goodness no. It takes a lot to get me irritated. I am usually very friendly.

_____

_____

3. Grant: All of the stories I've heard about bees are **terrifying**.

Frank: Let me calm you down. Have you ever met a bee before?

_____

_____

Name _____

A. Read each sentence. Circle the words that include a digraph. Then underline the digraph in each word.

1. My dad will choose the patch we buy.

2. Did you snatch the bar graph I did for homework?

3. Our chef came in fifth place at the cooking contest.

4. We will have to rush to get inside the kitchen.

5. Did you touch the bottle of ketchup?

6. Did you by chance see the family photo?

B. Write the singular possessive and plural possessive forms for each noun.

Noun	Singular Possessive	Plural Possessive
1. pitcher	_____	_____
2. table	_____	_____
3. orange	_____	_____
4. theater	_____	_____
5. bus	_____	_____
6. horse	_____	_____

Name _____

Evidence is details and examples from a text that support a writer's ideas. The student who wrote the paragraph below cited evidence to show how well the author used the elements of a play to tell a story.

Topic sentence →   In "Grant and the Flower Stem," I think the author did a good job of using the elements of a play to tell a story. The setting, stage directions, and the dialogue tell

Evidence → the reader what is happening in the play. For example, in the beginning, the stage directions say that Grant is whispering. I can tell he is nervous because he is whispering. From the dialogue, I can tell that Beatrice tries to make Grant feel less nervous. I think the author's

Concluding statement → use of dialogue and stage directions really helped me to understand the characters and the events in the play.

Write a paragraph about the text you have chosen. Cite evidence from the text to show how well the author used the elements of a play to tell a story. Remember to use evidence to support your opinion and use nouns correctly.

Write a topic sentence: _____

_____

Cite evidence from the text: _____

_____

_____

_____

End with a concluding statement: _____

_____

Name _____

A. Read the draft model. Use the questions that follow the draft to help you think about what everyday, conversational words and phrases you can add.

Draft Model

Hello, Dear Reader, my name is Theodore Baker. I have been alive almost 11 years. I am the youngest royal cake maker on the planet. Yesterday, the Queen requested that I bake her a special anniversary cake.

---

1. What is a more informal way for Theodore Baker to introduce himself?

2. How could Theodore Baker tell how old he is in a way that sounds more like conversation?

3. How might the Queen's request be written as dialogue?

B. Now revise the draft by adding everyday words and phrases that will make the story sound less formal and more like conversation.

_____

_____

_____

_____

_____

_____

_____

_____

_____

Name _____

flourished	fragile	droughts	ripples
extinct	crumbled	imbalance	ecosystem

Use a word from the box to answer each question. Then use the word in a sentence.

1. What does water in a pool do when you jump in? _____

    _____

2. What is another word for *delicate*? _____

    _____

3. What word might describe when something broke into small pieces?

    _____

4. What is another word for *no longer in existence*? _____

    _____

5. What might be the result if there is too much weight on one side of a boat?

    _____

6. What is the name of all the living and nonliving things in an area?

    _____

7. What is another word for *thrived*? _____

    _____

8. What might cause a farm that grows corn to have problems?

    _____

Name _____

Read the selection. Complete the main idea and details graphic organizer.

Main Idea
Detail
Detail
Detail

Name _____

A. Reread the passage and answer the questions.

1. What are three key details found in paragraphs 4, 6, and 7?

_____

_____

_____

_____

2. How are these details connected?

_____

_____

3. What is the main idea of the whole passage?

_____

_____

B. Work with a partner. Read the passage aloud. Pay attention to accuracy. Stop after one minute. Fill out the chart.

	Words Read	–	Number of Errors	=	Words Correct Score
First Read		–		=	
Second Read		–		=	

Name _____

Dad and I See Green Worms

"Look, Dad!" I said. "These bugs are eating the lupine flowers!"

"Those are Karner Blue butterfly larvae," Dad said. "The adult butterfly lays its eggs on the lupine's stem. When the larvae hatch from their eggs, they feed only on lupine leaves until they enter the pupa stage. In recent years, the wild lupine's habitat has been shrinking, and today the Karner Blue butterfly is endangered."

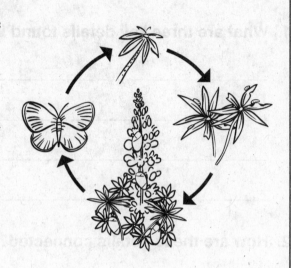

Answer the questions about the text.

1. How do you know this text is narrative nonfiction?

   _____

2. What text features does the text include?

   _____

3. What does the heading tell you? How would you change the heading to make it more effective?

   _____

   _____

   _____

4. What information does the flow chart give you?

   _____

   _____

Name _____

Read the sentences below. Underline the context clues that help you understand the meaning of each word in bold. Then write the word's meaning on the line.

1. But he is not alone in his **mission** for a nice garden.

   _____

2. As the worms **burrow** through the soil they create passages that allow air and water to pass through.

   _____

3. Bill begins to **plow** the area to get ready for planting seeds. He makes grooves in the dirt with his tool.

   _____

4. They bring down **organic** matter, or something that has to do with or comes from living things, from the surface.

   _____

5. This substance contains **nutrients** that plants need for healthy living.

   _____

Name _____

A. Read each sentence. Circle the word that has a three-letter blend. Then write it on the line to complete the sentence.

1. The tiny _____ came up from the ground.

   sprout   blossom   plant

2. I heard the owl _____ in the night.

   cry   screech   squeal

3. I have a sore _____ today.

   shoulder   throat   thumb

4. He will _____ his tie before he goes on stage.

   bring   clean   straighten

5. The kids were _____ in the pool.

   splashing   swimming   playing

B. Use -er or -est to write the correct form of the adjective.

1. wide (comparative -er ending)   _____

2. smart (comparative -er ending)   _____

3. loud (superlative -est ending)   _____

4. mad (comparative -er ending)   _____

5. cute (superlative -est ending)   _____

6. quick (superlative -est ending)   _____

Name _____

Evidence is details and examples from a text that support a writer's ideas. The student who wrote the paragraph below cited evidence that shows how the author used a text feature to provide more details about the topic.

Topic sentence →   In "Dad and I See Green Worms," the author includes a diagram to show information about the topic in a

Evidence → visual way. The text describes the different stages of the Karner Blue butterfly's life cycle. The author includes a diagram that shows what the different stages look like.

Concluding statement → The diagram of the life cycle makes the text easier to understand because it helps the reader to visualize the information.

Write a paragraph about the text you have chosen. Show how the author uses text features to add more details about the topic. Cite evidence from the text. Remember to clearly state the topic and use irregular plural nouns correctly.

Write a topic sentence: _____

_____

Cite evidence from the text: _____

_____

_____

_____

_____

_____

End with a concluding statement: _____

_____

Name _____

A. Read the draft model. Use the questions that follow the draft to help you think about what supporting details you can add.

Draft Model

Bees and flowers need each other. The bee helps the flower. Then the flower helps the bee. Bees need the pollen that flowers have.

---

1. How exactly do bees and flowers benefit each other?

2. How do bees get pollen from flowers? What do bees do with the pollen?

3. How do the actions of the bees help flowers survive?

4. Without bees, how would flowers suffer? Without flowers, how would bees suffer?

B. Now revise the draft by adding supporting details that help readers understand the connection between bees and flowers.

_____

_____

_____

_____

_____

_____

_____

Name _____

pounce	prey	dribbles	poisonous
extraordinary	vibrations	camouflaged	predator

Use the context clues in each sentence to help you decide which vocabulary word fits best in the blank.

Cyril the snake was not like the other snakes in his family. He didn't like to hunt for his meals, so he wasn't much of a _____.

"I don't care to hunt and eat mice," he told his mother. "They are not my _____ . They are my friends."

"We love to hunt mice!" said Cyril's brothers and sisters. "Cyril does not. His mouth waters at the thought of fruits and vegetables. He just _____ and drools when he sees a good salad."

Even though Cyril had teeth that could give a _____ bite and cause something harm, he never used them.

"Your brothers and sisters use their special coloring to be _____ and blend in with the brown grass and leaves," said his mother. "They shake their tails back and forth to cause _____ and make a rattling noise. This makes the mice frightened."

"I would never suddenly _____ on any mouse, big or small," said Cyril. "They are all my friends."

Because a friendly snake was so unusual to the mice, they all thought Cyril was an _____ friend.

Name _____

Read the selection. Complete the main idea and details graphic organizer.

Main Idea
Detail
Detail
Detail

Name _____

Read the passage. Use the summarize strategy to write a brief statement about the main ideas.

The Birds

	Do you know why some birds have bright feathers? Have you ever
12	wondered why some birds swim better than others? Different features
22	have made life easier for birds. These are all physical adaptations
33	birds have made in order to survive.
40	**The Web**
42	Many birds that live near water spend a lot of their time in the
56	water. These birds, called waterfowl, have webbed feet. Why is this
67	helpful? Webbed feet are like the paddles on a boat, which help the
80	waterfowl move through the water faster.
86	**Big Mouth**
88	The shape of a bird's beak is useful for specific tasks. The
100	spoonbill has a spoon-shaped beak. Why a spoon shape? This bird
111	spends a lot of time in the water. The spoon shape helps the bird stir
126	the water. The stirring causes little whirlpools. Small fish and insects
137	get pulled into the whirlpools, making it easy for the bird to snap up
151	a meal.
153	**Light as a Feather**
157	It is not uncommon to see birds with pretty feathers. Feathers are
169	for more than looking good, though. For the penguin, they do two
181	things. The outer part of the feather is waterproof. This keeps the
193	penguin dry. The inner part of the feather, called the down, traps
205	air that keeps it warm. This is important since penguins don't fly.
217	Instead, they swim in freezing water. Without waterproof feathers,
226	they would be at a disadvantage.

Name _____

True Colors

Bright colors help some birds stand out. The golden pheasant has red, green, and gold feathers. The toucan's large beak can be many colors at once. Bright colors help these two birds get noticed. This attention helps them find a mate.

The toucan's beak can be many colors.

There are some birds who are just the opposite. They do not want to be seen at all! The potoo has coloring that makes it look just like part of a tree. This camouflage helps the potoo avoid unwanted attention.

Voices Carry

Birds have different ways of talking. They have calls to find a mate, warn other birds, and to say "I live here!"

The killdeer has a special reason for one of its calls. This bird builds its nest on the ground. This can be unsafe. When a predator is too close to the nest, the killdeer gives a loud call. The bird hops around and pretends to be injured. This loud call and unusual act distract the predator. The predator will now go after the injured bird rather than look for the nest. When the predator gets too close the bird flies to safety, then to its nest. The killdeer's call and act help protect its nest.

The club-winged manakin has an interesting call, too. This bird uses its wings to "talk." It moves its feathers back and forth over one another. It can sound like a violin.

Birds have to adapt to their environments. Different environments require different features. Whether it's a certain way of moving, eating, or talking, various adaptations help birds to survive.

Name _____

A. Reread the passage and answer the questions.

1. What is the main idea in the third paragraph?

_____

_____

2. What are the key details in the fourth paragraph?

_____

_____

_____

3. How are these details connected?

_____

_____

B. Work with a partner. Read the passage aloud. Pay attention to rate. Stop after one minute. Fill out the chart.

	Words Read	−	Number of Errors	=	Words Correct Score
First Read		−		=	
Second Read		−		=	

Name _____

Giraffes' Adaptations

Where giraffes live there are few kinds of plants for animals to eat. So giraffes' bodies have adapted to eat the plants that are available. Giraffes mainly eat the leaves of the acacia tree. The acacia tree's branches are hard and thorny, but the giraffe's long, flexible tongue allows it to reach around the thorns and pluck the leaves. Even if a thorny branch does get into a giraffe's mouth, it has thick saliva that coats the thorns and protects its mouth from cuts.

Creatas/PunchStock

The giraffe's flexible tongue reaches between the thorns to remove the leaves.

Answer the questions about the text.

1. **How do you know this text is expository text?**

_____

_____

2. **What text features does the text include?**

_____

3. **What is the heading? Give an example of the topic it introduces.**

_____

_____

4. **How do the caption and photo help you understand the text better?**

_____

_____

Name _____

Read each sentence below. Then answer each question about the word in bold.

1. The prefix *un-* means "not." What does **uncommon** mean in the following sentence? "It is not **uncommon** to see birds with pretty feathers."

_____

2. What does **unwanted** mean in the following sentence? "This camouflage helps the potoo avoid **unwanted** attention."

_____

3. What does **unusual** mean in the following sentence? "This loud call and **unusual** act distract the predator."

_____

4. The prefix *dis-* means "opposite or lack of." What does **disadvantage** mean in the following sentence? "Without waterproof feathers, they would be at a **disadvantage**."

_____

5. The prefix *re-* means "again." What does **reproduce** mean in the following sentence? "This attention helps them find a mate and **reproduce**."

_____

Name _____

A. Circle the word with the /är/ or /ôr/ sound to complete each sentence. The /är/ sound is found in the word *star*. The /ôr/ sound is found in the word *fort*.

1. The boys saw a _____ on the roof of the house.

   hawk   stork   owl

2. The deck will _____ because of all the rain.

   warp   break   bend

3. I liked the new _____ that was in the bedroom.

   light   chair   carpet

4. It is always helpful to have _____ friends.

   kind   smart   many

5. They wanted to have the party in the _____.

   backyard   evening   basement

B. The suffix *-ful* means "full of" or "having." The suffix *-less* means "without." Add the suffix to each word on the first line. Then write the meaning of each word on the second line.

1. pity + less =   _____   _____

2. wonder + ful =   _____   _____

3. sense + less =   _____   _____

4. care + ful =   _____   _____

5. doubt + ful   _____   _____

6. penny + less =   _____   _____

Name _____

> *Evidence* is details and examples from a text that support a writer's opinion. The student who wrote the paragraph below cited evidence that shows how well the author used photographs and captions in the text.

Topic sentence →   In "Giraffe's Adaptations," the author included an interesting photograph and an informative caption to illustrate the text. The photograph shows a giraffe eating

Evidence → leaves from a thorny plant. I can see from the photograph the leaves are hard to get at. The caption explains how the giraffe is able to get to the leaves and avoid the

Concluding statement → thorns. I am glad that the author included the photograph and caption. It gave me more details about the giraffe and helped me understand the information in the text.

Write a paragraph about the text you have chosen. Show how well the author used photographs and captions. Cite evidence from the text. Remember to include text evidence that supports your opinion and to use possessive nouns correctly.

Write a topic sentence: _____

_____

Cite evidence from the text: _____

_____

_____

_____

_____

End with a concluding statement: _____

_____

Name _____

A. Read the draft model. Use the questions that follow the draft to help you think about what logical order to use to present details.

Draft Model

A giraffe has spots on its coat. Giraffes are tall animals from Africa. They are between 14 and 19 feet tall.

---

1. How could ideas be rearranged to help readers better understand what the text is about?

2. What other animals are giraffes related to?

3. What animals are giraffes taller than?

4. What other animal has spots on its coat?

B. Now revise the draft by rearranging ideas and presenting them in a logical order to help readers better understand giraffes.

_____

_____

_____

_____

_____

_____

_____

Name _____

> brittle   creative   descriptive   outstretched

Finish each sentence using the vocabulary word provided.

1. **(creative)** The artist is respected _____

    _____ .

2. **(outstretched)** Before she made the amazing catch, _____

    _____ .

3. **(descriptive)** I really like the author's writing because _____

    _____ .

4. **(brittle)** The old newspaper I found in the attic _____

    _____ .

Name _____

Read the selection. Complete the point of view graphic organizer.

Details

↓

Point of View

Name _____

Read the poem. Check your understanding as you read by asking yourself how the speaker thinks and feels.

Deer

6	The headlights turn their dark eyes green.
7	We see them sitting under trees
13	at night, in my yard, like a photo of
22	a family.
24	Then they dart away, their tails held
31	high,
32	six white arrows point at the sky.
39	We don't even get to say good-bye.
47	Into the night they disappear,
52	and though they move as quick as spears
60	a little later they'll be back here.
67	Our lights go off, we're warm inside,
74	they come out then, from where they hide.
82	Their secret place is a point of pride.
90	Calm as ponds, they never fight,
96	they stand and leave when the sky gets bright.
105	But the question never sat quite right—
112	where do they go when it gets light?

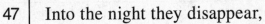

Name _____

A. Reread the passage and answer the questions.

1. What point of view is the poem told from?

_____

_____

2. How do you know which point of view it is told from?

_____

_____

3. What does the speaker think about the deer?

_____

_____

B. Work with a partner. Read the passage aloud. Pay attention to expression and phrasing. Stop after one minute. Fill out the chart.

	Words Read	–	Number of Errors	=	Words Correct Score
First Read		–		=	
Second Read		–		=	

Name _____

The Nautilus

The strangest creature in the sea?
Some say the eight-legged octopus.
The oddest always seemed to me
To be the baffling nautilus.

He peeks out from his spiral shell
While sailing on a backward trip.
He doesn't seem to know too well
How best to steer his puzzling ship.

Answer the questions about the text.

1. What makes this poem a lyric poem?

_____

2. What is the rhyme scheme of this poem?

_____

3. What does the poet think about the nautilus?

_____

_____

Name _____

> **Meter** is the rhythm of syllables in a line of poetry. It is created by the arrangement of accented and unaccented syllables.
>
> Words **rhyme** when their endings sound the same.

Read the lines of the lyric poem below. Then answer the questions.

Deer

Then they dart away, their tails held high,

six white arrows point at the sky.

We don't even get to say good-bye.

Into the night they disappear,

and though they move as quick as spears

a little later they'll be back here.

1. **Find two examples of rhyme in the poem. Write them below.**

_____

2. **What kind of meter appears in the poem?**

_____

3. **How do the meter and rhyme affect the poem?**

_____

_____

4. **Write another stanza for this poem that includes meter and rhyme.**

_____

_____

_____

Name _____

Read each passage. Underline the simile or metaphor in the sentence. Then write the two things that are being compared on the lines.

1. We see them sitting under trees

at night, in my yard, like a photo of a family.

_____

_____

2. Then they dart away, their tails held high,

six white arrows point at the sky.

_____

_____

3. Into the night they disappear,

and though they move as quick as spears

a little later they'll be back here.

_____

_____

Name _____

A. Read each sentence. Circle the word that has a suffix. Write the base word and the suffix on the lines.

1. We had a great time listening to the classical music.

   Base Word: _____   **Suffix:** _____

2. I could see the teacher walking up the steep stairs.

   Base Word: _____   **Suffix:** _____

3. My dad thinks that your answer is acceptable.

   Base Word: _____   **Suffix:** _____

4. A quality education is something that will always help you.

   Base Word: _____   **Suffix:** _____

5. There is a visitor waiting for you downstairs.

   Base Word: _____   **Suffix:** _____

B. Read each word pair. Write the contraction on the line.

1. was not   _____   5. we would   _____

2. they are   _____   6. were not   _____

3. he will   _____   7. has not   _____

4. should not   _____   8. they will   _____

Name _____

> *Evidence* is details and examples from a text that support a writer's ideas. The student who wrote the paragraph below cited evidence that shows how the author uses precise language in the poem.
>
> Topic sentence → In "The Nautilus," the author uses precise language to help the reader picture the images in the poem.
>
> Evidence → The author's use of the words *peeks* and *spiral* helps the reader to picture the nautilus in its shell. The phrase *steer his puzzling ship* compares the nautilus to a ship.
>
> Concluding statement → Without the use of precise language, the reader would not be able to understand that the author is comparing the nautilus to a ship that is sailing backwards.

Write a paragraph about the text you have chosen. Show how the author uses precise language to create an image. Cite evidence from the text. Remember to use precise language to inform about or explain the topic and combine sentences when necessary.

Write a topic sentence: _____

_____

Cite evidence from the text: _____

_____

_____

_____

_____

End with a concluding statement: _____

_____

Name _____

A. Read the draft model. Use the questions that follow the draft to add precise language that will help the reader create a picture in his or her mind.

Draft Model

We have a hamster named Teddy. He is small. We keep Teddy in a cage with a water bottle and a wheel. Teddy likes to run in his wheel for hours at a time.

---

1. What does Teddy look like? How small is he?

2. How long has the writer had this pet?

3. What words can be used to better describe Teddy's cage?

4. What strong verbs or descriptive adjectives can be added to describe what Teddy is like and how the writer feels about the pet?

B. Now revise the draft by adding precise language to help the reader create a picture in his or her mind.

_____

_____

_____

_____

_____

_____

_____

_____

Name _____

acquaintance	complementary	logical	scrounging
cautiously	jumble	scornfully	trustworthy

Use a word from the box to answer each question. Then use the word in a sentence.

1. What were the mice doing when they were looking on the ground for food?

   _____

2. Which word could you use to describe a mess? _____

   _____

3. What do you call a person you know? _____

   _____

4. How was the judge acting when she told the politician he had broken the law?

   _____

5. What is another word for *carefully*? _____

   _____

6. How would you describe someone you can rely on? _____

   _____

7. Which word would describe someone who is very sensible? _____

   _____

8. What is another word for *making whole*? _____

   _____

Name _____

Read the selection. Complete the point of view graphic organizer.

Details

↓

Point of View

Name _____

Read the passage. Use the visualize strategy to help you understand the fantasy story.

The Oak Tree and the Tiny Bird

	Far out in the country, in the middle of a grassy field, there lived
14	a beautiful oak tree. The oak tree loved her home, there in the field.
28	She loved the feel of squirrels jumping from limb to limb. She loved
41	watching the sun rise every morning and dip below the horizon
52	each night. She liked the feeling of wind in her branches. During
64	rainstorms, she enjoyed feeling the water run down her trunk.
74	One morning, the tree heard a tiny bird chirping sadly in her
86	branches. The tree looked and saw a baby bluebird there, trembling.
97	He was alone in a nest of twigs and feathers. The baby bird was
111	shaking with fright.
114	"What is the matter, little bird?" asked the tree.
123	The tiny bird jumped. He looked surprised, startled by the tree's
134	question. The bird choked back a few tears before saying, "It's my
146	mother. She left the nest two nights ago to go get me some food, and
161	she still hasn't come back."
166	The tree had seen this happen before. Sometimes mama birds leave
177	their nest to get food and run into danger. And sometimes, they stay
190	away longer than they planned.
195	"Well, your mother may be gone, but you still have me," said the
208	tree. "First things first. Let's get some food in that belly."
219	The oak tree saw some squirrels scrounging around on the ground.
230	They were running all over, picking up food.
238	"You there, squirrel," whispered the tree. "Will you share some of
249	your nuts and berries with this good little bluebird?"

Name _____

"Sure!" said the squirrel. He dashed into his home in the tree. He reappeared just as fast with his paws full of food. The squirrel ran again to the bird's nest and tossed in nuts and berries. The tiny bird ate everything up and felt much better.

"You must be thirsty," said the tree. The tree carefully shook her limbs. She cautiously bent her branches, and morning dew from her leaves trickled down to the bird's open mouth.

With the help of the squirrels and occasionally other animals, the oak tree kept the tiny bird fed and watered. Every once in a while, an owl helped out. Sometimes a rainstorm passed over the grassy field, and the tree would gently put her limbs around the tiny bird to protect him from the wind and rain.

This went on for weeks. Slowly but surely, the tiny bird began to grow.

One day, the tree went to check on the tiny bluebird, but the bird was not in his nest. The tree searched all over her limbs and trunk, and even the ground, but she could not see the tiny bird anywhere. "What could have happened?" thought the tree. Just then, with a flutter of wings, the bluebird, which the tree had loved and cared for all these weeks, flew and landed among the branches. He had a mouthful of nice, juicy worms.

"Why, you're all grown up," exclaimed the tree. "And you can fly!"

"All thanks to you," replied the not-so-tiny bluebird with a smile.

Name _____

A. Reread the passage and answer the questions.

1. What two pronouns are used in the first paragraph? Which character do the pronouns refer to?

_____

_____

2. Does the narrator take part in the events of the story? Explain. What point of view is the story told from?

_____

_____

3. What is the narrator's point of view about animals and nature? Give evidence or details from the story.

_____

_____

_____

B. Work with a partner. Read the passage aloud. Pay attention to expression. Stop after one minute. Fill out the chart.

	Words Read	–	Number of Errors	=	Words Correct Score
First Read		–		=	
Second Read		–		=	

Name _____

A Perfect Room

"What do you think of the room we made for you?" the gooey creatures asked their new robot friend. "Most of the rooms here are made out of ooze and slime, but we thought you might like something different."

The robot looked around. The floor was made of bright, gleaming metal. The furniture had perfectly straight edges. The closets' contents were all clearly labeled. "I love it!" she beeped.

Answer the questions about the text.

1. What is the genre of this text?

_____

_____

2. How does the illustration help you to identify the genre?

_____

_____

3. Describe one of the characters in the text. Could the character you chose exist in real life?

_____

_____

4. Describe the setting of the text. Could the setting exist in real life?

_____

_____

Name _____

Read each passage. Underline the context clues that help you figure out the meaning of each word in bold. Then write the word's meaning on the line.

1. The tree looked and saw a baby bluebird there, **trembling**. He was alone in a nest of twigs and feathers. The baby bird was shaking with fright.

   _____

2. The tiny bird jumped. He looked surprised, **startled** by the tree's question.

   _____

3. "Sure!" said the squirrel. He **dashed** into his home in the tree. He reappeared just as fast with his paws full of food. The squirrel ran again to the bird's nest and tossed in nuts and berries.

   _____

4. The tree carefully shook her limbs. She **cautiously** bent her branches, and morning dew from her leaves trickled down to the bird's open mouth.

   _____

5. With the help of the squirrels and **occasionally** other animals, the oak tree kept the tiny bird fed and watered. Every once in a while, an owl helped out.

   _____

Name _____

A. To complete each sentence, circle the word that has the /ûr/ sound found in *shirt*. Then write the word on the line.

1. I watched the acrobat _____ the ribbon in the air.

      hold   roll   twirl

2. We had to go home because my mom forgot her _____.

      ring   purse   form

3. The _____ at the zoo scared my little sister.

      lion   tiger   shark

4. After the game, my shirt was _____.

      dirty   ripped   torn

5. The brave woman pulled a _____ from the basket.

      snake   flame   serpent

B. Read the words in the box. Sort them according to the number of closed syllables.

cargo	pillow	pencil	raven	garlic	panda

Words with One Closed Syllable	Words with Two Closed Syllables
1.	4.
2.	5.
3.	6.

Name _____

Evidence is details and examples from a text that support a writer's ideas. The student who wrote the paragraph below cited evidence that shows how the author used the third-person narrator to tell a story.

Topic sentence →   In "The Oak Tree and the Tiny Bird," the author uses a third-person narrator to tell the story. The narrator's point of view shows how the narrator thinks and feels

Evidence → about the characters and events. Since the author uses the pronouns *she* and *her* to describe the oak tree, I know the story has a third-person narrator. In the first paragraph, I learn how the oak tree feels about her home. Later, I find out that the oak tree knows exactly what to do when she finds a baby bird in her branches. By using

Concluding statement → a third-person narrator, the author lets the reader know how the oak tree feels about helping the baby bird.

Write a paragraph about the text you have chosen. Cite evidence from the text that shows what point of view the story is narrated from. Remember to use precise language and to include action verbs.

Write a topic sentence: _____

_____

Cite evidence from the text: _____

_____

_____

_____

End with a concluding statement: _____

_____

Name _____

A. Read the draft model. Use the questions that follow the draft to help you think about what transitions you can add.

Draft Model

Liz was nervous about her first day at the underwater school. She fidgeted inside her airtight pod. Her teacher, a lobster, greeted her. She made friends with a fish. She had a good day.

---

1. What transition words or phrases might show a cause-and-effect relationship between Liz's nervousness and her fidgeting?

2. What transition words or phrases might help connect the ideas in the rest of the passage?

3. What transition words or phrases could be added to make clear the order of events?

B. Now revise the draft by adding transition words and phrases to help tell the order of events and to connect ideas.

_____

_____

_____

_____

_____

_____

_____

Name _____

| mature | assigned | residents | gingerly |
| selective | scattered | generosity | organizations |

Use the context clues in each sentence to help you decide which vocabulary word fits best in the blank.

The students of the two volunteer _____ were excited to be going on a trip. Due to all their hard work and the _____ they showed by helping others, the students were rewarded with a trip to an apple orchard.

After about an hour drive, the students arrived at their destination. They were welcomed by a few of the _____ who lived at the orchard all year long. The manager explained how they would help gather apples, which the students planned to give to those in need.

"I'm really excited to have you here," the manager said. "I have _____ each of you to a part of the orchard. This way you won't be picking apples from the same trees. I need you to be very _____ and only pick apples that are _____ and ripe."

After some more instructions, the students were _____ to different parts of the orchard. The students had a great time as they _____ climbed ladders in order to pick the best apples.

Name _____

Read the selection. Complete the point of view graphic organizer.

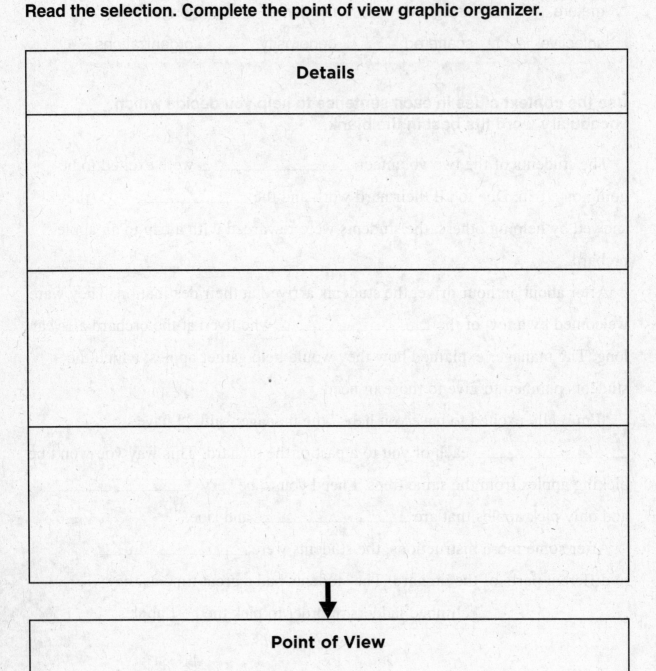

Details

↓

Point of View

Name _____

Read the passage. Use the visualize strategy to make sure you understand what you read.

How Vera Helped

"Excuse me. Are you going to drink that extra juice box?"

11	Brad turned around to see who was speaking to him. It was Vera.
24	Not again, Brad thought. "Um, I guess not. Here you go." Brad
36	handed Vera the second apple juice his mother always packed. She put
48	it in the reusable shopping bag she was carrying.
57	"Thank you so much," she said, smiling, then marched to the next
69	table.
70	Brad rotated back to his friends who sat with him at his lunch table,
84	rolled his eyes, and said, "She's so weird, always walking from table
96	to table, asking people for their food. Do you think she eats it all?"
110	His friends laughed. They wondered the same thing.
118	Vera had been collecting food since the beginning of the school
129	year. The first time she had asked Brad for his leftover food had been
143	back in September. Brad had been in the middle of deciding whether
155	to eat his extra apple, when Vera had asked him if she could have it.
170	He had been so surprised by her request, that he had just handed it to
185	her. It was November now, and Brad was curious about what happened
197	to all those juice boxes and food he gave away.
207	"Do you guys want to find out where all that food goes?" Brad
220	asked his friends. They didn't seem very interested. But it was a
232	Friday afternoon, and there wasn't any homework to do. So he decided
244	to go alone. He'd follow Vera after school and see what happened.

Name _____

After the last bell rang, Brad said good-bye to his friends. Then he waited around until he saw Vera leave. Her shopping bag was bulging. The edges of boxes were pushing out against the bag. Brad didn't know where she lived, so he stuck close behind.

When Vera walked into her house, Brad said out loud, "Wow, maybe she does eat it all. Maybe her family needs the food." He felt unsure as he said it. Her family had a beautiful house with a trimmed yard. But he was truly confused. He didn't know what to make of what he was seeing.

Brad was getting ready to go home when Vera came out of her house. She was carrying a small brown cardboard box. In it, Brad recognized all of the extra food she had collected at lunch!

Vera walked down her block to a house that was four doors down, as Brad quietly followed. She knocked on the front door. A moment later, an elderly man opened the door. Brad couldn't hear what the older man said to Vera, but they both smiled. He took the box from her, went back inside, and closed the door.

As Vera turned onto the sidewalk to walk back to her house, Brad was in front of her. "Hi, Brad," Vera said, looking a little puzzled. "What are you doing here?"

Brad said, "I wanted to know what you did with all that food! You just collect what other kids don't want. That is kind of odd."

Vera explained that her family was friendly with some of the older people in her neighborhood, and she collected the food to bring to them. "Sometimes it is hard for them to leave their homes," she explained.

"Okay, that's not odd. That's a great idea," Brad said. "What can I do to help?"

Name _____

A. Reread the passage and answer the questions.

1. What kind of narrator does the story use? How do you know?

_____

_____

_____

2. What details at the end of the story help you figure out the narrator's point of view?

_____

_____

_____

3. What is the narrator's point of view?

_____

_____

B. Work with a partner. Read the passage aloud. Pay attention to expression. Stop after one minute. Fill out the chart.

	Words Read	–	Number of Errors	=	Words Correct Score
First Read		–		=	
Second Read		–		=	

Name _____

The Bag Parade

Jane was receiving the Citizenship Award during her eighth-grade graduation. As she stood on the stage with the other award winners, she thought about the actions she took that led her to this award.

Four years ago, Jane and her friends were walking home from school. They saw litter all over the sidewalk. Her friend Alex said, "We need to do something. What if we organize a Garbage Bag Parade?" Jane didn't know what she meant. Alex explained that they could invite neighbors to help clean up the street next Saturday. After they filled the bags, they could take them to the dumpsters at the community center. It would be like a parade!

Jane smiled and listened to the end of the principal's introduction. Then she walked across the stage to accept the award.

Answer the questions about the text.

1. How do you know this text is realistic fiction?

_____

_____

2. How do you know that there is a flashback in this text?

_____

_____

3. How do you recognize dialogue in the text?

_____

4. Identify two ways that the characters in the text seem like real people.

_____

_____

Name _____

Read the following sentences from the passage. Underline the context clues that help you figure out the meaning of each word in bold. Write a short definition of the word on the line. Then use the word correctly in a sentence.

1. Vera had been collecting food since the beginning of the school year. . . . It was November now, and Brad was **curious** about what happened to all those juice boxes and food he gave away.

_____

_____

2. Her shopping bag was **bulging**. The edges of boxes were pushing out against the bag.

_____

_____

3. When Vera walked into her house, Brad said out loud, "Wow, maybe she does eat it all. Maybe her family needs the food." He felt unsure as he said it. Her family had a beautiful house with a trimmed yard. But he was truly **confused**. He didn't know what to make of what he was seeing.

_____

_____

4. She knocked on the front door. A moment later, an **elderly** man opened the door. Brad couldn't hear what the older man said to Vera, but they both smiled.

_____

_____

Name _____

A. Read each sentence. Circle the words that have silent letters.

1. I watched the newborn lambs wriggle free from their mother.

2. We asked the plumber to be careful while using the old wrench.

3. She knew the group would look away from the ghastly sight.

4. I was doubtful that he would give us a truthful answer.

5. The honest worker had to resign when he made too many mistakes.

B. Read each word. Circle the open syllables. Underline the closed syllables. Then check the correct box.

	Only Open Syllables	Only Closed Syllables	Both Open Syllables and Closed Syllables
1. spoken	☐	☐	☐
2. planet	☐	☐	☐
3. label	☐	☐	☐
4. banjo	☐	☐	☐
5. refund	☐	☐	☐
6. photo	☐	☐	☐

Name _____

Evidence is details and examples from a text that support a writer's opinion. The student who wrote the paragraph below cited evidence that supports his or her opinion about how well the author used realistic characters and events in the story.

Topic sentence →   In "How Vera Helped," I think the author did a good job of making the characters and the events of the story seem realistic. Brad thinks Vera is weird because she

Evidence → collects food at school. He decides to follow Vera to see what she does with the food. He finds out that she is giving it to some of the residents on her street who are elderly and cannot go out in the cold weather. I think the

Concluding statement → story is realistic because it is about a kid who is curious. I like the ending because Brad realizes that Vera is helping people and that makes him want to help. That is what I would have felt like if I were Brad.

Write a paragraph about the text you have chosen. Cite evidence from the text to show how well the author used realistic characters and events. Remember to support your opinion with details and examples.

Write a topic sentence: _____

_____

Cite evidence from the text: _____

_____

_____

_____

End with a concluding statement: _____

_____

Name _____

A. Read the draft model. Use the questions that follow the draft to help you think about what strong words you can add.

Draft Model

Lawrence saw the ship. He steered his canoe toward the ship. As he got closer, he could hear the cries for help. Lawrence saw two people on the ship.

---

1. What strong words would tell when and how Lawrence first saw the ship?

2. What specific verbs or concrete details would show how Lawrence steered the canoe?

3. What strong descriptive words would give readers a clearer picture of the passengers and the ship?

B. Now revise the draft by adding strong words to make the story about the ship clearer and more interesting to read.

_____

_____

_____

_____

_____

_____

_____

Name _____

> mistreated   encouragement   qualified   boycott
> fulfill   registered   protest   injustice

Finish each sentence using the vocabulary word provided.

1. **(protest)** We didn't want them to shut the library down _____

    _____ .

2. **(registered)** The new baseball league starts next week _____

    _____ .

3. **(fulfill)** My sister picked me up from school _____

    _____ .

4. **(qualified)** To have a good president of our school _____

    _____ .

5. **(boycott)** When my mother was younger, _____

    _____ .

6. **(mistreated)** When we got blamed for _____

    _____ .

7. **(encouragement)** My brother was having trouble with his painting _____

    _____ .

8. **(injustice)** The police officer told us _____

    _____ .

Name _____

Read the selection. Complete the author's point of view graphic organizer.

Details

↓

Author's Point of View

Name _____

Read the passage. Use the reread strategy to help you understand and remember information.

A Child's Fight for Rights

	At age 12, Craig Kielburger of Ontario, Canada, read a terrible
11	news story that changed his life. He read about Iqbal Masik. Iqbal
23	was a boy from Pakistan who was forced to work in a rug factory.
37	Craig read that children were taken from their homes. They were put
49	to work at very young ages. Craig was free. The thought of being
62	captive shocked him.

65	**Iqbal's Story**
67	Iqbal was the same age as Craig. He had been working constant
79	12-hour days since age four. Non-stop working kept Iqbal from going
90	to school. He was not treated well and lived behind large fences and
103	walls.
104	Iqbal was later set free by police. He tried to make his story known
118	and spoke to the press.

123	**Free the Children**
126	Craig was moved by Iqbal's story. It caused him and his friends
138	to write requests and reach out to world leaders to raise money for a
152	wonderful cause.
154	In 1996, Craig founded Free the Children. It was started as a group
167	of young people who wanted to stop the use of child labor around the
181	world.

Name _____

Craig Kielburger and Free the Children

Craig, Age 12-Starts
Free the Children

Craig, Age 14-Frees
children in South Asia

Craig, today-Continues to
fight for children's rights

Many people were not aware that children were being forced to work in factories. Free the Children helped make sure that Canada checked the rugs that were brought into the country. The rugs that were not made by children were labeled.

When Craig was 14, he went with police in South Asia to search for children who were being forced to work. The children were returned to their parents. Craig spoke with the parents and learned the families' stories.

Conflict and Results

Some people disagreed with Craig. They didn't agree with him because they thought he was too young. They didn't like that he was talking about these things.

That didn't stop Craig's group though. After two years, the group used the money they had raised to pay for a center in Pakistan. The center provided shelter and education for children who had escaped capture.

Free the Children still thrives today. It grows because countries like the United States and Germany have learned of Craig's mission. They have taken action. Children raise money with car washes and bake sales.

Craig has helped to build over 100 schools and centers for children in need. With his help and that of other interested people, Craig's group can complete its goal of fighting for children's rights—a very worthy cause.

Name _____

A. Reread the passage and answer the questions.

1. **What are two details from paragraphs 1 and 4 that tell us the author's point of view?**

_____

_____

2. **How are the two details similar?**

_____

_____

3. **What is the author's point of view in the passage? Give evidence or reasons from the passage.**

_____

_____

_____

B. Work with a partner. Read the passage aloud. Pay attention to accuracy. Stop after one minute. Fill out the chart.

	Words Read	–	Number of Errors	=	Words Correct Score
First Read		–		=	
Second Read		–		=	

Name _____

Talia Leman and Randomkid.org

In 2005, Hurricane Katrina hit the Gulf Coast of the United States hard. Ten-year-old Talia Leman helped raise over $10 million to help the victims.

Leman then founded the Web site RandomKid.org. It helps a variety of causes across the globe and has won awards and widespread recognition. Over 12 million young people in 20 countries have joined its effort.

In 2011, Leman won the National Jefferson Award for global change. It was her reward for all of her public service.

Important Events in Talia Leman's Life

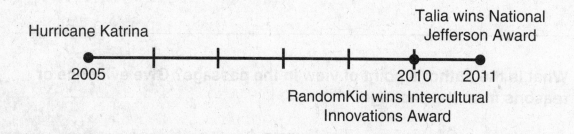

Answer the questions about the text.

1. **How do you know this text is a biography?**

_____

2. **What is one text feature included in this text?**

_____

3. **How does the time line help you understand the text better?**

_____

_____

4. **How can you tell that the events in the text are in the order that they happened?**

_____

Name _____

Read the sentences below. Underline the word in the second sentence that is a synonym or an antonym of the word in bold. Then write the best definition of the word you underlined on the line.

1. Craig was **free**. The thought of being captive shocked him.

   _____

2. He had been working **constant** 12-hour days since age four. Non-stop working kept Iqbal from going to school.

   _____

3. Craig was **moved** by Iqbal's story. It caused him and his friends to write requests and reach out to world leaders to raise money for a wonderful cause.

   _____

4. In 1996, Craig **founded** Free the Children. It was started as a group of young people who wanted to stop the use of child labor around the world.

   _____

5. Some people **disagreed** with Craig. They didn't agree with him because they thought he was too young.

   _____

Name _____

A. Read each sentence. Circle the word with the soft c or soft g to complete the sentence. Then write the word on the line.

1. The performers were a big hit at the _____.

   game   carnival   circus

2. The kids were _____ their plan to stay up late would work.

   certain   positive   sure

3. _____ are a great source of vitamins.

   Grapes   Oranges   Mangoes

4. The wet _____ fell on the kitchen floor.

   sponge   glue   grease

5. Did you see the _____ car drive down the street?

   silver   colorful   police

B. Read each sentence. Circle the word with the final VCe pattern. Then write that final e syllable on the line.

                                                        Final e Syllable

1. Did you complete your homework yet?   _____

2. The ballet dancer is very agile.   _____

3. The hikers want to escape the jungle.   _____

4. Does it excite you to play sports?   _____

5. Which reptile do you want to see first?   _____

6. You must include all of your work.   _____

Name _____

Evidence is details and examples from a text that support a writer's ideas. The student who wrote the paragraph below cited evidence that shows the author's point of view.

Topic sentence →   In "A Child's Fight for Rights," I can tell that the author admires Craig Kielburger's fight to stop the use of child labor around the world. The author says that

Evidence → Craig started a group called Free the Children. In two years, his group raised enough money to pay for a center in Pakistan that houses and educates child laborers. So far, the group has helped to build over 100 schools and

Concluding statement → centers for children. The author supports his point of view by including details about the difference Craig's group has made in the lives of children all over the world.

Write a paragraph about the text you have chosen. Cite evidence from the text to show how you identified the author's point of view. Remember to group related information and use main and helping verbs correctly.

Write a topic sentence: _____

_____

Cite evidence from the text: _____

_____

_____

_____

_____

End with a concluding statement: _____

_____

Name _____

A. Read the draft model. Use the questions that follow the draft to help you think about what reasons and evidence you can add.

Draft Model

Miss Cardenas made a big difference in our community. She started a nursing school five years ago. There was a shortage of skilled nurses in our town before the school opened.

---

1. What efforts did Miss Cardenas make to start the nursing school?

2. What concrete details would describe the problem with the nurse shortage?

3. What reasons and evidence would show how the school helped end the shortage?

4. What examples would show how things got better?

B. Now revise the draft by adding reasons and evidence that will help convince readers to agree with the writer's opinion.

_____

_____

_____

_____

_____

_____

_____

_____

Name _____

haste	divided	shattered	tension
opposed	perish	proclamation	address

Use a word from the box to answer each question. Then use the word in a sentence.

1. What word might be used to describe mental strain? _____

   _____

2. What is an official public announcement? _____

   _____

3. If something is in two separate pieces, what is it? _____

   _____

4. What is another word for *quickness*? _____

   _____

5. What word might describe something broken in many pieces?

   _____

6. If you do not take care of a plant, what might it do? _____

   _____

7. What is another word for *against*? _____

   _____

8. What might a politician give to a crowd of people? _____

   _____

Name _____

Read the selection. Complete the author's point of view graphic organizer.

Details

Author's Point of View

Name _____

Read the passage. Use the reread strategy to make sure you understand the text.

A True Declaration

      Do you like to write? What if you wrote words that helped form

13   laws? This is what Thomas Jefferson did. He was the third president

25   of the United States, but he might be best known for writing the

38   Declaration of Independence.

41   **A Strong Start**

44   Jefferson was born on April 13, 1743. At the age of nine, he began

58   to study Latin, Greek, and French. He would one day be able to speak

72   five languages and read seven.

77   When he went to school he studied law. In 1769 he was part of

91   the House of Burgesses, which was the first group of chosen law-

103 makers in our nation. While there, he was not known as a great public

116 speaker. It is not only spoken words that can make a change, though.

129 Sometimes written words can be just as valuable. People liked the

140 way he wrote about information from meetings while he was there.

151 They knew that he could write very well.

159   When the people wanted to be free from Britain, they asked

170 Jefferson to help. They asked him to write about why people wanted

182 to rebel against Britain. So he wrote the Declaration of Independence.

Name _____

The Power of Words

The Declaration said that we are all created equal. It said that we all have certain rights, including "life, liberty, and the pursuit of happiness." This means that we should all have the right to freedom and happiness. Jefferson wrote these words when the people had a lot of criticism for British law. They wanted to be free from these laws. The people did not agree with the king. They wanted to protect their happiness. They wanted to be in charge of making their own laws.

The words that Jefferson wrote were the thoughts of many people. The people did not want to live under British rule. They felt that it was not fair. Instead, they wanted to have a life of liberty. They wanted a life where all people were equal, where people could search for happiness. This is why Jefferson wrote that if a government is not working, "it is the right of the people to alter or to abolish it." This meant that the people had the power. They could change how they were ruled.

Jefferson's words gave a voice to the people. His words filled them with optimism. His words gave them strength, too. The people felt ready to say they were free of Britain. The day on which they made this official is a special day. Do you know what day it is? It is the Fourth of July.

Jefferson was in law and politics. Yet, he is also known as a great writer. The Declaration that he wrote helped in the development of our nation. It came when the people needed it most. Without his strong words, America might not have been able to find its freedom when it did.

Name _____

A. Reread the passage and answer the questions.

1. **Which detail in the first paragraph tells you what the author thinks Jefferson's biggest accomplishment is?**

_____

_____

_____

2. **What does the seventh paragraph tell you about how the author feels about the words Jefferson wrote?**

_____

_____

_____

_____

3. **How do your feelings about what Jefferson did for our country compare with the author's?**

_____

_____

_____

B. Work with a partner. Read the passage aloud. Pay attention to expression. Stop after one minute. Fill out the chart.

	Words Read	–	Number of Errors	=	Words Correct Score
First Read		–		=	
Second Read		–		=	

Name _____

Encouraging Change

John F. Kennedy did not plan to be a politician. He wanted to have a job in academics or the news. However, from 1947–1953 he was in the House of Representatives. He was a Senator from 1953–1960. In 1960 he was elected president. The words in his speech in 1961 helped bring change. He said, "Ask not what your country can do for you—ask what you can do for your country." He wanted people to better each other's lives.

NASA Headquarters-Greatest Images of NASA (NASA-HQ-GRIN)

President John F. Kennedy gives a speech to Congress in 1961.

Answer the questions about the text.

1. How do you know this text is a biography?

_____

_____

2. What text features does the text include?

_____

_____

3. What does the caption tell you about the photograph?

_____

_____

4. How do you know the photograph is a primary source?

_____

_____

Name _____

Suffix	Meaning
-able	capable of
-ation	action or process
-ism	the act or state of
-ment	act or process of

Using the information in the box above, circle the word in each sentence below with a Latin or Greek suffix. Write the meaning of the word on the line. Use a dictionary if necessary.

1. He was the third president of the United States, but he might be best known for writing the Declaration of Independence.

_____

2. Sometimes written words can be just as valuable.

_____

3. People liked the way he wrote about information from meetings while he was there.

_____

4. Jefferson wrote these words when the people had a lot of criticism for British law.

_____

5. His words filled them with optimism.

_____

6. What Jefferson wrote helped in the development of our nation.

_____

Name _____

A. Read each sentence. On the line, write the correct plural form of the noun in parentheses.

1. **(prop)** The play included many _____ to make it look real.

2. **(hobby)** I have two _____ that I enjoy doing after school.

3. **(mistake)** Did you make any _____ on your homework?

4. **(moss)** There are different kinds of _____ and plants.

5. **(arch)** We drove under two huge _____ when we entered the city.

6. **(day)** There are seven _____ in each week.

B. The suffixes -*ment*, -*ness*, -*age*, -*ance*, and -*ence* all mean "the state of" or "the act of" something. Write the meaning of each word below.

1. storage _____

2. brightness _____

3. punishment _____

4. guidance _____

5. patience _____

6. excitement _____

Name _____

Evidence is details and examples from a text that support a writer's ideas. The student who wrote the paragraph below cited text evidence that shows how the author supported his point of view.

Topic sentence ⟶   In "A True Declaration," the author states that Thomas Jefferson was a great writer. To support his viewpoint, the author says that by writing the Declaration of

Evidence ⟶ Independence, "Jefferson's words gave a voice to the people." The author supports this statement by explaining that people did not want to live under British law. They wanted liberty. Jefferson was able to express this in the Declaration of Independence. By discussing the

Concluding statement ⟶ importance of the Declaration of Independence, the author supports his viewpoint that Jefferson was a great writer.

Write a paragraph about the text you have chosen. Cite evidence from the text to show how the author supported his point of view. Remember to include a strong opening and concluding statements and to use linking verbs correctly.

Write a topic sentence: _____

_____

Cite evidence from the text: _____

_____

_____

_____

_____

End with a concluding statement: _____

_____

Name _____

A. Read the draft model. Use the questions that follow the draft to help you think about what details you can add to give the narrative a strong conclusion.

Draft Model

I had blamed my brother for ruining one of my books. He insisted that he hadn't even gone in my room. Then I saw the book's cover in our puppy's mouth. I learned an important lesson.

1. What details would tell why the narrator blamed the brother for ruining the book?

2. What did the puppy look like when the writer found it?

3. What details would provide a sense of closure and summarize the lesson the narrator learned?

B. Now revise the draft by adding a strong conclusion to help give readers a sense of closure.

_____

_____

_____

_____

_____

_____

_____

Name _____

> characteristics   concerns   disagreed   advancements
>
> resistance   prevalent   inherit   agriculture

Finish each sentence using the vocabulary word provided.

1. **(characteristics)** Fruits such as lemons and limes _____

    _____ .

2. **(prevalent)** During the wintertime _____

    _____ .

3. **(agriculture)** She went to college to _____

    _____ .

4. **(inherit)** Many parents hope their children _____

    _____ .

5. **(disagreed)** Some of the fans at the soccer game _____

    _____ .

6. **(concerns)** At the neighborhood meeting, _____

    _____ .

7. **(advancements)** Computers and cell phones _____

    _____ .

8. **(resistance)** To avoid getting sick, _____

    _____ .

Name _____

Read the selection. Complete the author's point of view graphic organizer.

Details

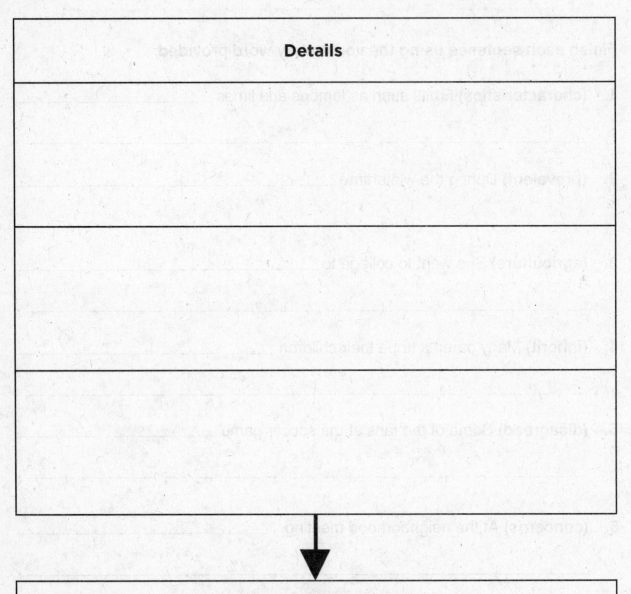

Author's Point of View

Name _____

Read the passage. Use the reread strategy to help you understand the text.

Is Nuclear Energy Safe?

12	Atoms are the tiny things that make up everything in the universe. At the center of an atom is the nucleus. The energy that holds the
26	nucleus together is called nuclear energy. Scientists have discovered
35	how to use that energy as power in our everyday lives. This energy is
49	cheap and clean. But there are dangers as well.

58	**Going Nuclear**
60	In the 1930s, physicists learned how to use the energy inside atoms.
72	They split the atom. This released a huge amount of energy. This was
85	exciting to many people. We get much of our power from oil and coal.
99	But people knew that oil and coal would not last forever. Nuclear
111	energy was much easier to come by. It was a great discovery!
123	Nuclear power plants have many benefits. They do not release
133	harmful chemicals into the air. The waste that is produced is in solid
146	form. This makes it easier to control. Also, there is a very small
159	amount of waste compared to other ways of making energy.
169	Nuclear power plants last much longer than coal plants. They can
180	sometimes last sixty years. Plus, nuclear power plants use only a tiny
192	amount of fuel to make energy. That means we could make nuclear
204	energy for many generations.

Name _____

Problems with Waste

Sadly, there are serious problems with nuclear power. The first problem is the waste that is produced. It is true, the waste is very small. Yet it is highly toxic. Physicians have discovered it can cause severe illness. It has to be contained. Sometimes though, the waste leaks out. It can get into drinking water. The waste can cause cancer in humans.

Japan Earthquake Disaster

It is true that accidents are rare. However, they can be very bad if they happen. In 2011, there was a large earthquake in Japan. As a result, one of the nuclear power plants was destroyed. The event is too recent to know all the effects it might have. Still, scientists believe that when the disaster is finally chronicled, it will prove to be one of the worst nuclear disasters ever.

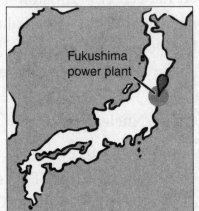

Fukushima power plant

Five days after the earthquake, the U.S. government advised Americans within 50 miles of the plant to leave.

Thousands of people had to be moved away from the plant. Waste leaked into the ocean. The cleanup will be long. It will take decades and it will be very costly.

Being Careful

There is no doubt that nuclear energy can be very good. It can give us energy. It can be safe and cheap. But it can also be dangerous. If we must use it, then we must use it carefully.

Name _____

A. Reread the passage and answer the questions.

1. According to paragraph 2, what is one way that nuclear energy is better than energy from coal and oil?

_____

_____

2. According to paragraphs 3 and 4, what is one of the benefits of nuclear power?

_____

_____

3. List two problems with nuclear energy that the author names in the text.

_____

_____

_____

4. What is the author's point of view on nuclear energy?

_____

_____

B. Work with a partner. Read the passage aloud. Pay attention to rate. Stop after one minute. Fill out the chart.

	Words Read	–	Number of Errors	=	Words Correct Score
First Read		–		=	
Second Read		–		=	

Name _____

Should We Use a Virus to Stop Fire Ants?

The fire ant has been an unwelcome guest in the United States ever since its arrival in 1930. Each year, fire ant colonies cause billions of dollars of damage. This much money could be put to better use.

Luckily, scientists have discovered a virus that may help control fire ant colonies. The SINV-1 virus is capable of destroying an infected colony in three months. Scientists' efforts to turn SINV-1 into a pesticide will save citizens a lot of money.

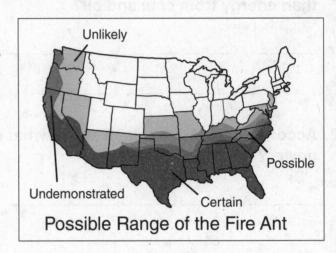

Possible Range of the Fire Ant

Answer the questions about the text.

1. **How do you know this text is a persuasive article?**

   _____

2. **What is the author's opinion about the SINV-1 virus?**

   _____

   _____

3. **What text feature is included? According to the text feature, how is the range of the fire ant changing?**

   _____

   _____

Name _____

> ### Greek Root Meanings
>
> *phys* – nature or body   *dec* – ten
>
> *gen* – birth or kind   *chron* – time

Read each passage below. Use the Greek roots from the box above along with context clues to find the meaning of each word in bold. Write the meaning on the line.

1. In the 1930s, **physicists** learned how to use the energy inside atoms. They split the atom.

   _____

2. Nuclear power plants last much longer than coal plants. They can sometimes last sixty years. Plus, nuclear power plants use only a tiny amount of fuel to make energy. That means we could make nuclear energy for many **generations**.

   _____

3. Waste leaked into the ocean. The cleanup will be long. It will take **decades** and it will be very costly.

   _____

4. A nuclear weapon was used in World War II. John Hersey **chronicled** the events in his true story, *Hiroshima*.

   _____

Name _____

A. Read each sentence and circle the compound word. Then write the meaning of the compound word based on the smaller words.

1. There was a terrible snowstorm yesterday.

   Meaning: _____

2. This new jacket is both warm and waterproof.

   Meaning: _____

3. Did you like to eat peanut butter and jelly sandwiches?

   Meaning: _____

4. She jumped off the diving board and landed with a splash.

   Meaning: _____

B. Read the words in the box. Sort them under their related roots below.

refresher	movement	collection	familiarize
collectible	unfamiliar	freshen	remove

collect

1. _____

2. _____

family

3. _____

4. _____

fresh

5. _____

6. _____

move

7. _____

8. _____

Name _____

Evidence is details and examples from a text that support a writer's opinion. The student who wrote the paragraph below cited evidence that supports the opinion that the author did a good job of presenting information in a compare-and-contrast text structure.

Topic sentence →   In "Is Nuclear Energy Safe?" I think the author does a good job of comparing and contrasting the benefits and dangers of nuclear energy. In the section "Going Nuclear,"

Evidence →   the author discusses the advantages of nuclear power. For example, nuclear power plants last longer than coal plants. In the section "Problems with Waste," the author explains that the waste produced by nuclear power plants is toxic

Concluding statement →   and can cause cancer. I think the author does a good job of using a compare-and-contrast text structure to show what is good and bad about nuclear energy.

Write a paragraph about the text you have chosen. Tell how well the author used a compare-and-contrast text structure to present information about a topic. Cite evidence from the text. Remember to link your opinions and reasons using words and phrases while using irregular verbs correctly.

Write a topic sentence: _____

_____

Cite evidence from the text: _____

_____

_____

_____

_____

End with a concluding statement: _____

_____

Name _____

A. Read the draft model. Use the questions that follow the draft to help you think about the writer's audience.

Draft Model

Technology is cool. It's got this way of making things easier. It does stuff like help people keep up with pals and find important info.

---

1. Who might be the audience for this writing?

2. What words and details could be added or deleted to make the purpose clearer?

3. What words in the model could be replaced to create a more formal tone?

4. What words and details could be added or deleted to appeal to the audience even more?

B. Now revise the draft by adding or replacing language to make the tone more formal.

_____

_____

_____

_____

_____

_____

_____

Name _____

| democracy | commitment | privilege | legislation |
| version | eventually | amendments | compromise |

Use a word from the box to answer each question. Then use the word in a sentence.

1. What word might describe an agreement reached by two different sides?

   _____

   _____

2. What is a system of government where the people decide what happens?

   _____

3. If there are formal changes made to a law, what are the changes called?

   _____

   _____

4. What is another word for *finally*? _____

   _____

5. If a community creates its own laws, what is it responsible for? _____

   _____

6. What is another word for *a sense of obligation*? _____

   _____

7. What do you call a special right that a person has? _____

   _____

8. What is another word for *an account given in a particular way*?

   _____

Name _____

Read the selection. Complete the cause and effect graphic organizer.

Cause	➤	Effect
	➤	
	➤	
	➤	
	➤	

Name _____

Read the passage. Use the ask and answer questions strategy to understand difficult parts of the text.

We the People

	Ms. Quibble stood by the chalkboard in front of her fourth-grade
11	class. "Who can tell me why the American colonies wanted to
22	separate from England and become their own country?"
30	The class was quiet. Some students scribbled in their notebooks
40	or shuffled their feet. Finally, a single hand shot up. Ms. Quibble
52	adjusted her spectacles. "Yes, Kwan?"
57	"People wanted to separate because they wanted liberty,"
65	Kwan said. "They felt that they didn't have a voice in the British
78	government."
79	"Very good!" Ms. Quibble said. "What was the name of the
90	document that declared the colonies' freedom?"
96	Kwan was the only volunteer. "It was the Declaration of
106	Independence," she said.
109	"Kwan, I can tell you will ace this test." Ms. Quibble sounded
121	impressed. "I *highly* suggest that everyone else study during lunch."
131	Sam Jones ran to catch up with Kwan after class. "You sure know a
145	lot about history," he said.
150	"That's because I'm studying for my naturalization exam. I've been
160	memorizing a lot about America," she said.
167	"Your *what* exam?" Sam asked.
172	"It's a test to become an American citizen," Kwan said. "My
183	parents have been studying with me for months. We are so excited for
196	the chance to become citizens!"

Name _____

The Document that Launched a Country

Sam and Kwan sat together at lunch. They inspected a copy of the Constitution that was printed in their textbooks. Kwan explained that the Constitution sets the rules for the government. It also explains the three branches of government. The legislative branch makes laws. The executive branch makes sure laws are followed. The judicial branch makes sense of the laws.

"All of the branches have checks and balances on each other," Kwan said. "This is so no one branch has complete power."

Rights for All People

"I'm still not sure why a piece of paper from hundreds of years ago is still so important," Sam said.

"Do you know the first three words of the Constitution, Sam?"

"We the people…"

To amend the Constitution, both houses of Congress or three-fourths of the states must approve.

"Right! The government of the United States is supposed to speak for all the people in every community. But there are times when the government has needed to make a change or addition to the Constitution. We call these changes *amendments*. The Bill of Rights is made up of the first ten amendments to the Constitution. Do you know what the Bill of Rights is?"

"I think it gives Americans freedoms, like the freedoms of speech and religion," Sam said.

"Exactly! So, the Bill of Rights makes sure everyone is free."

Sam and Kwan placed their trays on the cafeteria counter. "Good luck on the test today, Sam. I think you're going to do great," Kwan said and winked.

Name _____

A. Reread the passage and answer the questions.

1. **What is the cause in the following sentence from the passage?**
   People wanted to separate because they wanted liberty.

   _____

   _____

2. **What is the effect in the following sentence from the passage?**
   People wanted to separate because they wanted liberty.

   _____

   _____

3. **In paragraphs 8–10, what is the cause of the situation Kwan describes?**
   What is the effect?

   _____

   _____

   _____

B. Work with a partner. Read the passage aloud. Pay attention to phrasing and rate. Stop after one minute. Fill out the chart.

	Words Read	–	Number of Errors	=	Words Correct Score
First Read		–		=	
Second Read		–		=	

Name _____

An Interview with a State Representative

"I know that your main responsibilities are writing bills and voting them into effect. Do you have any other responsibilities?" I asked the representative.

"Like every other representative, I serve on two **committees** (kuh•MIT•tees)," he told me.

"What does a committee do?" I asked.

"A committee is a group of Congress members. They study a specific subject, like the military or education, and become experts on that subject. When a bill related to that subject is written, the committee reads the bill. Then it reports to Congress on the bill. Each committee provides valuable advice about changes that should be made to bills before they are passed."

Answer the questions about the text.

1. **How do you know this text is narrative nonfiction?**

_____

2. **What text features are included in this piece of narrative nonfiction?**

_____

3. **Choose one text feature. How does it add to your understanding of this text?**

_____

_____

4. **What opinion does the author express in the text?**

_____

_____

Latin Root	Meaning
commun	common
mem	remember
nat	to be from
scrib	write
spect	look

A. Look at each word below and identify the Latin root. Circle the roots and write the meaning of each word. Use the information above to help you.

1. community _____

2. scribbled _____

3. spectacles _____

4. naturalization _____

5. memorizing _____

6. inspected _____

B. Using what you know about the roots *spect* and *scrib*, write the meaning of each word below. Use a dictionary, if necessary.

7. spectator

_____

8. inscribe

_____

Name _____

A. Read each verb. Then write the correct -ed and -ing forms for each verb.

Verb	+ ed	+ ing
1. scare	_____	_____
2. tap	_____	_____
3. discuss	_____	_____
4. taste	_____	_____
5. force	_____	_____
6. skip	_____	_____

B. Read each word. Draw a slanted line (/) to divide it into syllables. Then write the vowel team on the line.

1. coaster _____

2. bookend _____

3. repeat _____

4. southwest _____

5. needle _____

6. unload _____

Name _____

Evidence is details and examples from a text that support a writer's ideas. The student who wrote the paragraph below cited evidence that shows how the author connected events using cause-and-effect relationships.

Topic sentence → In "We the People," the author uses cause-and-effect relationships to connect the events in the text. A fourth-grade teacher asks her class American history questions

Evidence → to help them review for a test. The main character, Kwan, has been studying for his exam to become an American citizen. The effect of this is that he is the only student in the class who can answer the teacher's questions. Kwan

Concluding statement → then helps his friend Sam study which has the effect of Sam understanding the material. The author uses cause and effect to connect the events in the text and tell a story.

Write a paragraph about the text you have chosen. Tell how the author used cause-and-effect relationships to present information about a topic. Cite evidence from the text. Remember that good explanatory writing includes transition words and uses pronouns and antecedents correctly.

Write a topic sentence: _____

_____

Cite evidence from the text: _____

_____

_____

_____

_____

End with a concluding statement: _____

_____

Name _____

A. Read the draft model. Use the questions that follow the draft to help you think about the topic sentence and the supporting sentences.

Draft Model

Schools have rules. Games have rules. There are rules in my home also. I have to clean my room once a week.

---

1. What is the topic of the draft model? What would be a clearer way to state it?

2. What words could you add to show how the supporting sentences relate to the main idea?

3. What other supporting sentences could you add to strengthen the text?

B. Now revise the draft by adding a topic sentence and supporting sentences to help readers learn more about the importance of rules.

_____

_____

_____

_____

_____

_____

_____

_____

Name _____

accompanies	campaign	governor	intend
opponent	overwhelming	tolerate	weary

Use the context clues in each sentence to help you decide which vocabulary word fits best in the blank.

Elections don't happen every year, so getting to vote is very important for

my dad. When the _____ begins to show who may be the next

_____ of our state, my dad becomes very involved. He usually

has a favorite, but he always learns about the _____ so he has all

information to make a good decision.

The amount of election mail we get is _____, but my dad

carefully goes through it all. He won't _____ it if we tell him we are

_____ of all the news he watches. He insists on knowing as much as

possible.

Every Election Day, we _____ to go together so he can vote after

he gets off of work. But every time, he comes home and has already voted. He likes

the little "I Voted" sticker that _____ him through his day. He says he

has done his duty as a United States citizen, and that makes him happy.

Name _____

Read the selection. Complete the point of view graphic organizer.

Details

↓

Point of View

Name _____

Read the passage. Use the make predictions strategy to predict what will happen later on in the text.

The Sheep in the Wilderness

14	Our herd of sheep was ruled by a cruel shepherd for years. At last we couldn't stand it any longer. We began to stay awake each night
27	until the shepherd had gone to bed. Then we would plan our escape.
40	Finally, the time came to make our move. Late one night, our herd
53	crept quietly out of the pasture while the shepherd and his dogs slept.
66	*We are finally free*! I thought as we entered the dark forest.
78	Life was hard when we lived with the shepherd, but I learned that it
92	was even harder on our own. Trouble came when we needed to find a
106	place to graze. Our group came to a fork in the path. "There's a wide,
121	green pasture that way," an old gray sheep said, pointing to the path
134	that led downhill. "I remember the shepherd took us there once to
146	graze. There was plenty for everyone to eat."
154	"We can't go there!" a younger brown sheep said. "If the shepherd
166	took you to graze in that pasture, he knows where it is. Besides, it's
180	completely surrounded by forest. We would never see the shepherd
190	coming if he tried to sneak up on us." The brown sheep pointed to
204	the other path. It led uphill. "There are fewer trees on the mountain.
217	There must be a pasture there. And if the shepherd comes looking for
230	us, we'll see him before he sees us."

Each of the other sheep took the side of either the old gray sheep or the young brown sheep. The herd argued for hours, but we still could not decide where to graze. Finally we all got so tired of arguing that we fell asleep.

Just before I fell asleep, I had an idea. We could choose one sheep to be our leader! This sheep could hear the other sheep's ideas and decide what to do. This way, we wouldn't have to spend all of our time arguing. I would tell the other sheep in the morning.

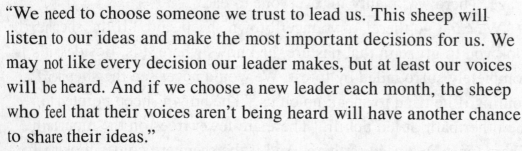

When I woke up, the others had already taken up where they had left off and were arguing over where to graze. So I shouted, "Quiet, everyone!" The herd fell silent and looked at me.

"We can't argue every time we need to make a decision," I began. "We need to choose someone we trust to lead us. This sheep will listen to our ideas and make the most important decisions for us. We may not like every decision our leader makes, but at least our voices will be heard. And if we choose a new leader each month, the sheep who feel that their voices aren't being heard will have another chance to share their ideas."

The herd liked my idea, so we set out to choose a leader. The sheep would vote by putting a brown leaf into a pile if they wanted the young ram to lead, a green leaf if they wanted the old gray sheep, and a red leaf if they wanted me. Each sheep voted. When we counted the leaves, I had won the most votes!

Name _____

A. Reread the passage and answer the questions.

1. What kind of narrator tells the story? How do you know?

_____

_____

_____

2. Is the narrator part of the story? What do we learn about the narrator in the first paragraph?

_____

_____

_____

3. What is the narrator's point of view about leadership? Cite evidence from the text.

_____

_____

_____

B. Work with a partner. Read the passage aloud. Pay attention to phrasing and expression. Stop after one minute. Fill out the chart.

	Words Read	–	Number of Errors	=	Words Correct Score
First Read		–		=	
Second Read		–		=	

Name _____

The *Aurora*'s First Mission

Construction on the *Aurora* ended in 2412. Over a mile in length, it was unlike any space cruiser ever built. The ship's advanced computer controlled the billions of instruments on board. Now the ship needed a captain. Two candidates were favored. Dr. Yanic had designed the ship's computer. He knew how it worked and how to fix it. The other candidate, Admiral Clark, had been in the Galactic Navy and knew how to run a ship.

Answer the questions about the text.

1. **How do you know this text is fantasy?**

   _____

2. **What in the text could not happen in real life?**

   _____

   _____

3. **What text feature is included?**

   _____

4. **How does the text feature help show that the text is fantasy?**

   _____

   _____

Name _____

Read each passage. Underline the words that help you figure out the meaning of each idiom in bold. Then write the idiom's meaning on the line.

1. Finally, the time came to **make our move**. Late one night, our herd crept quietly out of the pasture while the shepherd and his dogs slept.

   _____

   _____

2. Life was hard when we lived with the shepherd, but I learned that it was even harder **on our own**.

   _____

   _____

3. Each of the other sheep **took the side of** either the old gray sheep or the young brown sheep. The herd argued for hours, but we still could not decide where to graze.

   _____

   _____

Name _____

A. Change the *y* to *i* and add the indicated ending to each word. Write the new word on the line.

1. empty + er = _____

2. sorry + est = _____

3. reply + ed = _____

4. carry + es = _____

5. funny + er = _____

6. silly + est = _____

B. Read each sentence. Underline the word with an *r*-controlled vowel syllable. Then circle the *r*-controlled vowel syllable.

1. I think this is the best birthday present she has given me.

2. The small boat dropped its anchor late last night.

3. I put a leash and collar on my dog when we take a walk.

4. We went to see the mayor make an election speech.

5. My brother finished his juice and then went to bed.

Name _____

Evidence is details and examples from a text that support a writer's ideas. The student who wrote the paragraph below cited evidence to show how the point of view helps the author develop the main character.

Topic sentence →   In "The Sheep in the Wilderness," the first-person point of view helps the reader understand what the main character experiences. The main character of the story

Evidence → is a sheep. He tells the story, so we know only what he thinks, sees, and hears. He wants all the sheep to stop arguing and make a decision. Through his eyes, we see him propose that a new leader is elected every month. We feel his surprise when he is elected the leader. The

Concluding statement → author's use of first-person point of view helps bring the narrator's thoughts and feelings alive.

Write a paragraph about the story you have chosen. Cite evidence from the text to show how the point of view affects your understanding of the main character. Remember to use evidence to support your ideas, and use precise language and pronouns correctly.

Write a topic sentence: _____

_____

Cite evidence from the text: _____

_____

_____

_____

_____

End with a concluding statement: _____

_____

Name _____

A. Read the draft model. Use the questions that follow the draft to help you think about using dialogue to develop characters.

Draft Model

Today, I gave a speech at the rally. I talked about some of the changes I plan to make as mayor. I talked about improving our parks.

---

1. Where could dialogue be added to help bring the narrator to life?

2. What dialogue could be added to reveal exactly what the narrator is thinking?

3. What other details of the narrator's plans could be revealed through dialogue?

B. Now revise the draft by using dialogue to develop the main character in the story.

_____

_____

_____

_____

_____

_____

_____

Name _____

gleaming	decade	tinkering	engineering
scouted	squirmed	directing	technology

Use a word from the box to answer each question. Then use the word in a sentence.

1. What did the boy do when he twisted his body to avoid being tagged?

    _____

2. What word describes what a light is doing when it is shining? _____

    _____

3. What profession uses scientific knowledge for practical use? _____

    _____

4. What did the eagle do when it flew in search of food? _____

    _____

5. What is another word for a *period of ten years*? _____

    _____

6. What is the coach doing when he is giving instructions to the team?

    _____

7. What is another word for *puttering*? _____

    _____

8. What word means *the use of science for practical purposes*? _____

    _____

Name _____

Read the selection. Complete the point of view graphic organizer.

Details

↓

Point of View

Name _____

Read the passage. Use the make predictions strategy to help you make predictions about what will happen next.

Leonardo's Mechanical Knight

12	Leonardo scrambled out of bed early one clear spring day in 1464. He was excited to get out to the barn where he was working on a new
28	invention.
29	For months he had begged and pleaded with his father to get him a
43	suit of armor. On April 15—Leonardo's twelfth birthday—he got his
55	wish! He had set the armor up in the barn that day. The barn quickly
70	filled with Leonardo's notes and equipment as he worked and toiled
81	on his new invention: a mechanical knight.
88	High atop a rickety ladder, Leonardo was deep in concentration.
98	All his focus was on fixing the mechanical knight's arm, but it wasn't
111	easy work. No matter what he did, the knight's arm refused to lift!
124	Leonardo frowned and scowled at it.
130	"Leonardo!" yelled a voice. He jumped in surprise and shock as the
142	ladder teetered and shook under his feet.
149	"Oh no!" he exclaimed, losing his balance. He tumbled off the
160	ladder and into a pile of hay. The mechanical knight's arm lay broken
173	on the ground.
176	His good friend Albiera peered down at him. "Leonardo, are you
187	all right?"
189	"I'm fine," he said. He wasn't hurt, just upset that his mechanical
201	knight was broken.
204	Albiera glanced at the knight with the missing arm, the stacks of
216	notebooks, and the piles of papers. "What on earth are you doing in
229	here?" she asked.
232	"I was working on a new invention, but it's not going so well."

Name _____

Albiera knew the best way to cheer Leonardo up was to get him talking about his favorite subject: science. She picked up the mechanical knight's arm from the ground. "This looks interesting. Will you tell me about it?"

Sure enough, Leonardo's face lit up in a smile.

"This is my new invention. It's a mechanical knight," he said. "Watch what it can do!"

He cranked a handle behind the mechanical knight and stepped back to watch. Suddenly, the mechanical knight began to move on its own! It turned its head from side to side. It opened and closed its mouth. The attached arm clicked and ticked as it rose above the mechanical knight's head.

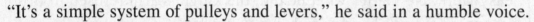

Albiera clapped her hands. *"Bravo!* That's amazing!"

"It's a simple system of pulleys and levers," he said in a humble voice.

"Don't be so modest. I've never seen anything like it before!"

"It's not finished yet. When it's completed, my mechanical knight will sit up, and maybe even walk, just as a human does."

"That would be quite a feat! But I don't understand what you can do with a mechanical knight. Why do we need machines like this at all?" asked Albiera.

Leonardo's face brightened with excitement. "There are so many reasons! Just think about it. A mechanical person will go where we can't go. A machine could explore the bottom of the sea or even the stars! There's so much we could learn from machines."

Albiera laughed. "You have such crazy ideas, Leonardo!"

"You never know," he said. "One day there might be a machine that helps people fly!"

Name _____

A. Reread the passage and answer the questions.

1. What pronouns are used in the first two paragraphs? Which character do these pronouns refer to?

_____

_____

2. What kind of narrator tells the story? Is the narrator part of the story?

_____

3. In paragraph 7, how is Leonardo feeling? In paragraph 10, what does Albiera do to make Leonardo feel better?

_____

4. What is the narrator's point of view about machines? Cite evidence from the text.

_____

_____

_____

_____

B. Work with a partner. Read the passage aloud. Pay attention to expression. Stop after one minute. Fill out the chart.

	Words Read	–	Number of Errors	=	Words Correct Score
First Read		–		=	
Second Read		–		=	

Name _____

Starting Work on the Brooklyn Bridge

I met the head of my work crew, Mr. Calloway. He told me about the caissons on the bridge's foundations, where I'll be working.

"The caissons are locked chambers at the bottom of the river, where workers dig down to the bedrock so the foundations can be placed. The pay's good because it's so dangerous down there," Mr. Calloway said.

"Dangerous? Because of flooding?" I asked.

"No, because the caissons are filled with high-pressure air to keep water from filling the work area," Mr. Calloway replied. "Some guys work down in the caissons too long and come to the surface too fast. The change in pressure gives them terrible pains, called caisson disease. It has killed two workers since 1870," Mr. Calloway explained.

Answer the questions about the text.

1. **How do you know this text is historical fiction?**

   _____

   _____

2. **During which historical event does the story take place?**

   _____

3. **What literary element is included in this piece of historical fiction?**

   _____

4. **What does the literary element add to your understanding of the text?**

   _____

   _____

Name _____

Read each passage. Underline the synonym that helps you figure out the meaning of each word in bold. Then write the definition of the word in bold on the line.

1. For months he had begged and **pleaded** with his father to get him a suit of armor.

_____

2. The barn quickly filled with Leonardo's notes and equipment as he worked and **toiled** on his new invention: a mechanical knight.

_____

3. High atop a rickety ladder, Leonardo was deep in **concentration**. All his focus was on fixing the mechanical knight's arm, but it wasn't easy work.

_____

4. No matter what he did, the knight's arm refused to lift! Leonardo frowned and **scowled** at it.

_____

5. "It's a simple system of pulleys and levers," he said in a **humble** voice. "Don't be so modest. I've never seen anything like it before!"

_____

Name _____

A. Read the words in the box below. Sort the words based on their vowel sounds.

bruised	huge	should	issue	crook	stoop

Vowel sound in *spoon*	Vowel sound in *cube*	Vowel sound in *book*
1. _____	3. _____	5. _____
2. _____	4. _____	6. _____

B. Divide each word into its syllables with a slanted line (/). Then write the consonant + *le* syllable on the line. Remember that an *le* syllable may also be spelled with a consonant + *al, el, il,* or *ol*.

1. tonsil _____

2. formal _____

3. tumble _____

4. bridle _____

5. symbol _____

6. channel _____

Name _____

Evidence is details and examples from a text that support a writer's opinion. The student who wrote the paragraph below cited evidence that supports his or her opinion about how well the author used historical events and realistic characters in the story.

Topic sentence →   In "Leonardo's Mechanical Knight," I think the author did a good job of using people and events from the past to make the characters and the events of the story realistic.

Evidence →   The story is set in 1464. The main character is called Leonardo, and he is working on building a mechanical knight. The author based him on a famous inventor who lived in the fifteenth century named Leonardo da Vinci. Leonardo really did invent a mechanical knight. I thought the dialogue between Leonardo and his friend was realistic.

Concluding statement →   I think the author did a good job of making the character of Leonardo come alive by including realistic dialogue.

Write a paragraph about the text you have chosen. Cite evidence from the text to show how well the author used realistic characters and historical events. Remember to support your opinion with reasons and details and to use pronoun-verb agreement correctly.

Write a topic sentence: _____

_____

Cite evidence from the text: _____

_____

_____

_____

End with a concluding statement: _____

_____

Name _____

A. Read the draft model. Use the questions that follow the draft to help you think about adding setting details to develop the plot.

Draft Model

    I woke up and went downstairs for breakfast. My brother and I went swimming in the lake. Then we went to help our dad with the horses in the barn. After that, we all went inside to do household chores.

---

1. What details could be added to show when and where the story takes place?

2. What setting details could describe the lake?

3. How could you better describe the barn?

4. How could setting details be strengthened to help drive the plot of the story?

B. Now revise the draft by adding details about the setting to help develop the story's plot.

_____

_____

_____

_____

_____

_____

_____

Name _____

rotates	crescent	sliver	astronomer
telescope	series	phases	specific

Finish each sentence using the vocabulary word provided.

1. **(phases)** The large apartment building next door to us _____

   _____.

2. **(astronomer)** Since she likes studying the planets and stars, _____

   _____.

3. **(series)** There was a _____

   _____.

4. **(rotates)** I like when the basketball player _____

   _____.

5. **(specific)** We arrived at his house _____

   _____.

6. **(telescope)** I discovered a new star _____

   _____.

7. **(sliver)** We avoided stepping on glass at the beach _____

   _____.

8. **(crescent)** We looked up at the night sky _____

   _____.

Name _____

Read the selection. Complete the cause and effect graphic organizer.

Cause	→	Effect
	→	
	→	
	→	
	→	

Name _____

Read the passage. Use the ask and answer questions strategy to understand new information in the text.

Stars: Lights in the Night Sky

12	Long ago, people thought the stars were lights attached to a big dome over Earth. The stars moved across the sky each night.
23	As a result, it looked as if the dome were rotating around Earth.
36	But now we know that this isn't true. Stars are actually huge,
48	glowing balls of plasma, or ionized atoms. Some stars look like
59	little pinpricks. Most are so far away that they can't be seen with the
73	naked eye.

75	**What's a Star?**
78	Stars are made of a mixture of plasmas like hydrogen. As you can
91	imagine, a star's core is extremely hot. When lots of pressure squeezes
103	the star's hot center, the hydrogen changes into helium. This process
114	produces lots of energy. As a result, the star shines a bright light
127	through space.
129	When you look up at the stars, you may think that most of them
143	produce a white light. Take another look. Stars generally lie on a
155	color spectrum. This range of colors goes from red to yellow to blue.
168	But what do the colors mean? Well, blue stars are much hotter. If you
182	compare the two stars Betelgeuse (BEE-tehl-jooz) and Rigel
190	(RIGH-jehl), you will see that Betelgeuse is reddish and Rigel is
201	bluish. Rigel has the higher core temperature.

Name _____

The Sun

The sun is the star at the center of our solar system. It looks bigger than other stars. That's because it's closer to Earth. The sun is actually an ordinary, middle-aged star. If you compare the actual size of the sun to the sizes of other stars, you'll realize that the sun is quite average. But the sun does a huge job for a star its size. It provides Earth with most of the energy it needs to support life. Without the sun, Earth would be just a barren rock floating in space! None of the life now on Earth's surface could exist.

Turning Out the Lights

Stars don't last forever. After billions of years, a star will use up all its hydrogen. A small star simply stops shining. This will happen to the sun one day. Of course, this won't happen for billions of years.

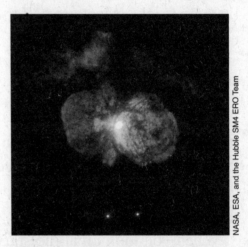

After a large star goes supernova, it may become a black hole.

A large star, however, ends in a big explosion. When a star does this, it is called a supernova (soo-per-NO-va). After the explosion, all of the star's material gets crushed and stops shining. Especially large stars will then become large objects called black holes. In a black hole, the crushed material becomes so dense that it develops a gravitational (grav-i-TAY-shun-al) pull strong enough to keep even light from escaping. To this day, we still don't know what happens in a black hole.

The sun and other stars have fascinated astronomers for centuries. Stars light up the sky at night, and they make life on Earth possible. But they have a life of their own. Next time you're out on a clear night, look up at the stars. Which one do you think might be the next supernova?

Name _____

A. Reread the passage and answer the questions.

1. Reread paragraph 2. What causes a lot of energy to be produced in a star's core?

   _____

   _____

2. What effect does this cause have on a star?

   _____

   _____

3. Under the heading "Turning Out the Lights," what is one example of a cause and an effect? Use text evidence to support your answer.

   _____

   _____

   _____

B. Work with a partner. Read the passage aloud. Pay attention to accuracy. Stop after one minute. Fill out the chart.

	Words Read	−	Number of Errors	=	Words Correct Score
First Read		−		=	
Second Read		−		=	

Name _____

How Rainbows Work

Have you ever used a prism? Drops of water in the air can act like prisms. Light passes into a raindrop. Then all the colors that make up white light separate. Some of the colors are **reflected** (ree•FLEC•ted), or bounced back, by the other side of the raindrop. The colors spread out at different angles, so only one color from each raindrop reaches your eye.

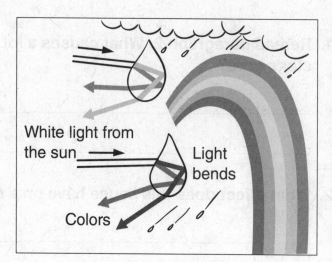

Light passes into many raindrops at the same time. This lets you see all of the colors of the rainbow.

Answer the questions about the text.

1. How do you know this text is expository text?

   _____

2. What text features are included in this piece of expository text?

   _____

3. How does the diagram help you understand the text?

   _____

   _____

4. Which text feature helps you understand the text the most?

   _____

   _____

Name _____

Read each passage below. Underline the context clues that help you understand the meaning of each word in bold. Then write the definition for each word on the line.

1. Stars are made of a mixture of plasmas like hydrogen. As you can imagine, a star's **core** is extremely hot. When lots of pressure squeezes the star's hot center, the hydrogen changes into helium.

   _____

2. When you look up at the stars, you may think that most of them produce a white light. Take another look. Stars generally lie on a color **spectrum**. This range of colors goes from red to yellow to blue.

   _____

3. The sun does a huge job for a star its size. It provides Earth with most of the energy it needs to support life. Without the sun, Earth would be just a **barren** rock floating in space! None of the life now on Earth's surface could exist.

   _____

4. A large star ends in a big explosion. When a star does this, it is called a **supernova**. After the explosion, all of the star's material gets crushed and stops shining.

   _____

5. In a black hole, the crushed material becomes so dense that it develops a **gravitational** pull strong enough to keep even light from escaping.

   _____

Name _____

A. Read each sentence. Circle the word with the same vowel sound found in boy or cow. Then write the letters that make the vowel sound on the line.

1. The voices in the hall would make it hard to study for the test. _____

2. The tree will tower over the plants once it begins to grow. _____

3. I must carefully pack for the long voyage ahead of me. _____

4. There were over two thousand people at the show last night. _____

5. The students were howling with laughter at my comedy act. _____

6. The icy snow was beginning to annoy the birds in the tree. _____

B. Read the definitions below. Then read each word and circle the Greek or Latin root. Write the meaning of the root on the line.

> The Greek root *graph* means "write." The Latin root *spec* means "look."
>
> The Greek root *phon* means "sound." The Latin root *aqua* means "water."

1. megaphone _____

2. speculate _____

3. aquamarine _____

4. geography _____

5. inspection _____

6. homograph _____

Name _____

Evidence is details and examples from a text that support a writer's ideas. The student who wrote the paragraph below cited evidence that shows how the author used headings to tell the reader what each section will be about.

Topic sentence → In "Stars: Lights in the Night Sky," the author uses headings to indicate what each section of the text will be about. For example, the first heading in the text is

Evidence → "What's a Star?" The heading lets the reader know that this text will give information that explains what a star is. The second heading is "The Sun." This lets the reader know that this section will be about the sun. The

Concluding statement → author's use of headings helps the reader to know what to expect in each section of text.

Write a paragraph about the text you have chosen. Show how the author uses precise words to link ideas. Cite evidence from the text. Remember to include a strong opening and a concluding statement and to use possessive pronouns correctly.

Write a topic sentence: _____

_____

Cite evidence from the text: _____

_____

_____

_____

_____

_____

End with a concluding statement: _____

_____

Name _____

A. Read the draft model. Use the questions that follow the draft to help you think about using figurative language to help the reader visualize the text.

Draft Model

The night sky is dark. The stars twinkle high in the sky. Sometimes there are clouds in the sky. The stars are reflected in rivers and lakes.

---

1. What figurative language could be added to describe the night sky?

2. What figurative language could be used to describe the clouds?

3. What other figurative language could be used to help readers visualize the scene?

B. Now revise the draft by adding figurative language to help readers visualize the night sky.

_____

_____

_____

_____

_____

_____

_____

Name _____

> attain   dangling   hovering   triumph

Use the context clues in each sentence to help you decide which vocabulary word fits best in the blank.

When we left for our walk that morning, I never thought that I would be making

history. I happened to grab my camera that was _____ off

my doorknob by its strap before we left for the woods, and it was a lucky chance!

About an hour into our walk, I spied a hummingbird _____

above a large bush with tiny yellow flowers. I took a picture, thinking it was a

personal _____, since I usually forget to take my camera. I put

my photo on a bird Web site, asking if anyone knew what kind it was. A couple of

days later, I got an e-mail saying it was a rare Wolf-Neck Hummingbird and that

no one had ever taken a photo of it before! I was able to _____

something no one else had. It just goes to show, it never hurts to be in the right

place at the right time!

Name _____

Read the selection. Complete the theme graphic organizer.

Detail

↓

Detail

↓

Detail

↓

Theme

Name _____

As you read the poem, ask yourself what message the author wants you to understand.

Spelling Bee

	Letters trip over each other
5	as they race to leave my mouth.
12	My tongue lines them up in order
19	as they march to the microphone:
25	A-S-
26	I am almost alone on the stage.
33	One last kid sags with his head
40	in his hands. He is mouthing
46	each letter as I say it:
52	C-E-N-
53	The hours I have spent on the floor
61	of my room with books
66	in my lap like wounded birds and cramping
74	wrists now seem worth it:
79	D-A-
80	There are lists of words
85	scribbled in my cursive and spelled
91	out in my parents' print
96	on top of dictionaries and thesauruses:
102	N-C-Y
103	There is applause and I smile.
109	I shake the seventh-grade boy's hand
115	and whisper, "I'll meet you back
121	here next year for a rematch."
127	A-S-C-E-N-D-A-N-C-Y

A-S-C-E-N

Name _____

A. Reread the passage and answer the questions.

1. What is this poem about?

_____

_____

_____

2. What is the theme of this poem?

_____

_____

_____

3. What in the poem lets you know what the theme is?

_____

_____

_____

B. Work with a partner. Read the passage aloud. Pay attention to rate. Stop after one minute. Fill out the chart.

	Words Read	–	Number of Errors	=	Words Correct Score
First Read		–		=	
Second Read		–		=	

Name _____

The Principal's Office

"Ms. Lee will see you now," the assistant said.
I swallowed hard and opened the door.
I've really done it, I thought.
As I stepped in, Ms. Lee looked up
And took an envelope from her desk.
"Daniel Birnbaum," she began.
"I just think that you ought to know"
—my heart was pounding in my chest—
"How proud we all are of your work."
Surprised, I saw the envelope read,
"District Youth Robotics Team."
"You made the district team!" she said.
I've really done it! I thought.

Answer the questions about the text.

1. What makes this text a narrative poem?

_____

2. Briefly summarize the text's events.

_____

_____

_____

3. What words repeat in the text?

_____

4. How does the repetition show that the narrator's feelings have changed?

_____

Name _____

> A **stanza** is two or more lines of poetry that together form a unit of the poem. Stanzas can be the same length and have a rhyme scheme, or vary in length and not rhyme.
>
> **Repetition** is the use of repeated words and phrases in a poem. Poets use repetition for rhythmic effect and emphasis.

Read the lines of the narrative poem below. Then answer the questions.

Letters trip over each other
as they race to leave my mouth.
My tongue lines them up in order
as they march to the microphone:
                A-S-

I am almost alone on the stage.
One last kid sags with his head
in his hands. He is mouthing
each letter as I say it:
                C-E-N-

1. **Are there stanzas in this part of the poem? If so, how many and how many lines does each have?**

_____

2. **What kind of repetition is in this poem? How does it affect the poem?**

_____

_____

_____

3. **Write another stanza for this poem that includes the same structure and repetition.**

_____

_____

_____

_____

Name _____

Read each passage. Each word in bold has a different connotation in the poem than its usual denotation. Explain the connotation on the lines.

1. Letters **trip** over each other as they race to leave my mouth.

   _____

   _____

2. One last kid **sags** with his head in his hands. He is mouthing each word as I say it:

   _____

   _____

3. My tongue lines them up in order as they **march** to the microphone:

   _____

   _____

Name _____

A. Read each sentence. Underline the word or words with the variant vowel /ô/ found in *hawk*. Then sort the words by their spellings in the chart below.

1. I love to eat strawberry shortcake.

2. The cat stalked the mouse in the yard.

3. I thought you might like to see the water at the beach.

4. The lady altered her shawl around her shoulders.

al	aw	wa	ough
5. _____	7. _____	9. _____	10. _____
6. _____	8. _____		

B. Circle the correct word in parentheses to complete each sentence. Use a dictionary to help you if necessary.

1. Did you (chose, choose) the red skateboard or the black one?

2. (Their, They're) waiting for us at the restaurant already.

3. I need some (advise, advice) about how to prepare for this test.

4. The baseball crashed (through, threw) the bedroom window.

5. I have (to, two) pairs of sneakers that I wear.

Name _____

Evidence is details and examples from a text that support a writer's ideas. The student who wrote the paragraph below cited evidence to show how the author of a poem communicated the theme.

Topic sentence →   The author of "Spelling Bee" uses a first-person narrator to communicate the theme of the poem. The narrator is in the final round of a spelling bee. Through

Evidence → the thoughts of the narrator we learn how hard she has worked to prepare for the spelling bee. Between each stanza of the poem, the author has the girl spelling part of the word. At the end of the poem, the author shows the whole word *ascendancy* spelled out. The girl's

Concluding statement → thoughts and the word she spells in the contest helped me to understand that the theme of the poem is that hard work leads to success.

Write a paragraph about the text you chose. Cite evidence from the text to show how the author uses details to develop the theme. Remember to include details about the characters and their actions. Use pronouns and homophones correctly.

Write a topic sentence: _____

_____

Cite evidence from the text: _____

_____

_____

_____

_____

End with a concluding statement: _____

_____

Name _____

A. Read the draft model. Use the questions that follow the draft to help you think about what sensory details you can add.

Draft Model

I was nervous.

I waited to hear the election results.

The loudspeaker came on.

I was excited when I heard the principal say my name.

---

1. What sensory details would better describe the speaker's nervousness in the first line?

2. What sensory details would more clearly show how the speaker "waited" to hear the election results?

3. What does the loudspeaker sound like to the speaker?

4. What sensory details would better describe the speaker's excitement in the last line?

B. Now revise the draft by adding sensory details to help readers feel what the narrator is feeling.

_____

_____

_____

_____

_____

_____

Name _____

> | bouquet | encircle | fussy | sparkles |
> | emotion | express | portraits | whirl |

Finish each sentence using the vocabulary word provided.

1. **(bouquet)** On Mother's Day _____

   _____.

2. **(emotion)** Watching the sad movie _____

   _____.

3. **(encircle)** When we play the game in the school yard, _____

   _____.

4. **(express)** Some artists I know _____

   _____.

5. **(fussy)** Whenever we go shopping, _____

   _____.

6. **(portraits)** At the art museum _____

   _____.

7. **(sparkles)** When I am in art class, _____

   _____.

8. **(whirl)** I saw the couple on the dance floor _____

   _____.

Name _____

Read the selection. Complete the problem and solution graphic organizer.

Characters

Setting

Problem

Event

Solution

Name _____

Read the passage. Use the visualize strategy to help you understand the story.

The Stray Dog

	Kwan was in his neighborhood, walking home from the bus stop,
11	when a medium-sized dog came running up to him. It was a shaggy
24	white dog with orange spots and floppy ears and looked as if it didn't
38	belong to anybody. Kwan bent down for a closer look. He didn't
50	recognize the animal from any of the families in the neighborhood.
61	The dog was a big fluffy ball of dirt and had no tags, so there was
77	little doubt. The dog was a stray. Kwan wondered what he should do.
90	Kwan walked the rest of the way to his house, the dog following
103	behind him. When Kwan reached his front door, he picked up the dog
116	and walked inside. The dog wagged his tail frantically with pleasure
127	at being held. He felt like a huge sack of marbles in Kwan's arms
141	as Kwan carried him into the kitchen. His father was there pouring
153	orange juice into a glass. He took one look at Kwan and the dog and
168	nearly dropped the carton of juice.
174	"You can't keep it, Kwan," his father said. "I've already explained
185	to you that we don't have the time or space for a dog."
198	"I know, Dad," said Kwan, putting the dog down on the floor. "But
211	he's definitely a stray, and I really want to help him." The dog ran
225	over to the kitchen door where Kwan's dad kept a pair of running
238	shoes. He took both shoes in his mouth and ran back over to Kwan
252	and plopped the shoes down in front of him. The dog sat there with
266	his tongue hanging out, wagging his tail. Just then, Kwan's mom
277	walked in.

Name _____

"I guess he likes shoes," she said, smiling. "Why don't you take him to Uncle Bae's and see if he wants the dog?" She looked at Kwan pointedly and said, "He gets so few visitors."

"Okay, okay. I'll go see Uncle Bae," said Kwan. He grabbed an old belt from the closet to use for a leash and walked out the door.

Uncle Bae was Kwan's least favorite relative, mainly because he was a real grump. He was about as warm as a block of ice. As a young man, Uncle Bae had fought in the army and had his vision severely damaged so that now he could barely see.

"Come in!" his uncle called when Kwan rang the bell. Kwan walked into the living room with the dog, saying, "Hi, Uncle Bae. It's me, Kwan." His uncle was sitting in an easy chair.

"This stray dog followed me home this afternoon and Mom and Dad said I couldn't keep it," Kwan announced. "We thought you might like to keep him."

"What am I going to do with a dog?" said Uncle Bae angrily. "Get him away. But first, go get my shoes. They're in my bedroom."

Kwan smiled knowingly at the dog. He walked the dog into Uncle Bae's bedroom and brought him over to a pair of loafers. The dog grabbed the shoes in his mouth and ran back into the living room. He plopped the loafers right in Uncle Bae's lap. Uncle Bae's face lit up like the sun. It was the first time in a long time that Kwan saw his Uncle Bae smile. Uncle Bae looked at Kwan and said, "What should I name him?"

Name _____

A. Reread the passage and answer the questions.

1. What is the main problem Kwan faces in the story?

_____

_____

_____

2. What is Kwan's mother's suggestion?

_____

_____

3. What is Uncle Bae's first reaction to the dog?

_____

_____

4. What is the solution to Kwan's problem?

_____

_____

B. Work with a partner. Read the passage aloud. Pay attention to expression. Stop after one minute. Fill out the chart.

	Words Read	–	Number of Errors	=	Words Correct Score
First Read		–		=	
Second Read		–		=	

Name _____

A Change of Heart

"I'm just plain sick of helping Eric with reading," Jen told her father after school one day. "Sometimes he can be a real brat."

"Well," said Jen's father with a knowing smile, "before you quit, look in your room."

Jen went into her room and there on her bed was a little handmade book. It was titled "Best Sister." It was about a boy who gets an "A" in reading and thanks his sister for her help. Jen went to her father. "Maybe I'll read this book with Eric next," she said with a smile.

Answer the questions about the text.

1. How can you tell this is realistic fiction?

_____

_____

2. How are the characters in this text like characters from real life?

_____

_____

3. How does the author foreshadow that Jen will change her mind?

_____

_____

4. How does Jen feel about reading to her brother at the end of the text?

_____

_____

Name _____

Read each passage. Find and underline the simile or metaphor. Then identify what is being compared and if it is a simile or a metaphor.

1. Kwan bent down for a closer look. He didn't recognize the animal from any of the families in the neighborhood. The dog was a big fluffy ball of dirt and had no tags, so there was little doubt. The dog was a stray.

   Simile or metaphor? _____

   What is being compared? _____

   _____

2. Uncle Bae was Kwan's least favorite relative, mainly because he was a real grump. He was about as warm as a block of ice.

   Simile or metaphor? _____

   What is being compared? _____

   _____

3. He plopped the loafers right in Uncle Bae's lap. Uncle Bae's face lit up like the sun. It was the first time in a long time that Kwan saw his Uncle Bae smile.

   Simile or metaphor? _____

   What is being compared? _____

   _____

Name _____

A. Read each sentence. Underline the word that has two closed syllables. Write the word on the line and divide the syllables with a slanted line (/).

1. I am a member of the chess club at school. _____

2. The blanket is on top of the sofa. _____

3. The student dug a fossil out of the sand. _____

4. The child is going to get the plastic toy. _____

5. There is a lot of traffic at this time on Friday. _____

B. Read the definitions in the box below. Write the prefix and the root on the lines. Then write the meaning of the prefix on the line below each word.

> The Latin prefix *extra-* means "outside" or "beyond."
>
> The Latin prefix *inter-* means "between."

1. extracurricular _____ _____

Prefix Meaning: _____

2. interstate _____ _____

Prefix Meaning: _____

3. intermission _____ _____

Prefix Meaning: _____

4. extraordinary _____ _____

Prefix Meaning: _____

Name _____

> *Evidence* is details and examples from a text that support a writer's ideas. The student who wrote the paragraph below cited evidence to show how the author used problem and solution to develop the plot.

Topic sentence →   In "The Stray Dog," the author develops the plot by having Kwan solve the problem of what to do with a stray dog.

Evidence → At the beginning of the story, a stray dog follows Kwan home. Kwan's father tells him that he cannot keep the dog. Kwan's problem is that he wants to help the dog. His mother tells him to take the dog to his uncle's house. At first his uncle does not want the dog, but Kwan comes up with a solution that makes his uncle want to keep the dog.

Concluding statement → The author used the steps that Kwan takes to solve his problem to make up the story's events, or the plot, of the story.

Write a paragraph about the text you have chosen. Cite evidence that shows how the author used problem and solution to develop the plot.

Write a topic sentence: _____

_____

Cite evidence from the text: _____

_____

_____

_____

_____

End with a concluding statement: _____

_____

Name _____

A. Read the draft model. Use the questions that follow the draft to help you think about how you can grab the reader's attention with a strong beginning.

Draft Model

Dad and I always help each other. Sometimes I help Dad in the kitchen. Other times, Dad helps me work on my bike or finish my homework.

---

1. How does the narrator help Dad in the kitchen?

2. How does Dad help with the bike?

3. How does Dad help with homework?

4. What opening sentence would introduce the topic and grab the reader's attention?

B. Now revise the draft by adding a strong beginning that introduces the topic clearly.

_____

_____

_____

_____

_____

_____

Name _____

| territories | withered | plunging | settlement |
| scoffed | prospector | topple | shrivel |

Use the context clues in each sentence to help you decide which vocabulary word fits best in the blank.

At school Belinda learned about Nellie Cashman, a famous _____ who explored Alaska for gold. Belinda was inspired. Nellie had left her home to explore _____ like Alaska and other large regions to look for gold.

"I'm going to be like Nellie Cashman," she told her sister, Jane.

Jane just _____, mocking her sister. "Sure, like you're actually going to find something! You'll get lost out in the sun and _____ up like a raisin!"

"I'll find something. Just you wait and see," said Belinda. She knew she could find minerals just like Nellie. It might not be gold she'd find, but she didn't plan on becoming dried up and _____ in the sun like Jane thought she would.

Belinda and her family lived in an area that had woods, rivers, and streams. She felt that the _____ where Nellie lived must have been almost the same. *Where would Nellie have looked?* Belinda asked herself. There was a small stream behind the house. Belinda remembered that people in Alaska found gold in streams and rivers. "I'll look there first!"

Belinda walked along the bank of the stream. Suddenly something in the shallow water caught her eye. She had to get down there and grab it. "Maybe it's gold!" Since the bank was steep, she walked carefully so she wouldn't _____ over. The last thing she wanted was to go _____ or diving into the cold stream.

Belinda made it to the stream and saw what was shining in the water. It was three shiny quarters sitting on the rocks and sand. Belinda swiped them up and put them in her pocket. "Well," she said as she climbed the bank, "it's not gold. But it's a good start!"

Name _____

Read the selection. Complete the cause-and-effect graphic organizer.

Cause	→	Effect
	→	
	→	
	→	
	→	

Name _____

Read the passage. Use the visualize strategy to make sure you understand what you read.

Working on the Weather

	Now, back in the days of wagon trains and gold rushes, many
12	people were leaving the Midwest to live in California. They had heard
24	the weather was beautiful the whole year. The soil never got too dry.
37	They thought they could plant crops and never worry they would die
49	from the heat.
52	The summer of 1849 was so hot that even now in the Midwest,
65	150 years later, it is called the Great Heat. To add to the troubles, at the
81	beginning of September, it began to rain. It rained for the next month
94	straight! The problem was that when the rain got close to the ground,
107	the heat turned it to steam.
113	The steam did cool enough to turn into fog, though. The country
125	was covered in fog. The fog was so thick that ranchers could not see
139	to give their animals water. It didn't matter, though. The animals just
151	drank the fog right out of the air! Farmers weren't so happy, however.
164	The sun couldn't get through. The seeds didn't know which way was
176	up. They grew down into the ground!
183	Febold Feboldson decided to fix things when it came to the
194	weather. He ordered some fog scissors from London. They know their
205	fog. Unfortunately, the English sent them on a slow boat. Febold didn't
217	get the scissors until Thanksgiving.

Name _____

Febold finally got to work. He cut the fog out of the air in strips. He laid them down along the roads. That way they wouldn't drown the fields. After a while, the dust covered the roads. You couldn't even tell where Febold buried the fog. Everyone was excited at the time. However, many mail carriers in the middle of the country have whispered Febold's name in anger ever since. Every spring, even today, when it rains or thaws, the fog comes leaking out of the ground. It turns country roads into rivers of mud!

There's also another problem here in the Midwest. Sometimes there is just not enough rain. The next year, in 1850, there was a terrible drought. The sun shone for weeks. There were no clouds to cover the people in Nebraska.

Febold was annoyed, because he loved fishing. It was too sunny and hot to sit and wait for the fish to bite. So he decided to make some rain fall.

He collected all the wood and dry grass he could find. Then he went from lake to lake. He was building the biggest bonfires you've ever seen. He thought if he could get the fires really hot, they'd make the water in the lakes evaporate and form clouds. Soon there were many clouds in the sky from all the water rising out of the lakes. They bumped into each other and the rain began to fall!

Once Febold started the rain, it rained regularly again. The only problem was that the people on the plains had nowhere to swim, since there was no water in the lakes!

Name _____

A. Reread the passage and answer the questions.

1. What happened when the rain got close to the ground during the Great Heat?

_____

_____

2. Why did the seeds grow down into the ground?

_____

_____

3. According to the third paragraph on the second page of the passage, what caused Febold to try to make some rain fall?

_____

_____

4. What was one effect of Febold making rain?

_____

_____

B. Work with a partner. Read the passage aloud. Pay attention to intonation and phrasing. Stop after one minute. Fill out the chart.

	Words Read	–	Number of Errors	=	Words Correct Score
First Read		–		=	
Second Read		–		=	

Name _____

The Mighty John Henry

When Americans started moving west, the country needed a railroad for faster travel. John Henry worked to help build that railroad. He was the strongest man to ever live.

The railroad needed to pass through Big Bend Mountain, and the boss wanted to use a powered drill to get through the rock. But that drill would put John Henry out of work! So John Henry challenged the mechanical drill to a digging competition. With two twenty-pound hammers in each hand, John Henry dug 15 feet in 35 minutes. He beat the machine and saved the day!

Answer the questions about the text.

1. **How can you tell this is a tall tale?**

   _____

   _____

2. **What is one example of hyperbole in the text?**

   _____

   _____

3. **In what way is John Henry a larger-than-life hero?**

   _____

   _____

4. **Why does the author include details about how far John Henry and the machine dug?**

   _____

   _____

Name _____

Read each sentence below. Underline the context clues that help you understand the meaning of each homograph in bold. Then write the correct definition of the homograph on the line.

1. Now, back in the days of wagon trains and gold rushes, many people were leaving the Midwest to **live** in California.

_____

2. To add to the troubles, at the beginning of **fall**, it began to rain.

_____

3. The problem was that when the rain got **close** to the ground, the heat turned it to steam.

_____

4. They grew down into the **ground**!

_____

5. He was **building** the biggest bonfires you've ever seen.

_____

Name _____

A. Read the words below. Use a slanted line (/) to divide each word into its syllables. On the line, write whether the first syllable is "open" or "closed."

1. prevent　　　　_____

2. famous　　　　_____

3. ribbon　　　　_____

4. bookend　　　　_____

5. cider　　　　_____

6. vacancy　　　　_____

B. Draw a line to match each singular noun with its correct plural rule. Then write the plural form of the noun on the line.

1. hoof　　　　change middle vowels　　　　_____

2. woman　　　　change middle vowels
　　　　　　　　and consonant　　　　_____

3. tooth　　　　make no change　　　　_____

4. mouse　　　　change ending to *-ves*　　　　_____

5. deer　　　　change ending to *-en*　　　　_____

Name _____

Evidence is details and examples from a text that support a writer's opinion. The student who wrote the paragraph below cited evidence that shows how well the author uses exaggeration to develop the main character.

Topic sentence →   In "Working on the Weather," the author does a good job of using exaggeration to show that Febold Feboldson is always trying to fix the weather. The author uses

Evidence → exaggeration to describe Febold's actions when he cuts the fog into strips and then buries it on the roads. But there was a problem. In the spring, the fog came to the surface and turned the roads to rivers of mud. I think the author's use

Concluding statement → of exaggeration made Febold a funny character. Every time he tried to fix the weather, he made something else worse.

Write a paragraph about a tall tale you have chosen. Cite evidence from the text to show how well an author uses exaggeration to develop the main character. Remember to use reasons and evidence to support your opinion and to use articles correctly.

Write a topic sentence: _____

_____

Cite evidence from the text: _____

_____

_____

_____

End with a concluding statement: _____

_____

Name _____

A. Read the draft model. Use the questions that follow the draft to help you think about what sentence types you can use.

> ## Draft Model
>
> Tall tales teach about life. Tall tales entertain. My grandmother tells me tall tales. I think tall tales are clever and fun to read, and I love tall tales.

1. How could you combine the first two sentences to make one longer sentence?

2. How could you rewrite the third sentence to provide more detail?

3. How could you rewrite the last sentence as two sentences to strengthen the narrator's final point?

B. Now revise the draft by using different types of sentences to make it more interesting to read.

_____

_____

_____

_____

_____

_____

_____

Name _____

mischief	procedure	dizzy	politician
genuine	nowadays	hilarious	experiment

Use a word from the box to answer each question. Then use the word in a sentence.

1. How can a spinning ride at the playground make you feel? _____

   _____

2. What is another word for *real*? _____

   _____

3. What word can be used to compare something with the past? _____

   _____

4. What might a scientist use as a test to discover something? _____

   _____

5. What would you call a person who seeks public office? _____

   _____

6. How might you describe your favorite comedian on television? _____

   _____

7. What can someone create if they cause harm or trouble? _____

   _____

8. How would you describe a series of steps used to accomplish an action?

   _____

   _____

Name _____

Read the selection. Complete the problem and solution graphic organizer.

Problem	Solution

Name _____

Read the passage. Use the summarize strategy to find the most important ideas in the passage.

Breaking the Silence

	American Sign Language is used by millions of people. The
10	hearing impaired have used it for years. A young science student
21	named José Hernández-Rebollar noticed that few people who could
30	hear knew ASL. They couldn't communicate with the hearing
39	impaired. He set out to make a new tool that would help solve this
53	problem. With it, he also saw a new way for the hearing impaired to
67	communicate.
68	**Early Years**
70	Hernández-Rebollar worked as an engineer in his native Mexico.
79	He even had a part in making what became the largest telescope in
92	the world!
94	In 1998, he received a grant to study in the United States. He chose
108	to get his Ph.D. degree at George Washington University, where he
119	studied electrical engineering. In 2000, he began work on his school
130	project. It was an idea for a new glove.
139	**His Invention**
141	Hernández-Rebollar called his tool the AcceleGlove. What was
149	the logic? People used their hands to sign. The glove could turn sign
162	language into spoken or printed words.
168	This process of turning movement into voice involves many steps.
178	It starts when the glove is put on the hand and strapped to the arm.
193	The glove sends signals made by where and how the hand and wrist
206	move. The glove compares where the wrist and hand are to where the
219	body is.

Name _____

A computer receives the signals. It then categorizes and links the hand movement with the correct word. An automatic computer voice then says the word.

Dr. Hernández-Rebollar's AcceleGlove helps hearing and non-hearing people communicate.

Uses for the Glove

The AcceleGlove can do many things. It can be helpful when something is urgent. People can exchange words quickly. It can also be used to teach ASL or for other forms of sign language.

The glove can translate ASL into Spanish as well as English. This can help people who move to this country. There is hope that one day the glove will help create one common sign language. Each country would not need its own.

Also, the total number of words that the glove knows will increase as more studies are done. There will be fewer mistakes.

There are other uses for the glove for people who can hear. People in the armed forces use a communication technique that involves silent gestures out in the field. The glove can help them send wireless notes back and forth. They would only need to move their hands.

It can also be used for fun in the online world of games. To move within a video game or direct a game with the glove are new ways a person can play.

Hernández-Rebollar's AcceleGlove has a wide range of uses. It is a tool that could end up meeting the needs of the hearing and non-hearing alike.

Name _____

A. Reread the passage and answer the questions.

1. **What problem is presented in paragraph 1?**

   _____

   _____

2. **What solution is presented to the problem in paragraph 1?**

   _____

   _____

3. **What is another example of a possible problem and its solution in paragraph 8?**

   _____

   _____

   _____

   _____

B. Work with a partner. Read the passage aloud. Pay attention to rate and accuracy. Stop after one minute. Fill out the chart.

	Words Read	–	Number of Errors	=	Words Correct Score
First Read		–		=	
Second Read		–		=	

Name _____

Thomas Edison

Thomas Edison was one of the world's greatest inventors. He was born in 1847 in Milan, Ohio. As a child, Edison was curious about the way things worked. Many of Edison's inventions led to machines that we still use today. In 1877, he invented the phonograph, which later became the record player. In 1879 he made a long-lasting light bulb. His Kinetograph of 1891 later became the movie camera.

Thomas Edison thought up over 1,000 inventions.

Answer the questions about the text.

1. How can you tell this text is a biography?

   _____

2. What text feature is included in this text?

   _____

3. How do the photo and caption help you understand the text better? What information do they give you?

   _____

   _____

4. In what order are the events of the text told?

   _____

   _____

Name _____

Greek root	Meaning
tele	far
log	thought
mis	wrongly
auto	self
techn	art, skill

Read the sentences below. Then look at the Greek roots and their meanings above. Underline the word in each sentence that contains a Greek root and write the Greek root on the line. Then write the definition of the underlined word on the line.

1. He even had a part in making what became the largest telescope in the world!

   _____

2. What was the logic?

   _____

3. An automatic computer voice then says the word.

   _____

4. There will be fewer mistakes.

   _____

5. People in the armed forces use a communication technique that involves silent gestures out in the field.

   _____

Name _____

A. Read each sentence. Underline the word with a vowel team syllable. On the line, write the letters that make the vowel team.

1. My trainer helped me practice for the game. _____

2. Is he giving a discount for this scratched item? _____

3. I will study to increase my chances of getting a better grade. _____

4. I will not reveal the secret of her amazing magic trick. _____

5. A baboon is an interesting type of animal. _____

6. The staircase rose endlessly to the sky. _____

B. Read the meanings of the roots. Draw a line to match the words with the same root. Then write the meaning of the root on the line.

> The Greek root *scop* means "see."   The Latin root *ped* means "foot."
>
> The Greek root *bio* means "life."   The Latin root *aud* means "listen."
>
> The Greek root *photo* means "light."

1. autobiography   periscope   _____

2. pedestrian   telephoto   _____

3. telescope   pedal   _____

4. auditorium   biological   _____

5. photocopier   audible   _____

Name _____

Evidence is details and examples from a text that support a writer's opinion. The student who wrote the paragraph below cited evidence that shows how the author uses photographs and captions in a text.

Topic sentence →   In "Thomas Edison," the author included an interesting photograph and caption that provide more details about the topic. The photograph that the author

Evidence → used shows Thomas Edison standing in his laboratory. The photograph lets me see what Thomas Edison looked like. The caption tells me that Edison had thought up more than

Concluding statement → 1,000 inventions. I like the fact that the caption the author included gives me information that is not in the text. Seeing what Edison looked like makes him seem more real to me.

Write a paragraph about a text you have chosen that contains photographs and captions. Cite evidence from the text to show how well the author uses photos and captions to add more details about the topic. Remember to use reasons and evidence to support your opinion and use adjectives that compare correctly.

Write a topic sentence: _____

_____

Cite evidence from the text: _____

_____

_____

_____

_____

End with a concluding statement: _____

_____

Name _____

A. Read the draft model. Use the questions that follow the draft to help you use transitions to connect ideas.

Draft Model

   Why is the smartphone the most important invention? It helps people stay connected. It allows people to look up information easily. You can use it to get directions. It is not just a phone—it is a tiny computer.

1. How many supporting sentences are there for this draft model?

2. Is there a logical flow from one idea to the next?

3. What transition words would fit well at the beginning of some of the supporting sentences?

B. Now revise the draft by adding transitions to move smoothly from one idea to another.

_____

_____

_____

_____

_____

_____

_____

_____

Name _____

cling   humid   magnify   mingle

microscope   dissolves   typical   gritty

Finish each sentence using the vocabulary word provided.

1. **(gritty)** After a day at the beach, _____

_____.

2. **(humid)** I was not used to _____

_____.

3. **(typical)** Even though she was not _____

_____.

4. **(microscope)** In order to see the _____

_____.

5. **(dissolves)** If you add water _____

_____.

6. **(magnify)** His glasses _____

_____.

7. **(cling)** In the tall tree _____

_____.

8. **(mingle)** At the school party _____

_____.

Name _____

Read the selection. Complete the sequence graphic organizer.

```
┌──────────────────────────────────────────────┐
│                                              │
│                                              │
│                                              │
│                                              │
└──────────────────────────────────────────────┘
                      │
                      ▼
┌──────────────────────────────────────────────┐
│                                              │
│                                              │
│                                              │
│                                              │
└──────────────────────────────────────────────┘
                      │
                      ▼
┌──────────────────────────────────────────────┐
│                                              │
│                                              │
│                                              │
│                                              │
└──────────────────────────────────────────────┘
                      │
                      ▼
┌──────────────────────────────────────────────┐
│                                              │
│                                              │
│                                              │
│                                              │
└──────────────────────────────────────────────┘
```

Name _____

Read the passage. Use the summarize strategy to make sure you understand the text.

At Your Fingertips

	What makes you different? Is it your hair or is it your name? Is
14	it the shape of your eyes and nose? All of these may be important.
28	However, there is one thing that truly sets you apart from everyone:
40	your fingerprints. You might not think of your fingerprints as part
51	of your identity. But they have replaced other uncertain methods of
62	identification. If you look closely, you can see that fingerprinting
72	is a reliable way of identifying people.
79	As we age, our looks change. Our hair and height may change and
92	even our face may change shape. There is one thing that stays the
105	same: our fingerprints. Unless you injure your fingertips, your prints
115	will be the same for your entire life, not just part of it. You will have
131	the same prints as an adult that you did as a child.
143	No two people are known to have the same prints. A quick look at
157	your fingertips might not prove much. Take a detailed look, though.
168	There are swirls and ridges. All of those shapes are specific to you.
181	The shapes you see are not the same for anyone else. Your prints are
195	unique. This is how they help to identify people. It took many years
208	for us to know the importance of fingerprints, though.

Name _____

In 1858, Sir William Herschel of England had people sign papers with handprints. He then used fingerprints. The more fingerprints he saw, the more he noticed how no prints were the same. It seemed no two prints were identical. He saw that prints might be used to identify people.

In 1892, scientist Sir Francis Galton wrote a book about prints. He proved that they do not alter during a person's life. They remain the same. He said that it was not likely for two people to have the same prints. The odds of two people having the same prints were 1 in 64 billion!

Galton's proof was used by police to help solve crimes. In 1901, the London police began using prints to find people. They found this was the best way. They could be sure they had found the right person to arrest. In 1903, the New York State Prison system began using prints to identify criminals, too.

Fingerprints can be used for more than identifying criminals. Fingerprints have since been used for identification by the U.S. Navy, the U.S. Marine Corps, and the F.B.I. Fingerprint scans can also act as a "key" to unlock a door or open files on a computer. Since they are unique, fingerprints are a sure way of keeping certain offices and files

Stockbyte/Getty Images

Every fingerprint has a unique set of swirls and ridges.

safe. Did you know that children are often fingerprinted to keep them from getting lost?

The importance of fingerprints has proved to be a great discovery. Whether used to sign papers, identify criminals, or unlock doors, prints are a reliable way to identify people. When we want to know who people are, we can look at their faces or ask their names. If we want to be sure, we have to look closely at the swirls and ridges on their fingertips.

Name _____

A. Reread the passage and answer the questions.

1. What did Sir William Herschel discover in 1858?

_____

_____

_____

2. According to the text, what was the next discovery after Herschel's?

_____

_____

_____

3. How do you know that the information in the text is presented in time order?

_____

_____

_____

B. Work with a partner. Read the passage aloud. Pay attention to rate. Stop after one minute. Fill out the chart.

	Words Read	–	Number of Errors	=	Words Correct Score
First Read		–		=	
Second Read		–		=	

Name _____

Scott Aldrich's Micro Art

Scott Aldrich uses microscopes and light to make art. Aldrich was trained as a chemist. He often used microscopes to look at chemicals. The shapes he saw inspired his art. Aldrich uses light filters. The filters allow certain colors to pass through chemicals. Then he takes pictures of the substances using a camera with a built-in microscope. The pictures often look like familiar objects and animals!

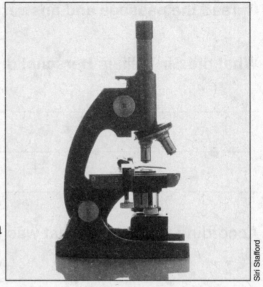

Siri Stafford

In his photography, Aldrich reveals the world as seen through a microscope.

Answer the questions about the text.

1. How do you know this is an expository text?

_____

2. What text features does the text include?

_____

3. What does the photograph show? How does it add to the text?

_____

_____

4. What information does the caption give you?

_____

_____

Name _____

A. Draw lines to match each word in Column 1 with an antonym in Column 2.

Column 1

Column 2

1. identical

a. simple

2. reliable

b. maintain

3. entire

c. different

4. alter

d. part

5. specific

e. general

6. detailed

f. unsteady

B. Rewrite each sentence below using an antonym for the underlined word.

1. We stayed to watch the <u>entire</u> movie.

_____

2. My mother did <u>not alter</u> the soup recipe.

_____

3. The math lesson was so <u>detailed</u> that I had to take notes.

_____

Name _____

A. Read each sentence. Underline any words that have *r*-controlled vowel syllables. Then circle the letters that make the *r*-controlled vowel syllable.

1. The popular singer was going to play a show in my town.

2. When I enter the shop, I always notice a strange odor.

3. That object can be a danger to people walking along the harbor.

4. My daughter loves to ride up and down on the elevator.

5. I prefer real chili peppers to the powder that is available.

6. He could not pull up his coat zipper because it was broken.

B. Circle the correct word in parentheses to complete each sentence. Use a dictionary to help you if necessary.

1. My sister is better at math (then, than) my brother.

2. Do you understand the (moral, morale) of the story?

3. Please (lay, lie) the book down on the table.

4. I immediately saw the (affect, effect) of the sun on my skin.

5. The wind caused the (lose, loose) tile to fall from the rooftop.

Name _____

> *Evidence* is details and examples from a text that support a writer's ideas. The student who wrote the paragraph below cited evidence that shows how the author uses key details to support the main idea.
>
> **Topic sentence** ⟶   In "At Your Fingertips," the author provides key details to support the main idea that fingerprints are a reliable way to identify people. The author gives
>
> **Evidence** ⟶ examples of how fingerprints are used to identify people. Two examples the author gives are that fingerprints are used by police to help solve crimes, and fingerprint scans can be used for security purposes. The author's
>
> **Concluding statement** ⟶ use of key details supports the main idea that everyone's fingerprints are unique and are a way to identify people.

Write a paragraph about the text you have chosen. Show how the author uses key details to support the main idea. Cite evidence from the text. Remember to include a strong opening and concluding statement.

Write a topic sentence: _____

_____

Cite evidence from the text: _____

_____

_____

_____

_____

End with a concluding statement: _____

_____

Name _____

A. Read the draft model. Use the questions that follow the draft to help you use a formal voice.

Draft Model

The teacher uses this thing a lot. You can't pick it up, but you can write all over it. It gets totally dusty with chalk. It's not a super cool thing, but it does the job.

---

1. What are some examples of conversational language in the first sentence?

2. What formal language can be used to replace these words in the first sentence?

3. How will formal language improve the draft model?

4. Where else in the draft model can formal language be used to replace conversational words or slang?

B. Now revise the draft by adding words and phrases that show a formal voice.

_____

_____

_____

_____

_____

_____

Name _____

uncover	era	tremendous	evidence
expedition	document	permanent	archaeology

Use a word from the box to answer each question. Then use the word in a sentence.

1. What is the scientific study of the way people lived in the past?

_____

_____

2. What word might be used to describe an elephant? _____

_____

3. What could a group of people looking for lions be called? _____

_____

4. What is important to have to convince people that you saw an alien? _____

_____

5. What is another way to say you keep a record of something? _____

_____

6. What is something that is intended to last without change? _____

_____

7. What is another word for *disclose*? _____

_____

8. What could the time period of the dinosaurs be considered? _____

_____

Name _____

Read the selection. Complete the sequence graphic organizer.

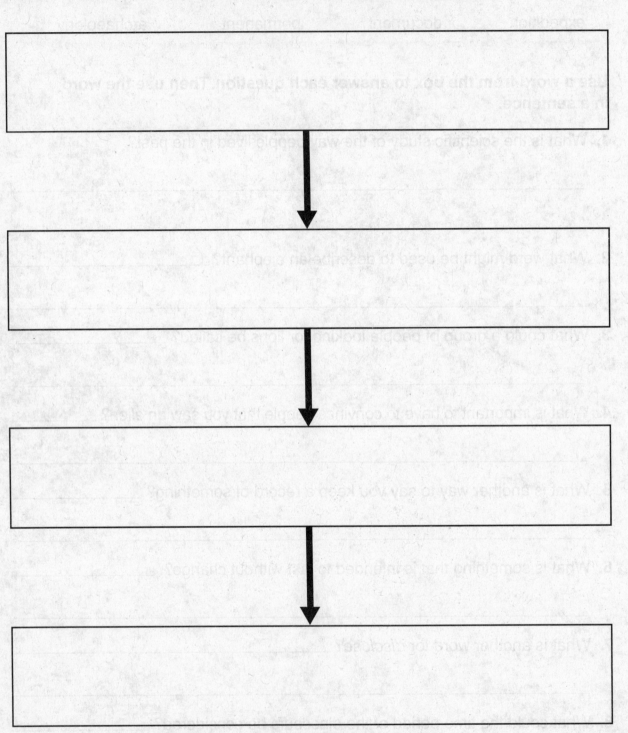

Name _____

Read the passage. Use the summarize strategy to find the most important ideas in the passage.

Eastern Influence

11	The first Asian immigrants to enter the United States were from China and some came as early as the 1700s. But most came looking
24	for gold in California in the mid-1800s. The Chinese brought their
35	culture. They also brought the skills to perform many jobs. Their
46	influence in those early years is still felt today.

Culture and Adapting

55	**Culture and Adapting**
58	In 1848, word spread across the world that gold had been found in
71	the United States. The Gold Rush began in the West. Thousands of
83	people rushed to California dreaming of a better life. The Chinese
94	came as well.
97	The Chinese brought their culture to America. They had their own
108	language and belief systems to share. They shared their customs and
119	food with the West.
123	In the search for gold, it was every man for himself. At first the
137	Chinese had no trouble finding gold. But then, all good things must
149	come to an end. The people looking for gold increased. Gold became
161	harder to find. At last, the Chinese found themselves looking for other
173	ways to make money. They opened shops for work. They also ran
185	cleaning and laundry services.

Sharing Skills

189	**Sharing Skills**
191	Many of the Chinese that came were from farming areas in China.
203	In the 1850s, they used their skills in California. They grew food
215	close to home and sold it door-to-door. Citrus fruits, peanuts, and rice
227	were among the things they grew.

Name _____

The Chinese also helped to make California a good place for fishing. Many of the Chinese were experts. They fished for cod, flounder, and shark. They also took oysters and mussels from the water. They sold their food in local markets. They also salt-dried it and shipped it to other areas.

A Strong Work Ethic

The Chinese showed that hard work pays off. They played a vital role in the first transcontinental railroad in America. It was built from 1863 to 1869. It was the first railroad to connect the East and the West.

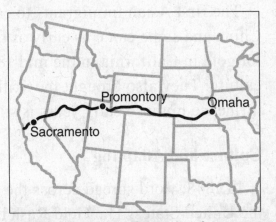

Chinese immigrants played an important role in the building of the first transcontinental railroad.

By 1868, most of the thousands of workers on the railroad were Chinese. They laid track across rivers and valleys. They built tunnels through mountain ranges. Harsh weather and long days were part of the job.

With the railroad came trade across the country. The West had crops that the East wanted. Farms grew in size and farmers were needed. The Chinese were called upon to help farm the land. Crops were then sent east.

The Chinese had a big influence on life in the West. They helped shape the country into what it is today.

A Different Kind of Medicine

Medicine and cures in the 1800s in America were not advanced. Rules for drugs were not set. The Chinese brought time-tested herbs for medicine. They had herbal treatments that had been around for thousands of years. Herbs from Asia are often still used today. People believe that they have little or no side effects.

Name _____

A. Reread the passage and answer the questions.

1. According to the sequence of the text, what happened first in 1848?

_____

_____

_____

2. What important event happened later from 1863 to 1869?

_____

_____

_____

3. How do you know that the information in the text is presented in time order?

_____

_____

_____

B. Work with a partner. Read the passage aloud. Pay attention to rate and expression. Stop after one minute. Fill out the chart.

	Words Read	–	Number of Errors	=	Words Correct Score
First Read		–		=	
Second Read		–		=	

Name _____

A Visit to the Past

To learn more about early United States history, you should visit Pilgrim Memorial State Park in Plymouth, Massachusetts. This park is home to Plymouth Rock, where according to tradition the Pilgrims first set foot in the New World. A reconstruction of the *Mayflower*, the ship the Pilgrims sailed on, is docked nearby. Every year nearly one million people from all over the world come to see these symbols of America's past.

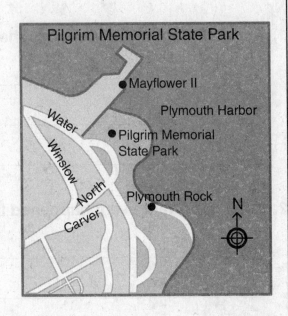

Answer the questions about the text.

1. **How do you know this is an informational text?**

   _____

2. **What is the topic of the text?**

   _____

3. **What text feature is included? How does it add to the text?**

   _____

   _____

4. **How could visiting Plymouth help you learn about the past?**

   _____

   _____

Name _____

Read each group of sentences below. Underline the context clues that help you understand the meaning of the proverb or adage in bold. Then write the meaning of the proverb or adage in bold.

1. In the search for gold, it was **every man for himself**. The people looking for gold increased. Gold became harder to find.

   _____

2. At first the Chinese had no trouble finding gold. But then, **all good things must come to an end**. At last, the Chinese found themselves looking for other ways to make money.

   _____

3. The Chinese showed that **hard work pays off**. They played a vital role in the first transcontinental railroad in America. They laid track across rivers and valleys. They built tunnels through mountain ranges.

   _____

4. People heard about gold being discovered in the United States. But **seeing is believing**. Immigrants came to the West from many countries to find out for themselves.

   _____

5. The Chinese fished for many types of fish for years. **Practice makes perfect**, and the Chinese became experts.

   _____

Name _____

A. Read each sentence. Underline any words that end with a consonant + *le* **syllable. Then circle the final syllable in the word.**

1. My uncle plays the fiddle in a band.

2. A single pebble made me trip and hurt my ankle.

3. I do not want to tangle my hair in the buckle on this hat.

4. Do not cuddle with any of the animals in this jungle!

5. He had trouble cleaning the marble countertop.

6. I have a freckle on the bottom of my foot.

B. The Latin suffixes *-ible* **and** *-able* **mean "can be done" or "the quality or state of" something. The Latin suffix** *-ment* **means "the state, action, or result of." Write the meaning of each word below.**

1. wonderment _____

2. convincible _____

3. establishment _____

4. punishable _____

5. sellable _____

6. permissible _____

Name _____

Evidence is details and examples from a text that support a writer's opinion. The student who wrote the paragraph below cited evidence to show how well an author supports his or her position on a topic.

Topic sentence →   I think that the author of "A Visit to the Past" does a good job of supporting his or her position. In "A Visit to the Past," the author includes facts and information to

Evidence → support the point that Pilgrim Memorial State Park is a good place to learn about American history. The author points out that Plymouth Rock and a reconstruction of the *Mayflower*, the ship the Pilgrims sailed on, can be

Concluding statement → seen at this park. I think these symbols—the rock and the ship—support the author's points and make the author's argument convincing.

Write a paragraph about the text you have chosen. Cite evidence from the text to show how well an author supports his or her position. Remember to include a concluding statement and use comparative adjectives correctly.

Write a topic sentence: _____

_____

Cite evidence from the text: _____

_____

_____

_____

End with a concluding statement: _____

_____

Name _____

A. Read the draft model. Use the questions that follow the draft to help you think about how you can end an informational article with a strong concluding statement.

Draft Model

Thomas Edison was an American inventor. He invented over 1,000 different things. Because he invented the electric light bulb, I don't have to do my homework by candle light!

1. What main idea might the concluding statement sum up?

2. What might be other reasons Edison's invention of the electric light bulb was important?

3. What idea or detail would best sum up the writer's thoughts?

B. Now revise the draft by adding a strong concluding sentence that sums up the writer's thoughts.

_____

_____

_____

_____

_____

_____

Name _____

> intensity   forfeit   retreated   ancestors
>
> endurance   irritating   despised   honor

Finish each sentence using the vocabulary word provided.

1. **(intensity) During the football game,** _____

   _____ .

2. **(endurance) It is important for athletes** _____

   _____ .

3. **(forfeit) As a result of not having enough players,** _____

   _____ .

4. **(irritating) When I'm watching a movie** _____

   _____ .

5. **(retreated) When it started to rain,** _____

   _____ .

6. **(despised) As a younger kid** _____

   _____ .

7. **(ancestors) The pictures on our walls** _____

   _____ .

8. **(honor) At the awards ceremony,** _____

   _____ .

Name _____

Read the selection. Complete the theme graphic organizer.

Detail

↓

Detail

↓

Detail

↓

Theme

Name _____

Read the passage. Use the reread strategy to understand difficult parts of the text.

The Generation Belt

	Kanti snuck behind her village's circle of wigwams. One Algonquin
10	family was repairing their home with fresh birch bark strips. Kanti
21	stayed in the shadow of the trees until she reached the lake. She could
35	see her father's sleek canoe far off in the distance. He was fishing for
49	their dinner. Her cousins were splashing merrily near the shore and
60	waved to her. She stepped into the water.
68	"Kanti!" an irritated voice said.
73	Kanti felt her heart drop to her stomach. She was caught. Kanti's
85	mother walked quickly toward her. "Kanti, you know that your
95	grandmother is going to teach you today."
102	"It's so steamy outside. Why can't I swim with my cousins?"
113	she whined.
115	Her mother looked sympathetic, but firm. "Sometimes we have to
125	set aside play so we can learn. Come, I think you will like this lesson
140	better than you predict."
144	Kanti's grandmother looked dignified sitting cross-legged in the
152	center of their wigwam. Around her lay wide beaded belts of white
164	and purple with all kinds of vivid designs. In front of her was a loom
179	shaped like an archer's bow with a few rows of beads strung.
191	"Thanks for coming, Kanti." There was a mischievous glint in her
202	grandmother's eye. She held a few small purple beads. "Do you know
214	what these are?"
217	"That's easy, they're wampum." Sometimes Kanti would help
225	collect the quahog, or clams, the beads were made from.

Name _____

"I actually meant, what do the beads stand for?" Kanti's grandmother said. "Here, let me show you."

She held out one of the most elaborate belts for Kanti to see. The purple beads made a pattern of triangles on the right side. On the left side, two figures stood holding hands next to a wigwam. "These people are your great-great grandmother and grandfather," she said. "They traveled over the mountains to find a place to settle." She traced the triangles with her fingers, stopping at one with the outline of a majestic bird hovering over it. "Your great-great grandmother saw an eagle that led them through the mountains." A circle at the edge of the mountains represented the lake that fed the village. "When they found a wide lake, they knew it would support many people. This is how our village began."

Despite herself, Kanti was drawn in by the story the belt portrayed. Suddenly, the belts' patterns jumped out at her, all holding adventures of their own. She looked at the loom with a scant five rows completed. "What story will this belt tell?" she asked.

"This belt will tell your story," her grandmother said. "I started it for you and you can continue to add to it as you grow." With that, her grandmother carefully stacked the belts and left.

Kanti immediately set to work, concentrating on finding just the right shades of purple wampum before stringing together rows. The purple beads became a figure about to leap into a calm lake. She couldn't wait for her cousins to come back so she could show them her new belt.

Name _____

A. Reread the passage and answer the questions.

1. Why can't Kanti swim with her cousins?

_____

_____

_____

2. What does Kanti learn about the belts?

_____

_____

_____

3. What is the theme of this story?

_____

_____

_____

B. Work with a partner. Read the passage aloud. Pay attention to rate and accuracy. Stop after one minute. Fill out the chart.

	Words Read	−	Number of Errors	=	Words Correct Score
First Read		−		=	
Second Read		−		=	

Name _____

A Roman Tradition

"Come help me pick flowers from the garden," Cornelia's mother called. Cornelia got up and followed her mother outside. Their house stood on a hill outside the city of Rome, and from their garden they could look out over the empire's capital.

"What do we need the flowers for?" Cornelia asked.

"To decorate the *lararium*," her mother said. She turned and pointed to the house's courtyard. A small building stood in the corner. It looked like a tiny temple. Columns held up its triangular roof, and a group of small statues and oil lamps sat inside.

"Three times a month, we bring flowers and honey to the spirits of the household. That way they'll protect our house and our crops," she explained.

Answer the questions about the text.

1. **How do you know this text is historical fiction?**

   _____

   _____

2. **What literary element is included in this piece of historical fiction?**

   _____

3. **Do you think the dialogue is fictional or historical?**

   _____

4. **What tradition does Cornelia's family have?**

   _____

   _____

Name _____

Read each sentence below. For each word in bold, write the denotation on the line. Then write its connotation.

1. She could see her father's **sleek** canoe far off in the distance.

   _____

   _____

2. It's so **steamy** outside.

   _____

   _____

3. "Why can't I swim with my cousins?" she **whined**.

   _____

   _____

4. Kanti's grandmother looked **dignified** sitting cross-legged in the center of their wigwam.

   _____

   _____

5. She looked at the loom with a **scant** five rows completed.

   _____

   _____

Name _____

**A. Read each sentence. Circle the word that ends with the same sound as
on in *person*. Then sort the words in the chart below.**

1. Today I am going to visit my cousin who lives in the city.

2. The group searched endlessly for the sunken treasure.

3. Did you know that a raisin is a grape that is partially dried out?

4. It was difficult to choose a gift, but I finally decided on the woven shirt.

5. The dinosaur skeleton at the museum was as big as a house!

-in	*-en*	*-on*
6. _____	8. _____	10. _____
7. _____	9. _____	

**B. Read the definitions for the prefixes below. Then read each word and
circle the prefix. Write the meaning of the word based on the prefix.
Use a dictionary to help you if necessary.**

uni-, mono-	=	one	*deca-* = ten
bi-	=	two	*cent-* = hundred
tri-	=	three	

1. monotone _____

2. bimonthly _____

3. centimeter _____

4. unicolor _____

Name _____

> *Evidence* is details and examples from a text that support a writer's ideas. The student who wrote the paragraph below cited evidence to compare the themes of two different stories.
>
> **Topic sentence** →   Both "The Generation Belt" and "A Roman Tradition" have similar themes, even though they have different settings. In "The Generation Belt," a young Algonquin girl learns a traditional craft from her grandmother. In "A Roman Tradition," Cornelia's mother teaches her to decorate the household *lararium*. One girl is Native American, and the other girl is from Ancient Rome, but they are both learning about their culture and traditions.
>
> **Evidence** →
>
> **Concluding statement** → The theme of each story is about the importance of cultural traditions.

Write a paragraph about the texts you have chosen. Cite evidence from the text that shows how the themes are similar or different. Remember to use precise language and adverbs correctly.

Write a topic sentence: _____

_____

Cite evidence from the text: _____

_____

_____

_____

End with a concluding statement: _____

_____

Name _____

A. Read the draft model. Use the questions that follow the draft to help you think about what strong words you can add.

Draft Model

Every winter, my family has "beach day" at home. We fill a plastic pool with sand and make sand castles. We listen to music and dance. Mom makes picnic food.

---

1. What strong words could be used to describe the plastic pool?

2. What strong words could be used to describe the sand castles?

3. What strong words could describe the music, the dancing, and the food?

B. Now revise the draft by adding strong words that create a clearer picture in readers' minds.

_____

_____

_____

_____

_____

_____

Name _____

| eldest | detested | ignored | treacherous |
| refuge | obedience | discarded | depicts |

Use a word from the box to answer each question. Then use the word in a sentence.

1. **What is a way to say "shows in pictures or words"?** _____

   _____

2. **What might a person seek during a bad storm?** _____

   _____

3. **What is another word for *oldest*?** _____

   _____

4. **What word might describe the things you find in a garbage can?**

   _____

5. **What is a dog usually rewarded for?** _____

   _____

6. **How might your sister feel if you did not pay attention to her?** _____

   _____

7. **What is another word for something that is disliked very much?**

   _____

Name _____

Read the selection. Complete the theme graphic organizer.

```
┌─────────────────────────────────────┐
│              Detail                 │
│                                     │
│                                     │
└─────────────────────────────────────┘
                  │
                  ▼
┌─────────────────────────────────────┐
│              Detail                 │
│                                     │
│                                     │
└─────────────────────────────────────┘
                  │
                  ▼
┌─────────────────────────────────────┐
│              Detail                 │
│                                     │
│                                     │
└─────────────────────────────────────┘
                  │
                  ▼
┌─────────────────────────────────────┐
│              Theme                  │
│                                     │
│                                     │
└─────────────────────────────────────┘
```

Name _____

Read the passage. Use the reread strategy to make sure you understand what you read.

The Lost Diary of Princess Itet

	Amelia peered down at the papyrus scrolls laid on the table. She
12	was standing inside a room full of them. They were bundled up
24	in rolls and spread over long tables. Strange symbols were drawn
35	on them in black ink. One looked like a bird. Another looked like
48	an open eye. The Egyptian hieroglyphs didn't look at all like the
60	English alphabet. She recognized the symbol *leb* that meant *heart*.
70	"Amelia, what are you doing?" Amelia's mother asked.
78	Amelia's mother was an archaeologist. She still had dust on her
89	clothes from digging in the pyramid that morning. It was 1905 and
101	exciting things were happening in Egypt. Amelia's mother and her
111	team of archaeologists found new artifacts every day.
119	"I'm reading the hieroglyphs," she said proudly.
126	"I bet you've learned a lot of new things from Mr. Breasted,"
138	her mother said. James Henry Breasted was her mother's boss and
149	Amelia's teacher. He knew a lot about ancient Egypt.
158	"Mom, do you think I could help your team at the pyramids?"
170	"I don't know, Amelia. Maybe when you're older," she said.
180	Amelia sighed and went back to reading the scrolls.
189	"Hello, Amelia," Mr. Breasted said. He walked up to Amelia,
199	smiling. "Are you translating the new papyrus scrolls we found?"
209	"I'm trying, but I don't know all of the symbols," said Amelia.
221	"Well, why don't we work on it together?" he suggested.
231	Amelia copied all the hieroglyphs on a piece of paper. Then
242	they translated each symbol into English. Soon they had translated
252	all the scrolls. Amelia read their finished work aloud.

Name _____

Day 32, the harvest season

    I asked Mother if I could go to Pharaoh's feast. She said I am not old enough. The trip through the desert is long. I am nine years old! My cousins are going and they're the same age as I am. Last year my cousin Nefer talked about the delicious dessert for days. I wish there was a way to change Mother's mind.

Day 34, the harvest season

    This morning Nefer had an idea. "Itet, you need to show your mother you can be useful at the harvest feast," she said. I'm a good writer, but I'm not sure if that will help.

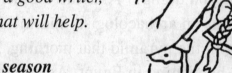

Day 37, the harvest season

    I have exciting news! I wrote a poem for Pharaoh. I tried very hard to write it from my heart. Mother loved it. She wants me to read it to Pharaoh at the feast. It will be a gift from our family. Nefer was right. I just needed to show her! And just in time too. We leave for the feast in an hour!

    "Wow. It's a diary!" said Amelia.

    "Not just any diary," said Mr. Breasted. "This is the lost diary of Princess Itet! Itet met the Pharaoh's son at this feast. They later married. Thank you, Amelia. I could not have done this without your help." Amelia had a sudden idea.

    "Mr. Breasted, could I show these papers to my mom?"

    "Of course! You earned it." Amelia ran off to show her mom.

    "You helped translate *all this*?" her mom asked. "This is very good work, Amelia. Maybe you are ready to help at the pyramids."

    "Thank you, Mom!" said Amelia.

    And thank you too, Nefer and Itet, she thought.

Name _____

A. Reread the passage and answer the questions.

1. What does Amelia want to do in the beginning of the passage?

_____

_____

2. What does Amelia do to help get what she wants?

_____

_____

3. What is the theme of this story?

_____

_____

_____

B. Work with a partner. Read the passage aloud. Pay attention to intonation. Stop after one minute. Fill out the chart.

	Words Read	–	Number of Errors	=	Words Correct Score
First Read		–		=	
Second Read		–		=	

Name _____

August 23, 1886: Arrival in America

My brother Pavol woke me up this morning. He shoved me and whispered loudly in my ear, "Aleksy! Wake up! We're almost there!" I rubbed my eyes, got out of bed, and followed him up on deck.

Once we had pushed our way through the crowd we were able to look out over the harbor for ourselves. I couldn't believe the sight that I saw! A giant statue the color of dull gold stood before the city. Workers crawled all over it like tiny ants.

Answer the questions about the text.

1. How do you know this text is historical fiction?

_____

_____

2. How is the story told?

_____

_____

3. Is Aleksy a historical figure or a fictional character?

_____

_____

4. Why do you think the author chose to tell this story in the form of a diary entry?

_____

_____

_____

Name _____

Read each sentence below. Underline the context clues that help you understand the meaning of each homophone in bold. Then write the correct definition of the homophone on the line.

1. "I bet you've learned a lot of **new** things from Mr. Breasted," her mother said.

   _____

2. Last year my cousin Nefer talked about the delicious **dessert** for days.

   _____

3. I wrote a poem for Pharaoh. I tried very hard to **write** it from my heart.

   _____

4. I brought the pencils! And I brought some paper, **too**.

   _____

5. We leave for the feast in an **hour**!

   _____

Name _____

A. Complete each sentence by filling in the blank with the correct homophone in parentheses ( ). Use context clues to help you.

1. The baker rolls the (**doe, dough**) _____ before twisting it into the shape of a pretzel.

2. Do you know (**whose, who's**) _____ coming to the party this evening?

3. I must get to the (**root, route**) _____ of the problem if I want to solve it.

4. The heavy (**bolder, boulder**) _____ tumbled off the mountain into the valley below.

5. I didn't like the (**moose, mousse**) _____ because it made my hair feel sticky.

6. She had to (**wade, weighed**) _____ into the shallow pond to get her kite.

B. Read each word. Write the base word and suffix on the lines.

	Base Word	Suffix
1. purify	_____	_____
2. cancellation	_____	_____
3. beautify	_____	_____
4. royalty	_____	_____
5. captivity	_____	_____
6. calculation	_____	_____

Name _____

Evidence is details and examples from a text that support a writer's opinion. The student who wrote the paragraph below cited evidence to show how well the author used sequence of events to develop the character and plot.

Topic sentence →   In "The Lost Diary of Princess Itet," I think the author did a good job of developing the characters and the plot. At the beginning of the story, Amelia wants

Evidence → to help her mother who is an archaeologist. Her mother thinks Amelia is too young. Then Amelia translates some hieroglyphs with the help of her mother's boss. She shows the translation to her mother. Impressed with Amelia's work, her mother tells her that she can

Concluding statement → help her at the pyramids. I think the clear sequence of events makes it easy to understand how Amelia is able to persuade her mother to change her mind.

Write a paragraph about the text you have chosen. Cite evidence from the text that shows how the author used sequence of events to develop the plot. Remember to use evidence to support your opinion.

Write a topic sentence: _____

_____

Cite evidence from the text: _____

_____

_____

_____

End with a concluding statement: _____

_____

Name _____

A. Read the draft model. Use the questions that follow the draft to help you organize ideas and events in the text.

Draft Model

Bring a gift to welcome your new neighbor. Tell your neighbor about your favorite places in town. Invite him or her to a community event, such as a concert in the park.

---

1. Of the ways the writer describes to help a new neighbor, which would the writer do first?

2. Of the ways the writer describes to help a new neighbor, which would the writer do last?

3. What sequence words can be added to help put the sentences in logical order?

B. Now revise the draft by organizing the ideas and events in the text using sequence words.

_____

_____

_____

_____

_____

_____

_____

Name _____

converted	renewable	coincidence	efficient
incredible	consume	consequences	installed

Use the context clues in each sentence to help you decide which vocabulary word fits best in the blank.

The class settled in as Ms. Gibson wrote the assignment for the group project on the board: Being Green.

"Being Green? What does that mean?" asked Tiffany. "Do we need to paint ourselves?"

Ricky smiled. "No, Tiffany. It means being better to the environment. For example, we should try to _____, or use, _____ resources, or resources that can be restored."

"Ricky's right," said Ms. Gibson. "I want all of you to find a way to tell your friends and family the _____ of our actions if we don't take care of the environment. It's important to let everyone know that we should be more _____ and create as little waste as possible."

"My parents _____ solar panels on our roof so that we can use power from the sun," said Lance. "The sunlight is _____ into electricity by the panels."

"I think taking care of the environment should be something that we all think about and plan carefully. Saving the environment shouldn't be something that is just a _____, or happens by chance," said Britney.

"It sounds like you all already know a lot about this topic," said Ms. Gibson. "Now, let's convince as many people as we can to feel the same way as we do. Being green should be something we actually do, not just an _____ way of life that nobody can achieve."

"Let's all be green!" said Tiffany. The class applauded, eager to begin the project.

Name _____

Read the selection. Complete the main idea and details graphic organizer.

Main Idea
Detail
Detail
Detail

Name _____

Read the passage. Ask and answer questions to understand new information in the text.

Energy from the Sea

	As I sat on the beach the other day, I saw the power of the waves
16	crash on the sand. The water splashed around me. Then the water
28	pulled along the shells that lay around me. This got me thinking.
40	We can use the wind and the sun to make power. We can use water,
55	too. Waterpower is also a renewable resource. It should be able to
67	help us solve our energy problems.
73	Waterpower has been in use for thousands of years. The earliest
84	use of hydropower can be traced to the waterwheel. It is a big wheel
98	with paddles on the rim. The force of the water turns the wheel. Then
112	the wheel runs machinery that is linked to it. Ancient Egyptians
123	used river currents to turn wheels way back in 2500 B.C. The ancient
136	Greeks and Romans used hydropower, too. It survived all the way
147	through medieval times.
150	But waterpower has evolved since then. Way back in 1628, the
161	Pilgrims used it to grind corn in mills. But by the 1800s, hot steam
175	replaced waterpower as the main power source. People used burning
185	coal to heat water. The boiling water then produced steam, which
196	ran engines and other machines.
201	By the end of the 1800s, waterpower came back into fashion.
212	Demand rose for electric energy. In 1882, the first hydroelectric plant
223	was built in Appleton, Wisconsin. It could make enough energy to light
235	a house and two paper mills. That's not much if you think about it. But
250	it was a start! As time went on, the demand for hydropower steadily
263	increased. One power plant now has the capacity of 7,600 megawatts.

Name _____

How Dams Work

You may think dams just hold water. But some dams are used to make waterpower. The amount of power they make depends on the height of the water. When the water is high, more pressure is put on the turbines down below. The more the turbines turn, the more power there is.

But there is a problem with hydropower. It is only useful in certain parts of the country. If there is not a large moving water source, then hydropower will not work. This is why some people believe waterpower is all nonsense. But there are states that do make lots of hydropower. Areas in California and the Pacific Northwest produce the most power.

I went to the library to find out how much of our energy comes from waterpower. About 7.8 percent of the power made in the United States is from hydropower. To my disbelief, a lot comes from fossil fuels and nuclear power, too. I had hoped to see higher numbers for renewable resources.

Perhaps one day we can learn to rely just on renewable resources. Look at countries like Brazil and Iceland. Iceland relies on geothermal power from hot springs. Brazil has one of the biggest dams in the world. These countries can give us a preview of how the United States can become a greener nation.

Name _____

A. Reread the passage and answer the questions.

1. What are three key details in paragraph 2?

_____

_____

_____

2. How are these details connected?

_____

_____

3. What is the main idea of the whole passage?

_____

_____

B. Work with a partner. Read the passage aloud. Pay attention to expression. Stop after one minute. Fill out the chart.

	Words Read	–	Number of Errors	=	Words Correct Score
First Read		–		=	
Second Read		–		=	

Name _____

Cooling our Homes

After electric fans came air conditioning. This kind of cooling had a big impact on how houses were built in America. Rooms became smaller so they would be easier to cool. Ceilings were lowered. Glass doors and picture windows replaced open porches.

Air conditioning also allowed cities to grow in new places. Harsh local climates no longer kept people from building comfortable homes. Desert cities like Phoenix, Los Angeles, and Las Vegas grew quickly after air conditioning was invented.

Dates in the History of Air Conditioning

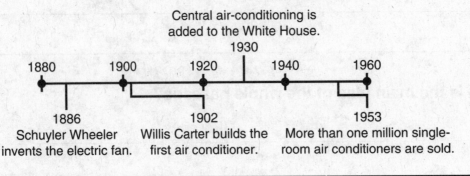

Answer the questions about the text.

1. How can you tell that this text is narrative nonfiction?

_____

_____

2. What text features are included in this text?

_____

_____

3. How does the time line help you understand the text?

_____

_____

_____

Name _____

Latin Prefix	Meaning	Greek Prefix	Meaning
non-	not	*hydro-*	water
pre-	before	*pre-*	before
		mega-	large
		geo-	earth

Read each sentence. Write the meaning of each word in bold on the line provided. Use the information about prefixes in the box above to help you.

1. The chapter **preview** in our book told us we would be studying marine life next week.

   _____

2. **Megawatts** are a greater unit of power than a watt.

   _____

3. Some ancient civilizations used rivers to create **hydropower**.

   _____

4. My friends looked at me in **disbelief** when I told them I met a movie star.

   _____

5. The **geothermal** temperature is hotter near Earth's core.

   _____

6. Some people used to think it was **nonsense** to say Earth was round!

   _____

Name _____

A. Read each sentence. Circle the words that have prefixes. Write the prefixes on the line.

1. My teacher was disappointed when she learned that I had misplaced my work.

_____   _____

2. One misstep and the mountain goat could fall from the rocky cliff.

_____

3. I was uncertain if the disc was mislabeled because it had an odd title.

_____   _____

4. I have never uncovered such silly nonsense in my entire life!

_____   _____

5. Never discourage your friends from trying new and interesting things.

_____

B. Read the words in the box below. Then read each definition of a word from mythology. Write a word from the box next to each definition to show that the two are related. Use each word from the box only once.

> chronology   fortune   panic   titanic   hydrant   typhoon

1. Typhon – a dangerous monster   _____

2. Pan – a frightening creature   _____

3. Cronos – god of time   _____

4. Titans – gigantic gods   _____

5. Hydra – a water snake   _____

6. Fortuna – the goddess of luck   _____

Name _____

> *Evidence* is details and examples from a text that support a writer's ideas. The student who wrote the paragraph below cited evidence that shows how the author uses key details to support the main idea.
>
> **Topic sentence** →   In "Energy from the Sea," the author provides key details to support the main idea that hydropower is a renewable energy source that can be used to help solve
>
> **Evidence** → our energy problems. The author gives key details presenting evidence that waterpower has been used for centuries. The author also points out that hydropower is a renewable source of energy. The author's use of key
>
> **Concluding statement** → details supports the main idea that hydropower is an important source of renewable energy.

Write a paragraph about the text you have chosen. Show how the author uses key details to support the main idea. Cite evidence from the text. Remember to use precise language and to use negatives correctly.

Write a topic sentence: _____

_____

Cite evidence from the text: _____

_____

_____

_____

_____

End with a concluding statement: _____

_____

Name _____

A. Read the draft model. Use the questions that follow the draft to help you think about what transition words you can add.

Draft Model

Gas has many important uses. People use gas to power their cars and to run buses and trains. I think people need to save energy. People should stop using so much gas.

---

1. What transition word would show that the second sentence is an example of the idea in the first sentence?

2. What transition word would show that the ideas in the second and third sentences are related?

3. What transition word would show a cause-and-effect relationship between the ideas in the last two sentences?

B. Now revise the draft by adding transition words to link ideas.

_____

_____

_____

_____

_____

_____

Name _____

| currency | global | marketplace | entrepreneur |
| economics | invest | transaction | merchandise |

Finish each sentence using the vocabulary word provided.

1. **(currency) In the United States** _____

   _____.

2. **(economics) Goods and services** _____

   _____.

3. **(global) Many businesses** _____

   _____.

4. **(invest) People say it is wise** _____

   _____.

5. **(marketplace) After the farmer harvests her corn,** _____

   _____.

6. **(transaction) Paying dollars for a piece of fruit** _____

   _____.

7. **(entrepreneur) With a new and creative idea,** _____

   _____.

8. **(merchandise) At the shopping mall** _____

   _____.

Name _____

Read the selection. Complete the main idea and details graphic organizer.

Main Idea
Detail
Detail
Detail

Name _____

Read the passage. Use the ask and answer questions strategy to better understand key details in the text.

American Money

Think about a dollar bill. On it is an image of George Washington.
But Washington was not always on the dollar. And the dollar was not
always green. American money has changed over time.

Continental Currency

The American Revolution cost money. The colonists thought of a
way to pay for the war. They printed a kind of paper money. These
bills were called Continentals. But Continentals were not backed by
gold or silver. After the war they lost their worth.

A New Country, A New Currency

If at first you don't succeed try, try again. The United States
had won the war. Now they needed their own money. The dollar
became the United States unit of currency in 1785. The first United
States pennies were made in 1793. They were worth one cent each.
One hundred pennies equaled one dollar. The first pennies showed
a woman with flowing hair. She was called Lady Liberty. Today,
President Lincoln is on the penny. Other presidents are on our money
too. George Washington is on the quarter. Thomas Jefferson is on
the nickel. Andrew Jackson is on the $20 bill.

Honoring American Leaders

Ben Franklin was a famous author, scientist, and statesman.
He is on the $100 bill. Sacagawea was a Native American woman.
She helped Lewis and Clark reach the West Coast of North America.
She is on a special dollar coin.

13
26
34
36
46
60
70
80
86
98
110
122
134
144
155
167
178
187
190
199
211
223

Name _____

Free Banking Era

A good name is better than riches. In 1836 most banks did not have good reputations. Any bank could print money called bank notes. Bank notes came in many colors, shapes, and sizes. A dollar note in Maine did not look the same as a dollar note in New York. Often bank notes could only be turned in for coins at the bank that made them. Some banks did not have gold or silver to back them up. There is a proverb that says, "Don't put all your eggs in one basket." Many people only had dollars from one bank. Soon people had dollars that they could not use.

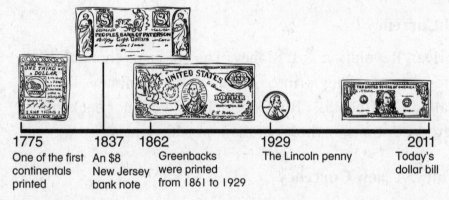

1775	1837	1862	1929	2011
One of the first continentals printed	An $8 New Jersey bank note	Greenbacks were printed from 1861 to 1929	The Lincoln penny	Today's dollar bill

Greenbacks

In 1861 the first greenbacks were made. These notes used green ink. They were the same in all the states. $5, $10, and $20 bills were the first greenbacks. Later, $1, $2, $50, $100, $500, and $1000 bills were printed too. The faces of presidents were shown on them. George Washington was on the dollar bill for the first time in 1862. The North used greenbacks during the Civil War. The South used their own paper money called Confederate dollars. History repeats itself. Just like Continentals, Confederate dollars lost their worth when the war ended.

American Money Today

The Federal Reserve is in charge of printing money today. In 1929, it started printing smaller dollars. We still use these dollars today. Our money has changed over time. Who knows what the dollar will look like in 100 years!

Name _____

A. Reread the passage and answer the questions.

1. What are two key details in paragraph 3?

_____

_____

2. What kind of money was being printed during the Free Banking Era?

_____

_____

3. Name two key details from the section called "Greenbacks."

_____

_____

4. What is the main idea of the whole passage?

_____

_____

B. Work with a partner. Read the passage aloud. Pay attention to accuracy. Stop after one minute. Fill out the chart.

	Words Read	–	Number of Errors	=	Words Correct Score
First Read		–		=	
Second Read		–		=	

Name _____

Where Does *Dollar* Come From?

We use dollars all the time, but where does the name come from? The word dollar actually comes from an older word, *thaler*, and its spelling has changed over time. Thalers are silver coins once widely used throughout Europe. They got their name from the place where the silver was mined, Joachimsthal, a town in what today is the Czech Republic. At first, these coins were called Joachimsthaler, but this long name was shortened to become *thaler*.

GLOSSARY

Thaler
any of numerous silver coins once used in some Germanic countries

Answer the questions about the text.

1. **How can you tell that this is an expository text?**

   _____

2. **What topic does the text tell you about?**

   _____

3. **What text feature is included? What does it tell you?**

   _____

   _____

4. **Where does the word *dollar* come from?**

   _____

Name _____

Read each passage. Underline the paragraph clues that help you understand the meaning of each proverb or adage in bold. On the line, write the meaning of the proverb or adage.

1. The colonists printed a kind of paper money. They were called Continentals. But Continentals were not backed by gold or silver. After the war they lost their worth. **If at first you don't succeed try, try again**. The United States had won the war. Now they needed their own money. The dollar became the United States unit of currency in 1785.

_____

_____

2. Some banks did not have gold or silver to back them up. There is a proverb that says, "**Don't put all your eggs in one basket**." Many people only had dollars from one bank. Soon people had dollars that they could not use.

_____

_____

3. The South used their own paper money called Confederate dollars. **History repeats itself**. Just like Continentals, Confederate dollars lost their worth when the war ended.

_____

_____

Name _____

A. Sort the words in the box below based on their suffixes.

sorrowful	tasteless	certainly	happiness
hairy	fitness	handful	wireless

-ful	-less	-ness	-y/-ly
1. _____	3. _____	5. _____	7. _____
2. _____	4. _____	6. _____	8. _____

B. Read the definitions below. Then read each word and circle the Greek or Latin root. Write the meaning of the root on the line.

The Greek root *astr* or *aster* means "star."

The Greek root *log, logo,* or *logy* means "word, topic, or speech."

The Latin root *port* means "carry."

The Latin root *vis* or *vid* means "see."

1. portable _____

2. video _____

3. asteroid _____

4. dialogue _____

5. visible _____

6. apology _____

Name _____

Evidence is details and examples from a text that support a writer's ideas. The student who wrote the paragraph below cited evidence that shows how well the author used a text feature to provide more details about the topic.

Topic sentence ⟶   In "American Money," the author does a good job using text features by including a time line to show information about the history of money in a visual way.

Evidence ⟶ The text describes how American money has changed over time. Each section discusses a new type of American currency. The author includes a time line that shows the reader when each type of currency was

Concluding statement ⟶ introduced. I thought that the author's use of a time line was good because it helped to sum up the information in the article.

Write an opinion paragraph about the text you have chosen. Show how the author uses text features to add more details about the topic. Cite evidence from the text. Remember to clearly state the topic.

Write a topic sentence: _____

_____

Cite evidence from the text: _____

_____

_____

_____

_____

End with a concluding statement: _____

_____

Name _____

A. Read the draft model. Use questions that follow the draft to help you think about what content words you can add.

Draft Model

It is important to work. When you work, you make money. This allows you to pay for things you need. Working teaches you to be responsible. It is a way to help society.

---

1. How do the words used in this model help you understand the main topic?

2. What word could be used to better explain what the writer means by "work"?

3. Where could the writer include words like *income* to help the reader better understand what the topic is about?

B. Now revise the draft by adding content words to help explain more specifically the importance of work.

_____

_____

_____

_____

_____

_____

_____

Name _____

> gobble   mist   individuality   roots

Use a word from the box to answer each question. Then use the word in a sentence.

1. What do both your family and a tree have in common? _____

_____

2. What is another word for "eat very quickly"? _____

_____

3. What is created when you spray a bottle of glass cleaner? _____

_____

4. When you show how you are different from others, what do you show?

_____

_____

Name _____

Read the selection. Complete the theme graphic organizer.

Detail

↓

Detail

↓

Detail

↓

Theme

Name _____

Read the poem. Pay attention to details that help you understand the author's message.

Me, As a Mountain

	I am not an island.
5	On my worst day, I am
11	Florida, the ocean tempting me away from the mainland
20	states that are my parents.
25	On the days I feel best,
31	I am the Rocky Mountains,
36	broad as the landscape, filling a window.
43	I command any attention to the horizon.
50	I rise into the air, my hair a
58	mist against the blue of the sky.
65	I rest on the Great Plains.
71	Plateaus and pine forests lift me.
77	They are my parents'
81	broad shoulders I stand on.
86	I try to use them wisely to build
94	myself
95	into a tower of rock, strong and
102	impossibly tall.

Name _____

A. Reread the passage and answer the questions.

1. What is this poem about?

_____

_____

2. What is the theme of this poem?

_____

_____

_____

3. What in the poem lets you know what the theme is?

_____

_____

_____

B. Work with a partner. Read the passage aloud. Pay attention to phrasing. Stop after one minute. Fill out the chart.

	Words Read	–	Number of Errors	=	Words Correct Score
First Read		–		=	
Second Read		–		=	

Name _____

Quiet Room

I love the quiet of my room,
silent but for the slightest sound of a breeze that stirs the curtains.

Some friends I have would scoff and say,
"Come on, this place is boring!
Where's the music? Where's the fun?"

But me, I like a place to think—
a place where I can share my thoughts with only me
and let my mind wander out the window to the wide, wide world beyond.

Answer the questions about the text.

1. **What makes this text a free verse poem?**

   _____

2. **Are the lines in this poem regular or irregular?**

   _____

3. **What does the speaker of the text like about the bedroom? What do the speaker's friends not like about it?**

   _____

   _____

   _____

Name _____

> **Imagery** is the use of specific language to create a picture in a reader's mind. **Personification** is giving human qualities to a non-human thing.

Read the lines of the free verse poem below. Then answer the questions.

Me, As a Mountain

I am not an island.
On my worst day, I am

Florida, the ocean tempting me away from the mainland
states that are my parents.

On the days I feel best,
I am the Rocky Mountains

broad as the landscape, filling a window.
I command any attention to the horizon.

1. **What is an example of imagery in this poem?**

_____

_____

2. **Point out an example of personification in this poem.**

_____

_____

3. **Write another stanza that includes imagery and personification.**

_____

_____

_____

_____

Name _____

Read each passage. Underline the metaphor in the passage. Then write the two things that are being compared on the lines.

1. On the days I feel best, I am the Rocky Mountains,

   _____

   _____

2. On my worst day, I am Florida, the ocean tempting me away from the mainland

   _____

   _____

3. I rise into the air, my hair a mist against the blue of the sky.

   _____

   _____

Name _____

A. Read each sentence. Circle any words that have prefixes or suffixes.

1. I happily prepaid for the new book that will arrive in the store next month.

2. Do not prejudge the witness and reverse your ideas about what went on.

3. This establishment has been unchanged in its appearance for years.

4. The driver became fearful when she saw the two roads begin to intersect.

5. My semiweekly visits to the doctor were finally over.

B. Read the words from English in the box below. Then read each word from another language in bold. Write the word from the box next to its similar word from another language.

waffle	iceberg	lagoon	pretzel	macaroni	canyon

1. **brezel** (German) _____

2. **ijsberg** (Dutch) _____

3. **cañon** (Spanish) _____

4. **laguna** (Italian) _____

5. **makkaroni** (Italian) _____

6. **wafel** (Dutch) _____

Name _____

> *Evidence* is details and examples from a text that support a writer's ideas. The student who wrote the paragraph below cited evidence to support his or her opinion about how well two poets used precise language.
>
> **Topic sentence** ⟶   I think the poet of "Quiet Room" did a better job of using precise language than the poet of "Me, As a Mountain." In "Quiet Room," the poet writes, "silent but for the slightest sound of a breeze that stirs the curtains." These sensory details create a picture in my mind. In "Me, As a Mountain," the poet writes, "I command any attention to the horizon." I find the meaning of these words confusing. The poet's use of precise language in "Quiet Room" creates a clearer picture in my mind than the words the poet used in "Me, As a Mountain."
>
> **Evidence** ⟶
>
> **Concluding statement** ⟶

Write a paragraph about two poems. Compare how well the poets use precise language. Tell which poet did a better job. Cite details that created a picture in your mind. Remember to use prepositions correctly.

Write a topic sentence: _____

_____

Cite evidence from the text: _____

_____

_____

End with a concluding statement: _____

_____

Name _____

A. Read the draft model. Use the questions that follow the draft to help you think about what concrete and descriptive details you can add.

Draft Model

I'm not very TALL at all
My hair is a MESS when I get out of bed
I like to display my collections
I always SING in the back seat of our car
My family is the BEST

---

1. What descriptive detail would tell how tall the speaker is?

2. What descriptive details would show how the speaker's hair is messy?

3. What concrete details would tell what the speaker collects?

4. What concrete details would tell what kinds of songs the speaker sings?

B. Now revise the draft by adding concrete supporting details that help build a clearer picture for readers.

_____

_____

_____

_____

_____

_____

_____

INSTRUCTIONS FOR PEDIATRIC PATIENTS

INSTRUCTIONS FOR PEDIATRIC PATIENTS

BARTON D. SCHMITT, M.D.

Professor of Pediatrics
University of Colorado School of Medicine;
Director of General Consultative Services
The Children's Hospital of Denver
Denver, Colorado

W.B. SAUNDERS COMPANY *Philadelphia/London/Toronto/Montreal/Sydney/Tokyo*
Harcourt Brace Jovanovich, Inc.

W. B. SAUNDERS COMPANY
Harcourt Brace Jovanovich, Inc.

The Curtis Center
Independence Square West
Philadelphia, Pennsylvania 19106

Library of Congress Cataloging-in-Publication Data

Schmitt, Barton D.,
　　Instructions for pediatric patients / Barton D. Schmitt.
　　　　p.　　cm.
　　ISBN 0-7216-3160-6
　　1. Child care--Popular works.　I. Title.
RJ61.S363　1992　　　　　　　　　　　　　　　　　　91-25787
618.92--dc20　　　　　　　　　　　　　　　　　　　　　CIP

Editor: Judith Fletcher

Instructions for Pediatric Patients　　　　　　　ISBN　0-7216-3160-6

Printed in the United States of America.

Last digit is the print number:　　9　8　7　6　5　4　3　2　1

CONTENTS

PART 3

PREVENTIVE PEDIATRICS

PART 4

COMMON INFECTIONS OF CHILDHOOD

PART 5

PEDIATRIC DERMATOLOGY

PART 6

MISCELLANEOUS PHYSICAL PROBLEMS

PART 7

BEHAVIOR PROBLEMS

PREFACE

This book contains printed instructions written for parents and covering the 137 most common health problems occurring in infants, children, and adolescents. The content comes from mainstream pediatrics and has been peer reviewed. Because the guidelines are printed on durable paper, you can use the master copy to make multiple office handouts. The instructions are written for use in pediatric offices, family practice offices, and other clinics where children are seen. These handouts can become a key part of your parent education program.

INFORMATION SHARING

The following is the philosophy behind educating parents about pediatric illnesses and conditions.

1. **Parents are a part of the medical care team.** They know their child better than anyone else. We need them as active participants in the child's treatment program.

2. **Informed parents are better parents.** The more they know about their child's health condition (e.g., asthma or encopresis), the better team members they can be. Smart, informed parents are easier to work with. Also, the quality of decisions made by parents depends on the quality of information they have available (e.g., the pros and cons of tonsillectomy and adenoidectomy).

3. **Parents already read about medical problems.** We can't provide all health information one-on-one. They receive ongoing health advice from friends, relatives, newspapers, magazines, radio, and television. Unfortunately, information from the media or non-professionals may be confusing, conflicting, or even alarming. Parents' fears and concerns usually can be allayed by the type of accurate, up-to-date, straightforward health advice found in these guidelines.

4. **Medical information should be shared.** There should be no barriers to public disclosure of accurate health information. Access to information is one of our basic freedoms (see the First Amendment).

BENEFITS OF PARENT HANDOUTS FOR PHYSICIANS AND PARENTS

Printed materials are the mainstay of any parent education program. They are an inexpensive form of intervention and have the following advantages:

1. **Increase the amount of information that can be transmitted to and absorbed by the parent.** Most parents would like to know everything about their child's condition. Most physicians want to be their educator, but time constraints in the office setting limit the amount of information the physician can discuss with the parents. The physician can highlight the more crucial aspects of home treatment and rest assured that the instruction sheets will cover the details. The information sheets supplement the physician's counseling and teaching. In a sense, these information sheets serve as a physician extender that expands his influence over his patients' health care.

2. **Increase the number of people who receive this information.** The patient instructions can be read by other caretakers who are not present during the office visit. These might include the father, grandmother, child caretaker, or babysitter.

3. **Improve parent compliance with treatment regimens.** Written instructions reinforce verbal ones. Forgetfulness is the most common cause of noncompliance. Most people can only remember two or three instructions. Normally 50% of what was said during an office visit is forgotten by 5 minutes after leaving the office. At times of crisis, people remember even less. Several studies have shown that compliance is increased if the specific recommendations are written out, but the physician rarely has time to write out all instructions. Written instructions are especially important with complex problems (e.g., enuresis, ADD, and asthma). To achieve a true understanding of such conditions, the parent needs to re-read and re-think the information. These printed instructions increase the parents' accountability by making it impossible for them to say that they were not instructed to provide a specific type of care. These printed instructions can serve as a form of contract if the physician requests that the parent read it, ask questions, and then sign it before leaving the office.

4. **Save physician time.** Printed instructions can increase office efficiency. Initially the physician saves the time required to write out instructions for each patient. Some of the time required for verbal presentation of the treatment plan is also saved, because the physician can now limit the verbal instructions to the two or three main points and let the parents

read the details later (on their time). If information sheets are given out before the physician sees the parent (e.g., fever or chickenpox), it reduces the amount of routine advice she needs to give in the office. Telephone calls about forgotten instructions are also avoided. If the routine information is covered in an instruction sheet (e.g., the common cold), the physician can use her time to address more complex issues (e.g., the nuts and bolts of how to suction the nose of a fussy 3-month-old). Instead of trying to cover everything, the physician has time to cover the parent's main agenda. Written instructions are especially helpful for first-time parents or those parents who need "constant" teaching.

5. **Prevent repetition and boredom.** First, we need sheets covering the most repetitive problems we deal with. During epidemics (e.g., diarrhea, coughs, and colds) the physician often can't remember whether he has already given the parent currently in his presence his routine spiel on that condition. During these times, routine information can be transmitted with printed instructions, often before we even examine the patient.

6. **Helps counteract office stressors.** The most common office stress is getting behind in our appointment schedule. Sometimes we feel that if we tried to answer all of each parent's questions, we won't have any time left to see more patients. Written information can improve office efficiency and get you back on schedule. Some physicians even have found that after they make a diagnosis, they can give the parent something to read, see another patient, and then come back to discuss specific questions with the previous parent. Written instructions can also help with demanding parents who clearly want more information from us than we thus far have provided. One option is to refer them to a subspecialist for a second opinion, but another is to give them printed instructions (e.g., ventilation tubes or infectious mononucleosis) and reappoint them for a follow-up visit.

7. **Protect against malpractice risk.** The printed instructions document our exact treatment instructions, drug dosages, and follow-up plan. For example, one of the more common ways for the delayed diagnosis of meningitis to present is in a child who is receiving antibiotics for an ear infection. The ear infection handout states clearly to call immediately if your child becomes worse, or if the fever or earache persists for more than 48 hours on antibiotics. Clarification of the indications for recontacting the physician is essential in providing quality medical care (e.g., croup and head trauma). In emergency room settings, parents can sign on the encounter form that they have received specific written instructions.

8. **Reduce unnecessary telephone calls.** The guidelines for common illnesses reduce unnecessary telephone calls that are "for information only," because they provide the details of home treatment that the parents are interested in. The ones for specific illnesses (e.g., asthma) prevent call backs about drug dosages. These guidelines clarify for each topic when to call the physician—immediately, during office hours, or not at all (i.e., when it is safe to continue to treat their child at home). The information sheets therefore encourage appropriate calls and discourage inappropriate ones. They prevent unnecessary calls about minor symptoms (over 50% of calls) from worried parents. More importantly, they prevent undercalling from parents who might overlook serious symptoms (e.g., a lethargic newborn, drooling, signs of dehydration, swollen scrotum, bulging soft spot, stiff neck, and purpura or petechiae). Keep in mind that parents also don't like to make unnecessary phone calls, since it often requires several attempts before they can get through to your office.

9. **Increase parent satisfaction.** Most parents love printed materials. They like to leave our office with a piece of paper. Giving parents something tangible is one way to show we care. Information sharing also shows them that we consider them a partner in health care, and that we respect their thinking and common sense. If given in the waiting room, information sheets show that we value their waiting time. For recurrent illnesses (e.g., colds and diarrhea), printed handouts save parents time and money. This is of interest to them, especially if they both work outside the home. If parents post handouts on their refrigerator and you have stamped your name on them, you may find the added spin-off that these handouts are a marketing tool that attracts new families to your practice.

10. **Help with the delegation of tasks to office staff.** These instruction sheets can serve as standard protocols (standing orders) in your office. The office nurse can use them to debrief the patient after the physician has arrived at a diagnosis. They can be used as standard protocols for triaging incoming telephone calls in an efficient and safe manner. The requests for telephone advice seem to be increasing, possibly because working parents don't want to come in unless absolutely necessary. The time-consuming routine task of telephone triage and giving advice can be delegated safely.

THE CONTENT OF THE PARENT HANDOUTS

Each topic is covered in depth so that parents will have the majority of their questions answered after reading it. The home treatment instructions are detailed so that parents should be able to reduce their child's symptoms and improve his comfort level. The names of specific drugs are not listed unless one main drug is prescribed for that particular disease (e.g., penicillin for strep throat or scarlet fever). For most diseases requiring a prescription drug, the physician who gives out the instruction sheet will need to fill in several blanks with the name of the drug, the dosage, the dosing interval, and the number of days of total therapy (e.g., sinus infection, ear infection, UTI, strep throat, scarlet fever, asthma, and scabies). Behavioral topics (e.g., tantrums, toilet training, and biting) and health promotion topics (e.g., cholesterol, passive smoking, frequent infections) have been highlighted because they are in demand by families. The preventive approach to various topics (e.g., the prevention of sleep problems, toilet training problems, spoiled children, sunburn, and tooth decay) is also stressed.

Some of these handouts are identical to those found in my book for parents, *Your Child's Health*, Bantam Books, 1991. Most, however, have been rewritten into an "after-the-office-visit" format. Some handouts describe diseases (e.g., pneumonia or mononucleosis) not covered in the parent book. The writing has been tested for clarity. The reading level is sixth to eighth grade. The information has been reviewed by many parents, and it contains no medical or psychiatric jargon.

ACCURACY OF THE CONTENT

The guidelines are as up-to-date as the pediatric literature available through the summer of 1991. The importance of the HIB vaccine beginning at 2 months of age is reviewed. The potential complications of Fifth Disease in the pregnant mother are described, as well as the more common occurrence of arthralgias. The risk of suffocation with a bead-filled pillow is included in the Colic guideline. The overconcern regarding fluoride and osteosarcoma is discussed in Tooth Decay Prevention. The UTI issue is covered with the pros and cons of circumcision. A balanced approach to cholesterol testing is reviewed. The accuracy has been achieved largely because of an excellent review panel of practicing pediatricians and academic pediatricians who are listed in the acknowledgment section.

MAKING CHANGES IN CONTENT

It would be surprising if you agreed with more than 95% of what is contained in these guidelines. Feel free to make changes in your master copy by whiting out the part you disagree with or drawing a line through it. You could also put a bracket around it and in the margin write "disagree." If you think the guideline is incomplete, type up additional special instructions and add them at the bottom of the page. Any changes you make, of course, are your legal responsibility. Keep in mind that prescription drugs are not listed, and it is your role to fill in the current drug of choice for your patient's condition.

DUPLICATING PARENT HANDOUTS

These guidelines are printed on durable paper and distributed in a book with perforated pages. You can selectively tear out the master copies, make multiple copies for use in your office setting, and preserve the originals in a loose-leaf binder for future use. The acknowledgment of the author and the publisher is listed as a footer on each page of each handout. Permission to duplicate (photocopy) handouts for non-commercial purposes (to give to your patients) is hereby granted. No special or additional permission is needed to distribute these parent handouts for this purpose. In granting this permission, the author and publisher expect that the practices involving multiple physicians and offices will maintain one set of original master copies in each office setting. We also encourage you to add your name and office telephone number to these handouts.

WHEN TO DISTRIBUTE PARENT HANDOUTS DURING PATIENT FLOW IN YOUR OFFICE

Everyone on the office team can be involved with helping parents obtain appropriate handouts. The office staff can use handouts to better utilize waiting time both in the waiting room and the exam rooms.

1. **In the waiting room.** A menu of selected handouts can be posted on the office bulletin board. Parents can request them from the front desk. They can also print copies of their own if a copying machine and a binder containing these handouts is available. During epidemics or seasonal illness, stacks of relevant handouts can be placed in the waiting room (e.g., influenza, hay fever, chickenpox). Just as toys are essential for children in the waiting room, so is reading material for the parents.

2. **After nursing contact.** After the nurse processes the patient and puts her into the exam room, she can provide one or two handouts that are appropriate for the child's illness. Again, selected handouts can be stocked in the exam room (e.g., fever, diarrhea, colds). The parent then can read the handout while waiting for the physician. A good spin-off of this procedure is that it reduces the number of routine questions the parent will have for the physician.

3. **After physician contact.** After the physician has examined the patient and made a specific diagnosis, he can write down or mark on a checklist the information sheet (e.g., asthma, bronchiolitis, pneumonia, or croup) that he wants the parents to receive. These can be given to the parent at the appointment desk. The front desk staff or the physician should write in the patient's name at the top of the handout, because this gesture makes it more likely that the family will read it.

4. **During the first visit.** Some of the instruction sheets cover

minor illnesses that are universal and that every child acquires on multiple occasions. These include cough, sore throat, diarrhea, fever, and others. These parent handouts can be given out as a packet on the first office visit. Thereafter they can be referred to for home treatment and save the health care provider considerable telephone time in discussing them.

5. **By mail.** When parents call in requesting information about particular topics, often these can be mailed out. Examples are Lyme disease, ADD, bedwetting, and sleepwalking.

Best wishes in all your efforts to enhance parent education.

BARTON D. SCHMITT, M.D., F.A.A.P.
Denver, Colorado
December 1991

ACKNOWLEDGMENTS

I am immeasurably indebted to my pediatric reviewers for their careful examination of my text for accuracy, safety, objectivity, clarity, and completeness. Their ongoing efforts have been extraordinary and their feedback invaluable.

Pediatric Review Board
Joseph H. Banks, M.D., Columbus, Ohio
John M. Benbow, M.D., Concord, North Carolina
Daniel D. Broughton, M.D. Rochester, Minnesota
Rosemary D. Casey, M.D., Philadelphia, Pennsylvania
David M. Christopher, M.D., Renton, Washington
Jessie R. Groothuis, M.D., Denver, Colorado
Robin L. Hansen, M.D., Sacramento, California
David L. Kerns, M.D., San Jose, California
Bruce J. McIntosh, M.D., Jacksonville, Florida
Robert D. Mauro, M.D., Denver, Colorado
Cajsa J. Schumacher, M.D., Albany, New York
Daniel R. Terwelp, M.D., Austin, Texas
Wallace C. White, M.D., Denver, Colorado

My appreciation and admiration to the following pediatric subspecialists and pediatric surgeons who have graciously helped me with specific topics and questions in their areas of expertise:

General Pediatrics:	Drs. Robert Mauro, Steven Poole, Richard Krugman, Stephen Berman, Richard Shiffman, and Burris Duncan
Adolescent Medicine:	Drs. David Kaplan, Kathleen Mammel, Ida Nakashima, and Henry Cooper
Emergency Pediatrics:	Dr. Michael Clemmens
Infectious Disease:	Drs. James Todd, Mary Glode, Mark Abzug, and Brian Lauer
Dermatology:	Dr. William Weston

Allergy:	Drs. James Lustig, Allen Bock, David Pearlman, James Shira, and Fred Leffert
Psychology:	Drs. Edward Christophersen, Jeffrey Dolgan, and Andrea Van Steenhouse
Neonatology:	Drs. Jacinto Hernandez and Susan Niermeyer
Breast-Feeding:	Drs. Marianne Neifert, Joy Seacat, and Jack Newman
Cardiology:	Drs. James Wiggins, Robert Wolfe, Henry Sondheimer, and Reginald Washington
Pulmonology:	Drs. Leland Fan and Frank Accurso
Gastroenterology:	Drs. Arnold Silverman, Ronald Sokol, Judy Sondheimer, and Sharon Taylor
Neurology:	Dr. Paul Moe
Ear, Nose and Throat:	Drs. James Jaskunas, Nigel Pashley, and Ray Wood
Ophthalmology:	Drs. Robert King and Robert Sargent
Dentistry:	Drs. William Mueller and Richard Abrams
Urology:	Dr. Martin Koyle
Orthopedics:	Drs. Robert Eilert, Frank Chang, and Gerard Glancy

My special thanks to the good people at W. B. Saunders Company who helped me complete this project: Lisette Bralow and Judith Fletcher, my editors; Lorraine Kilmer, the designer; and Jean Kenworth, in marketing.

PART 1

NEW
BABY CARE

Before the baby is born, most parents prepare a special room. They buy a layette including clothing, a place to sleep, feeding equipment, bathing equipment, and changing supplies. This preparation is called nesting behavior. The most common mistake parents on a limited budget can make during this time is buying something they don't need at all or buying an expensive (often fancy) version of an essential piece of equipment.

ESSENTIAL EQUIPMENT

Safety Car Seat. Child restraint seats are essential for transporting your baby in a car. They are required by law in most states. Consider buying one that is convertible and usable until your child reaches 40 pounds and 40 inches. Until your child weighs more than 20 pounds the car seat faces backward; after that time it is moved to a forward-facing position. Car seats must conform to federal safety standards; also, they are ranked by consumer magazines. Many hospitals have a rental program for car seats that can save you money unless you are going to have several children.

Crib. Since your baby will spend so much unattended time in the crib, make certain it is a safe one. Federal safety standards require that all cribs built after 1974 have spaces between the crib bars of 2⅜ inches or less. This restriction is to prevent a child from getting the head or body stuck between the bars. If you have an older crib, be sure to check this distance, which is approximately the width of three fingers. Also, check for any defective crib bars. The mattress should be the same size as the crib so that your baby's head can't get caught in the gap. It should also be waterproof. Bumper pads are unnecessary because infants rarely strike their heads on the railings. The pads have the disadvantage of keeping your baby from seeing out of the crib; they are also something to climb on at a later stage. During the first 2 or 3 months of life it may be more convenient to have your baby sleep in a drawer, a cardboard box, or a basket that is well padded with towels or blankets.

Bathtub. Small plastic bathtubs with sponge linings are available. A large plastic dishpan will also suffice for the purpose. A molded sponge lining can be purchased separately. As a compromise, a kitchen sink works well if you are careful about preventing your child from falling against hard edges or turning on the hot water, thereby causing a burn. Until the umbilical cord falls off, keep the water level below the navel. Most children can be bathed in a standard bathtub by 1 year of age.

Bottles and Nipples. If you are feeding your baby formula, you will need about ten 8-ounce bottles. Although clear plastic bottles cost twice as much as glass ones, you will be glad you bought the unbreakable type the first time you or your baby drops one. You will also need a corresponding number of nipples. If you prepare more than one bottle at a time, you will need a 1-quart measuring cup and a funnel for mixing a batch of formula.

Diapers: Reusable vs. Disposable. Let's compare disposable diapers to cloth diapers. The rate of diaper rashes is about the same. If you're concerned about using safety pins, worry not. Modern cloth diapers come with Velcro

straps. The main advantage of disposable diapers is that they are very convenient—freeing the family to travel easily and day-care centers to operate efficiently. The diapers made with super absorbent gel have the advantage of not letting urine leak. The main disadvantage of disposable diapers is that they cost more. Disposable diapers average about 20 cents per diaper vs. 12 cents per diaper from the diaper service or 3 cents per diaper if you wash your own diapers (after their initial purchase).

Because of the ecological ramifications of disposable diapers, which type of diaper to use is a controversial issue. Why not take advantage of both options. Use cloth diapers when you are home. Use disposable diapers when you are traveling or as a backup if you are out of the home. Use disposables when your child has diarrhea because they prevent leakage of watery stools. (Some parents also prefer disposable diapers at night because they are leakproof.) During the first 2 or 3 months of life, when most mothers are exhausted by new baby care, consider a diaper service rather than washing the diapers yourself. You will find that modern diaper services are very efficient, provide excellent sterilized diapers, and pick them up weekly.

Pacifier. A pacifier is useful in soothing many babies. To prevent choking, the pacifier's shield should be at least 1½ inches in diameter and the pacifier should be one single piece. Some of the newer ones are made of silicone (instead of rubber), which lasts longer because it doesn't dry out. The orthodontic-shaped pacifiers are accepted by some babies but not by others.

Nasal Suction Bulb. A suction bulb is essential for helping young babies with breathing difficulties caused by sticky or dried nasal secretions. A suction bulb with a blunt tip is more effective than the ones with long tapered tips (which are used for irrigating ears). The best ones on the market have a small clear plastic tip (mucous trap), that can be removed from the rubber suction bulb for cleaning.

Thermometer. A rectal thermometer is most helpful if your baby becomes sick. The digital thermometers that display the temperature in 30 seconds are worth the extra few dollars. If you buy a glass thermometer, the ones with four color zones are easier to read.

Humidifier. A humidifier will be helpful in dry climates or areas with cold winters. The new ultrasonic humidifiers are quieter and have other advantages. Do not buy a vaporizer (a gadget that produces steam) because it can cause burns in children and doesn't deliver humidity at as fast a rate as a humidifier.

Diaper and Bottle Bag. For traveling outside the home with your baby, you will need an all-purpose shoulder bag to carry the items that allow you to feed your baby and change diapers.

High Chair. During the first 6 months of life your baby can be held when being fed. Once your child can sit unsupported and take solid foods, a high chair is needed. The most important feature is a wide base that prevents tipping. The tray needs to have a good safety latch. The tray should also have adjustable positions to

(Continued on the reverse side)

Instructions for Pediatric Patients by Barton D. Schmitt, M.D., *Pediatrician*
Adapted from YOUR CHILD'S HEALTH, Copyright © 1991 by Barton D. Schmitt, M.D.
Reprinted by permission of Bantam Books.

adapt to your infant's growth. A safety strap is critical. Plastic or metal chairs are easier to clean than wooden chairs. Small, portable, hook-on high chairs that attach directly to the tabletop are gaining in popularity. They are convenient and reasonably priced. The ones with a special clamp that keeps your child from pushing the chair off the tabletop with his feet have a good safety record.

Food Grinder. The time comes when your baby must make the transition from baby foods to table foods. A baby-food grinder takes the work out of mashing up table foods. It's as effective as a blender, easier to clean, and less expensive. Food processors have the advantage of allowing you to make larger quantities faster than in a grinder.

Training Cup. By the time your child is 1 year old, he will want to hold his own cup. Buy a spill-proof one with a weighted base, double handles, a lid, and a spout.

Bib. To keep food off your baby's clothes, find a molded plastic bib with an open scoop on the bottom to catch the mess.

Safety Gadgets. Once your child is crawling, you will need electric-outlet safety plugs, cabinet door safety locks, bathtub spout protectors, plastic corner guards for sharp table edges, and so forth.

HELPFUL EQUIPMENT

The following items mainly provide your child with forms of transportation or special places to play.

Changing Table. Diapers need to be changed 10 to 15 times daily. Although a bed can be used for changing, performing this task without bending over prevents back strain. An old dining table or buffet can work as well as a special changing table.

Automatic Swing. Although swings are entertaining to most babies, they are especially helpful for crying babies. They come in windup-spring, pendulum-driven, or battery-powered models. The latter two have quieter mechanisms. Again, a sturdy base and crossbars are important for safety.

Front Pack or Carrier. Front packs are great for new babies. They give your child a sense of physical contact and warmth. In fact, they have been shown to promote bonding. They allow you freedom to use your hands. Buy one with head support. Carrying a baby in front after 5 or 6 months of age can cause a backache for the parent.

Backpack. Backpacks are useful in carrying babies who are 5 or 6 months old and have good head support. They are an inexpensive way to carry your baby outside when you go shopping, hiking, or walking anywhere. The inner seat can usually be adjusted to different levels.

Stroller. Another way to transport a baby who has outgrown the front pack is in a baby stroller. The most convenient ones are the umbrella type, which fold up. A safety belt is important to keep your baby from standing up and falling.

Infant Seat. An infant seat is a good place to keep a young baby who is not eating or sleeping. Infants prefer this inclined position so they can see what is going on around them. Buy one with a safety strap, but don't substitute it for a car seat. Once children reach 3 to 4 months of age, they can usually tip the infant seat over, so discontinue using it.

Playpen. A playpen is a handy and safe place to leave your baby when you need uninterrupted time to cook a meal or do the wash. Babies like playpens because the slatted or mesh sides afford a good view of the environment. Playpens can be used both indoors and outdoors. As with cribs, the slats should be less than 2⅜ inches apart. The playpens with a fine-weave netting are also acceptable although sometimes older infants can climb out of them. Bottomless playpens are gaining in popularity. Your baby should be introduced to the playpen by 4 months of age in order to build up positive associations with it. It is very difficult to introduce a playpen after a baby has learned to crawl. Avoid stringing any objects on a cord across the playpen, because your baby could become entangled in them and strangle.

Gates. A gate is essential if your house has stairways that your baby must be protected from. A gate also helps to keep a child in a specific room with you and out of the rest of the house, as when you are working in the kitchen. Many rooms can be closed off with doors. All gates should be climb resistant. The strongest gates are spring loaded.

UNNECESSARY EQUIPMENT

Some baby equipment is usually not worth the investment, but your judgment may be different. You can bathe your baby without a special bathinette. Nursery monitors or intercoms will not prevent crib deaths and may interfere with the learning of self-comforting behavior. Baby carriages or buggies generally have been replaced by baby strollers, front packs, or backpacks.

You can determine if your baby is being fed enough without a baby scale. An infant feeder is a bottle with a nipple on one end and a piston on the other and is used to feed young babies strained foods. They are advertised as a "natural" step between bottle- and spoon-feeding. Since babies don't need any food except formula or breast milk until at least 4 months of age (at which time spoon-feeding works fine), this item is unnecessary and can lead to forced feedings. You can prepare warm formula without a bottle warmer. Finally, shoes are not needed until your child has to walk outdoors.

POTENTIALLY HARMFUL EQUIPMENT: WALKERS

Over 40% of children who use walkers have an accident requiring medical attention. They get skull fractures, concussions, dental injuries, and lacerations. There have even been some deaths. Most of the serious walker injuries occur from falling down a stairway. When a crawling child falls down some unprotected steps, he tumbles and breaks his fall. When a child goes down a stairway in a walker, he accelerates and crash-lands at the bottom.

Some parents believe walkers help children learn to walk. On the contrary, walkers can delay both crawling and walking if used over 2 hours per day. Don't buy a walker. But if you have one, be sure to keep the door to any stairway locked. Children in walkers have crashed right through gates.

Instructions for Pediatric Patients by Barton D. Schmitt, M.D., *Pediatrician*
Adapted from YOUR CHILD'S HEALTH, Copyright © 1991 by Barton D. Schmitt, M.D.
Reprinted by permission of Bantam Books.

NEWBORN APPEARANCE

Even after your child's physician assures you that your baby is normal, you may find that he or she looks a bit odd. Your baby does not have the perfect body you have seen in baby books. Be patient. Most newborns have some peculiar characteristics. Fortunately they are temporary. Your baby will begin to look normal by 1 to 2 weeks of age.

This discussion of these transient newborn characteristics is arranged by parts of the body. A few minor congenital defects that are harmless but permanent are also included. Call our office if you have questions about your baby's appearance that this list does not address.

Head

Molding. Molding refers to the long, narrow, cone-shaped head that results from passage through a tight birth canal. This compression of the head can temporarily hide the fontanel. The head returns to a normal shape in a few days.

Caput. This refers to swelling on top of the head or throughout the scalp caused by fluid squeezed into the scalp during the birth process. Caput is present at birth and clears in a few days.

Cephalohematoma. This is a collection of blood on the outer surface of the skull. It is due to friction between the infant's skull and the mother's pelvic bones during the birth process. The lump is usually confined to one side of the head. It first appears on the second day of life and may grow larger for up to 5 days. It doesn't resolve completely until the baby is 2 or 3 months of age.

Anterior Fontanel. The "soft spot" is found in the top front part of the skull. It is diamond shaped and covered by a thick fibrous layer. Touching this area is quite safe. The purpose of the soft spot is to allow rapid growth of the brain. The spot will normally pulsate with each beat of the heart. It normally closes with bone when the baby is between 9 and 12 months of age.

Eyes

Swollen Eyelids. The eyes may be puffy because of pressure on the face during delivery. They may also be puffy and reddened if silver nitrate eye drops are used. This irritation should clear in 3 days.

Subconjunctival Hemorrhage. A flame-shaped hemorrhage on the white of the eye (sclera) is not uncommon. It is caused by birth trauma and is harmless. The blood is reabsorbed in 2 to 3 weeks.

Iris Color. The iris is usually blue, green, gray, or brown or variations of these colors. The permanent color of the iris is often uncertain until your baby reaches 6 months of age. White babies are usually born with blue-gray eyes. Black babies are usually born with brown-gray eyes. Children who will have dark irises often change eye color by 2 months of age; children who will have light-colored irises usually change by 5 or 6 months of age.

Blocked Tear Duct. If your baby's eye is continuously watery, he or she may have a blocked tear duct. This means that the channel that normally carries tears from the eye to the nose is blocked. It is a common condition, and more than 90% of blocked tear ducts open up by the time the child is 12 months old.

Ears

Folded Over. The ears of newborns are commonly soft and floppy. Sometimes one of the edges is folded over. The outer ear will assume normal shape as the cartilage hardens over the first few weeks.

Ear Pits. About 1% of normal children have a small pit or dimple in front of the outer ear. This minor congenital defect is not important unless it becomes infected.

Flattened Nose

The nose can become misshapen during the birth process. It may be flattened or pushed to one side. It will look normal by 1 week of age.

Mouth

Sucking Callus (or Blister). A sucking callus occurs in the center of the upper lip from constant friction at this point during bottle- or breast-feeding. It will disappear when your child begins cup feedings. A sucking callus on the thumb or wrist may also develop.

Tongue-tie. The normal tongue in newborns has a short tight band that connects it to the floor of the mouth. This band normally stretches with time, movement, and growth. Babies with symptoms from tongue-tie are rare.

Epithelial Pearls. Little cysts (containing clear fluid) or shallow white ulcers can occur along the gum line or on the hard palate. These are a result of blockage of normal mucous glands. They disappear after 1 to 2 months.

Teeth. The presence of a tooth at birth is rare. Approximately 10% are extra teeth without a root structure. The other 90% are prematurely erupted normal teeth. The distinction can be made with an x-ray. The extra teeth must be removed by a dentist. The normal teeth need to be removed only if they become loose (with a danger of choking) or if they cause sores on your baby's tongue.

Breast Engorgement

Swollen breasts are present during the first week of life in many female and male babies. They are caused by the passage of female hormones across the mother's placenta. Breasts are generally swollen for 4 to 6 months, but they may stay swollen longer in breast-fed and female babies. One breast may lose its swelling before the other one by a month or more. Never squeeze the breast because this can cause infection. Be sure to call our office if a swollen breast develops any redness, streaking, or tenderness.

(Continued on the reverse side)

Instructions for Pediatric Patients by Barton D. Schmitt, M.D., *Pediatrician*
Adapted from YOUR CHILD'S HEALTH, Copyright © 1991 by Barton D. Schmitt, M.D.
Reprinted by permission of Bantam Books.

© 1992 by W. B. Saunders Company

Female Genitals

Swollen Labia. The labia minora can be quite swollen in newborn girls because of the passage of female hormones across the placenta. The swelling will resolve in 2 to 4 weeks.

Hymenal Tags. The hymen can also be swollen because of maternal estrogen and can have smooth ½-inch projections of pink tissue. These normal tags occur in 10% of newborn girls and slowly shrink over 2 to 4 weeks.

Vaginal Discharge. As the maternal hormones decline in the baby's blood, a clear or white discharge can flow from the vagina during the latter part of the first week of life. Occasionally the discharge will become pink or blood tinged (false menstruation). This normal discharge should not recur once it stops.

Male Genitals

Hydrocele. The newborn scrotum can be filled with clear fluid. The fluid is squeezed into the scrotum during the birth process. This painless collection of clear fluid is called a "hydrocele." It is common in newborn males. A hydrocele may take 6 to 12 months to clear completely. It is harmless but can be rechecked during regular visits. If the swelling frequently changes size, a hernia may also be present and you should call our office during office hours for an appointment.

Undescended Testicle. The testicle is not in the scrotum in about 4% of full-term newborn boys. Many of these testicles gradually descend into the normal position during the following months. In 1-year-old boys only 0.7% of all testicles are undescended; these need to be brought down surgically.

Tight Foreskin. Most uncircumcised infant boys have a tight foreskin that doesn't allow you to see the head of the penis. This is normal and the foreskin should not be retracted.

Erections. Erections occur commonly in a newborn boy, as they do at all ages. They are usually triggered by a full bladder. Erections demonstrate that the nerves to the penis are normal.

Bones and Joints

Tight Hips. Your child's physician will test how far your child's legs can be spread apart to be certain the hips are not too tight. Outward bending of the upper legs until they are horizontal is called "90 degrees of spread." (Less than 50% of normal newborn hips permit this much spreading.) As long as the upper legs can be bent outward to 60 degrees and are the same on each side, they are fine. The most common cause of a tight hip is a dislocation.

Tibial Torsion. The lower legs (tibia) normally curve in because of the cross-legged posture your baby was confined to while in the womb. If you stand your baby up, you will also notice that the legs are bowed. Both of these curves are normal and will straighten out after your child has been walking for 6 to 12 months.

Feet Turned Up, In, or Out. Feet may be turned in any direction inside the cramped quarters of the womb. As long as your child's feet are flexible and can be easily moved to a normal position, they are normal. The direction of the feet will become more normal between 6 and 12 months of age.

Long Second Toe. The second toe is longer than the great toe as a result of heredity in some ethnic groups that originated along the Mediterranean, especially Egyptians.

"Ingrown" Toenails. Many newborns have soft nails that easily bend and curve. However, they are not truly ingrown because they don't curve into the flesh.

Hair

Scalp Hair. Most hair at birth is dark. This hair is temporary and begins to be shed by 1 month of age. Some babies lose it gradually while the permanent hair is coming in; others lose it rapidly and temporarily become bald. The permanent hair will appear by 6 months. It may be an entirely different color from the newborn hair.

Body Hair (Lanugo). Lanugo is the fine downy hair that is sometimes present on the back and shoulders. It is more common in premature infants. It is rubbed off with normal friction by 2 to 4 weeks of age.

NEWBORN BEHAVIOR

Some findings in newborns that concern parents are not signs of illness. Most of these harmless reflexes are due to an immature nervous system and will disappear in 2 or 3 months:

—Chin trembling
—Lower lip quivering
—Hiccups
—Irregular breathing: any irregular breathing pattern is normal if your baby is content, the rate is less than 60 breaths per minute, a pause is less than 6 seconds, and your baby doesn't turn blue; occasionally infants take rapid, progressively deeper, stepwise breaths to completely expand the lungs
—Passing gas (not a temporary behavior)
—Sleep noise from breathing and moving
—Sneezing
—Spitting up or belching
—Startle reflex or brief stiffening of the body (also called the Moro or embrace reflex) following noise or movement
—Straining with bowel movements
—Throat clearing (or gurgling sounds of secretions in the throat)
—Trembling or jitteriness of arms and legs during crying: common but convulsions are rare (During convulsions babies also jerk, blink their eyes, rhythmically suck with their mouths, and don't cry. If your baby is trembling and not crying, give him or her something to suck on. If the trembling doesn't stop during sucking, call our office immediately because your infant may be having a convulsion.)
—Yawning

 Instructions for Pediatric Patients by Barton D. Schmitt, M.D., *Pediatrician*   © 1992 by W. B. Saunders Company
Adapted from YOUR CHILD'S HEALTH, Copyright © 1991 by Barton D. Schmitt, M.D.
Reprinted by permission of Bantam Books.

After the first bath, your newborn will normally have a ruddy complexion from the extra high count of red blood cells. He can quickly change to a pale- or mottled-blue color if he becomes cold, so keep him warm. During the second week of life, the skin normally becomes dry and flaky. This guideline covers seven rashes and birthmarks. Save time by going directly to the one that pertains to your baby.

ACNE OF NEWBORN

More than 30% of newborns develop acne of the face, mainly small red bumps. This neonatal acne begins at 3 to 4 weeks of age and lasts until 4 to 6 months of age. The cause appears to be the transfer of maternal androgens (hormones) just before birth. Since it is temporary, no treatment is necessary. Baby oil or ointments will just make it worse.

DROOLING RASH

Most babies have a rash on the chin or cheeks that comes and goes. This often is due to contact with food and acid that has been spit up from the stomach. Some of this can be helped by placing an absorbent diaper under your baby's face during naps. Also rinse the face with water after all feedings.

Other temporary rashes on the face are heat rashes in areas held against the mother's skin during nursing (especially in the summertime). Change your baby's position more frequently and put a cool washcloth on the area. No baby has perfect skin. The babies in advertisements wear makeup.

ERYTHEMA TOXICUM

More than 50% of babies get a rash called erythema toxicum on the second or third day of life. The rash is composed of ½- to 1-inch red blotches with a small white lump in the center. They look like insect bites. They can be numerous, keep occurring, and be anywhere on the body surface. Their cause is unknown; they are harmless and resolve themselves by 2 weeks of age (rarely 4 weeks).

FORCEPS OR BIRTH CANAL TRAUMA

If delivery was difficult, a forceps may have been used to help the baby through the birth canal. The pressure of the forceps on the skin can leave bruises or scrapes or can even damage fat tissue anywhere on the head or face. Skin overlying bony prominences (such as the sides of the skull bone) can become damaged even without a forceps delivery by pressure from the birth canal. Fetal monitors can also cause scrapes and scabs on the scalp. The bruises and scrapes will be noted on day 1 or 2 and disappear by 1 to 2 weeks. The fat tissue injury won't be apparent until day 5 to 10. A thickened lump of skin with an overlying scab is the usual finding. This may take 3 or 4 weeks to resolve. If it becomes tender to the touch or soft in the center or shows other signs of infection, call our office.

MILIA

Milia are tiny white bumps that occur on the faces of 40% of newborn babies. The nose and cheeks are most often involved, but milia are also seen on the forehead and chin. Although they look like pimples, they are smaller and not infected. They are blocked-off skin pores and will open up and disappear by 1 to 2 months of age. No ointments or creams should be applied to them.

Any true blisters or pimples (especially of the scalp) that occur during the first month of life must be examined and diagnosed quickly. If they are caused by the herpes virus, treatment is urgent. If you suspect blisters or pimples, call our office immediately.

MONGOLIAN SPOTS

A mongolian spot is a bluish gray flat birthmark that is found in more than 90% of American Indian, Oriental, Hispanic, and black babies. Mongolian spots occur most commonly over the back and buttocks, although they can be present on any part of the body. They vary greatly in size and shape. Most fade away by 2 or 3 years of age, although a trace may persist into adult life.

STORK BITES (PINK BIRTHMARKS)

Flat pink birthmarks (also called capillary hemangiomas) occur over the bridge of the nose, the eyelids, or the back of the neck in more than 50% of newborns. The birthmarks on the bridge of the nose and eyelids clear completely by 1 to 2 years of age. Most birthmarks on the nape of the neck also clear, but 25% can persist into adult life.

Instructions for Pediatric Patients by Barton D. Schmitt, M.D., *Pediatrician*
Adapted from YOUR CHILD'S HEALTH, Copyright © 1991 by Barton D. Schmitt, M.D.
Reprinted by permission of Bantam Books.

NORMAL NEWBORN SKIN CARE

BATHING

Bathe your baby daily in hot weather and once or twice each week in cool weather. Keep the water level below the navel or give sponge baths until a few days after the cord has fallen off. Submerging the cord could cause infection or interfere with its drying out and falling off. Getting it a little wet doesn't matter. Use tap water without any soap or a nondrying soap such as Dove. Don't forget to wash the face; otherwise, chemicals from milk or various foods build up and cause an irritated rash. Also, rinse off the eyelids with water.

Don't forget to wash the genital area. However, when you wash the inside of the female genital area (the vulva), never use soap. Rinse the area with plain water and wipe from front to back to prevent irritation. This practice and the avoidance of any bubble baths before puberty may prevent many urinary tract infections and vaginal irritations. At the end of the bath, rinse your baby well; soap residue can be irritating.

CHANGING DIAPERS

After wet diapers are removed, just rinse your baby's bottom off with a wet washcloth. After soiled diapers, rinse the bottom under running warm water or in a basin of warm water. After you finish the rear area, cleanse the genital area by wiping front to back with a wet cloth. In boys, carefully clean the scrotum; and in girls, the creases of the vaginal lips (labia).

SHAMPOO

Wash your baby's hair once or twice weekly with a special baby shampoo that doesn't sting the eyes. Don't be con-cerned about hurting the anterior fontanelle (soft spot). It is well protected.

LOTIONS, CREAMS, AND OINTMENTS

Newborn skin normally does not require any ointments or creams. Especially avoid the application of any oil, ointment, or greasy substance, since this will almost always block the small sweat glands and lead to pimples or a heat rash. If the skin starts to become dry and cracked, use a baby lotion, hand lotion, or moisturizing cream twice daily. Cornstarch powder can be helpful for preventing rashes in areas of friction. Avoid talcum powder because it can cause a serious chemical pneumonia if inhaled into the lungs.

UMBILICAL CORD

Try to keep the cord dry. Apply rubbing alcohol to the base of the cord (where it attaches to the skin) twice each day (including after the bath) until 1 week after it falls off. Air exposure also helps with drying and separation, so keep the diaper folded down below the cord area or use a scissors to cut away a wedge of the diaper in front.

FINGERNAILS AND TOENAILS

Cut the toenails straight across to prevent ingrown toenails, but round off the corners of the fingernails to prevent unintentional scratches to your baby and others. Trim them weekly after a bath when the nails are softened. Use clippers or special baby scissors. This job usually takes two people unless you do it while your child is asleep.

Instructions for Pediatric Patients by Barton D. Schmitt, M.D., *Pediatrician*
Adapted from YOUR CHILD'S HEALTH, Copyright © 1991 by Barton D. Schmitt, M.D.
Reprinted by permission of Bantam Books.

DEFINITION

Circumcision means cutting off the foreskin or ring of tissue that covers the head (glans) of the penis. This surgical procedure is usually performed on the day of discharge from the hospital.

Fewer children in the United States are being circumcised now than several years ago. According to one survey, 60% of American newborn males were circumcised in 1986, whereas 90% were circumcised in 1979.

The following information should help you decide what is best for your son.

CULTURAL ASPECTS

Followers of the Jewish and Moslem faiths perform circumcision for religious reasons. Nonreligious circumcision became popular in English-speaking countries between 1920 and 1950 because it was thought that circumcision might help prevent sexually transmitted diseases. Circumcision never became a common practice in Asia, South America, Central America, or most of Europe. Over 80% of the world's male population is not circumcised. Circumcision rates have fallen to 1% of newborn males in Britain, 10% in New Zealand, and 40% in Canada.

PURPOSE OF THE FORESKIN

The presence of the foreskin is not some cosmic error. The foreskin protects the glans against urine, feces, and other types of irritation. Although rare events, infection of the urinary opening (meatitis) and scarring of the opening (meatal stenosis) occur almost exclusively in a circumcised penis. The foreskin may also serve a sexual function, namely protecting the sensitivity of the glans.

BENEFITS OF CIRCUMCISION

In 1989 the American Academy of Pediatrics issued a new statement on circumcision, clarifying that the procedure carried small potential risks and benefits that parents needed to consider. According to a recent study by Dr. T.E. Wiswell, circumcision may protect against urinary tract infections during the first year of life. However, there is only a 1% chance that an uncircumcised infant will get a urinary tract infection. Should we circumcise all infants to prevent such a small percentage of urinary tract infections (which are treatable)? Probably not.

Removal of the foreskin prevents infections under the foreskin (posthitis) and persistent tight foreskin (phimosis). However, both of these conditions are uncommon and usually due to excessive attempts to retract the foreskin.

In general, circumcision does not prevent sexually transmitted disease later in life. Although it does protect against cancer of the penis, good hygiene offers equal protection against this rare condition.

Another argument for circumcision is so the boy will look "like other boys in his school" or "like his father." However, the psychologic harm of being different from the father has never been documented. In general, boys don't mind looking different from other males in their family. However, they do mind being harassed in the locker room or shower, which may occur if most of their buddies are circumcised. It can be emotionally painful to be a trailblazer about the appearance of one's genitals.

In the final analysis, nonreligious circumcision is mainly cosmetic surgery.

RISKS OF CIRCUMCISION

Like any surgical procedure, circumcision may cause complications (in less than 1 per 100 circumcisions). Complications that might occur are skin infections, bloodstream infections, bleeding, gangrene, scarring, and various surgical accidents. A recent study showed that 1 of every 500 circumcised newborns suffered a serious side effect.

In addition, the procedure itself causes some pain. However, this pain can be minimized if physicians use a local anesthetic to block the nerves of the foreskin.

Finally, the cost of circumcision is about $100 per procedure in the United States. (A total of $200 million is spent on circumcisions each year.) You may have to pay for the procedure yourself because many medical insurance companies do not cover the costs of this procedure.

RECOMMENDATIONS

Circumcision of boys for religious purposes will continue. The need to circumcise other boys is open to question. Just because a father was circumcised doesn't mean that this optional procedure must be performed on the son. Because the foreskin comes as standard equipment, you might consider leaving it intact, unless your son will be attending a school where everyone else is likely to be circumcised. The risks and benefits are too small to swing the vote either way. This is a parental decision, not a medical decision.

Instructions for Pediatric Patients by Barton D. Schmitt, M.D., *Pediatrician*
Adapted from YOUR CHILD'S HEALTH, Copyright © 1991 by Barton D. Schmitt, M.D.
Reprinted by permission of Bantam Books.

DEFINITION

At birth the foreskin is normally attached to the head of the penis (glans) by a layer of cells. Over the next 5 to 10 years the foreskin will naturally separate from the head of the penis without any help from us. It gradually loosens up (retracts) a little at a time. Normal erections during childhood probably cause most of the change by stretching the foreskin.

The foreskin generally causes no problems. However, overzealous retraction before the foreskin has fully loosened can cause it to get stuck behind the head of the penis, resulting in severe pain and swelling. If retraction causes bleeding, scar tissue may form and interfere with natural retraction. Occasionally, the space under the foreskin becomes infected. Most of these problems can be prevented.

NORMAL FORESKIN RETRACTION

Some physicians feel that parents should not engage in any attempts at retraction, but this runs the risk of smegma collection and infection. In general, the foreskin requires minimal care. The following suggestions will help maintain good hygiene.

Only the outside of the foreskin needs to be cleaned during the first year. Gentle partial retraction can begin at 1 or 2 years of age. It can be done once each week during bathing. Perform retraction by gently pulling the skin on the shaft of the penis downward toward the abdomen. This will make the foreskin open up, revealing the end of the glans.

During retraction, the exposed part of the glans should be cleansed with water. Wipe away any whitish material (smegma) that you find there. Smegma is simply the accumulation of dead skin cells that are normally shed from the glans and lining of the foreskin throughout life. Do not use soap or leave soapy water under the foreskin because this can cause irritation and swelling. After cleansing, always pull the foreskin forward to its normal position. (NOTE: A collection of smegma that is seen or felt through the foreskin but that lies beyond the point to which the foreskin is retractable should be left alone until normal separation exposes it.)

Avoid vigorous retraction because this can cause the foreskin to become stuck behind the head of the penis (called "paraphimosis"). Retraction is excessive if it causes any discomfort or crying.

By the time your son is 5 or 6 years old, teach him to retract his own foreskin and clean beneath it once each week during baths to prevent poor hygiene and infection. Gentle reminders are necessary in the early years.

In summary, foreskin retraction is overdone in our society. Keep in mind that any degree of foreskin movement is normal as long as your boy has a normal urine stream. There should be no rush to achieve full retraction. Full retraction always occurs naturally by puberty. As the foreskin becomes retractable on its own, your son should cleanse beneath it to prevent infections.

CALL OUR OFFICE

IMMEDIATELY if
—The foreskin is pulled back and stuck behind the head of the penis.
—Your child can't pass any urine.
—The foreskin is red or tender to the touch.
—A fever (over 100° F) is present.

Within 24 hours if
—The foreskin is swollen.
—Any pus is coming from the end of the foreskin.
—The urine stream is weak or dribbly.
—You have other concerns or questions.

Instructions for Pediatric Patients by Barton D. Schmitt, M.D., *Pediatrician*
Adapted from YOUR CHILD'S HEALTH, Copyright © 1991 by Barton D. Schmitt, M.D.
Reprinted by permission of Bantam Books.

PREVENTING FATIGUE AND EXHAUSTION

For most mothers the first weeks at home with a new baby are often the hardest in their lives. You will probably feel overworked, even overwhelmed. Inadequate sleep will leave you fatigued. Caring for a baby can be a lonely and stressful responsibility. You may wonder if you will ever catch up on your rest or work. The solution is asking for help. No one should be expected to care for a young baby alone.

Every baby awakens one or more times each night. The way to avoid sleep deprivation is to know the total amount of sleep you need per day and to get that sleep in bits and pieces. Go to bed earlier in the evening. When your baby naps you must also nap. Your baby doesn't need you hovering while he or she sleeps. If sick, your baby will show symptoms. While you are napping take the telephone off the hook and put up a sign on the door saying "Mother and baby sleeping." If your total sleep remains inadequate, hire a babysitter or bring in a relative. If you don't take care of yourself, you won't be able to take care of your baby.

THE POSTPARTUM BLUES

More than 50% of women experience postpartum blues on the third or fourth day after delivery. The symptoms include tearfulness, tiredness, sadness, and difficulty in thinking clearly. The main cause of this temporary reaction is probably the sudden decrease of maternal hormones. Since the symptoms commonly begin on the day the mother comes home from the hospital, the full impact of being totally responsible for a dependent newborn may also be a contributing factor. Many mothers feel letdown and guilty about these symptoms because they have been led to believe they should be overjoyed about caring for their newborn. In any event, these symptoms usually clear in 1 to 3 weeks as hormone levels return to normal and the mother develops routines and a sense of control over her life.

There are several ways to cope with the postpartum blues. First, acknowledge your feelings. Discuss them with your husband or a close friend. Also discuss your sense of being trapped and your feeling that these new responsibilities are insurmountable. Don't feel you need to suppress crying or put on a "supermom show" for everyone. Second, get adequate rest. Third, get help with all your work. Fourth, mix with other people, don't become isolated. Get out of the house at least once every week—go to the hairdresser, go shopping, visit a friend, or see a movie. By the third week, setting aside an evening each week for a "date" with your husband is also helpful. If you don't feel better by the time your baby is 1 month old, see your physician about the possibility of needing counseling for depression.

HELPERS: RELATIVES, FRIENDS, SITTERS

As already emphasized, everyone needs extra help during the first few weeks alone with a new baby. Ideally, you were able to make arrangements for help before your baby was born. The best person to help (if you get along with her) is usually your mother or mother-in-law. If not, teenagers or adults can come in several times per week to help with housework or look after your baby while you go out or get a nap. If you have other young children, you will need daily help. Clarify that your role is looking after your baby. Your helper's role is to shop, cook, houseclean, and wash clothes and dishes. If your newborn has a medical problem that requires special care, ask for home visits by a community health nurse.

THE FATHER'S ROLE

The father needs to take time off from work to be with his wife during labor and delivery, as well as on the day she and his child come home from the hospital. If the couple has a relative who will temporarily live in and help, the father can continue to work after the baby comes home. However, when the relative leaves, the father can take saved-up vacation time as paternity leave. At a minimum he needs to work shorter hours until his wife and baby have settled in.

The age of noninvolvement of the father is over. Not only does the mother need the father to help her with household chores, but also the baby needs to develop a close relationship with the father. Today's father helps with feeding, changing diapers, bathing, putting to bed, reading stories, dressing, disciplining, homework, playing games, and calling the physician when the child is sick.

A father may avoid interacting with his baby during the first year of life because he is afraid he will hurt his baby or that he won't be able to calm the child when the baby cries. The longer a father goes without learning parenting skills, the harder it becomes to master them. At a minimum, a father should hold and comfort his baby at least once each day.

VISITORS

Only close friends and relatives should visit you during your first month at home. They should not visit if they are sick. To prevent unannounced visitors, the parents can put up a sign saying "Mother and baby sleeping. No visitors. Please call first." Friends without children may not understand your needs. During visits the visitor should pay special attention to older siblings.

(Continued on the reverse side)

Instructions for Pediatric Patients by Barton D. Schmitt, M.D., *Pediatrician*
Adapted from YOUR CHILD'S HEALTH, Copyright © 1991 by Barton D. Schmitt, M.D.
Reprinted by permission of Bantam Books.

FEEDING YOUR BABY: ACHIEVING WEIGHT GAIN

Your main assignments during the early months of life are loving and feeding your baby. All babies lose a few ounces during the first few days after birth. However, they should never lose more than 7% of their birth weight (usually about 8 ounces). Most bottle-fed babies are back to birth weight by 10 days of age and breast-fed babies by 14 days of age. Then infants gain approximately 1 ounce per day during the early months. If milk is provided liberally, the normal newborn's hunger drive ensures appropriate weight gain.

A breast-feeding mother often wonders if her baby is getting enough calories, since she can't see how many ounces the baby takes. Your baby is doing fine if he or she demands to nurse every 1½ to 2½ hours, appears satisfied after feedings, takes both breasts at each nursing, wets six or more diapers each day, and passes four or more soft stools per day. Whenever you are worried about your baby's weight gain, bring your baby to our office for a weight check. Feeding problems detected early are much easier to remedy than those of long standing. A special weight check 1 week after birth is a good idea for infants of a first-time breast-feeding mother or a mother concerned about her milk supply.

DEALING WITH CRYING

Crying babies need to be held. They need someone with a soothing voice and a soothing touch. You can't spoil your baby during the early months of life. Overly sensitive babies may need an even gentler touch. For additional help, request "The Crying Baby" handout.

TAKING YOUR BABY OUTDOORS

You can take your baby outdoors at any age. You already took your baby outside when you left the hospital, and you will be going outside again when you go for the baby's 2-week checkup.

Dress the baby with as many layers of clothing as an adult would wear for the outdoor temperature. A common mistake is overdressing a baby in summer.

In winter a baby needs a hat because there is often not much hair to protect against heat loss. Cold air or winds do not cause ear infections or pneumonia.

The skin of babies is more sensitive to the sun than the skin of older children. Keep sun exposure to small amounts (10 to 15 minutes at a time). Protect your baby's skin from sunburn with longer clothing and a bonnet.

Camping and crowds should probably be avoided during your baby's first month of life. Also, during your baby's first year of life try to avoid close contact with people who have infectious illnesses.

THE 2-WEEK MEDICAL CHECKUP

This checkup is probably the most important medical visit for your baby during the first year of life. By 2 weeks of age your baby will usually have developed symptoms of any physical condition that was not detectable during the hospital stay. Your child's physician will be able to judge how well your baby is growing from height, weight, and head circumference.

This is also the time your family is under the most stress of adapting to a new baby. Try to develop a habit of jotting down questions about your child's health or behavior at home. Bring this list with you to office visits to discuss with your child's physician. We welcome the opportunity to address your agenda, especially if your questions are not easily answered by reading or talking with other mothers.

If at all possible, have your husband join you on these visits. We prefer to get to know the father during a checkup rather than during the crisis of an acute illness.

If you think your newborn is sick between these routine visits, be sure to call our office for help.

 Instructions for Pediatric Patients by Barton D. Schmitt, M.D., *Pediatrician*
Adapted from YOUR CHILD'S HEALTH, Copyright © 1991 by Barton D. Schmitt, M.D.
Reprinted by permission of Bantam Books.

DEFINITION

Diagnostic Finding

Any rash in the skin area covered by a diaper

Causes

Almost every child gets diaper rashes. Most of them are due to prolonged contact with moisture, bacteria, and ammonia. The skin irritants are made by the action of bacteria from bowel movements on certain chemicals in the urine. Bouts of diarrhea cause rashes in most children. Diaper rashes occur equally with cloth and disposable diapers.

Expected Course

With proper treatment these rashes are usually better in 3 days. If they do not respond, a yeast infection (*Candida*) has probably occurred. Suspect this if the rash becomes bright red and raw, covers a large area, and is surrounded by red dots. We will need to prescribe a special cream for a yeast infection.

HOME CARE

Change Diapers Frequently. The key to successful treatment is keeping the area dry and clean so it can heal itself. Check the diapers about every hour, and if they are wet or soiled, change them immediately. Exposure to stools causes most of the skin damage. Make sure that your baby's bottom is completely dry before closing up the fresh diaper.

Increase Air Exposure. Leave your baby's bottom exposed to the air as much as possible each day. Practical times are during naps or after bowel movements. Put a towel or diaper under your baby. When the diaper is on, fasten it loosely so that air can circulate between it and the skin. Avoid airtight plastic pants for a few days. If you use disposable diapers, punch holes in them to let air in.

Rinse the Skin With Warm Water. Washing the skin with soap after every diaper change will damage the skin. Use a mild soap (such as Dove) only after bowel movements. The soap will remove the film of bacteria left on the skin. After using a soap, rinse well. If the diaper rash is quite raw, use warm water soaks for 15 minutes three times every day.

Nighttime Care. At night use the new disposable diapers that are made with materials that lock wetness inside the diaper and away from the skin. Avoid plastic pants at night. Until the rash is better, awaken once during the night to change your baby's diaper.

Creams and Powders. Most babies don't need any diaper creams or powders. If your baby's skin is dry and cracked, however, apply an ointment to protect the skin after washing off each bowel movement. A barrier ointment is also needed whenever your child has diarrhea.

Cornstarch reduces friction and can be used to prevent future diaper rashes after this one is healed. Recent studies show that cornstarch does not encourage yeast infections. Avoid talcum powder because of the risk of pneumonia if your baby inhales it.

Prevention of Diaper Rash. Changing the diaper immediately after your child has a bowel movement and rinsing the skin with warm water are the most effective things you can do to prevent diaper rash.

If you use cloth diapers and wash them yourself, you will need to use bleach (such as Clorox, Borax, or Purex) to sterilize them. During the regular cycle, use any detergent. Then refill the washer with warm water, add 1 cup of bleach, and run a second cycle. Unlike bleach, vinegar is not effective in killing germs.

CALL OUR OFFICE

IMMEDIATELY if
—The diaper rash develops any big (more than 1 inch across) blisters or open sores.
—The face becomes bright red and tender to the touch.
—Your child starts acting very sick.

Within 24 hours if
—The rash isn't much better in 3 days.
—The diaper rash becomes solid and bright red.
—Pimples, blisters, boils, sores, or crusts develop.
—The rash becomes raw or bleeds.
—The rash spreads beyond the diaper area.
—Your child is male and circumcised, *and* the end of the penis develops a sore or scab.
—An unexplained fever (over 100° F) occurs.
—The rash causes enough pain to interfere with sleeping.
—You have other concerns or questions.

Instructions for Pediatric Patients by Barton D. Schmitt, M.D., *Pediatrician*
Adapted from YOUR CHILD'S HEALTH, Copyright © 1991 by Barton D. Schmitt, M.D.
Reprinted by permission of Bantam Books.

JAUNDICE OF THE NEWBORN

DEFINITION

In jaundice the skin and the whites of the eyes (the sclera) are yellow because of increased amounts of a pigment called bilirubin in the body. Bilirubin is produced by the normal breakdown of red blood cells. Bilirubin accumulates if the liver doesn't excrete it into the intestines at a normal rate.

TYPES OF JAUNDICE

Physiological (Normal) Jaundice

Physiological jaundice occurs in more than 50% of babies. An immaturity of the liver leads to a slower processing of bilirubin. The jaundice first appears at 2 to 4 days of age. It usually disappears by 1 to 2 weeks of age and the levels reached are harmless.

Breast-milk Jaundice

Breast-milk jaundice occurs in 1% to 2% of breast-fed babies. It is caused by a special substance that some mothers produce in their milk. This substance (an enzyme) increases the resorption of bilirubin from the intestine. This type of jaundice starts at 4 to 7 days of age and may last from 3 to 10 weeks.

Blood Group Incompatibility (Rh or ABO Problems)

If a baby and mother have different blood types, sometimes the mother produces antibodies that destroy the newborn's red blood cells. This causes a sudden buildup in bilirubin in the baby's blood. This type of jaundice usually begins during the first 24 hours of life. Rh problems formerly caused the most severe form of jaundice but are now preventable with an injection of RhoGAM to the mother within 72 hours after delivery. This prevents her from forming antibodies that might endanger subsequent babies.

TREATMENT OF SEVERE JAUNDICE

High levels of bilirubin (usually above 20 mg/100 ml) can cause deafness, cerebral palsy, or brain damage in some babies. High levels usually occur with blood-type problems. These complications can be prevented by lowering the bilirubin using phototherapy (blue light that breaks down bilirubin in the skin). In many communities, phototherapy can be used in the home.

In rare cases where the bilirubin reaches dangerous levels, an exchange transfusion may be used. This technique replaces the baby's blood with fresh blood. Physiologic jaundice does not rise to levels requiring this type of treatment.

TREATMENT OF BREAST-MILK JAUNDICE

The bilirubin level can rise above 20 mg/100 ml in less than 1% of infants with breast-milk jaundice. Almost always elevations to this level can be prevented by more frequent feedings. Nurse your baby every 1½ to 2½ hours. Since bilirubin is carried out of the body in the stools, passing frequent bowel movements is helpful. If your baby sleeps more than 5 hours at night, awaken him for a feeding.

Occasionally the bilirubin will not come down with frequent feedings. In this situation the bilirubin level can be reduced by alternating each breast feeding with formula feeding for 2 or 3 days. Supplementing with glucose water is not as helpful as formula for moving the bilirubin out of the body. Whenever you miss a nursing, be sure to use a breast pump to keep your milk production flowing. Breast-feeding should never be permanently discontinued because of breast-milk jaundice. Once the jaundice clears, you can return to full breast-feeding and you need not worry about the jaundice coming back.

CALLING OUR OFFICE

Newborns often leave the hospital within 48 hours of their birth. Parents therefore have the responsibility to closely observe the degree of jaundice in their newborn. The amount of yellowness is best judged by viewing your baby unclothed in natural light by a window.

 ## CALL OUR OFFICE

IMMEDIATELY if
—Jaundice is noticed during the first 48 hours of life.
—Jaundice involves the arms or legs.
—Your baby develops a fever over 100° F (37.8° C) measured rectally.
—Your baby also starts to look or act sick.

During office hours if
—The color gets deeper after day 7.
—Jaundice is not gone by day 14.
—Your baby is not gaining weight well.
—You are concerned about the amount of jaundice.

Instructions for Pediatric Patients by Barton D. Schmitt, M.D., *Pediatrician*
Adapted from YOUR CHILD'S HEALTH, Copyright © 1991 by Barton D. Schmitt, M.D.
Reprinted by permission of Bantam Books.

DEFINITION

Diagnostic Findings of Spitting Up (Regurgitation)

Regurgitation is the effortless spitting up of one or two mouthfuls of stomach contents. It is usually seen shortly after feedings. It mainly occurs in children under 1 year of age and begins in the first weeks of life. More than half of all infants have it to some degree.

Cause

A lack of closure of the valve at the upper end of the stomach is responsible. This condition is also called "gastroesophageal reflux" (GE reflux) or "chalasia."

Expected Course

Spitting up improves with age. By the time your baby has been walking for 3 months it should be totally cleared up. Many babies get over it even sooner.

HOME CARE

Feed Smaller Amounts. Overfeeding always makes spitting up worse. If the stomach is filled to capacity, spitting up is more likely. Give your baby smaller amounts (at least 1 ounce less than you have been giving). Your baby doesn't have to finish a bottle. Wait at least 2½ hours between feedings because it takes that long for the stomach to empty itself.

Burp Your Child to Prevent Spitting Up. Burp your baby several times during each feeding. Do it when he pauses and looks around. Don't interrupt his feeding rhythm in order to burp him. Keep in mind that burping is less important than giving smaller feedings.

Positioning. After meals, try to hold your baby in an upright position using a front pack, backpack, or swing. Avoid infant seats because they increase the contact of stomach acid with the lower esophagus. When your infant is in a crib, always place him on his abdomen to protect the lower esophagus. Try to elevate the head of the bed a bit. After your child is 6 months old, a walker can be helpful for maintaining an upright posture after meals. To make the walker safe, try to remove the wheels. Make sure stairways are closed off securely.

Avoid Pressure on the Abdomen. Avoid tight diapers. They put added pressure on the stomach. Don't double your child up during diaper changes. Don't let people hug your child or play vigorously right after meals.

Cleaning Up. One of the worst aspects of spitting up in the past was the odor. This was caused by the effect of stomach acid on the butterfat in cow's milk. The odor is not present with commercial formulas because they contain vegetable oils. A more common concern is clothing stains from milk spots. Use the powdered formulas, they stain the least. Also, don't pick up your child when you have your best clothes on. Try to confine your baby to areas without rugs (for example, the kitchen).

 ## CALL OUR OFFICE

IMMEDIATELY if
—There is blood in the spit-up material
—The spitting up causes your child to choke or cough.

During office hours if
—Your baby doesn't seem to improve with this approach. (We can discuss how to thicken feedings with cereal and how to use a chalasia or reflux harness after meals.)
—Your baby does not gain weight normally.
—Your baby becomes cranky.
—The spitting up continues after your baby has been walking for more than 3 months.
—You have other concerns or questions.

BLOCKED TEAR DUCT

DEFINITION

Diagnostic Findings

—Continuously watery eye
—Tears running down the face even without crying
—During crying, nostril on blocked side remains dry
—Onset at birth to 1 month of age
—Eye not red and eyelid not swollen (unless the soggy tissues become infected)

Cause

Your child probably has a blocked tear duct on that side. This means that the channel that normally carries tears from the eye to the nose is blocked. Although the obstruction is present at birth, the delay in onset of symptoms can be explained by the occasional delay in tear production until the age of 3 or 4 weeks in some babies. Both sides are blocked 30% of the time.

Expected Course

This is a common condition, affecting 6% of newborns. Over 90% of blocked tear ducts open up spontaneously by the time the child is 12 months of age. If the obstruction persists beyond 12 months of age, an ophthalmologist (eye specialist) can open it with a probe.

HOME CARE FOR PREVENTING INFECTION

Because of poor drainage, eyes with blocked tear ducts become easily infected. The infected eye produces a yellow discharge. To keep the eye free of infection, massage the lacrimal sac (where tears collect) twice a daily. Always wash your hands carefully before doing this. The lacrimal sac is located in the inner lower corner of the eye. This sac should be massaged to empty it of old fluids and to check for infection. Start at the inner corner of the eye and press *upward* using a cotton swab. (CAUTION: Massaging downward is not helpful and may lead to infection.) If the eye becomes infected, it is very important to begin antibiotic eye drops.

 ## CALL OUR OFFICE

IMMEDIATELY if
—The eyelids are red or swollen.
—A red lump appears at the inner lower corner of the eyelid.

During office hours if
—The eyelids are stuck together with pus after naps.
—Much yellow discharge is present.
—Your child reaches 12 months of age and the eye is still watering.
—You have other concerns or questions.

Instructions for Pediatric Patients by Barton D. Schmitt, M.D., *Pediatrician*
Adapted from YOUR CHILD'S HEALTH, Copyright © 1991 by Barton D. Schmitt, M.D.
Reprinted by permission of Bantam Books.

DEFINITION

Teething is the normal process of new teeth working their way through the gums. Your baby's first tooth may appear any time between the ages of 3 months to 1 year old. Most children have completely painless teething. The only symptoms are increased saliva, drooling, and a desire to chew on things. It occasionally causes some mild gum pain, but it doesn't interfere with sleep. The degree of discomfort varies from child to child, but your child won't be miserable. When the back teeth (molars) come through (age 6 to 12 years), the overlying gum may become bruised and swollen. This is harmless and temporary.

Since teeth erupt continuously from 6 months to 2 years of age, many unrelated illnesses are blamed on teething. Fevers are also common during this time because after 6 months infants lose the natural protection provided by their mother's antibodies.

DEVELOPMENT OF BABY TEETH

Your baby's teeth will usually erupt in the following order:
1. Two lower incisors
2. Four upper incisors
3. Two lower incisors and all four first molars
4. Four canines
5. Four second molars

HOME CARE

Gum Massage. Find the irritated or swollen gum. Vigorously massage it with your finger for 2 minutes. Do this as often as necessary. If you wish, you may use a piece of ice to massage the gum.

Teething Rings. Your baby's way of massaging his gums is to chew on a smooth, hard object. Solid teething rings and ones with liquid in the center (as long as it's purified water) are fine. Most children like them cold. A wet washcloth placed in the freezer for 30 minutes will please many infants. He may also like some ice, Popsicle, frozen banana, or a frozen bagel. Avoid hard foods that your baby might choke on (such as raw carrots), but teething biscuits are fine.

Diet. Avoid salty or acid foods. Your baby probably will enjoy sucking on a nipple, but if he complains, use a cup for fluids temporarily. A few babies may need acetaminophen for pain relief for a few days.

Common Mistakes in Treating Teething

—Teething does not cause fever, sleep problems, diarrhea, diaper rash, or lowered resistance to any infection. It probably doesn't cause crying. If your baby develops fever while teething, the fever is due to something else.
—Special teething gels are unnecessary. Since many contain benzocaine, there is a risk that they may cause choking by numbing the throat or may cause a drug reaction.
—Don't tie the teething ring around the neck. It could catch on something and strangle your child. Attach it to clothing with a "catch-it" clip.

CALL OUR OFFICE

During regular hours if
—You have other questions or concerns.

Instructions for Pediatric Patients by Barton D. Schmitt, M.D., *Pediatrician*
Adapted from YOUR CHILD'S HEALTH, Copyright © 1991 by Barton D. Schmitt, M.D.
Reprinted by permission of Bantam Books.

© 1992 by W. B. Saunders Company

DEFINITION

Diagnostic Findings

—White, irregularly shaped patches that coat the inside of the mouth and sometimes the tongue, adhere to the mouth, and cannot be washed away or wiped off easily like milk (If the only symptom is a uniformly white tongue, it's due to a milk diet, not thrush.)
—Bottle-fed or breast-fed child

Cause

Thrush is caused by a yeast (called *Candida*) that grows rapidly on the lining of the mouth in areas abraded by prolonged sucking (as when a baby sleeps with a bottle or pacifier). A large pacifier or nipple can also injure the lining of the mouth. Thrush may also occur when your child has recently been on a broad-spectrum antibiotic. Thrush is not contagious since it does not invade normal tissue.

HOME CARE

Nystatin Oral Medicine. The drug for clearing this up is nystatin oral suspension. It requires a prescription. Give 1 ml of nystatin four times daily. Place it in the front of the mouth on each side (it doesn't do any good once it's swallowed). If the thrush isn't responding, rub the nystatin directly on the affected areas with a cotton swab or with gauze wrapped around your finger. Apply it after meals or at least don't feed your baby anything

for 30 minutes after application. Do this for at least 7 days or until all the thrush has been gone for 3 days. If you are breast-feeding, apply nystatin to any irritated areas on your nipples.

Decrease Sucking Time During Thrush. If eating and sucking are painful for your child, temporarily use a cup and spoon. In any event, reduce sucking time to 20 minutes or less per feeding.

Restrict Pacifier to Bedtime. Eliminate the pacifier temporarily except when it's really needed for going to sleep. If your infant is using an orthodontic-type pacifier, switch to a smaller, regular one. Soak all nipples in water at 130° F (55° C; the temperature of most hot tap water) for 15 minutes. If the thrush recurs and your child is bottle fed, switch to a nipple with a different shape and made from silicone.

Diaper Rash Associated with Thrush. If your child has an associated diaper rash, assume it is due to yeast. Request nystatin cream and apply it four times daily.

 ## CALL OUR OFFICE

During regular hours if
—Your child refuses to eat.
—The thrush gets worse on treatment.
—The thrush lasts beyond 10 days.
—An unexplained fever (over 100° F [37.8° C]) occurs.
—You have other concerns or questions.

 Instructions for Pediatric Patients by Barton D. Schmitt, M.D., *Pediatrician*   © 1992 by W. B. Saunders Company
Adapted from YOUR CHILD'S HEALTH, Copyright © 1991 by Barton D. Schmitt, M.D.
Reprinted by permission of Bantam Books.

PART 2

FEEDING
AND
EATING

Babies who are breast-fed have fewer infections and allergies during the first year of life than babies who are fed formula. Breast milk is also inexpensive and served at the perfect temperature. Breast-feeding becomes especially convenient when a mother is traveling with her baby. Overall, breast milk is nature's best food for young babies.

HOW OFTEN TO FEED

The baby should nurse for the first time in the delivery room. The second feeding will usually be at 4 to 6 hours of age, after he awakens from a deep sleep. Until your milk supply is well established and your baby is gaining weight (usually 2 weeks), nurse your infant whenever he cries or seems hungry ("demand feeding"). Thereafter, babies can receive adequate breast milk by nursing every 2 to 2½ hours. If your baby cries and less than 2 hours have passed, he can be rocked or carried in a front pack. However, waiting more than 2½ hours can lead to swollen breasts (engorgement), which decreases milk production. (Feeding less frequently is fine at night, but no more than 5 hours should pass between feedings.) Your baby will not gain adequately unless he nurses eight or more times per day initially. The risks of continuing to nurse at short intervals (less than 1½ hours) are that "grazing" will become a habit, your baby won't be able to sleep through the night, and you won't have much free time.

HOW LONG PER FEEDING

Nurse your baby 10 minutes on the first breast and as long as he wants on the second breast. Your goal is to have your baby nurse for a total of about 30 minutes at each feeding. Remember to alternate which breast you start with each time. Once your milk supply is well established (about 2 to 3 weeks after birth), 10 minutes of nursing per breast is fine when you are in a hurry (since your child usually gets over 90% of the milk in this time). However, try not to nurse for periods shorter than 20 minutes because it may lead to more frequent feedings and more nighttime awakenings.

HOW TO KNOW YOUR BABY IS GETTING ENOUGH BREAST MILK

In the first couple weeks, if your baby has four or more bowel movements per day and six or more wet diapers per day, he is receiving a good supply of breast milk. (CAUTION: Infrequent bowel movements are not normally seen before the second month of life.) In addition, most babies will act satisfied after completing a feeding. Your baby should be back to birth weight by 10 to 14 days of age if breast-feeding is going well. Therefore the 2-week checkup by your baby's physician is very important. The presence of a letdown reflex is another indicator of good milk production.

THE LETDOWN REFLEX

A letdown reflex develops after 2 to 3 weeks of nursing and is indicated by tingling or milk ejection in the breast just before feeding (or when you are thinking about feeding). It also occurs in the opposite breast while your baby is nursing. Letdown is enhanced by adequate sleep, adequate fluids, a relaxed environment, and reduced stress (such as low expectations about how much housework gets done). If your letdown reflex is not present yet, take extra naps and ask your husband and friends for more help. Also consider calling the local chapter of La Leche League, a support group for nursing mothers.

SUPPLEMENTAL BOTTLES

Do not offer your baby any bottles during the first 4 to 6 weeks after birth because this is when you establish your milk supply. Good lactation depends on frequent emptying of the breasts. Supplemental bottles take away from sucking time on the breast and reduce the appetite. If your baby is not gaining well, see your physician or a lactation specialist for a complete evaluation.

After your baby is 6 weeks old and nursing is well established, you may want to offer your baby a bottle of expressed milk or water once a day so that he can become accustomed to the bottle and the artificial nipple. Once your baby accepts bottle feedings, you can occasionally leave your baby with a sitter and go out for the evening or return to work outside the home. You can use pumped breast milk that has been refrigerated or frozen.

EXTRA WATER

Babies do not routinely need extra water. Even when they have a fever or the weather is hot and dry, breast milk provides enough water.

PUMPING THE BREASTS TO RELIEVE PAIN OR COLLECT MILK

Severe engorgement (severe swelling) of the breasts decreases milk production. To prevent engorgement, nurse your baby more often. Also, compress the area around the nipple (the areola) with your fingers at the start of each feeding to soften the areola. For milk release, your baby must be able to grip and suck on the areola as well as the nipple. Every time you miss a feeding (for example, if you return to work outside the home), pump your breasts. Also, whenever your breasts hurt and you are unable to feed your baby, pump your breasts until they are soft. If you don't relieve engorgement, your milk supply can dry up in 2 to 3 days.

A breast pump is usually unnecessary because pumping can be done by hand. Ask someone to teach you the Marmet technique.

Collect the breast milk in plastic containers or plastic bottles because some of the immune factors in the milk

(Continued on the reverse side)

stick to glass. Pumped breast milk can be saved for 48 hours in a refrigerator or up to 3 months in a freezer. To thaw frozen breast milk, put the plastic container of breast milk in the refrigerator (it will take a few hours to thaw) or place it in a container of warm water until it has warmed up to the temperature your baby prefers.

SORE NIPPLES

Clean a sore nipple with water after each feeding. Do not use soap or alcohol because they remove natural oils. At the end of each feeding, the nipple can be coated with some breast milk to keep it lubricated. Try to keep the nipples dry with loose clothing, air exposure, and nursing pads.

Sore nipples usually are due to poor latching on and a feeding position that causes undue friction on the nipple. Position your baby so that he directly faces the nipple without turning his neck. At the start of the feeding, compress the nipple and areola between your thumb and index finger so that your baby can latch on easily. Throughout the feeding, hold your breast from below so the nipple and areola aren't pulled out of your baby's mouth by the weight of the breast. Slightly rotate your baby's body so that his mouth applies pressure to slightly different parts of the areola and nipple at each feeding.

Start your feedings on the side that is not sore. If one nipple is extremely sore, temporarily limit feedings to 10 minutes on that side.

VITAMINS/FLUORIDE FOR THE BABY

Breast milk contains all the necessary vitamins and minerals except vitamin D and fluoride. Full-term dark-skinned babies and all premature babies need 400 units of vitamin D each day. White babies who have little sun exposure (less than 15 minutes twice per week) also need vitamin D supplements. From 2 weeks to 12 years of age, children need fluoride to prevent tooth decay; 0.25 mg of fluoride drops should be given each day. In the United States this is a prescription item that you can obtain from your child's physician.

VITAMINS FOR THE MOTHER

A nursing mother can take a multivitamin tablet daily if she is not following a well-balanced diet. She especially needs 400 units of vitamin D and 1200 mg of both calcium and phosphorus per day. A quart of milk (or its equivalent in cheese or yogurt) can also meet this requirement.

THE MOTHER'S MEDICATIONS

Almost any drug a breast-feeding mother consumes will be transferred in small amounts into the breast milk.

Therefore try to avoid any drug that is not essential, just as you did during pregnancy.

Some commonly used drugs that are safe for you to take while nursing are acetaminophen, penicillins, erythromycin, stool softeners, antihistamines, mild sedatives, cough drops, nose drops, eye drops, and skin creams. Aspirin and sulfa drugs can be taken if your baby is more than 2 weeks old *and* not jaundiced. Take drugs that are not harmful immediately after you breast-feed your child so that the level of drugs in the breast milk at the time of the next feeding is low.

Some of the dangerous drugs that can harm your baby are tetracyclines, chloramphenicol, antithyroid drugs, anticancer drugs, or any radioactive substance. Women who must take these drugs should not be breast-feeding or should request a safer form of therapy. Another group of drugs that should be avoided because they can suppress milk production are ergotamines (for migraine), birth control pills with a high estrogen content (most are not harmful), vitamin B_6 (pyridoxine) in large doses, and many antidepressants.

BURPING

Burping is optional. Its only benefit is to decrease spitting up. Air in the stomach does not cause pain. If you burp your baby, burping two times during a feeding and for about a minute is plenty. Burp your baby when switching from the first breast to the second and at the end of the feeding.

CUP FEEDING

Introduce your child to a cup at approximately 6 months of age. Total weaning to a cup will probably occur somewhere between 9 and 18 months of age, depending on your baby's individual preference. If you discontinue breast-feeding before 9 months of age, switch to bottle-feeding first. If you stop breast-feeding after 9 months of age, you may be able to go directly to cup feeding.

 ## CALL OUR OFFICE

During regular hours if
—Your baby doesn't seem to be gaining adequately.
—Your baby has less than six wet diapers per day.
—During the first month, your baby has less than four bowel movements per day.
—You suspect your baby has a food allergy.
—You need to take a medication that was not discussed.
—Your breasts are not full (engorged) before feedings by day 5.
—You have painful engorgement or sore nipples that do not respond to the recommended treatment.
—You have a fever (also call your obstetrician).

    Instructions for Pediatric Patients by Barton D. Schmitt, M.D., *Pediatrician*
Adapted from YOUR CHILD'S HEALTH, Copyright © 1991 by Barton D. Schmitt, M.D.
Reprinted by permission of Bantam Books.

Breast milk is best for babies, but breast-feeding isn't always possible. Use an infant formula if
—You decide not to breast-feed.
—You need to discontinue breast-feeding and your infant is less than 1 year of age.
—You need to occasionally supplement your infant after breast-feeding is well established.
—NOTE: If you want to breast-feed but feel your milk supply is insufficient, don't discontinue breast-feeding. Instead seek help from your physician or a lactation nurse.

COMMERCIAL FORMULAS

Infant formulas are a safe alternative to breast milk. Infant formulas have been designed to resemble breast milk and fulfill the nutritional needs of your infant by providing all known essential nutrients in their proper amounts. Most formulas are derived from cow's milk. A few are derived from soybeans and are for infants who may be allergic to the type of protein in cow's milk. Bottle-feeding can provide your child with all the emotional benefits and many of the health benefits of breast-feeding. Bottle-fed babies grow as rapidly and are as happy as breast-fed babies. A special advantage of bottle-feeding is that the father can participate.

Use a commercial formula that is iron fortified to prevent iron deficiency anemia, as recommended by the American Academy of Pediatrics. The amount of iron in iron-fortified formula is too small to cause any diarrhea or constipation. Don't use the low-iron formulas.

Most commercial infant formulas are available in three forms: powder, concentrated liquid, and ready-to-serve liquid. Powder and ready-to-serve liquids are the most suitable forms when a formula is occasionally used to supplement breast milk.

PREPARING COMMERCIAL FORMULAS

The concentrated formulas are mixed 1:1 with water. Two ounces of water are mixed with each level scoop of powdered formula. Never make the formula more concentrated by adding extra powder or extra concentrated liquid. Never dilute the formula by adding more water than specified. Careful measuring and mixing ensure that your baby is receiving the proper formula.

If you make one bottle at a time, you can use warm water directly from the tap rather than boiled water. This method saves you the time of warming up or cooling down the formula. Most city water supplies are quite safe. If you have well water, either boil it for 10 minutes (plus one minute for each 1000 feet of elevation) or use distilled water until your child is 6 months of age. If you prefer to prepare a batch of formula, you must use boiled or distilled water and closely follow the directions printed on the side of the formula can. This prepared formula should be stored in the refrigerator and must be used within 48 hours.

HOMEMADE FORMULAS FROM EVAPORATED MILK

If necessary, you can make your own formula temporarily from evaporated milk. Evaporated milk formulas have some of the same risks as whole cow's milk. This formula needs supplements of vitamins and minerals. It also requires sterilized bottles because it is prepared in a batch. If you must use it in a pinch, mix 13 ounces of evaporated milk with 19 ounces of boiled water and 2 tablespoons of corn syrup. Place this mixture in sterilized bottles and keep them refrigerated until use.

WHOLE COW'S MILK

Whole cow's milk should not be given to babies before 12 months of age because of increased risks of iron deficiency anemia and allergies. The ability to drink from a cup doesn't mean you should switch to cow's milk. While it used to be acceptable to introduce whole cow's milk after 6 months of age, recent studies have shown that infant formula is the optimal food during the first year of life for babies who are not breast-fed. Skim milk or 2% milk should not be given to babies before 2 years of age, because the fat content of regular milk (approximately 3.5% butterfat) is needed for rapid brain growth.

TRAVELING

When traveling, use powdered formula for convenience. Put the required number of scoops in a bottle, add warm tap water, and shake. A more expensive alternative is to use throwaway bottles of ready-to-use formula. This product avoids problems with contaminated water.

FORMULA TEMPERATURE

In summer many children prefer cold formula. In winter most prefer warm formula. By trying various temperatures, you can find out which your child prefers. If you do warm the formula, be certain to check the temperature before giving it to your baby. If it is too hot, it could burn your baby's mouth.

AMOUNTS AND SCHEDULES

The amount of formula that most babies take per feeding (in ounces) can be calculated by dividing your baby's weight (in pounds) in half. Another way to calculate the ounces per feeding is to add 3 to your baby's age (in months) with a maximum of 8 ounces per feeding at 5 or 6 months of age. The maximal amount per day is 32 ounces. If your baby needs more than this and is not overweight, consider starting solids.

In general, your baby will need six to eight feedings per day for the first month; five to six feedings per day

(Continued on the reverse side)

Instructions for Pediatric Patients by Barton D. Schmitt, M.D., *Pediatrician*
Adapted from YOUR CHILD'S HEALTH, Copyright © 1991 by Barton D. Schmitt, M.D.
Reprinted by permission of Bantam Books.

from 1 to 3 months; four to five feedings per day from 3 to 7 months; and three to four feedings per day thereafter. If your baby is not hungry at some of the feedings, the feeding interval should be increased.

LENGTH OF FEEDING

A feeding shouldn't take more than 20 minutes. If it does, you are overfeeding your baby or the nipple is clogged. A clean nipple should drip about 1 drop per second when the bottle of formula is inverted. At the end of each feeding, discard any formula left in the bottle, because it is no longer sterile.

EXTRA WATER

Babies do not routinely need extra water. They should be offered a bottle of water twice daily, however, when they have a fever or the weather is hot and dry.

BURPING

Burping is optional. Although it may decrease spitting up, air in the stomach does not cause pain. Burping two times during a feeding and for about 1 minute is plenty.

VITAMINS/IRON/FLUORIDE

Commercial formulas with iron contain all of your baby's vitamin and mineral requirements except for fluoride.

(NOTE: All soy-based formulas are iron fortified.) In the United States the most common cause of anemia in children under 2 years old is iron deficiency (largely because iron is not present in cow's milk). Iron also can be provided at 4 months of age by adding iron-fortified cereals to the diet.

From 2 weeks to 12 years of age, children need fluoride to prevent dental caries. If the municipal water supply contains fluoride and your baby drinks some water each day, this should be adequate. Otherwise, fluoride drops or tablets (without vitamins) should be given separately. This is a prescription item that can be obtained from your child's physician. Added vitamins are unnecessary after you child has reached 1 year of age and is on a regular balanced diet, but continue the fluoride.

CUP FEEDING

Introduce your child to a cup at approximately 4 to 6 months of age. Total weaning to a cup will probably occur somewhere between 9 and 18 months of age, depending on your baby's individual preference.

BABY-BOTTLE CARIES: PREVENTION

Sleeping with a bottle of milk, juice, or any sweetened liquid in the mouth can cause severe decay of the newly erupting teeth. Prevent this tragedy by not using the bottle as a pacifier or allowing your child to take it to bed.

 Instructions for Pediatric Patients by Barton D. Schmitt, M.D., *Pediatrician*
Adapted from YOUR CHILD'S HEALTH, Copyright © 1991 by Barton D. Schmitt, M.D.
Reprinted by permission of Bantam Books.

DEFINITION

Breast- or bottle-feeding can be considered prolonged after about 18 months of age, but delayed weaning is not always a problem. The older toddler who only occasionally nurses or drinks from a bottle doesn't necessarily need to be pressured into giving up the bottle or breast. Delayed weaning should be considered a problem only if it is causing one or more of the following types of harm:

—Refusal to eat any solids after 6 months of age
—Anemia confirmed by a routine screening test at 1 year of age
—Tooth decay or baby-bottle caries
—Obesity from overeating
—Daytime withdrawal and lack of interest in play because the child is always carrying a bottle around
—Frequent awakening at night for refills of a bottle
—Inability to stay with a babysitter because the child is exclusively breast-fed and refuses a bottle or cup

If any of these criteria apply to your baby, proceed to the following section. Otherwise, continue to breast- or bottle-feed your baby when she wants to (but less than four times each day) and don't worry about complete weaning at this time.

HOW TO ELIMINATE EXCESSIVE BREAST OR BOTTLE FEEDINGS

To decrease breast or bottle feedings to a level that won't cause any of the preceding side effects, take the following steps:

1. **Reduce milk feedings to three or four per day.** When your child comes to you for additional feedings, give him extra holding and attention instead. Get your child on a schedule of three main meals per day plus two or three nutritious snacks.

2. **Introduce cup feedings if this was not done at 6 months of age.** Cup feedings are needed as substitutes for breast- or bottle-feedings regardless of the age at which weaning occurs. The longer the infant goes without using a cup, the less willing he will be to try it. Starting daily cup feedings by 5 or 6 months of age is a natural way to keep breast- or bottle-feedings from becoming overly important.

3. **Immediately stop allowing your child to carry a bottle around during the day.** The companion bottle can interfere with normal development that requires speech or two-handed play. It also can contribute to problems with tooth decay. You can explain to your child that "it's not good for you" or "you're too old for that."

4. **Immediately stop allowing your child to take a bottle to bed.** Besides causing sleep problems, taking a bottle to bed carries the risk of causing tooth decay. You can offer the same explanations as in the preceding paragraph.

5. Once you have made these changes, you need not proceed further unless you wish to eliminate breast- or bottle-feedings completely. Attempt total weaning only if your family is not under stress (such as might be caused by moving or some other major change) and your child is not in crisis (from illness or trying to achieve bladder control, for example). Weaning from breast or bottle to cup should always be done gradually and with love. The "cold turkey," or abrupt withdrawal, approach will only make your child angry, clingy, and miserable. Although there is no consensus about the best time to wean, there is agreement about the appropriate technique.

HOW TO ELIMINATE BREAST-FEEDING COMPLETELY

1. **Offer formula in a cup before each breast-feeding.** If your child refuses formula, offer expressed breast milk. If that fails, add some flavoring he likes to the formula. If your child is older than 12 months, you can use whole milk. Some infants won't accept a cup until they've nursed for several minutes.

2. **Gradually eliminate breast-feedings.** First, eliminate the feeding that is least important to your child (usually the midday one). Replace it with a complete cup feeding. About once every week drop one more breast feeding. The bedtime nursing is usually the last to be given up, and there's no reason why you can't continue it for months if that's what you and your child want. Some mothers prefer to wean by decreasing the length of feedings. Shorten all feedings by 2 minutes each week until they are 5 minutes long. Then eliminate them one at a time.

3. **Relieve breast engorgement.** Since the breast operates on the principle of supply and demand, reduced sucking time eventually reduces milk production. In the meantime, express just enough milk to relieve breast pain resulting from engorgement. (This is better than putting your baby to the breast for a minute, because she probably won't want to stop nursing.) Remember that complete emptying of the breast increases milk production. An acetaminophen product also may help relieve discomfort.

4. **If your child asks to nurse after you have finished weaning, respond by holding her instead.** You can explain that "the milk is all gone." If she has a strong sucking drive, more pacifier time may help.

HOW TO ELIMINATE BOTTLE-FEEDING COMPLETELY

1. **Offer formula in a cup before each bottle-feeding.** Use whole milk if your child is 1 year of age or older.

2. **Make the weaning process gradual.** Eliminate one bottle feeding every 3 or 4 days, depending on your child's reaction. Replace each bottle feeding with a cup feeding and extra holding.

3. **Eliminate bottle-feedings in the following order: midday, late afternoon, morning, and bedtime.** The last feeding of the day is usually the most important one to

(Continued on the reverse side)

Instructions for Pediatric Patients by Barton D. Schmitt, M.D., *Pediatrician*
Adapted from YOUR CHILD'S HEALTH, Copyright © 1991 by Barton D. Schmitt, M.D.
Reprinted by permission of Bantam Books.

© 1992 by W. B. Saunders Company

WEANING PROBLEMS *Continued*

the child. When it is time to give up this feeding, gradually reduce the amount of milk each day over the course of a week.

4. **After you have completed the weaning process, respond to requests for a bottle by holding your child.** You can explain that bottles are for little babies. You may even want to have your child help you carry the bottles to a neighbor's house. If your child has a strong need to suck, offer a pacifier.

CALL OUR OFFICE

During regular hours if:
—Your child is over 6 months of age and won't eat any food except milk and won't drink from a cup.
—Your child has tooth decay.
—You think your child has anemia.
—This approach to weaning has not been successful after trying it for 1 month.
—Your child is over 3 years old.
—You have other questions or concerns.

Instructions for Pediatric Patients by Barton D. Schmitt, M.D., *Pediatrician*
Adapted from YOUR CHILD'S HEALTH, Copyright © 1991 by Barton D. Schmitt, M.D.
Reprinted by permission of Bantam Books.

DEFINITION

Weaning is the replacement of bottle- or breast-feedings (nipple feedings) with drinking from a cup and eating solid foods. Weaning occurs easily and smoothly unless the breast or bottle has become overly important to the child.

HOW TO PREVENT WEANING PROBLEMS

Children normally develop a reduced interest in breast- and bottle-feedings between 6 and 12 months of age if they are also taking cup and spoon feedings. If a child hasn't weaned by the age of 12 to 18 months, the parent often has to initiate it, but the child is still receptive. After 18 months of age, the child usually resists weaning because she has become overly attached to the breast or bottle. If your child shows a lack of interest in the breast or bottle at any time after 6 months of age, start to phase out these nipple feedings.

You can tell that your baby is ready to begin weaning when she throws the bottle down, takes only a few ounces of milk and then stops, chews on the nipple rather than sucking it, refuses the breast, or nurses for only a few minutes and then wants to play. The following steps encourage early natural weaning at 9 to 12 months:

1. **Keep formula feedings to four times per day or fewer after your child reaches 6 months of age.** Some breast-fed babies may need five feedings per day until 9 months of age. Even at birth, feedings should be kept to eight times daily or fewer.

2. **Give older infants their daytime milk at mealtime with solids.** Once your child is having just four milk feedings each day, be sure three of them are given at mealtime with solids rather than as part of the ritual before naps. Your child can have the fourth feeding before going to bed at night.

3. **After your baby is 6 weeks old and breast-feeding is well established, offer a bottle of expressed breast milk or water daily.** This experience will help your baby become accustomed to a bottle so that you can occasionally leave him with a sitter. This step is especially important if you will be returning to work or school. The longer after 2 months you wait to introduce the bottle, the more strongly your infant will initially reject it. If you wait until 4 months of age, the transition period may take up to 1 week. Once bottle feedings are accepted, you will need to continue them at least three times weekly.

4. **Hold your child for discomfort or stress instead of nursing her.** You can comfort your child and foster a strong sense of security and trust without nursing every time she is upset. If you always nurse your child in such situations, your child will learn to eat whenever upset. She will also be unable to separate being held from nursing, and you may become an "indispensable mother."

5. **Don't let the bottle or breast substitute for a pacifier.** Learn to recognize when your baby needs non-nutritive sucking. At these times, instead of offering your child food, encourage him to suck on a pacifier or thumb. Feeding your baby every time he needs to suck can lead to obesity.

6. **Don't let the bottle or breast become a security object at bedtime.** Your child should be able to go to sleep at night without having a breast or bottle in her mouth. She needs to learn how to put herself to sleep. If she doesn't, she will develop sleep problems that require the parents' presence during the night.

7. **Don't let a bottle become a daytime toy.** Don't let your child carry a bottle around as a companion during the day. This habit may keep him from engaging in more stimulating activities.

8. **Don't let your child hold the bottle or take it to bed.** Your child should think of the bottle as something that belongs to you; hence, she won't protest giving it up, since it never belonged to her in the first place.

9. **Offer your child formula or breast milk in a cup by 6 months of age.** For the first few months your child will probably accept the cup only after he has drunk some from the bottle or breast. However, by 9 months of age your child should be offered some formula or breast milk from a cup before breast or bottle feedings.

10. **Help your baby become interested in foods other than milk by 4 months of age.** Introduce solids with a spoon by 4 months of age to formula-fed babies and by 6 months to breast-fed infants. Introduce finger foods by 8 months of age. As soon as your child is able to eat finger foods, include her at the table with the family during mealtime. She will probably become interested in the foods that she sees you eating and will ask for them. Consequently, her interest in exclusive milk feedings will diminish.

Instructions for Pediatric Patients by Barton D. Schmitt, M.D., *Pediatrician*
Adapted from YOUR CHILD'S HEALTH, Copyright © 1991 by Barton D. Schmitt, M.D.
Reprinted by permission of Bantam Books.

SOLID (STRAINED) FOODS

AGE FOR STARTING SOLID FOODS

The best time to begin using a spoon to feed your child is when your baby can sit with some support and voluntarily move his head to engage in the feeding process. This time is usually between 4 and 6 months of age. Breast milk and commercial formulas meet all of your baby's nutritional needs until 4 to 6 months of age. Introducing strained foods earlier just makes feeding more complicated. Research has shown that it won't help your baby sleep through the night.

TYPES OF SOLID FOODS

Cereals are usually the first solid food introduced into your baby's diet. Generally these are introduced at 4 months of age in formula-fed infants and 6 months of age in breast-fed infants.

Start with rice cereal, which is less likely to cause allergies than other cereals. Barley and oatmeal may be tried 1 or 2 weeks later. A mixed cereal should be added to your baby's diet only after each kind of cereal in the mixed cereal has been separately introduced.

Strained or pureed vegetables and fruits are the next solid foods introduced to your baby. Although the order of foods is not important, introduce only one new food at a time and no more than three per week. If your infant doesn't seem to like the taste of cereals, start with a fruit (such as bananas).

Between 8 and 12 months of age, introduce your baby to mashed table foods or junior foods (although the latter are probably unnecessary). If you make your own baby foods in a baby-food grinder or electric blender, be sure to add enough water to get a consistency that your baby can easily swallow.

Although there is controversy about them, egg whites, wheat, peanut butter, fish, and orange juice may be more likely to cause allergies than other solids and should be avoided until 1 year of age (especially in infants with allergies).

SPOON FEEDING

Spoon feeding is begun at 4 to 6 months of age. By 8 to 10 months of age, most children want to try to feed themselves and can do so with finger foods. By 15 to 18 months of age, most children can use a spoon independently for foods they can't pick up with their fingers, and the parent is no longer needed in the feeding process.

Place food on the middle of the tongue. If you place it in front, your child will probably push it back at you. Some infants get off to a better start if you place the spoon between their lips and let them suck off the food. Some children constantly bat at the spoon or try to get a grip on it during feedings. These children need to be distracted with finger foods or by having a spoon of their own to play with.

FINGER FOODS

Finger foods are small bite-sized pieces of soft foods. Most babies love to feed themselves. Finger foods can be introduced between 9 and 10 months of age or whenever your child develops a pincer grip. Since most babies will not be able to feed themselves with a spoon until 15 months of age, finger foods keep them actively involved in the feeding process. Good finger foods are dry cereals (such as Cheerios or Rice Krispies), slices of cheese, pieces of scrambled eggs, slices of canned fruit (peaches, pears, or pineapple) or soft fresh fruits, slices of banana, crackers, cookies, and breads.

SNACKS

Once your baby goes to eating three meals a day or at 5-hour intervals, small snacks will often be necessary to tide him over to the next meal. Most babies go to this pattern between 6 and 9 months of age. The midmorning and midafternoon snack should be a nutritious, nonmilk food. Fruits and dry cereals are recommended. If your child is not hungry at mealtime, the snacks should be made smaller or eliminated.

TABLE FOODS

Your child should be eating the same meals as you do by approximately 1 year of age. This assumes that your diet is well balanced and that you carefully dice any foods that would be difficult for your baby to chew. Avoid foods such as raw carrots that could be choked on.

IRON-RICH FOODS

Throughout our lives we need iron in our diets to prevent anemia. Certain foods are especially good sources of iron. Red meats, fish, and poultry are best. Some young children will only eat lunch meats, and the low-fat ones are fine. Adequate iron is also found in iron-enriched cereals, beans of all types, egg yolks, peanut butter, raisins, prune juice, sweet potatoes, and spinach.

VITAMINS

Added vitamins are unnecessary after your child has reached 1 year of age and is on a regular balanced diet. If he's a picky eater, give him one chewable vitamin pill per week.

Instructions for Pediatric Patients by Barton D. Schmitt, M.D., *Pediatrician*
Adapted from YOUR CHILD'S HEALTH, Copyright © 1991 by Barton D. Schmitt, M.D.
Reprinted by permission of Bantam Books.

DEFINITION

Characteristics of a child with a normal decline in appetite:
—It seems to you that your child doesn't eat enough, is never hungry, or won't eat unless you spoon feed her yourself.
—Your child is between 1 and 5 years old.
—Your child's energy level remains normal.
—Your child is growing normally.

Cause

Between 1 and 5 years of age many children normally gain only 4 or 5 pounds each year even though they probably gained 15 pounds during their first year. Children in this age range can normally go 3 or 4 months without any weight gain. Because they are not growing as fast, they need less calories and they seem to have a poorer appetite (this is called "physiologic anorexia"). How much a child chooses to eat is governed by the appetite center in the brain. Kids eat as much as they need for growth and energy. Many parents try to force their children to eat more than they need because the parents fear that poor appetite might cause poor health or a nutritional deficiency. This is not true, however, and forced feedings interfere with the normal pleasure of eating and actually decrease a child's appetite.

Expected Course

Once you allow your child to be in charge of how much is eaten, the unpleasantness at mealtime and your concerns about her health should disappear in 2 to 4 weeks. Your child's appetite will improve when she becomes older and needs to eat more.

HELPING A POOR EATER REDISCOVER HER APPETITE

1. **Put your child in charge of how much she eats.** Trust your child's appetite center. The most common reason for some children never appearing hungry is that they have so many snacks and meals that they never become truly hungry. Offer your child no more than two small snacks of nutritious food each day, and provide them only if your child requests them. If your child is thirsty between meals, offer water. Limit the amount of juice your child drinks to less than 6 ounces each day. Let your child miss one or two meals if she chooses and then watch her appetite return. Skipping a meal is harmless.

2. **Never feed your child if she is capable of feeding herself.** The greatest tendency for parents of a child with a poor appetite is to pick up the spoon, fill it with food, smile, and try to trick the child into taking it. Once your child is old enough to use a spoon independently (usually 15 to 18 months), never again pick it up for her. If your child is hungry, she will feed herself.

3. **Offer finger foods.** Finger foods can be started at 8 to 10 months of age. Such foods allow your child to feed herself at least some of the time, even if she is not yet able to use a spoon.

4. **Limit milk to less than 16 ounces each day.** Milk contains as many calories as most solid foods. Drinking too much milk can fill kids up and dull their appetites.

5. **Serve small portions of food—less than you think your child will eat.** A child's appetite is decreased if she is served more food than she could possibly eat. If you serve your child a small amount on a large plate, she is more likely to finish it and gain a sense of accomplishment. If your child seems to want more, wait for her to ask for it. Avoid serving your child any foods that she strongly dislikes (such as some vegetables).

6. **Consider giving your child daily vitamins.** Although vitamins are probably unnecessary, they are not harmful in normal dosages and may allow you to relax about your child's eating patterns.

7. **Make mealtimes pleasant.** Draw your children into the conversation. Avoid making mealtimes a time for criticism or struggle over control.

8. **Avoid conversation about eating.** Don't discuss how little your child eats in her presence. Trust your child's appetite center to look after her food needs. Also, don't praise your child for eating a lot. Children should eat to please themselves.

9. **Don't extend mealtime.** Don't make your child sit at the dinner table after the rest of the family is done eating. This will only cause your child to develop unpleasant associations with mealtime.

10. **Avoid common mistakes.** Parents who are worried that their child isn't eating enough may start some irrational patterns of feeding. Some awaken the child at night to feed her. Some offer the child snacks at 15- to 20-minute intervals throughout the day. Some try to make the child feel guilty by talking about other children in the world who are starving. Others threaten, "If you don't eat what I cook, it means you don't love me." Some parents force their child to sit in the high chair for long periods of time after the meal has ended. The most common mistake is picking up a child's spoon or fork and trying various ways to get food into her mouth.

PREVENTION OF FEEDING STRUGGLES

The main way to prevent feeding struggles is to teach your child how to feed herself at as early an age as possible. You can wait for your infant to show you when she is ready to eat (by leaning forward, for example) and to pace the feeding herself (for example, by turning her head). Do not put food into a child's mouth just because she has inadvertently opened it. Do not insist that your child empty the bottle, finish a jar of baby food, or clean the plate. By the time your child is 8 to 10 months old, start giving her finger foods. By 12 months of age, your child will begin to use a spoon and she should be able to feed herself completely by 15 months of age.

(Continued on the reverse side)

Instructions for Pediatric Patients by Barton D. Schmitt, M.D., *Pediatrician*
Adapted from YOUR CHILD'S HEALTH, Copyright © 1991 by Barton D. Schmitt, M.D. Reprinted by permission of Bantam Books.

CALL OUR OFFICE

During regular hours if
—Your child is losing weight.
—Your child has not gained any weight in 6 months.

—Your child has associated symptoms of illness (such as diarrhea, fever).
—Your child gags on or vomits some foods.
—Someone is punishing your child for not eating.
—This approach has not improved mealtimes in your house within 1 month.
—You have other questions or concerns.

Instructions for Pediatric Patients by Barton D. Schmitt, M.D., *Pediatrician*   © 1992 by W. B. Saunders Company
Adapted from YOUR CHILD'S HEALTH, Copyright © 1991 by Barton D. Schmitt, M.D.
Reprinted by permission of Bantam Books.

Cholesterol is the normal way fat is carried in the bloodstream. Cholesterol has become a health issue because high cholesterol levels carry an increased risk of coronary heart disease (CHD). A 1% decrease in blood cholesterol leads to a 2% decrease in risk of CHD in adults. Societies with low serum cholesterol usually have a low incidence of CHD. The amount of cholesterol and saturated fats we eat contributes to the level of cholesterol in our bloodstreams. The level of cholesterol in childhood tends to persist (track) into adulthood in about 50% of children. This ability of the child's level of cholesterol to predict the adult level increases with each passing year. Further, reducing the cholesterol and saturated fat in the diet does reduce the level of cholesterol in the bloodstream. One major goal of preventive medicine is to lower cholesterol to healthy levels.

TYPES OF CHOLESTEROL

Cholesterol is composed of high density lipoprotein (HDL), low density lipoprotein (LDL), and triglycerides. The HDL is called the "good" cholesterol because it carries cholesterol away from the arteries and to the liver for elimination. LDL is referred to as the "bad" cholesterol. An excess of LDL deposits cholesterol on the inner walls of the arteries over time. In addition to reducing total cholesterol levels, we would like to see you increase your HDL and decrease your LDL. A 1% rise in HDL may give a 3% reduction in CHD in adults.

NORMAL AND ABNORMAL CHOLESTEROL LEVELS

Normal cholesterol levels remain rather constant between 120 and 170 throughout childhood. After 18 years of age they tend to rise about 1 point per year of age. For total cholesterol and LDL, a healthy or desirable level is below the 75th percentile. A borderline high level is between the 75th and 95th percentile. A high or abnormal level is above the 95th percentile. In general, levels above the 75th percentile should be lowered because the normal values in the United States are considerably higher than normal values in countries with a low incidence of CHD.

		CHILDREN	ADULTS
Total	>95th	>200	>240
Cholesterol	>75th	>170	>200
	Desirable	<170	<200
LDL	>95th	>130	>160
	>75th	>110	>130
	Desirable	<110	<130

The desired level for HDL, which we want to be high since it is protective, is above the 25th percentile. A borderline low value is between the 5th and 25th percentile. A low or abnormal value is below the 5th percentile.

		CHILDREN	ADULTS
HDL	<5th	<35	<30
	<25th	<45	<40
	Desirable	>45	>40

HIGH-RISK CHILDREN: WHAT AGE TO TEST?

The American Academy of Pediatrics and the American Heart Association are in complete agreement that all children who have risk factors for CHD should be screened soon after 2 years of age. The reason children aren't tested before 2 years is that during this period of rapid growth and development, the diet needs to be high in fat. Two main risk factors should be considered: (1) a family history of high blood cholesterol and (2) a family history of CHD. The latter includes an early (less than 50 years of age in men or less than 60 years of age in women) history of heart attack, angina, stroke, or bypass surgery. The family history is considered positive if these diseases have occurred in parents, grandparents, aunts, or uncles. Information must be obtained about the grandparents since the parents are often too young to have entered the high-risk age group for CHD. Over 50% of children with high cholesterol levels are identified by screening these high-risk children.

ALL OTHER CHILDREN: WHAT AGE TO TEST?

The practice of performing cholesterol testing on all children is controversial. The main reason for universal testing is to identify all children with high cholesterol levels. Eating and exercise patterns in children need to be established early if they are to be followed throughout life. The main arguments against testing all children are that testing is costly, high cholesterol levels do not persist into adulthood 50% to 60% of the time, and healthy diets can be started on all children without knowing cholesterol levels. If routine testing is done, it's usually performed between 2 and 5 years of age, often on school entry.

RETESTING CHILDREN WITH HIGH CHOLESTEROL LEVELS

If your child's cholesterol value is borderline high or high, the test will be repeated in 1 to 2 weeks to confirm that the value is high. There is some normal day-to-day variation in cholesterol levels. If the level remains high, it's assumed to be accurate. Children with confirmed high total cholesterol levels (greater than the 95th percentile) will then have blood drawn for a lipid profile or panel. This test measures not only total cholesterol, but also LDL, HDL, and triglycerides. Depending on the results, diet and exercise treatment will be initiated and

(Continued on the reverse side)

Instructions for Pediatric Patients by Barton D. Schmitt, M.D., *Pediatrician*
Adapted from YOUR CHILD'S HEALTH, Copyright © 1991 by Barton D. Schmitt, M.D.
Reprinted by permission of Bantam Books.

the level repeated in approximately 2 to 4 months. If your child has a high-normal total cholesterol level (greater than the 75th percentile), treatment can be started without additional tests. The test for total cholesterol will probably be repeated yearly. The reason we don't obtain routine lipid panels on all children is that they cost approximately $50, in contrast to $15 for a total cholesterol test. In addition, the lipid panel requires blood drawn from a vein (which can be a more difficult procedure in a child) rather than a simple finger stick.

RETESTING CHILDREN WITH NORMAL CHOLESTEROL LEVELS

Children with cholesterol levels below the 75th percentile do not need their cholesterol rechecked until they become adolescents. Most physicians who treat adults repeat cholesterol levels every 5 years as long as they remain within normal range.

TESTING FAMILY MEMBERS

If your child's value is high (greater than 95th percentile) we recommend that you have everyone else in your family tested for total cholesterol. A child with a high level is a good way to detect parents or siblings with high levels. In over 80% of cases, other family members also have high values. This will provide you with additional reasons to start your family on a healthier diet and exercise program. If your child's cholesterol level is high or high-normal, see the information sheet entitled "Treating High Cholesterol Levels."

 Instructions for Pediatric Patients by Barton D. Schmitt, M.D., *Pediatrician*
Adapted from YOUR CHILD'S HEALTH, Copyright © 1991 by Barton D. Schmitt, M.D.
Reprinted by permission of Bantam Books.

If your child's cholesterol level is high or borderline high, start the programs listed in this information sheet. (If your child's cholesterol level is normal, it still would be a good idea to place your family on the same programs.) High cholesterol levels are not the only risk factor for coronary heart disease (CHD). The following risk factors are just as harmful as being on a high-cholesterol diet: physical inactivity, obesity, and smoking. The more risk factors that you and your child have, the higher the risk of CHD. Living a long and healthy life requires healthy eating and exercise patterns. It is easier to start these habits as a child than to have to adopt them as an adult. Review with your family the following ways to reduce cholesterol levels. If you already are carrying out the majority of these recommendations, you are protecting your child's heart and blood vessels.

A LOW-FAT DIET

The American Heart Association recommends that all children over 2 years of age be on a low-cholesterol, low-saturated fat diet. Currently, most Americans take in 40% of their daily calories as fat. A healthy (prudent) diet keeps fat to 30% of total calories. The goal is eating fat in moderation, not eliminating fat entirely. Lowering your child's fat intake to 30% of daily calories carries no risk for children over 2 years old. (None of the following recommendations apply to children less than 2 years.) Foods of plant origin, such as fruits, vegetables, and grains, do not contain cholesterol. Foods of animal origin, such as meats, eggs, and milk products, do contain cholesterol. Our blood cholesterol is raised by consuming cholesterol itself or by eating saturated fats that stimulate the production of cholesterol. Even without any fat intake, the liver produces a small amount of cholesterol each day. Therefore we will always have a blood cholesterol level. Serving a low-fat diet in your house is rather easy:
—Serve more fish, turkey, and chicken, since they have less fat than red meats. Buy lean ground beef for hamburgers. Use lean ham or turkey for sandwiches.
—Trim the fat from meats and remove the skin from poultry before eating.
—Avoid the meats with the highest fat content, such as bacon, sausages, salami, pepperoni, and hot dogs.
—Limit the number of eggs eaten to three or four per week.
—Limit the amount of all meats to portions of moderate size.
—Use 1% or skim (0.5%) milk instead of whole milk (which is 3.5% fat).
—Use a margarine product instead of butter.
—Avoid deep-fat fried food or food fried in butter or fat. If you prefer to fry meats, use margarine or nonstick cooking sprays.
—Increase your child's fiber intake. Fiber is found in most grains, vegetables, and fruits.

FAMILY EXERCISE PROGRAM

Exercise is the best way to raise your HDL level. Your goal should be 20 to 30 minutes of vigorous exercise three times per week. Vigorous exercise must involve the large muscles of the legs and cause your heart to beat faster (aerobic exercise). Vigorous exercise also improves your heart's response to work. A child is much more likely to exercise if you exercise with him. Encourage your child to try the following forms of exercise:
—Walk or bike instead of riding in a car.
—Use stairs instead of elevators.
—Take the dog for a walk, jump rope, or play ball if bored.
—Join a team (such as soccer) or learn a new sport (such as roller skating) that requires vigorous (aerobic) activity. Swimming and jogging are sports that burn lots of calories. Sports such as baseball and football do not exercise the heart.
—Exercise to a videotape or music.
—Limit television and video game time to 2 hours or less per day. These sitting activities interfere with physical fitness.
—Use an exercise bike, dance, or run in place while watching television.
—Support better physical education programs and aerobics classes in your schools.

IDEAL BODY WEIGHT

Children who are overweight tend to have a low HDL level and a high LDL level. Helping your child return to ideal body weight will improve the blood cholesterol levels. Decreasing fat in a person's diet automatically decreases the calories consumed because fat has twice as much calories as the same amount of protein or carbohydrates. A low-fat diet *and* exercise are the key ingredients for losing weight. If your child is overweight, also request the guideline entitled "Overweight."

SMOKE-FREE HOME

A good way to raise your HDL level is to stop smoking. Also avoid exposing your child to passive smoking. If someone in your home has a problem with smoking, request the guideline "Passive Smoking."

SETTING A GOOD EXAMPLE

If your child needs to lower his cholesterol level, he will need help from his family. You cannot put him on a special diet without putting the entire family on it. You cannot put him on a special exercise program without having other family members participate. Eat healthy foods and snacks, so your child will eat similarly. Play more sports and watch fewer television sports shows—as you would like your child to do.

(Continued on the reverse side)

MEDICATIONS TO LOWER CHOLESTEROL

Medications to lower cholesterol are rarely used in children unless they have a rare form of high cholesterol related to disease rather than diet. If your child's level remains high despite your initial efforts, request a consultation with a nutritionist regarding special diets. Also, join an exercise program at a local gym or fitness center. These additional steps will usually help your child.

WHEN TO RECHECK YOUR CHILD'S CHOLESTEROL LEVEL

Generally, for high cholesterol levels (above the 95th percentile), the level is rechecked approximately 2 to 4 months after starting a program to lower it. If the cholesterol level is borderline high (above the 75th percentile), it is usually rechecked yearly.

Your child's next cholesterol test is on _____.

Instructions for Pediatric Patients by Barton D. Schmitt, M.D., *Pediatrician*
Adapted from YOUR CHILD'S HEALTH, Copyright © 1991 by Barton D. Schmitt, M.D.
Reprinted by permission of Bantam Books.

A popular misconception suggests that eating sugar is harmful or at least a weakness. Many well-educated parents worry needlessly about sugar, candy, and desserts. For purposes of discussion, sweets can be identified as any food where sucrose, fructose, glucose, corn syrup, honey, or other sugars are listed as the first ingredient on the packaging. Sweets are not bad. The body needs sugar to function and the brain needs glucose to think. Sweets just need to be eaten in moderation. If you want to protect your child's health, get after the Cholesterol Monster, not the Sugar Monster and the Cookie Monster.

THE NORMAL SWEET TOOTH

Soon after birth infants show a preference for sweet solutions (such as breast milk) over unsweetened solutions. Many humans are born with a "sweet tooth," probably on a genetic basis. Most adults also naturally seek out and enjoy sweets. Giving candy as a gift for holidays or birthdays is a common symbol of affection. Many members of the animal kingdom also show a craving for sweets.

People forget that the recommended daily amount of calories from carbohydrates (sugar and starches) is 55%. The amount from refined sugars (sucrose) should not exceed 10% of the daily calories. Sugar is present naturally in most foods except the meat group. Lactose is the sugar present in milk, fructose is the sugar present in fruits, and maltose is the sugar present in grain products. Sucrose, the sugar found in sugar cane and sugar beets, has no greater adverse effect on body functioning than any of the other sugars.

SIDE EFFECTS OF SUGAR

The main risk of sugar is its ability to increase tooth decay. Tooth decay is also the only permanent harm from consuming too much sugar. This risk can be greatly reduced by brushing the teeth after sugar-containing foods are eaten and drinking fluoridated water. The foods causing the most dental cavities (caries) are those that stick to the teeth (for example, raisins). The greatest risk factor for causing severe dental caries is falling asleep or walking around with a bottle of sugar solution in the mouth. The solution can be fruit juice, Kool-Aid, or milk. This type of tooth decay is called "baby-bottle caries."

A temporary side effect may be seen 2 to 4 hours after excessive sugar consumption. The reaction is probably due to a rapid fall in blood sugar and consists of sweating, hunger, dizziness, tiredness, or sleepiness. This reaction to a sugar binge is brief and harmless and can be relieved by the passage of time and eating a food containing some sugar such as a fruit juice. These symptoms do not occur after eating a normal amount of sweets, and they do not occur in everyone.

MYTHS ABOUT SUGAR

Eating sugar is basically not harmful. Candy does not cause cancer, heart disease, or diabetes mellitus. The following are some common overconcerns.

1. **Obesity.** Obesity is due to overeating in general and not specifically to eating sugars. Fatty foods have twice the calories per amount as sugary foods and are much more related to obesity. Recent studies have shown that lean people tend to eat more sugar than overweight people.

2. **Hyperactivity.** Extensive research has shown that sugar does not cause or worsen hyperactivity. In fact, a high intake of refined sugar may cause a relaxed state or even drowsiness.

3. **Junk food.** The term "junk food" has led to considerable confusion in the United States. Some people define any sweet or dessert as a junk food. Others define fast foods as junk foods. Let's junk this negative term that implies if a food is sweet or purchased from a fast-food chain, it's bad for your health. It's not that simple.

RECOMMENDATIONS FOR THE SAFE USE OF SUGAR

1. **Allow sugar in moderation.** In general, eating foods in moderation is healthy, but eating foods in excess is unhealthy. One precaution is to avoid sweets if possible during the first year of life. If they are introduced too early, they may interfere with a willingness to try new foods that are unsweetened. (NOTE: These guidelines about sugar in moderation may not apply to children with diabetes mellitus.)

2. **Don't try to forbid sugar.** Some parents do this in hopes of preventing a preference for sweet foods. Since this preference is present at birth, we have little influence over it. If we forbid sweets entirely, children may become fascinated with them. With candy and other sweets so readily available in stores and vending machines, a sugar embargo cannot be monitored and becomes unenforceable as a child grows up. If we make an issue of it, this becomes an unnecessary battleground.

3. **Limit the amount of sweets you buy.** The more sweets there are in the house, the more your child will eat. Try to purchase breakfast cereals and cookies in which sugar is not the main ingredient.

4. **Limit how much sweets are eaten.** Whereas one candy bar is fine, eating an entire bag of candy is unacceptable. Try to eliminate binging on candy or sweets. Do this mainly by setting a good example. Exceptions of allowing extra candy can be made on Halloween, other holidays, birthdays and other parties. The worst that could happen is that your child could become extra sleepy or have a mild stomachache.

5. **Allow sweets for desserts.** As stated earlier sweets only cause symptoms if they are eaten in excess. As long

(Continued on the reverse side)

Instructions for Pediatric Patients by Barton D. Schmitt, M.D., *Pediatrician*
Adapted from YOUR CHILD'S HEALTH, Copyright © 1991 by Barton D. Schmitt, M.D.
Reprinted by permission of Bantam Books.

as they follow a well-balanced meal, they cause no symptoms. An acceptable dessert, therefore, can be just about anything, including candy.

6. **Discourage sweets for snacks**. Candy, soft drinks, or other sweets are not a good choice for a snack. Since very little else is eaten with the snack, consuming mainly refined sugar may cause some rebound symptoms several hours later. Teach your child that if he does take a soft drink or Kool-Aid as a snack, he should eat something else from the grain or fruit food group along with it. An occasional sweet drink with a sugar substitute is fine. Stock up on nutritious snacks (such as fruit juices, yogurt, graham crackers, oatmeal cookies, and popcorn). In fact, most cookies are not sweets since the main ingredient is flour. Also, set a good example by what you eat for snacks.

7. **Insist that the teeth are brushed after eating sweets**. Encourage your child to rinse her mouth with some water after eating when she's away from home. Unless you encourage this good habit, a "sweet tooth" can become a "decayed tooth."

SPECIAL BENEFITS OF SUGAR

Using candy occasionally as a reward is not habit forming. The joy of eating sweets is a natural preference, not enhanced by this practice. Candy and other sweet treats are a powerful incentive. Whether we like it or not, the best motivators are always items that children crave. In addition, candy is inexpensive and easy to purchase. Because of the many types of candy, the child also has many choices. Candy may bring about a breakthrough with a negative child who has not responded to other approaches. Star charts and praise should be used simul-

taneously for improved behavior and continued after the candy has been phased out.

Second, sugar can be useful in helping a finicky eater try an essential new food. Some children who have been breast-fed until almost 1 year of age will not accept any milk products. One way of helping them make this transition is by sweetening the cow's milk temporarily with honey or other flavorings. (**CAUTION**: Avoid giving honey before 1 year of age because of the small risk of botulism for this age group.) After the child is drinking adequate amounts of milk the sweetener can be gradually phased out.

Third, some children will take bitter medicines easier when they are mixed with a sweet flavoring such as Kool-Aid powder or chocolate pudding.

OVERVIEW

Let's be honest. Most adults and children enjoy sweets. Most children spend part of their allowance on sweets. And eating sweets in moderation is fine. A well-balanced diet can include some daily sweets.

 ## CALL OUR OFFICE

During regular hours if
— Your child frequently binges on sweets.
— You find yourself repeatedly reminding your child about sweets.
— You think your child has a problem with sugar.
— You have other questions or concerns.

 Instructions for Pediatric Patients by Barton D. Schmitt, M.D., *Pediatrician*   © 1992 by W. B. Saunders Company
Adapted from YOUR CHILD'S HEALTH, Copyright © 1991 by Barton D. Schmitt, M.D.
Reprinted by permission of Bantam Books.

Although food allergies tend to be overdiagnosed, about 5% of children have true reactions to foods. Suspect that your child may have a food allergy if the following three characteristics are present:

1.   Your child has allergic symptoms after eating certain foods. The most common reactions involve the mouth (for example, swelling), gastrointestinal tract (for example, diarrhea), or skin (for example, hives). Rarely, a child has a severe allergic reaction (anaphylactic reaction) that may be life threatening. Common anaphylactic symptoms are a rapid onset of difficult breathing, difficult swallowing, or a fall in blood pressure (shock).

2.   Your child has other allergic conditions, such as eczema, asthma, or hay fever. Children with these conditions have a much higher rate of associated food allergies than nonallergic children.

3.   Other family members (parents or siblings) have food allergies. Food allergies are often inherited.

Cause

Allergic children produce antibodies against certain foods. When these antibodies come in contact with the allergic food, the reaction releases numerous chemicals that cause the symptoms. The tendency to be allergic is inherited. If one parent has allergies, about 40% of the children will develop allergies. If both parents have allergies, about 75% will. Sometimes the child is allergic to the same food as the parent.

Expected Course

At least half of the children who develop a food allergy during the first year of life outgrow it by 2 or 3 years of age. Some food reactions (such as to milk) are more commonly outgrown than others. Whereas 3% to 4% of infants have a cow's milk allergy, less than 1% of them develop a lifelong allergy to milk. Allergies to peanuts, tree nuts, fish, and shellfish (shrimp, crab, and lobster) often persist for life.

COMMON SYMPTOMS OF FOOD ALLERGIES

The following symptoms are all commonly seen with food allergies. In some cases the food aggravates the underlying allergic condition.
—Swelling of lips, tongue, or mouth
—Diarrhea or vomiting
—Hives
—Itchy red skin (especially with underlying eczema)

Some less common symptoms are
—Sore throat or throat clearing
—Nasal congestion, runny nose, sneezing, or sniffing (especially with underlying hay fever)

An occasional child with asthma, migraine headaches, colic, or recurrent abdominal pain may have some attacks triggered by food allergies. These children, however, also have some of the typical symptoms (in the preceding lists) that occur with food reactions. Attention deficit disorder and behavioral disorders, as isolated symptoms, have not been scientifically linked to food allergies.

COMMON ALLERGIC FOODS

Overall, the most allergic food is the peanut. In infants, egg and milk products are more common. The following five foods account for over 80% of food reactions: peanuts (and peanut butter), eggs, cow's milk products, soybeans (and soy formula), and wheat. Eight foods (fish, shellfish, tree nuts, and the preceding five foods) account for over 95% of food reactions. Four foods (chocolate, strawberries, corn, and tomatoes) are highly overrated as triggers of symptoms. Although commonly mentioned, they rarely cause any allergic symptoms.

DIAGNOSING A FOOD ALLERGY

1.   **Keep a diary of symptoms and recently eaten foods**. If the ingestion of a particular food is clearly the cause of particular symptoms, go directly to step 2. Otherwise, be a good detective and keep a symptom/food diary for 2 weeks. Anytime your child has symptoms, write down the foods eaten during the preceding meal. After 2 weeks, examine the diary for foods that were repeatedly consumed on days your child had symptoms. Expect some inconsistency, depending on the amount of food consumed. Although anaphylactic reactions can be triggered by small amounts of allergic foods, other symptoms (such as diarrhea) usually increase as the amount of the allergic food increases, but not to the point of being serious. Reactions to food may be worse when a child is also reacting to other substances in the environment such as pollens. Therefore food allergies may flare up during pollen season.

2.   **Eliminate the suspected food from the diet for 2 weeks**. Record any symptoms that occur during this time. If you have eliminated the correct food, all symptoms should disappear. Most children improve within 2 days and almost all of them improve after 1 week of avoiding the allergic food.

3.   **Rechallenge your child with the suspected food**. (CAUTION: This step should never be carried out if your child has experienced a severe or anaphylactic reaction to a food.) The purpose of rechallenging is to prove that the suspected food is definitely the cause of your child's symptoms. Give your child a small amount of the suspected food. The same symptoms should appear anywhere from 10 minutes to 2 hours after the food is consumed. Call us before doing this.

TREATMENT OF FOOD ALLERGIES

1.   **Avoid the allergic food**. This should keep your child free of symptoms. If you are breast-feeding, elim-

(Continued on the reverse side)

inate the food your child is allergic to from your diet until breast-feeding is discontinued. Food allergens can be absorbed from your diet and enter your breast milk. Talk to a nutritionist if you have questions.

2. **Consider avoiding other foods in that food group.** Some children are allergic to two or more foods. Occasionally the foods belong to the same food group. The most common cross-reaction involves children allergic to ragweed pollen. They commonly react to watermelon, cantaloupe, muskmelon, honeydew melon, or other foods in the gourd family. Children allergic to peanuts may rarely cross-react with soybean, peas, or other beans. Surprisingly, most tree nuts are unrelated to each other and do not cross-react with peanuts.

3. **Provide substitutes for any missing vitamins or minerals.** Eliminating single foods usually does not cause any side effects. If a major food group (such as milk products) is eliminated, however, your child will develop vitamin D and calcium deficiency unless he receives appropriate supplements. Talk to your physician or a nutritionist about this.

4. **Rechallenge your child with the food in about 3 to 6 months.** (CAUTION: Never rechallenge a child who has had a severe or anaphylactic reaction to a food. Such a child should avoid that food for the rest of his life and keep an emergency kit with an epinephrine-loaded syringe at home, at school, and in the car.) Many food allergies are temporary. For children under 3 years of age, challenge them every 6 months until they are 3 years old. If they continue to react each time, have them evaluated by a board-certified allergist before permanently eliminating that food from the diet.

PREVENTING FOOD ALLERGIES IN HIGH-RISK CHILDREN

High-risk or allergy-prone children are those who have parents or siblings with asthma, eczema, severe hay fever, or documented food allergies. The risk is highest if both parents are allergic to foods. The onset of allergies in these children may be delayed by being somewhat careful about their diet. If possible they should breast-feed during the first year of life. The mother should avoid milk products, peanuts, and eggs in her diet during this time. If the mother cannot breast-feed, there are two choices: a formula made from protein hydrolysate (known as an elemental formula) or a soy protein formula. The allergy-prone child should avoid all solid foods until 6 months old. Try to avoid milk products, eggs, peanut butter, soy protein, fish, wheat, and citrus fruits during the entire first year of life. Try to avoid the most allergic foods (peanuts and fish) until 2 years of age.

 ## CALL AN EMERGENCY RESCUE SQUAD (911)

IMMEDIATELY if
—Your child develops any serious symptoms such as wheezing, croupy cough, difficult breathing, passing out, or tightness in the chest or throat.

 ## CALL OUR OFFICE

IMMEDIATELY if
—Widespread hives, swelling, or itching occurs.
—Other mild symptoms occur within 30 minutes of eating a suspected food.

During regular hours if:
—You suspect your child has a food allergy.
—You want to rechallenge your child with a food you suspect.
—You have other questions or concerns.

RECOMMENDED READING

S. Allan Bock: Food Allergy: A Primer for People. Vantage Press, N.Y., 1988.

DEFINITION

—Your child appears overweight to an objective person.
—Your child weighs more than 20% over the ideal weight for her height.
—The skin fold thickness (fat layer) of his upper arm is more than 1 inch (25 mm), as measured with a special instrument.
—More than 25% of American children are overweight.

Causes

The tendency to be overweight is usually inherited. If one parent is overweight, half of the children will be overweight. If both parents are overweight, most of their children will be overweight. If neither parent is overweight, the children have a 10% chance of being overweight.

Heredity alone (without overeating) accounts for most mild obesity (defined as less than 30 pounds overweight in an adult). Moderate obesity is usually due to a combination of heredity, overeating, and underexercising. Some overeating is normal in our society, but only those who have the inherited tendency to be overweight will gain significant weight when they overeat. It is therefore not reasonable to blame your child for being overweight.

Less than 1% of obesity has an underlying medical cause. Your physician can easily determine this by a simple physical examination.

Expected Course

Losing weight is very difficult. Keeping the weight off is also a chore. The best time for losing weight is when a child is over 15 years old, that is, when she becomes very concerned with appearance. The self-motivated teenager can follow a diet and lose weight regardless of what the family eats. Helping children lose weight between 5 and 15 years of age is very difficult because they have access to so many foods outside the home and are not easily motivated to lose weight. It is not quite as difficult to help a child less than 5 years old to lose weight because the parents have better control of the foods offered to the child.

HOW TO HELP OLDER CHILDREN AND TEENAGERS LOSE WEIGHT

Readiness and Motivation

Teenagers can increase their motivation by joining a weight-loss club such as TOPS or Weight Watchers. Sometimes schools have classes for helping children lose weight. A child's motivation can often be improved if diet and exercise programs are undertaken by the entire family. A cooperative parent-child weight loss program with individual goals is usually more helpful than a competitive program focused on who can loose weight faster.

Protecting Your Child's Self-esteem

Self-esteem is more important than an ideal body weight. If your child is overweight, he is probably already disappointed in himself. He needs his family to support him and accept him as he is. Self-esteem can be reduced or destroyed by parents who become overconcerned about their child's weight. Avoid the following pitfalls:
—Don't tell your child he's fat. Don't discuss his weight unless he brings it up.
—Never try to put your child on a strict diet. Diets are unpleasant and should be self-imposed.
—Never deprive your child of food if he says he is hungry. Withholding food eventually leads to overeating.
—Don't nag him about his weight or eating habits.

Setting Weight-loss Goals

Pick a realistic target weight, depending on your child's bone structure and degree of obesity. The loss of 1 pound per week is an attainable goal, but your child will have to work quite hard to maintain this rate of weight loss for several weeks. Have your child weigh himself no more than once each week; daily weighings generate too much false hope or disappointment. Keeping a record of weekly weights may provide added motivation. When losing weight becomes a strain, have your child take a few weeks off from the weight-loss program. During this time, try to help your child stay at a constant weight.

Once your child has reached the target weight, the long-range goal is to try to stay within 5 pounds of that weight. Staying at a particular weight is possible only through a permanent moderation in eating and maintaining a reasonable exercise program. Your child will probably always have the tendency to gain weight easily and it's important that she understand this.

Diet: Decreasing Calorie Consumption

Your child should eat three well-balanced meals of average-size portions every day. There are no forbidden foods; your child can have a serving of anything family or friends are eating. However, there are forbidden portions. While your child is reducing, she must leave the table a bit hungry. Your child cannot lose weight if she eats until full (satiated).

Encourage average portions and discourage seconds. Shortcuts such as fasting, crash dieting, or diet pills rarely work and may be dangerous. Liquid diets are only safe if used according to directions. If you have any questions, consult a dietician.

Calorie counting is helpful for some people, but it is usually too time consuming. Consider the following guidelines on what to eat and drink:
—Fluids: Because milk has lots of calories, your child should drink no more than 16 ounces of skim or low fat milk each day. Since fruit juices and 2% milk have similar calories per ounce, keep juice consumption to 8 ounces or less per day. All other

(Continued on the reverse side)

drinks should be either water or diet drinks. Encourage your child to drink six glasses of water each day.

—Meals: Serve fewer fatty foods (e.g., eggs, bacon, sausage, and butter). A portion of fat has twice as many calories as the same portion of protein or carbohydrate. Trim the fat off meats. Serve more baked, broiled, boiled, or steamed foods and fewer fried foods. Serve more fruits, vegetables, salads, and grains.

—Desserts: Encourage smaller-than-average portions. Encourage more gelatin and fresh fruits as desserts. Avoid rich desserts. Do not serve seconds.

—Snacks: Serve only low-calorie foods such as raw vegetables (carrot sticks, celery sticks, raw potato sticks, pickles, etc.), raw fruits (apples, oranges, cantaloupe, etc.), popcorn, or diet soft drinks. Limit snacks to two each day.

—Vitamins: Give your child one multivitamin tablet daily during the weight-loss program.

Eating Habits

To counteract the tendency to gain weight, your youngster must be taught eating habits that will last for a lifetime. You can help your child lose and keep off unwanted pounds by doing the following:

—Discourage skipping any of the three basic meals.

—Encourage drinking a glass of water before meals.

—Serve smaller portions.

—Suggest chewing the food slowly.

—Offer second servings only if your child has waited for 10 minutes after finishing the first serving.

—Don't purchase high-calorie snack foods such as potato chips, candy, or regular soft drinks.

—Do purchase and keep available diet soft drinks and fresh fruits and vegetables.

—Leave only low-calorie snacks out on the counter—fruit, for example. Put away the cookie jar.

—Store food only in the kitchen. Keep it out of other rooms.

—Offer no more than two snacks each day. Discourage your child from continual snacking ("grazing") throughout the day.

—Allow eating in your home only at the kitchen or dining-room table. Discourage eating while watching television, studying, riding in a car, or shopping. Once eating becomes associated with these activities, the body learns to expect it.

—Discourage eating alone.

—Help your child reward herself for hard work or studying with a movie, television, music, or a book rather than food.

—Put up reminder cards on the refrigerator and bathroom mirror that state: *Eat less.*

Exercise: Increasing Calorie Expenditure

Daily exercise can increase the rate of weight loss as well as the sense of physical well-being. The combination of diet and exercise is the most effective way to lose weight. Try the following forms of exercise:

—Walk or bike instead of riding in a car.

—Use stairs instead of elevators.

—Learn new sports. Swimming and jogging are the sports that burn the most calories. Your child's school may have an aerobic class.

—Take the dog for a long walk.

—Spend 30 minutes daily exercising or dancing to records or music on television.

—Use an exercise bike or Hula Hoop while watching television. (Limit television sitting time to 2 hours or less each day.)

Social Activities: Keeping the Mind off Food

The more outside activities your child participates in, the easier it will be for her to lose weight. Spare time fosters nibbling. Most snacking occurs between 3 and 6 PM. Help your child fill after-school time with activities such as music, drama, sports, or scouts. A part-time job after school may help. If nothing else, encourage your child to call or visit friends. An active social life almost always leads to weight reduction.

CALL OUR OFFICE

During regular hours if

—Your child has not improved his eating and exercise habits after trying this program for 2 months.

—Your child is a compulsive overeater.

—You find yourself frequently nagging your child about his eating habits.

—Your child is trying to lose weight and doesn't need to do so.

—You think your child is depressed.

—Your child has no close friends.

—You have other questions or concerns.

DEFINITION

An overweight baby is one with a weight gain far out of proportion to height gain. An overweight baby looks fat. Such a baby is not necessarily a healthy one. The infants who continue to be overweight as children and adults usually have parents, siblings, or grandparents who are overweight. Any infant with a strong family tendency toward obesity needs help. Overfeeding teaches a child to overeat. Some physicians wait until such a child shows signs of being overweight before making any alterations in the diet, but prevention is easier than treatment.

DIETARY PRECAUTIONS TO PREVENT AN EXCESSIVE WEIGHT GAIN IN INFANTS

If someone in your family has a problem with easy weight gain, consider the following dietary precautions to prevent your baby from becoming overweight. If your child is already overweight, these guidelines will also be helpful. The goal for growing children is always slowing the rate of weight gain (not weight loss).

—From the beginning, try to teach your child to stop eating before she reaches a point of satiation. Help her stop before she has a sense of complete fullness and a reluctance to eat another bite. When she closes her mouth, turns her head, or wants to play, she's losing interest in feeding.

—Try to breast-feed. Breast-fed babies tend to be lighter in weight.

—If you are breast-feeding, avoid grazing. Grazing is nursing at frequent intervals, sometimes hourly. Such infants learn to eat when they are upset and to use food as a stress reliever.

—If you are bottle-feeding, don't allow your child to keep a bottle as a companion during the day or night. Children who are allowed to carry a bottle around with them learn to eat frequently and use food as a comforting device.

—Don't feed your baby every time he cries. Most crying babies want to be held and cuddled or may be thirsty and just need some water.

—Also teach your infant to use human contact (rather than food) to relieve stress and discomfort.

—Don't assume a sucking baby is hungry. Your baby may just want a pacifier or help with finding her thumb. Also, don't use teething biscuits or other foods in place of a teething ring.

—Don't insist that your baby finish every bottle. Unless your baby is underweight, he knows how much formula he needs.

—Don't enlarge the hole in the nipple of a baby bottle. The formula will come out of the bottle too fast.

—Feed your infant no more often than every 2 hours at birth and no more often than every 3 hours from 2 to 6 months of age.

—Feed your child slowly rather than rapidly. Don't do anything to hurry your child's pace of eating. It takes 15 to 20 minutes for the sensation of fullness to develop. The rapid-eating habit in adults has been associated with obesity.

—Avoid solids until your child is 4 months old (6 months old in breast-fed babies).

—Change to three meals daily by 6 months of age.

—Don't insist that your child clean his plate or finish a jar of baby food.

—Don't encourage your child to eat more after she signals she is full, by turning her head or not opening her mouth.

—Discontinue breast- and bottle-feeding by 12 months of age. A recent study by Dr W.S. Agras found that delayed weaning was associated with more obesity.

—Avoid sweets until at least 12 months of age.

—Don't give your child food as a way to distract him or keep him occupied. Instead, give him something to play with when you need some free time.

—Use praise and physical contact instead of food as a reward for good behavior.

CAUTION: Also don't underfeed your infant. Don't put your baby on low fat milk or skim milk before 2 years of age. Your baby's brain is growing rapidly and needs the fat content of whole milk. While overfeeding is more common than underfeeding in infancy, underfeeding is more harmful.

CALL OUR OFFICE

During regular hours if
—You are uncertain whether your infant is overweight.
—You are concerned about your infant's weight gain.

Instructions for Pediatric Patients by Barton D. Schmitt, M.D., *Pediatrician*
Adapted from YOUR CHILD'S HEALTH, Copyright © 1991 by Barton D. Schmitt, M.D.
Reprinted by permission of Bantam Books.

PART 3

PREVENTIVE PEDIATRICS

CAR SAFETY SEATS
TOOTH DECAY PREVENTION
IMMUNIZATIONS FOR PREVENTION
PASSIVE (INVOLUNTARY) SMOKING
SUNBURN—See Part 5, Pediatric Dermatology

The major killer as well as the major crippler of children in the United States is motor vehicle crashes. Approximately 700 children under the age of 5 years are killed each year, and about 60,000 are injured. Proper use of car safety seats can reduce traffic fatalities by at least 80%. All 50 states have passed laws that require children to ride in approved child passenger safety seats.

A parent cannot protect a child by holding him or her tightly. In a 30-mph crash, the child will either be crushed between the parent's body and the dashboard or ripped from the parent's arms and possibly thrown from the car. Car safety seats also help to control a child's misbehavior, prevent motion sickness, and reduce the number of accidents caused by a child distracting the driver.

CHOOSING A CAR SEAT

Government Safety Standards

Since January 1981, all manufacturers of child safety seats have been required to meet stringent government safety standards, including crash testing. Choose a seat that has met Federal Motor Vehicle Safety Standard 213, with 1981 or later as the year of manufacture. If the seat was manufactured between 1971 and 1981, it may not meet the government safety standard. When in doubt, contact the National Highway Traffic Safety Administration hotline (1-800-424-9393) for information. The American Academy of Pediatrics also publishes a list of infant/child safety seats that is updated yearly. To obtain this list, write to

American Academy of Pediatrics
Division of Public Education
141 Northwest Point Boulevard
PO Box 927
Elk Grove Village, IL 60009-0927

Types of Car Safety Seats

There are three types of car safety seats:
—Infant safety seats are installed in a rear-facing position only and can be used from birth until a child weighs approximately 20 pounds.
—Convertible safety seats can be used in both rear- and forward-facing positions.
—Booster safety seats are forward facing and have a removable shield.

Before you buy a car safety seat, look at several different models. Make sure that the car seat will fit in your car and that your seat belts will work with the seat.

Matching Car Safety Seats with Your Child's Weight

—Birth to 20 pounds: Use an infant safety seat until your child is over 20 pounds and able to sit up alone. Keep your child facing backward as long as possible because it protects him from neck injuries.
—Over 20 pounds: Use a convertible car seat in the forward-facing position.
—Over 40 pounds and over 40 inches tall: Use a booster

safety seat. This will also help your child see out the window.
—Over 60 pounds: Use the regular car seat without a booster seat and with a lap belt low across the hips. When your child is also over 4 feet (48 inches) tall, add a shoulder strap. Using a shoulder strap before your child is 4 feet tall can cause neck injuries. If the shoulder strap runs across the neck (rather than the shoulder), put it behind your child. Never put the shoulder belt under both arms.

USING A CAR SEAT PROPERLY*

If used consistently and properly, your child's car seat can be a lifesaver. Your attitude toward safety belts and car seats is especially important. If you treat buckling up as a necessary, automatic routine, your child will follow your lead and also accept car seats and seat belts. To keep your child safe and happy, follow these guidelines:
—**ALWAYS FOLLOW THE MANUFACTURER'S DIRECTIONS** for installation and use of the car seat: improper installation or use will not protect your child.
—Always use the safety seat. Use the safety seat on the first ride home from the hospital, and continue using it for every ride.
—Whenever possible put the safety seat in the back seat of the car, which is much safer than the front seat.
—If the seat belt in your car has a shoulder harness, you will need a seat belt–locking clip that keeps the seat belt from moving when it is used with your child's safety seat. These locks often are sold with the safety seat. Baby specialty stores also sell them separately.
—Everyone buckles up! Allow *no* exceptions for older kids and adults. If adults ride unprotected, the child quickly decides that safety is just kid stuff.
—Give frequent praise for appropriate behavior in the car.
—Remember that a bored child can become disruptive. Keep a supply of favorite soft toys and munchies on hand.
—*Never* let a fussy child out of the car seat or safety belt while the car is in motion. If your child needs a break, *stop* the car. Responding to complaints by allowing your child to ride unprotected is a disastrous decision that will make it harder to keep him or her in the seat on the next ride.
—If a child tries to get out of the seat, stop the car and firmly but calmly explain that you won't start the car until he or she is again buckled in the car seat.
—Make a vinyl seat pad more comfortable in hot weather by covering it with a cloth pad or towel.
—When your child travels in another person's car (such as a babysitter's or grandparent's), insist that the driver also use the safety seat.
—For long-distance trips, plan for frequent stops and try to stop before your child becomes restless. Cuddle a young child; let an older child snack and run around for 10 to 15 minutes.

*Adapted from the American Academy of Pediatrics with permission, 1986.

TOOTH DECAY PREVENTION

Tooth decay causes toothaches, lost teeth, malocclusion, and costly visits to the dentist. Fortunately, modern dentistry can prevent 80% to 90% of tooth decay.

FLUORIDE

Fluoride builds strong, decay-resistant enamel. Fluoride is needed from 2 weeks to 12 years of age. Drinking fluoridated water (containing 0.7 to 1.2 parts per million) or taking a prescription fluoride supplement is the best protection against tooth decay, reducing cavities by 70%.

If fluoride is consumed in drinking water, a child must take at least 1 pint per day (preferably 1 quart per day by school age).

If your city's water supply doesn't have fluoride added or you are breast-feeding, ask your physician for a prescription for fluoride drops or tablets during your next routine visit. The dosage of fluoride required for prevention of tooth decay is 0.25 mg per day in the first 2 years; 0.5 mg from 2 to 3 years of age; and 1.0 mg over age 3. Give fluoride on an empty stomach, because mixing it with milk reduces its absorption to 70%.

Bottled water usually doesn't contain adequate fluoride. Call the producer for information. If your child drinks bottled water containing less than 0.7 parts per million of fluoride, ask your child's physician for a fluoride supplement.

Fluoride is safe. Over half of all Americans drink fluoridated water. Consumer Reports (July/August 1978) states: "The simple truth is that there is no scientific controversy over the safety of fluoridation. The practice is safe, economical and beneficial. The survival of any controversy is one of the major triumphs of quackery over science in our generation."

One concern about fluoride is white spots or mottling on the teeth (fluorosis). This can occur when a child ingests 2 mg or more per day. The preventive dose is 1 mg or less. Children can ingest excessive fluoride if they receive supplements when it is already present in the city water supply. Occasionally they ingest it by eating toothpaste. A ribbon of toothpaste contains about 1 mg of fluoride. Therefore people of all ages should use only a drop of toothpaste the size of a pea. This precaution and encouraging your child not to swallow most of the toothpaste will prevent fluorosis.

TOOTHBRUSHING AND FLOSSING

The purpose of toothbrushing is to remove plaque from the teeth. Plaque is an invisible scum that forms on the surface of teeth. Within this plaque, mouth bacteria change sugars to acids, which in turn etches the enamel.
—Toothbrushing should begin before 1 year of age.
—Help your child brush at least until after 6 years of age. Most children don't have the coordination or strength to brush their own teeth adequately before then.
—Try to brush after each meal, but especially after the last meal or snack of the day.
—To prevent mouth bacteria from changing food caught in the teeth into acid, brush the teeth within the first 5 to 10 minutes after meals.
—Brush the molars (back teeth) carefully. Decay usually starts in the pits and crevices there.
—If your child is negative about toothbrushing, have him brush your teeth first before you brush his.
—A fluoride toothpaste is beneficial. People of all ages tend to use too much toothpaste; a drop the size of a pea is all that is needed.
—If your child is in a setting where he can't brush his teeth, teach him to rinse his mouth with water after meals instead.
—Dental floss is very useful for cleaning between the teeth where a brush can't reach. This should begin when your child's molars start to touch. In the early years, most of the teeth have spaces between them.

DIET

A healthy diet from a dental standpoint is one that keeps the sugar concentration in the mouth at a low level. The worst foods contain sugar and also stick to the teeth.
—Prevent baby-bottle caries by not letting your infant sleep with a bottle of milk or juice. If your baby, after the teeth erupt, must have a bottle at night, it should contain only water. It is better to put your child to bed after finishing the bottle.
—Discourage prolonged contact with sugar (for example, hard candy) or any sweets that are sticky (for example, caramels or raisins).
—Avoid frequent snacks.
—Give sugar-containing foods only with meals.
—Parents worry needlessly about soft drinks. The sugar in these products does not bind to the teeth and is cleared rather rapidly from the mouth.
—Since no one can keep children away from candy completely, try to teach your child to brush after eating it.

DENTIST VISITS

The American Dental Association recommends that dental checkups begin at 3 years of age (sooner for dental symptoms or abnormal-looking teeth).

DENTAL SEALANTS

The latest breakthrough in dental research is dental sealing of the pits and fissures of the biting surfaces of the molars. Fluoride does little to prevent decay on these surfaces. A special plastic seal can be applied to the top surfaces of the permanent molars at about 6 years of age. The seal may protect against decay for a lifetime. Ask your child's dentist about the latest recommendations.

Instructions for Pediatric Patients by Barton D. Schmitt, M.D., *Pediatrician*
Adapted from YOUR CHILD'S HEALTH, Copyright © 1991 by Barton D. Schmitt, M.D.
Reprinted by permission of Bantam Books.

These immunizations protect your child against several serious, life-threatening diseases. If your child's shots are not up-to-date, call our office for an appointment.

IMMUNIZATION SCHEDULE*

AGE OF CHILD	IMMUNIZATION
2 mo	DTP, OPV, Hib
4 mo	DTP, OPV, Hib
6 mo	DTP, Hib
15 mo	MMR, Hib
18 mo	DTP, OPV
5 yr	DTP, OPV
12 yr	MMR
15 yr	Td

*DTP = diphtheria, tetanus, pertussis (whooping cough); Hib = *Haemophilus influenzae* type B; MMR = measles, mumps, rubella; OPV = oral polio virus; Td = adult tetanus and diphtheria (needed every 10 years throughout life).

MEASLES REVACCINATION

In 1989 the American Academy of Pediatrics recommended that all children receive a second MMR vaccine before they enter middle school (when they are about 11 or 12 years old). The best age for giving this MMR booster is controversial. In some places it is given to children as young as 5 years of age.

Recent outbreaks of measles in high schools and colleges have made this change in policy necessary. The measles, mumps, and rubella vaccine is being used rather than a single measles vaccine because cases of mumps have also increased in recent years.

If your child has been exposed to measles and has not received two MMR vaccines after he or she was 12 months old, call our office during office hours for additional information.

VACCINE AGAINST *HAEMOPHILUS INFLUENZAE*, TYPE B (HIB)

Haemophilus influenzae is a strain of bacteria that causes several life-threatening diseases (for example, meningitis, epiglottitis, and pneumonia) in young children. Over 10,000 children in the United States develop *haemophilus* meningitis each year. About 500 of them die and 3800 have mental retardation, blindness, deafness, and cerebral palsy as a result of the disease.

The first Hib vaccine became available in 1985 and was only effective in children over 2 years old. In late 1990 a new Hib vaccine was approved that could be started in infants as young as 2 months old.

The complete series of four Hib vaccines gives up to 99% protection against these devastating diseases. The side effects are minor (a sore injection site and low-grade fever) and only occur in 1.5% of children. If your child is over 15 months old, the vaccine can still be helpful if it is given some time before the age of 6 years.

The Hib vaccine does not protect against viral influenza or viral meningitis.

REACTIONS TO IMMUNIZATIONS

Polio, Measles, Mumps, Rubella, and *Haemophilus influenzae*, Type b, Vaccines

There are no common reactions to polio, mumps, rubella, or Hib vaccines. A small percentage of children have brief joint pain or swelling about 14 days after they receive the rubella vaccine. There is a small risk that children with poor immunity or living with adults who have poor immunity (for example, AIDS) might acquire or pass on polio following the live oral polio vaccine (OPV). They should receive the inactivated polio vaccine (IPV).

The measles vaccine can result in a 101° to 103° F (38.3° to 39.4° C) fever and pink rash about 7 to 10 days after the injection. The symptoms last 2 or 3 days and need no treatment. The rash from the measles vaccine is not contagious.

DTP Vaccines

Vaccines against diphtheria, tetanus, and pertussis (whooping cough) often cause fever and tenderness, redness, and swelling in the area where the child got the shot. These symptoms may last 1 to 2 days. Give acetaminophen for these symptoms. If your child has severe pain with the first DTP vaccine, with future vaccines give acetaminophen at the time of the injection and continue it four times per day for six dosages. Call our office if your child cries for more than 3 hours, has a fever over 105° F (40.6° C), or has any other unusual reaction. Call also if the redness, swelling, or fever lasts for more than 48 hours.

The pertussis vaccine scare has made some parents postpone their child's immunizations. Keep in mind that pertussis is a very dangerous disease, especially for infants. The American Academy of Pediatrics has stated clearly that "the risk of suffering and death caused by whooping cough is far greater than the possible side effects of the vaccine."

A child who has not been immunized against pertussis has a chance of 1 in 3000 of getting whooping cough. In contrast, a child who has received the vaccine has a chance of one in 2 million of having neurologic damage with the vaccine. In fact, a new study (1990) by Dr. M.R. Griffin found no brain damage or epilepsy to be caused by the pertussis vaccine. The panic over pertussis vaccine may all have been a tempest in a teapot. In the meantime, the risk of children getting pertussis increases as fewer of them are immunized.

(Continued on the reverse side)

The pertussis vaccine should be withheld initially only if a child has seizures or serious neurologic disease. If you remain opposed, at least give your child the benefits of the tetanus and diphtheria (Td) vaccine.

Egg Allergies

Children who are allergic to eggs can receive all the routine immunizations except measles and mumps.

These vaccines are grown in chick cell culture, and some children who are allergic to eggs have had allergic reactions to these vaccines.

If a child's reaction to eggs is mild, the vaccines can still be given. If a reaction to eggs has occurred rapidly (within 2 hours after the child ate eggs) or has been severe (for example, causing difficult breathing or swallowing), an allergist should skin test your child to determine if the measles vaccine would be safe.

Instructions for Pediatric Patients by Barton D. Schmitt, M.D., *Pediatrician*   © 1992 by W. B. Saunders Company

Adapted from YOUR CHILD'S HEALTH, Copyright © 1991 by Barton D. Schmitt, M.D.
Reprinted by permission of Bantam Books.

Nonsmoking children who live in homes with smokers are involuntarily exposed to cigarette smoke. The smoke comes from two sources—secondhand smoke and side-stream smoke. Secondhand smoke is exhaled by the smoker. Side-stream smoke rises off the end of a burning cigarette and accounts for most of the smoke in a room. Side-stream smoke contains two or three times more harmful chemicals than secondhand smoke because it does not pass through the cigarette filter. At worst, a child in a very smoky room for 1 hour with several smokers inhales as many bad chemicals as he would by smoking 10 or more cigarettes. In general, children of smoking mothers absorb more smoke into their bodies than children of smoking fathers because they spend more time with their mothers. Children who are breast-fed by a smoking mother are at the greatest risk because chemicals are found in the breast milk as well as the surrounding air.

HARMFUL EFFECTS OF PASSIVE SMOKING ON CHILDREN

Children who live in a house where someone smokes have an increased rate of all respiratory infections. Their symptoms are also more severe and last longer than those of children who live in a smoke-free home. The impact of passive smoke is worse during the first 5 years of life when children spend most of their time with their parents. The more smokers there are in a household and the more they smoke, the more severe a child's symptoms. Passive smoking is especially hazardous to children who have asthma. Exposure to smoke causes more severe asthma attacks, more emergency room visits, and increased admissions to the hospital. These children are also less likely to outgrow their asthma. The following conditions are worsened by passive smoking:
—Pneumonia
—Coughs or bronchitis
—Croup or laryngitis
—Wheezing or bronchiolitis
—Asthma attacks
—Influenza
—Ear infections
—Middle ear fluid and blockage
—Colds or upper respiratory infections
—Sinus infections
—Sore throats
—Eye irritation
—Crib deaths (SIDS)
—School absenteeism for all of the above

HOW TO PROTECT YOUR CHILD FROM *PASSIVE SMOKING*

1. **Give up active smoking**. Sign up for a stop-smoking class or program. Giving up smoking is even more urgent if you are pregnant because your unborn baby has twice the risk for prematurity and newborn complications if you smoke during pregnancy. It is also important to avoid smoking if you are breast-feeding because smoke-related, harmful chemicals get into your breast milk. You can stop smoking if you get help. If you need some self-help reading materials, call your local American Lung Association or American Cancer Society office. The Surgeon General would like us to become a smoke-free society by the year 2000. For more information call the National Cancer Institute on their toll-free line: 1-800-4-CANCER. If you want your child not to smoke, set a good example.

2. **Never smoke inside your home**. Some parents find it difficult to give up smoking, but all parents can change their smoking habits. Restrict your smoking to times you are away from home. If you have to smoke when you are home, smoke only in your garage or on the porch. If these options are not available to you, designate a smoking room within your home. Keep the door to this room closed and periodically open the window to let fresh air into the room. Wear a special overshirt in this room to protect your underlying clothing from collecting the smoke. Never allow your child inside this room, and don't smoke in other parts of the house. Apply the same rule to visitors.

3. **Never smoke while holding your child**. If your smoking habit cannot be controlled to the degree mentioned above, at a minimum protect your child from smoking when you are close to him. This precaution will reduce his exposure to smoke and protect him from cigarette burns. Never smoke in a car when your child is a passenger. Never smoke when you are feeding or bathing him. Never smoke in your child's bedroom. Even doing this much will help your child to some degree.

4. **Avoid leaving your child with a caretaker who smokes.** Inquire about smoking when you are looking for day-care centers or babysitters. If your child has asthma, this safeguard is crucial.

PART 4

COMMON INFECTIONS OF CHILDHOOD

DEFINITION

Diagnostic Findings

—Wheezing: a high-pitched whistling sound produced during breathing out
—Rapid breathing with a rate of over 40 breaths/minute
—Tight breathing (your child has to push the air out)
—Coughing, often with very sticky mucus
—Onset of lung symptoms often preceded by fever and a runny nose
—An average age of 6 months, always less than 2 years
—Symptoms similar to asthma

Cause

The wheezing is caused by a narrowing of the smallest airways in the lung (bronchioles). This narrowing results from inflammation (swelling) caused by any of a number of viruses, usually the respiratory syncytial virus (RSV). RSV occurs in epidemics almost every winter. Whereas infants with RSV develop bronchiolitis, children over 2 years of age and adults just develop cold symptoms. This virus is found in nasal secretions of infected individuals. It is spread by sneezing or coughing at a range of less than 6 feet or by hand-to-nose or hand-to-eye contact. People do not develop permanent immunity to the virus.

Expected Course

Wheezing and tight breathing (difficulty breathing out) become worse for 2 or 3 days and then begin to improve. Overall, the wheezing lasts approximately 7 days and the cough about 14 days. The most common complication of bronchiolitis is an ear infection, occurring in some 20% of infants. Bacterial pneumonia is an uncommon complication. Only 1% or 2% of children with bronchiolitis are hospitalized because they need oxygen or intravenous fluids. In the long run, approximately 30% of the children who develop bronchiolitis go on to develop asthma. Recurrences of wheezing (asthma) occur mainly in children who come from families where close relatives have asthma. Asthma is very treatable with current medications.

HOME TREATMENT FOR BRONCHIOLITIS

Medicines. Some children with bronchiolitis respond to asthma medicines, others do not. Your child's medicine is _____. Give _____ every ____ hours. Continue the medicine until your child's wheezing is gone for 24 hours. In addition, your child can be given acetaminophen every 4 to 6 hours if the fever is over 102° F (39° C).

Warm Fluids for Coughing Spasms. Coughing spasms are often caused by sticky secretions in the back of the throat. Warm liquids usually relax the airway and loosen the secretions. Offer warm lemonade or apple juice. In addition, breathing warm moist air helps to loosen the sticky mucus that may be choking your child.

You can provide warm mist by placing a warm wet washcloth loosely over your child's nose and mouth, or you can fill a humidifier with warm water and have your child breathe in the warm mist it produces. Avoid steam vaporizers because they can cause burns.

Humidity. Dry air tends to make coughs worse. Use a humidifier in your child's bedroom. The new ultrasonic humidifiers not only have the advantage of quietness, but also kill molds and most bacteria that might be in the water.

Suction of a Blocked Nose. If the nose is blocked up, your child will not be able to drink from a bottle or nurse. Most stuffy noses are blocked by dry or sticky mucus. Suction alone cannot remove dry secretions. Warm tap water nose drops are better than any medicine you can buy for loosening up mucus. Place three drops of warm water in each nostril. After about 1 minute, use a soft rubber suction bulb to suck it out. You can repeat this procedure several times until your child's breathing through the nose becomes quiet and easy.

Feedings. Encourage your child to drink adequate fluids. Eating is often tiring, so offer your child formula or breast milk in smaller amounts at more frequent intervals. If your child vomits during a coughing spasm, feed the child again.

No Smoking. Tobacco smoke aggravates coughing. The incidence of wheezing increases greatly in children who have an RSV infection *and* are exposed to passive smoking. Don't let anyone smoke around your child. In fact, try not to let anybody smoke inside your home.

 ## CALL OUR OFFICE

IMMEDIATELY if
—Breathing becomes labored or difficult.
—The wheezing becomes severe (tight).
—Breathing becomes faster than 60 breaths/minute (when your child is not crying).
—The retractions (tugging in between the ribs) become worse.
—Your child stops breathing or passes out.
—The lips become bluish.
—Your child starts acting very sick.

Within 24 hours if
—Your child is unable to sleep because of the wheezing.
—Your child is not drinking enough fluids.
—There is any suggestion of an earache.
—A nasal discharge becomes yellow for more than 24 hours.
—Any fever (over 100° F [37.8° C]) lasts more than 72 hours.
—You feel your child is getting worse.

During regular hours if
—The cough lasts more than 3 weeks.
—You have other questions or concerns.

CHICKENPOX (VARICELLA)

DEFINITION

Diagnostic Findings of Chickenpox

—Multiple small, red bumps that progress to thin-walled water blisters; then cloudy blisters or open sores, which are usually less than ¼ inch across; and finally dry, brown crusts (all within 24 hours)
—Repeated crops of these sores for 4 to 5 days
—Rash on all body surfaces but usually starts on head and back
—Some ulcers (sores) in the mouth, eyelids, and genital area
—Fever (unless the rash is mild)
—Exposure to a child with chickenpox 14 to 16 days earlier

Cause

Chickenpox is caused by exposure to a highly contagious virus 14 to 16 days earlier. A chickenpox vaccine should be available for general use in 1991.

Expected Course

New eruptions continue to crop up daily for 4 to 5 days. The fever is usually the highest on the third or fourth day. Children start to feel better and stop having a fever once they stop getting new bumps. The average child gets a total of 500 sores.

Chickenpox rarely leaves any permanent scars unless the sores become badly infected with impetigo or your child repeatedly picks off the scabs. However, normal chickenpox can leave temporary marks on the skin that take 6 to 12 months to fade. One attack gives lifelong immunity. Very rarely, a child may develop a second mild attack.

HOME CARE

Itching and Cool Baths. The best treatment for skin discomfort and itching is a cool bath every 3 to 4 hours for the first few days. Baths don't spread the chickenpox. Calamine lotion can be placed on itchy spots after the bath. If the itching becomes severe or interferes with sleep, give your child a nonprescription antihistamine (Benadryl).

Fever. Acetaminophen may be given in the dose appropriate for your child's age for a few days if your child develops a fever over 102° F (39° C). Aspirin should be avoided in children and adolescents with chickenpox because of the link with Reye's syndrome.

Sore Mouth. Since chickenpox sores also occur in the mouth and throat, your child may be picky about eating. Encourage cold fluids. Offer a soft, bland diet and avoid salty foods and citrus fruits. If the mouth ulcers become troublesome, have your child gargle or swallow 1 tablespoon of an antacid solution four times daily after meals.

Sore Genital Area. Sores also normally occur in the genital area. If urination becomes very painful, apply some 2½% lidocaine (Xylocaine) or 1% Nupercainal ointment (no prescription needed) to the genital ulcers every 2 to 3 hours to relieve pain.

Prevention of Impetigo (Infected Sores). To prevent the sores from becoming infected with bacteria, trim your child's fingernails short. Also, wash the hands with an antibacterial soap (such as Dial or Safeguard) frequently during the day. For young babies who are scratching badly, you may want to cover their hands with cotton socks.

Contagiousness and Isolation. Children with chickenpox are contagious until all the sores have crusted over, usually about 6 to 7 days after the rash begins. To avoid exposing other children, try not to take your child to the physician's office. If you must, leave your child in the car with a sitter while you check in. Your child does not have to stay home until all the scabs fall off (this may take 2 weeks).

Most adults who think they didn't have chickenpox as a child had a mild case. Only 4% of adults are not protected. If you lived in the same household with siblings who had chickenpox, consider yourself protected. Siblings will come down with chickenpox in 14 to 16 days. The second case in a family always has many more chickenpox than the first case.

 ## CALL OUR OFFICE

IMMEDIATELY if
—Your child develops a patch of red, tender skin.
—Your child develops a speckled red rash that looks like scarlet fever.
—Your child becomes confused or difficult to awaken.
—Your child develops trouble walking.
—The neck becomes stiff.
—Breathing becomes difficult or fast.
—Vomiting occurs three or more times.
—Bleeding occurs into the chickenpox.
—Your child starts acting very sick.

Within 24 hours if
—The scabs become larger.
—The scabs become soft and drain pus. (**NOTE:** Use an antibiotic ointment on these sores until your child is seen by a physician.)
—The fever lasts over 4 days.
—A lymph node becomes larger and more tender than others.
—The itching is severe and doesn't respond to treatment.
—Your child develops severe pain when urinating.
—You have other concerns or questions.

Instructions for Pediatric Patients by Barton D. Schmitt, M.D., *Pediatrician*   © 1992 by W. B. Saunders Company
Adapted from YOUR CHILD'S HEALTH, Copyright © 1991 by Barton D. Schmitt, M.D.
Reprinted by permission of Bantam Books.

DEFINITION

Diagnostic Findings of a Cold (Upper Respiratory Infection [URI])

—Runny or stuffy nose
—Usually associated with fever and sore throat
—Sometimes associated with a cough, hoarseness, red eyes, and swollen lymph nodes in the neck

Similar Conditions

1. *Vasomotor rhinitis*. Many children and adults have a profusely runny nose in the winter when they are breathing cold air. This usually clears within 15 minutes of coming indoors. It requires no treatment beyond a handkerchief and has nothing to do with infection.

2. *Chemical rhinitis*. Chemical rhinitis is a dry stuffy nose from excessive and prolonged use of vasoconstrictor nose drops (more than 1 week). It will be better within a day or two of stopping the nose drops.

Cause

A cold or upper respiratory infection is a viral infection of the nose and throat. The cold viruses are spread from one person to another by hand contact, coughing, and sneezing—not by cold air or drafts. Since there are up to 200 cold viruses, most healthy children get at least six colds each year.

Expected Course

Usually the fever lasts less than 3 days, and all nose and throat symptoms are gone by 1 week. A cough may last 2 to 3 weeks. The main things to watch for are secondary bacterial infections such as ear infections, yellow drainage from the eyes, thick pus from the nose (often indicating a sinus infection), or difficulty breathing (often caused by pneumonia). In young infants, a blocked nose can interfere so much with the ability to suck that dehydration can occur.

HOME CARE

Not much can be done to affect how long a cold lasts. However, we can relieve many of the symptoms. Keep in mind that the treatment for a runny nose is quite different from the treatment for a stuffy nose.

Treatment for a Runny Nose with Profuse Clear Discharge: Suctioning or Blowing. The best treatment is clearing the nose for a day or two. Sniffing and swallowing the secretions are probably better than blowing because blowing the nose can force the infection into the ears or sinuses. For younger babies, use a soft rubber suction bulb to remove the secretions gently.

Nasal discharge is the nose's way of eliminating viruses. Medicine is not helpful unless your child has a nasal allergy.

Treatment for a Dry or Stuffy Nose with Only a Little Discharge

Warm-Water Nose Drops and Suctioning. Most stuffy noses are blocked by dry mucus. Blowing the nose or suction alone cannot remove most dry secretions. Nose drops of warm tap water are better than any medicine you can buy for loosening mucus. If you prefer normal saline nose drops, mix ¼ teaspoon of table salt in 8 ounces of water. Make up a fresh solution every few days and keep it in a clean bottle. Use a clean dropper to insert drops. Water can also be dripped or splashed in using a wet cotton ball.

—For the younger child who cannot blow his nose: Place three drops of warm water in each nostril. After 1 minute use a soft rubber suction bulb to suck out the loosened mucus gently. To remove secretions from the back of the nose, you will need to seal off both nasal openings completely with the tip of the suction bulb and your fingers. You can get a suction bulb at your drugstore for about two dollars.

—For the older child who can blow his nose: Use three drops as necessary in each nostril while your child is lying on his back on a bed with his head hanging over the side. Wait 1 minute for the water to soften and loosen the dried mucus. Then have your child blow his nose. This can be repeated several times in a row for complete clearing of the nasal passages.

—Errors in using warm-water nose drops: The main errors are not putting in enough water, not waiting long enough for secretions to loosen up, and not repeating the procedure until the breathing is easy. The front of the nose can look open while the back of the nose is all gummed up with dried mucus. Obviously, putting in warm-water nose drops without suctioning or blowing the nose afterward is of little value.

Decongestant Nose Drops. If nasal congestion interferes with breathing despite warm-water nose drops, buy some nonprescription vasoconstrictor nose drops or spray. Use them only after the nose has been cleaned out. Don't use them again unless the nasal congestion recurs *and* your child is uncomfortable.

—For 6 months to 2 years of age: ⅛% Neo-Synephrine nose drops every 2 to 3 hours as needed (especially before feedings)

—For 2 to 6 years of age: pediatric-strength, long-acting nose drops every 8 to 12 hours as needed

—Over 6 years of age: adult-strength, long-acting nose drops every 8 to 12 hours as needed

—**WARNING**: Don't use vasoconstrictor nose drops or spray for more than 5 days because the vasoconstrictor medicine can irritate the nose and make it more congested. Vasoconstrictor nose drops can be restarted only if the nose has had 2 or more days of rest from them.

The Importance of Clearing the Nose in Young Infants. A child can't breathe through the mouth and suck on something at the same time. If your child is

(Continued on the reverse side)

Instructions for Pediatric Patients by Barton D. Schmitt, M.D., *Pediatrician*
Adapted from YOUR CHILD'S HEALTH, Copyright © 1991 by Barton D. Schmitt, M.D.
Reprinted by permission of Bantam Books.

breast- or bottle-feeding, you must clear his nose so he can breathe while he's sucking. Clearing the nasal passages is also important before putting your child down to sleep.

Treatment for Associated Symptoms of Colds

—Fever: Use acetaminophen for aches or mild fever (over 102° F [38.9° C]).
—Sore throat: Use hard candies and saltwater gargles for children over 4 years old.
—Cough: Use cough drops for children over 4 years old and corn syrup for younger children. Run a humidifier.
—Red eyes: Rinse frequently with wet cotton balls.
—Poor appetite: Encourage fluids of the child's choice.

Prevention of Colds. A cold is caused by direct contact with someone who already has one. Over the years, we all become exposed to many colds and develop some immunity to them. Since complications are more common in children during the first year of life, try to avoid undue exposure of young babies to other children or adults with colds, to day-care nurseries, and to church nurseries. A humidifier prevents dry mucous membranes, which may be more susceptible to infections. Vitamin C, unfortunately, has not been shown to prevent or shorten colds. Large doses of vitamin C (for example, 2 grams) cause diarrhea.

Common Mistakes in Treating Colds. Most over-the-counter cold remedies or tablets are worthless. Nothing can shorten the duration of a cold. If the nose is really running, consider a pure antihistamine (such as chlor-pheniramine products). Especially avoid drugs that have several ingredients because they increase the risk of side effects. Avoid oral decongestants if they make your child jittery or keep him from sleeping at night. Use acetaminophen for a cold only if your child also has fever, sore throat, or muscle aches. Leftover antibiotics should not be given for uncomplicated colds because they have no effect on viruses and may be harmful.

CALL OUR OFFICE

IMMEDIATELY if
—Breathing becomes difficult *and* no better after you clear the nose.
—Your child starts acting very sick.

During regular hours if
—The fever lasts more than 3 days.
—The discharge lasts more than 10 days.
—The discharge becomes thick yellow for more than 24 hours.
—The skin under the openings of the nose becomes raw or scabbed over.
—The eyes develop a yellow discharge.
—You can't unblock the nose enough for your infant to take adequate fluids.
—There is any suggestion of an earache or sinus pain.
—The throat becomes quite sore (get a throat culture).
—You feel your child is getting worse.
—You have other questions or concerns.

 Instructions for Pediatric Patients by Barton D. Schmitt, M.D., *Pediatrician*
Adapted from YOUR CHILD'S HEALTH, Copyright © 1991 by Barton D. Schmitt, M.D.
Reprinted by permission of Bantam Books.

DEFINITION

Diagnostic Findings

—The cough reflex expels air from the lungs with a sudden explosive noise.
—Cough can be dry and hacking or wet and productive.
—A coughing spasm is more than 5 minutes of continuous coughing.

Similar Conditions

—Croup

Cause

Most coughs are due to a viral infection of the trachea (windpipe) and bronchi (larger air passages). These infections are called tracheitis and bronchitis, respectively. Most children get this infection a couple of times every year as part of a cold. Keep in mind that coughing clears the lungs and protects them from pneumonia. Bronchitis isn't serious. The role of milk in thickening the secretions is doubtful.

Expected Course

Usually bronchitis gives a dry tickly cough that lasts for 2 to 3 weeks. Sometimes it becomes loose (wet) for a few days and your child coughs up a lot of phlegm (mucus). This is usually a sign that the end of the illness is near.

HOME CARE

Medicines to Loosen the Cough and Thin the Secretions

—Cough drops: Most coughs in children over 4 years of age can be controlled by sucking on cough drops freely. Any brand will do.
—Homemade cough syrup: For children under age 4 years, use 1 teaspoon of honey or corn syrup instead. (Don't use honey for babies under 1 year of age.)
—Warm liquids for coughing spasms: Warm liquids usually relax the airway and loosen the mucus. Start with warm lemonade, warm apple juice, or warm tea. Add some honey (corn syrup for babies under 1 year of age). Avoid adding any alcohol because inhaling the alcohol fumes stimulates additional coughing and also because there is a risk of intoxication from unintentional overdosage.

Cough Suppressants. Cough suppressants reduce the cough reflex, which protects the lungs. They are only indicated for dry coughs that interfere with sleep, school attendance, or work. They also help children who have chest pain from coughing spasms. They should not be given to infants under 12 months of age or for wet coughs.

A nonprescription cough suppressant is dextromethorphan (DM). Ask your pharmacist for help in choosing a brand that contains DM without any other active in-gredients. Dosage is 0.2 mg/lb every 4 to 6 hours as needed. It usually comes as a liquid in the strength of 15 mg/teaspoon. The following table shows the dosages of DM that you can give a child according to weight or age.

WEIGHT OF CHILD	DOSAGE OF DM (IN MG)
20 lb	4
30 lb	6
4-6 yr	7.5
7-12 yr	15
Adults	30

Often corn syrup or cough drops can be given during the day and DM given at bedtime and during the night. DM is also available as a cough lozenge for easy carrying and as a long-acting (12-hour) liquid.

Humidifiers in the Treatment of Cough. Dry air tends to make coughs worse. Dry coughs can be loosened by encouraging a good fluid intake and using a humidifier in your child's bedroom.

The new ultrasonic humidifiers are very quiet, and they kill molds and most bacteria found in the water. If possible, use distilled water instead of tap water in the humidifier. The Environmental Protection Agency reported in 1988 that tap water may contain harmful minerals (such as lead and asbestos). These minerals are present in the mist produced by ultrasonic humidifiers. Frequent inhaling of these particles may cause chronic lung problems. Don't add medication to the water in the humidifier because it irritates the cough in some children.

Active and Passive Smoking. Teenagers will find that physical education classes and exercise trigger coughing spasms when they have bronchitis. If so, such physical activity should be avoided temporarily. Don't let anyone smoke around your coughing child. Remind the teenager who smokes that his cough may last weeks longer than it normally would without smoking.

Common Mistakes in Treating Cough. Antihistamines, decongestants, and antipyretics are found in many cough syrups. These ingredients are of unproven value, and the antihistamines carry the risk of sedation. Expectorants are of unproven value but harmless. Stay with the simple remedies mentioned above or use dextromethorphan (DM). Milk does not need to be eliminated from the diet, since restricting it only improves the cough if your child is allergic to milk. Also, never stop breastfeeding because of a cough.

CALL OUR OFFICE

IMMEDIATELY if
—Breathing becomes difficult *and* is not better after you clear the nose.

(Continued on the reverse side)

COUGH *Continued*

—Breathing becomes fast or labored (when your child is not coughing).
—Your child passes out with coughing spasms.
—The lips turn bluish with coughing spasms.
—Any blood-tinged sputum is coughed up.
—Your child starts acting very sick.

During regular hours if
—A fever (over 100° F [37.8° C]) lasts more than 72 hours.

—The cough lasts more than 3 weeks.
—Coughing spasms cause exhaustion or lost sleep.
—The coughing causes vomiting three or more times.
—The coughing causes bad chest pains.
—The cough causes your child to miss 3 or more days of school.
—Your child develops sinus congestion or pain.
—You have other concerns or questions.

Instructions for Pediatric Patients by Barton D. Schmitt, M.D., *Pediatrician*   © 1992 by W. B. Saunders Company
Adapted from YOUR CHILD'S HEALTH, Copyright © 1991 by Barton D. Schmitt, M.D.
Reprinted by permission of Bantam Books.

DEFINITION

Diagnostic Findings of Croupy Cough

—There is a distinctive cough that occurs with infections of the voice box (larynx).
—The cough is tight, metallic, and like a barking seal.
—The voice is usually hoarse.

Diagnostic Findings of Stridor

—A harsh, raspy, vibrating sound is heard when your child breathes in.
—Breathing in becomes very difficult.
—Stridor only occurs with severe croup.
—Stridor is usually only present with crying or coughing.
—As the disease becomes worse, stridor also occurs when a child is sleeping or relaxed.

Cause

Croup is a viral infection of the vocal cords. It is usually part of a cold. The hoarseness is due to swelling of the vocal cords.

Stridor occurs as the opening between the cords becomes more narrow.

Expected Course

Croup usually lasts for 5 to 6 days and generally gets worse at night. During this time, it can change from mild to severe many times. The worst symptoms are seen in children under 3 years of age.

FIRST AID FOR ATTACKS OF STRIDOR WITH CROUP

If your child suddenly develops stridor or tight breathing, do the following:

Inhalation of Warm Mist. Warm, moist air seems to work best to relax the vocal cords and break the stridor. The simplest way to provide this is to have your child breathe through a warm, wet washcloth placed loosely over his nose and mouth. Another good way, if you have a humidifier (not a hot vaporizer), is to fill it with warm water and have your child breathe deeply from the stream of humidity.

The Foggy Bathroom. In the meantime, have the hot shower running with the bathroom door closed. Once the room is all fogged up, take him in there for at least 10 minutes. Try to allay fears by cuddling your child.

Results of First Aid. Most children settle down with the above treatments and then sleep peacefully through the night.

NOTE: If the stridor continues in your child, call our office IMMEDIATELY. If your child turns blue, passes out, or stops breathing, call the rescue squad (911).

HOME CARE FOR A CROUPY COUGH

Mist. Dry air usually makes coughs worse. Keep the child's room humidified. Use a cool mist humidifier if you have one. Run it 24 hours daily. Otherwise, hang wet sheets or towels in your child's room.

Warm Fluids for Coughing Spasms. Coughing spasms are often due to sticky mucus caught on the vocal cords. Warm, clear fluids, such as apple juice, lemonade, or tea, may help relax the vocal cords and loosen the mucus.

Cough Medicines. Medicines are less helpful than either mist or swallowing clear fluids. Older children can be given cough drops for the cough, and younger children can be given some corn syrup. If your child has a fever (over 102° F [38.9° C]), you may give him acetaminophen.

Close Observation. While your child is croupy, sleep in the same room with him. Croup can be a dangerous disease. By all means, don't let anyone smoke around your child; smoke can make croup worse.

Contagiousness. The viruses that cause croup are quite contagious until the fever is gone or at least until 3 days into the illness. Since spread of this infection can't be prevented, your child can return to school or child care once he feels better.

CALL OUR OFFICE

IMMEDIATELY and begin first aid for stridor if
—Breathing becomes difficult.
—Your child develops drooling, spitting, or great difficulty in swallowing.
—Your child develops retractions (tugging in) between the ribs.
—The lips turn bluish or dusky.
—Your child can't sleep because of the croup.
—The warm mist fails to clear up the stridor in 20 minutes.
—You feel your child is getting worse.

Within 24 hours if
—The coughing spasms are getting worse.
—The attacks of stridor occur more than three times.
—Your child is not drinking much.
—A fever (over 104° F [40° C]) occurs.
—You have other concerns or questions.

Instructions for Pediatric Patients by Barton D. Schmitt, M.D., *Pediatrician*
Adapted from YOUR CHILD'S HEALTH, Copyright © 1991 by Barton D. Schmitt, M.D.
Reprinted by permission of Bantam Books.

© 1992 by W. B. Saunders Company

EAR INFECTION (OTITIS MEDIA)

DEFINITION

An ear infection is a bacterial infection of the middle ear (the space behind the eardrum). It usually is a complication of a cold, occurring after the cold blocks off the eustachian tube (the passage connecting the middle ear to the back of the throat). The pain is due to pressure and bulging of the eardrum from trapped, infected fluid.

Most children (75%) will have one or more ear infections, and over 25% of these will have repeated ear infections. In 5% to 10% of children, the pressure in the middle ear causes the eardrum to rupture and drain. This small tear usually heals over the next week. The peak age range for ear infections is 6 months to 2 years, but they continue to be a common childhood illness until 8 years of age.

If the following treatment is carried out, there should be no permanent damage to the ear or to the hearing.

HOME TREATMENT

Antibiotics.   Your child's antibiotic is _____ .

Your child's dose is _____ given _____

times each day during waking hours for _____ days. This medicine will kill the bacteria that are causing the ear infection.

Try to remember all doses. If your child goes to school or a babysitter, arrange for someone to give the afternoon dose. If the medicine is a liquid, store it in the refrigerator and use a measuring spoon to be sure that you give the right amount. Give the medicine until all the pills are gone or the bottle is empty. (An antibiotic should not be saved from one illness to the next because it loses its strength.) Even though your child will feel better in a few days, give the antibiotic until it is completely gone to keep the ear infection from flaring up again.

Pain Relief.   Acetaminophen can be given for a few days for the earache or for fever over 102° F (39° C). Earaches tend to hurt more at bedtime.

Restrictions.   Your child can go outside and does not need to cover the ears. Swimming is permitted as long as there is no perforation (tear) in the eardrum or drainage from the ear. Air travel or a trip to the mountains is safe; just have your child swallow fluids, suck on a pacifier, or chew gum during descent. Your child can return to school or day care when he or she is feeling better and the fever is gone. Ear infections are not contagious.

Follow-up Visits.   Your child has been given a return appointment in 2 to 3 weeks. At that visit we will look at the eardrum to be certain that the infection is cleared up and more treatment isn't needed. We may also want to test your child's hearing. Follow-up exams are very important, particularly if the eardrum is perforated.

CALL OUR OFFICE

IMMEDIATELY if
—The fever or pain is not gone after your child has taken the antibiotic for 48 hours.
—Your child develops a stiff neck.
—You feel your child is getting worse.

Instructions for Pediatric Patients by Barton D. Schmitt, M.D., *Pediatrician*

DEFINITION

Diagnostic Findings

Diarrhea is the sudden increase in the frequency and looseness of bowel movements. Mild diarrhea is the passage of a few loose or mushy stools. Moderate diarrhea gives many watery stools. The best indicator of the severity of the diarrhea is its frequency. A green stool also points to very rapid passage and moderate to severe diarrhea.

The main complication of diarrhea is dehydration from excessive loss of body fluids. Symptoms are a dry mouth, the absence of tears, a reduction in urine production (for example, none in 8 hours), and a darker, concentrated urine. It's dehydration you need to worry about, not the presence of diarrhea.

Cause

Diarrhea is usually caused by a viral infection of the intestines (gastroenteritis). Occasionally it is caused by bacteria or parasites. Diarrhea can be due to excessive fruit juice or to a food allergy. If only one or two loose stools are passed, the cause was probably something unusual your child ate.

Expected Course

Diarrhea usually lasts from several days to a week, regardless of the treatment. The main goal of therapy is to prevent dehydration by giving enough oral fluids to keep up with the fluids lost in the diarrhea. Don't expect a quick return to solid stools. Since one loose stool can mean nothing, don't start dietary changes until there have been at least two.

HOME CARE: DIET

Dietary changes are the mainstay of home treatment for diarrhea. The optimal diet depends on your child's age and the severity of the diarrhea. Go directly to the part that pertains to your child.

Diet for Mild Diarrhea (Mushy Stools) in Children Less Than 2 Years Old. Give extra fluids by mixing your baby's formula or milk with 1 or 2 ounces of extra water per bottle. If your baby is on solids, offer only the ABCs (that is, Applesauce, strained Bananas, and strained Carrots), rice, potatoes, and other high-fiber foods for the next few days. Fiber is helpful for both diarrhea and constipation.

Diet for Moderate Diarrhea (Watery or Frequent Stools) in Children Less Than 1 Year Old

Clear Fluids (Oral Electrolyte Solutions) for 24 Hours. Have your baby take one of the following special clear fluids (oral electrolyte solutions) for the first 24 hours: Pedialyte, Resol, or Ricelyte. These are available without a prescription in most pharmacies and super-markets. Until you obtain this special solution, half-strength Gatorade or another sports drink will do. As a last resort, Jell-O water can be used. Jell-O water must be mixed (one package per quart of water, or twice as much water as usual). Don't use any red-colored Jell-O water because it can look like blood. Give your baby as much of the liquid as he wants. Diarrhea makes children thirsty and your job is to prevent dehydration.

Soy Formula. After being on clear fluids for 6 to 24 hours your baby will be hungry, so begin his regular formula. If the diarrhea is severe, begin a soy formula. Change to a soy formula later if the diarrhea doesn't improve after 3 days on regular formula. There is often less diarrhea with soy formulas than with cow's milk formulas because they don't contain milk sugar (lactose). Mix the formula with 1 or 2 ounces of extra water per bottle until the stools are no longer watery. Plan on keeping your baby on soy formula until the diarrhea is gone for 3 days.

Solids. The foods most easily absorbed are composed of starch. If your baby wants solids, offer applesauce, strained bananas, strained carrots, mashed potatoes, and rice cereal with water.

Diet for Moderate Diarrhea (Watery or Frequent Stools) in Children 1 to 2 Years Old. Babies 1 to 2 years old don't need formula or milk of any kind for the first week. During this week water or Kool-Aid can be used for fluids (avoid fruit juice). Gradually phase in the following special solids:

Day 1: Clear fluids and Popsicles. If your toddler is hungry, add some foods from the day 2 list.
Day 2: Saltine crackers, toast with honey, rice, mashed potatoes, carrots, applesauce, bland soups, or other high-fiber foods.
Day 3: Lean meats, soft-boiled eggs, noodles, soft cooked fruits and vegetables, and active culture yogurt.
Day 6: Regular diet but no milk products.
Day 8: Milk and milk products can gradually be added.

NOTE: Avoid cheeses, which contain 80% of the lactose found in milk, until day 8. By contrast, the lactose in active culture yogurt will be digested by the *Lactobacillus* organisms.

Diet for Mild or Moderate Diarrhea in Children Over 2 Years Old. For the child who is toilet trained for bowel movements, the approach to diarrhea is the same as what any adult would do; namely, eat a regular diet with a few simple changes.
—Increase the intake of foods containing starch since these are easily absorbed during diarrhea. Examples are breads, crackers, rice, mashed potatoes, and noodles.
—Increase the intake of water or clear fluids (those you can see through).

(Continued on the reverse side)

Instructions for Pediatric Patients by Barton D. Schmitt, M.D., *Pediatrician*
Adapted from YOUR CHILD'S HEALTH, Copyright © 1991 by Barton D. Schmitt, M.D.
Reprinted by permission of Bantam Books.

—Reduce or eliminate the intake of milk and milk products (**EXCEPTION:** active-culture yogurt is fine).

—Avoid raw fruits and vegetables, beans, spices, and any other foods that cause loose BMs.

—Resume normal diet 1 day after the diarrhea is gone, which is usually in 3 or 4 days.

Diet for Breast-Feeding Babies with Diarrhea

Definition/Special Considerations. No matter how it looks, the stool of the breast-fed infant must be considered normal unless it contains mucus or blood. In fact, breast-fed babies can normally pass some green stools or stools with a water ring. Frequency of movements is also not much help. During the first 2 or 3 months of life, the breast-fed baby may normally have one stool after each feeding. The presence of something in the mother's diet that causes rapid passage should always be considered in these babies (for example, coffee, cola, or herbal teas). Diarrhea can be diagnosed if your baby's stools abruptly increase in number.

Diet. If your breast-fed baby has diarrhea, treatment is straightforward. Breast-feeding should never be discontinued because of mild to moderate diarrhea. The only treatment necessary is to offer extra water between breast feedings. Breast-feeding may have to be temporarily discontinued if your baby requires intravenous fluids for severe diarrhea and dehydration. Pump your breasts to maintain milk flow until you can breast-feed again (usually within 12 hours).

HOME CARE: OTHER ASPECTS

Common Mistakes. Using boiled skim milk or any concentrated solution can cause serious complications for babies with diarrhea because they contain too much salt. Kool-Aid and soda pop should not be used as the only foods because they contain little or no salt. Use only the fluids mentioned. Clear fluids alone should only be used for 6 to 24 hours because the body needs more calories than they can provide. Likewise, a diluted formula should not be used for more than 24 hours. The most dangerous myth is that the intestine should be "put to rest"; restricting fluids can cause dehydration. Keep in mind that there is no effective, safe drug for diarrhea and that extra water and diet therapy work best.

Prevention. Diarrhea is very contagious. Hand washing after diaper changing or using the toilet is crucial for keeping everyone in the family from getting diarrhea.

Diaper Rash from Diarrhea. The skin near your baby's anus can become "burned" from the diarrhea stools. Wash it off after each BM and then protect it with a thick layer of petroleum jelly or other ointment. This protection is especially needed during the night and during naps. Changing the diaper quickly after BMs also helps.

Overflow Diarrhea in a Child Not Toilet Trained. For children in diapers, diarrhea can be a mess. Place a cotton washcloth inside the diaper to trap some of the more watery stool. Use disposable suberabsorbent diapers temporarily to cut down on cleanup time. Use the ones with snug leg bands or cover the others with a pair of plastic pants. Wash your child under running water in the bathtub. Someday he will be toilet trained.

 ## CALL OUR OFFICE

IMMEDIATELY if

—Your child does not urinate in more than 8 hours.

—Crying produces no tears.

—The mouth becomes dry rather than moist.

—Any blood appears in the diarrhea.

—Severe abdominal cramps occur.

—The diarrhea becomes severe (such as a bowel movement every hour for more than 8 hours).

—The diarrhea is watery *and* your child vomits the clear fluids three or more times.

—Your child becomes dizzy with standing.

—Your child starts acting very sick.

NOTE: If your child has vomited more than once, treatment of the vomiting has priority over the treatment of diarrhea until your child has gone 8 hours without vomiting.

During regular hours if

—Mucus or pus appears in the stools.

—The diarrhea causes loss of bowel control.

—A fever (over 100° F [37.8° C]) has been present for more than 72 hours.

—The diarrhea does not improve after 48 hours on the special diet.

—Mild diarrhea lasts more than 1 week.

—You have other concerns or questions.

Instructions for Pediatric Patients by Barton D. Schmitt, M.D., *Pediatrician*   © 1992 by W. B. Saunders Company
Adapted from YOUR CHILD'S HEALTH, Copyright © 1991 by Barton D. Schmitt, M.D.
Reprinted by permission of Bantam Books.

DEFINITION

Diagnostic Findings

—Redness of the sclera (white part of the eye)
—Redness of the inner eyelids
—A watery discharge
—No yellow discharge or matting of eyelids
—Not caused by crying or allergy
Also called "bloodshot eyes" or "conjunctivitis."

Causes

Red eyes are usually caused by a viral infection, and they commonly accompany colds. If a bacterial superinfection occurs, the discharge becomes yellow and the eyelids are commonly matted together after sleeping. These children need antibiotic eye drops even if the eyes are not red.

The second most common cause is an irritant in the eye. The irritant can be shampoo, smog, smoke, or chlorine from a swimming pool. More commonly in young kids it comes from touching the eyes with hands carrying dirt, food, or soap.

Expected Course

Viral conjunctivitis usually lasts as long as the cold (4 to 7 days). Red eyes from irritants usually are cured within 4 hours after washing out the irritating substance.

HOME CARE

Washing with Soap. Wash the face, and then wash the eyelids once with soap and water. Rinse them carefully with water. This will remove any irritants.

Irrigating with Water. For viral infections, rinse the eyes with warm water as often as possible, at least every 1 to 2 hours while your child is awake. Use a fresh, wet cotton ball each time. This usually will keep a bacterial infection from occurring. For mild chemical irritants, irrigate the eye with warm water for 5 minutes.

Vasoconstrictor Eye Drops. Viral conjunctivitis is not helped by eye drops.

Red eyes from irritants usually feel much better after the irritant has been washed out. If the eyes remain uncomfortable and bloodshot, instill some long-acting vasoconstrictor eye drops (a nonprescription item). Your

child's eye drops are _____. Use

2 drops every _____ hours as necessary.

CALL OUR OFFICE

IMMEDIATELY if
—The eyelids become red or swollen.
—The vision becomes blurred.

Within 24 hours if
—A yellow discharge develops.
—The eyelids become matted together with pus.
—The redness lasts for more than 7 days.
—You have other concerns or questions.

DEFINITION

Diagnostic Findings

—Yellow discharge in the eye
—Eyelids stuck together with pus, especially after naps
—Dried eye discharge on the upper cheek
—Eyes usually red or pink
Also called "bacterial conjunctivitis," "runny eyes," or "mattery eyes."

NOTE: A small amount of cream-colored mucus in the inner corner of the eyes after sleeping is normal.

Cause

Eye infections with pus are caused by various bacteria and can be a complication of a cold. Red eyes without a yellow discharge, however, are more common and are due to a virus.

Expected Course

With proper treatment, the yellow discharge should clear up in 72 hours. The red eyes (which are due to the cold) may persist for several more days.

HOME TREATMENT

Cleaning the Eye. Before putting in any medicines, remove all the pus from the eye with warm water and wet cotton balls. Unless this is done, the medicine will not have a chance to work.

Antibiotic Eye Drops or Ointments. Bacterial conjunctivitis must be treated with an antibiotic eye medicine. Your child's eye medicine is _____ .

Put in _____ , _____ times each day.

Putting eye drops or ointment in the eyes of younger children can be a real battle. It is most easily done with two people. One person can hold the child still while the other person opens the eyelids with one hand and puts in the medicine with the other. One person can do it alone if she sits on the floor holding the child's head (face up) between the knees to free both hands to put in the medication.

If we have prescribed antibiotic eye drops, put 2 drops in each eye every 2 hours while your child is awake. Do this by gently pulling down on the lower lid and placing the drops there. As soon as the eye drops have been put in the eyes, have your child close them for 2 minutes so the eye drops will stay inside. If it is difficult to separate your child's eyelids, put the eye drops over the inner corner of the eye while he is lying down. As your child opens the eye and blinks, the eye drops will flow in. Continue the eye drops until your child has awakened two mornings in a row without any pus in the eyes.

If we have prescribed antibiotic eye ointment, the ointment needs to be used just four times daily because it can remain in the eyes longer than eye drops. Separate the eyelids and put in a ribbon of ointment from one corner to the other. If it is very difficult to separate your child's eyelids, put the ointment on the lid margins. As it melts, it will flow onto the eyeball and give equally good results. Continue until two mornings have passed without any pus in the eye.

Contagiousness. The pus from the eyes can cause eye infections in other people if they get some of it on their eyes. Therefore it is very important for the sick child to have his own washcloth and towel. He should be encouraged not to touch or rub his eyes, because it can make his infection last longer and it puts many germs on his fingers. Your child's hands should also be washed often to prevent spreading the infection.

 ## CALL OUR OFFICE

IMMEDIATELY if
—The outer eyelids become red or swollen.
—Your child starts acting very sick.

Within 24 hours if
—The infection isn't cleared up in 72 hours.
—Your child develops an earache.
—The eyes become itchy or more red after eye drops are begun.
—You have other concerns or questions.

DEFINITION

Diagnostic Findings

Your child has a fever if his
—Rectal temperature is over 100.4° F (38.0° C).
—Oral temperature is over 99.5° F (37.5° C).
—Axillary (armpit) temperature is over 98.6° F (37° C).

The body's average temperature when it is measured orally is 98.6° F (37° C), but it normally fluctuates during the day. Mild elevation (100.4° to 101.3° F or 38° to 38.5° C) can be caused by exercise, excessive clothing, a hot bath, or hot weather. Warm food or drink can also raise the oral temperature. If you suspect such an effect on the temperature of your child, take his temperature again in one-half hour.

Causes

Fever is a symptom, not a disease. Fever is the body's normal response to infections and plays a role in fighting them. Fever turns on the body's immune system. The usual fevers (100° to 104° F [37.8° to 40° C]) that all children get are not harmful. Most are caused by viral illnesses; some are caused by bacterial illnesses. Teething does not cause fever.

Expected Course

Most fevers with viral illnesses range between 101° and 104° F (38.3° to 40° C) and last for 2 to 3 days. In general, the height of the fever doesn't relate to the seriousness of the illness. How sick your child acts is what counts. Fever causes no permanent harm until it reaches 107° F (41.7° C). Fortunately, the brain's thermostat keeps untreated fevers below this level.

Although all children get fevers, only 4% develop a brief febrile convulsion. Since this type of seizure is generally harmless, it is not worth worrying about, especially if your child has had high fevers without seizures.

HOME CARE

Acetaminophen Products for Reducing Fever. Children older than 2 months of age can be given any one of the acetaminophen products. Tylenol, Anacin-3, Liquiprin, Panadol, and Tempra all have the same dosage.

Remember that fever is helping your child fight the infection. Use drugs only if the fever is over 102° F (39° C) and preferably only if your child is also uncomfortable. Give the correct dosage for your child's age every 4 to 6 hours, but no more often.

Two hours after they are given, these drugs will reduce the fever 2° to 3° F. Medicines do not bring the temperature down to normal unless the temperature was not very elevated before the medicine was given. Repeated dosages of the drugs will be necessary because the fever will go up and down until the illness runs its course. If your child is sleeping, don't awaken him for medicines.

CAUTION: The dropper that comes with one product should not be used with other brands.

Dosages of Acetaminophen. See table below.

Liquid Ibuprofen. Liquid ibuprofen was approved by the U.S. Food and Drug Administration (FDA) in 1989 for treating fever in children 6 months to 12 years old. It is available only by prescription. (Ibuprofen pills, a nonprescription product, have been used for many years to treat menstrual cramps and sports injuries.)

Ibuprofen and acetaminophen are similar in their abilities to lower fever, and their safety records are similar. One advantage that ibuprofen has over acetaminophen is a longer-lasting effect (6 to 8 hours instead of 4 to 6 hours). However, acetaminophen is still the drug of choice for controlling fever in most conditions. Children with special problems requiring a longer period of fever control may do better with ibuprofen.

Cautions about Aspirin. The American Academy of Pediatrics has recommended that children (through 21 years of age) not take aspirin if they have chickenpox or influenza (any cold, cough, or sore throat symptoms).

BRAND	CONCENTRATION	AGE AND DOSAGE							
		2-4 mo	5-11 mo	12-23 mo	2-3 yr	4-5 yr	6-8 yr	9-11 yr	12 yr and older
Acetaminophen drops	80 mg/0.8 ml	0.4 ml	0.8 ml	1.2 ml	1.6 ml	2.4 ml			
Acetaminophen syrup	160 mg/5 ml		½ tsp	¾ tsp	1 tsp	1½ tsp	2 tsp	2½ tsp	4 tsp
Chewable acetaminophen	80 mg tabs			1½ tabs	2 tabs	3 tabs	4 tabs	5-6 tabs	8 tabs
Adult acetaminophen	325 mg tabs						1 tab	1-1½ tabs	2 tabs

mg = milligrams; ml = milliliters; tsp = teaspoon; tabs = tablets.

(Continued on the reverse side)

Instructions for Pediatric Patients by Barton D. Schmitt, M.D., *Pediatrician*
Adapted from YOUR CHILD'S HEALTH, Copyright © 1991 by Barton D. Schmitt, M.D.
Reprinted by permission of Bantam Books.

This recommendation is based on several studies that have linked aspirin to Reye's syndrome, a severe encephalitis-like illness. Most pediatricians have stopped using aspirin for fevers associated with any illness.

On the other hand, aspirin may be a better drug for relief from muscle and bone pains. For such pains not caused by flu use the same dosage of aspirin as given above for acetaminophen.

CAUTION: A hidden source of aspirin that is commonly overlooked is Pepto-Bismol. Don't give your child Pepto-Bismol if he has a fever.

Sponging. Sponging is usually not necessary to reduce fever. Never sponge your child without giving him acetaminophen first. Sponge immediately only in emergencies such as heatstroke, delirium, a seizure from fever, or any fever over 106° F (41.1° C). In other cases sponge your child only if the fever is over 104° F (40° C), the fever stays that high when you take the temperature again 30 minutes after your child has taken acetaminophen, and your child is uncomfortable. Until acetaminophen has taken effect (by resetting the body's thermostat), sponging will just cause shivering, which is the body's attempt to raise the temperature.

If you do sponge your child, sponge him in lukewarm water (85° to 90° F [29° to 32° C]). (Use slightly cooler water for emergencies.) Sponging works much faster than immersion, so sit your child in 2 inches of water and keep wetting the skin surface. If your child shivers, raise the water temperature or wait for the acetaminophen to take effect. Don't expect to get the temperature below 101° F (38.3° C). Don't add rubbing alcohol to the water; it can cause a coma if breathed in.

Extra Fluids. Encourage your child to drink extra fluids, but do not force him to drink. Popsicles and iced drinks are helpful. Body fluids are lost during fevers because of sweating.

Less Clothing. Bundling can be dangerous. Clothing should be kept to a minimum because most heat is lost through the skin. Do not bundle up your child; it will cause a higher fever. During the time your child feels cold or is shivering (the chills), give him a light blanket.

CALL OUR OFFICE

IMMEDIATELY if
—Your child is less than 2 months old.
—The fever is over 105° F (40.6° C).
—Your child is crying inconsolably.
—Your child is difficult to awaken.
—Your child's neck is stiff.
—Any purple spots are present on the skin.
—Breathing is difficult *and* no better after you clear the nose.
—Your child is unable to swallow anything and drooling saliva.
—Your child looks or acts very sick (if possible, check your child's appearance 1 hour after your child has taken acetaminophen).

Within 24 hours if
—Your child is 2 to 4 months old (unless the fever is due to a DPT shot).
—The fever is between 104° and 105° F (40° to 40.6° C; especially if your child is less than 2 years old).
—Burning or pain occurs with urination.
—Your child has had a fever more than 24 hours without an obvious cause or location of infection.

During regular hours if
—Your child has had a fever more than 72 hours.
—The fever went away for more than 24 hours and then returned.
—Your child has a history of febrile seizures.
—You have other concerns or questions.

 Instructions for Pediatric Patients by Barton D. Schmitt, M.D., *Pediatrician*   © 1992 by W. B. Saunders Company
Adapted from YOUR CHILD'S HEALTH, Copyright © 1991 by Barton D. Schmitt, M.D.
Reprinted by permission of Bantam Books.

TAKING THE TEMPERATURE

Obtaining an accurate measurement of your child's temperature requires some practice. If you have questions about this procedure, ask a physician or nurse to demonstrate how it's done and then to observe you doing the same.

Shaking a Glass Thermometer. Shake until the mercury line is below 98.6° F (37° C).

Where to Take the Temperature

—Rectal temperatures are the most accurate. Oral temperatures are also accurate if done properly. Armpit temperatures are the least accurate but are better than no measurement.
—For a child younger than 5 years old a rectal temperature is preferred. An axillary (armpit) temperature is adequate for screening if it is taken correctly. If the armpit temperature is over 98.6° F (37° C), check it by taking the rectal temperature.
—For a child 5 years old or older, take the temperature orally (by mouth).

Taking Rectal Temperatures

—Have your child lie stomach down on your lap.
—Before you insert the thermometer, apply some petroleum jelly to the end of the thermometer and to the opening of the anus.
—Insert the thermometer into the rectum about 1 inch but never force it.
—Hold your child still while the thermometer is in.
—Leave the thermometer in your child's rectum for 2 minutes.

Taking Armpit Temperatures

—Place the tip of the thermometer in a dry armpit.
—Close the armpit by holding the elbow against the chest for 4 or 5 minutes. You may miss detecting a fever if the thermometer is removed before 4 minutes.
—If you're uncertain about the result, check it with a rectal temperature.

Taking Oral Temperatures

—Be sure your child has not taken a cold or hot drink within the last 10 minutes.
—Place the tip of the thermometer under one side of the tongue and toward the back. An accurate temperature depends on proper placement. Ask a physician or nurse to show you where it should go.
—Have your child hold it in place with the lips and fingers (not the teeth) and breathe through the nose, keeping the mouth closed.
—Leave it inside for 3 minutes.
—If your child can't keep his mouth closed because his nose is blocked, suction out the nose.

Reading a Glass Thermometer. Find where the mercury line ends by rotating the thermometer until you can see the mercury.

TYPES OF THERMOMETERS

Glass (with Mercury) Thermometers. This type of thermometer has been the standard since 1870. Although these are the least expensive thermometers, they record the temperature slowly and are often hard to read. If you have difficulty reading a glass thermometer, purchase one with four color zones.

Glass thermometers come in two forms, oral with a thin tip and rectal with a rounder tip. This difference is not too important. If necessary, a rectal thermometer can be used in the mouth and an oral thermometer can be used in the rectum, as long as the thermometer is cleaned with rubbing alcohol and you are extra careful with rectal insertion.

Digital Thermometers. Digital thermometers record temperatures with a heat sensor and run on a button battery. They measure quickly, usually in less than 30 seconds. The temperature is displayed in numbers on a small screen. A study in *Consumer Reports* (January 1988) found they were more accurate than glass thermometers. The same thermometer can be used to take both rectal and oral temperatures. I encourage you to buy one for your family; they cost about $10.00.

Ear Thermometers. Many hospitals and medical offices now take your child's temperature using an infrared thermometer that reads the temperature of the eardrum. In general, the eardrum temperature provides a measurement that is as accurate or more accurate than the rectal temperature. The outstanding advantage of this instrument is that it measures temperatures in less than 2 seconds. It also requires no cooperation by the child and causes no discomfort. An ear thermometer for home use is being developed.

Temperature Strips. Liquid crystal strips applied to the forehead and temperature-sensitive pacifiers have been studied and found to be inaccurate. They do not detect an elevated temperature in most children with fever. Touching the forehead is somewhat reliable for detecting fevers over 102° F (38.9° C) but tends to miss mild fevers.

CONVERSION OF DEGREES FAHRENHEIT (F) TO DEGREES CENTIGRADE (C)

98.6° F = 37.0° C
99.5° F = 37.5° C
100.0° F = 37.8° C
100.4° F = 38.0° C
101.0° F = 38.3° C
102.0° F = 38.9° C
103.0° F = 39.5° C
104.0° F = 40.0° C
105.0° F = 40.6° C
106.0° F = 41.1° C
107.0° F = 41.7° C

Instructions for Pediatric Patients by Barton D. Schmitt, M.D., *Pediatrician*
Adapted from YOUR CHILD'S HEALTH, Copyright © 1991 by Barton D. Schmitt, M.D.
Reprinted by permission of Bantam Books.

© 1992 by W. B. Saunders Company

Some emergency symptoms are either difficult to recognize or are not considered serious by some parents. Most parents will not overlook or underestimate the importance of a major burn, major bleeding, choking, a convulsion, or a coma. However, if your child has any of the following symptoms, also contact our office immediately.

Sick Newborn. If your baby is less than 1 month old and sick in any way, the problem could be serious.

Severe Lethargy. Fatigue during an illness is normal, but watch to see if your child stares into space, won't smile, won't play, is too weak to cry, is floppy, or is hard to awaken. These are serious symptoms.

Severe Pain. If your child cries when you touch or move him or her, this can be a symptom of meningitis. A child with meningitis also doesn't want to be held. Constant screaming or inability to sleep also point to severe pain.

Can't Walk. If your child has learned to walk and then loses the ability to stand or walk, he or she probably has a serious injury to the legs or an acute problem with balance. If your child walks bent over, holding his abdomen, he or she probably has a serious abdominal problem such as appendicitis.

Tender Abdomen. Press on your child's belly while he or she is sitting in your lap and looking at a book. Normally you should be able to press an inch or so in with your fingers in all parts of the belly without resistance. It is significant if your child pushes your hand away or screams. If the belly is also bloated and hard, the condition is even more dangerous.

Tender Testicle or Scrotum. The sudden onset of pain in the groin can be from twisting (torsion) of the testicle. This requires surgery within 8 hours to save the testicle.

Labored Breathing. You should assess your child's breathing after you have cleaned out the nose and when he or she is not coughing. If your child has difficulty in breathing, tight croup, or obvious wheezing, he or she needs to be seen immediately. Other signs of respiratory difficulty are a breathing rate of more than 60 breaths/ minute, bluish lips, or retractions (pulling in between the ribs).

Bluish Lips. Bluish lips or cyanosis can indicate a reduced amount of oxygen in the bloodstream.

Drooling. The sudden onset of drooling or spitting, especially associated with difficulty in swallowing, can mean that your child has a serious infection of the tonsils, throat, or epiglottis (top part of the windpipe).

Dehydration. Dehydration means that your child's body fluids are low. Dehydration usually follows severe vomiting or diarrhea. Suspect dehydration if your child has not urinated in 8 hours; crying produces no tears; the mouth is dry rather than moist; or the soft spot in the skull is sunken. Dehydration requires immediate fluid replacement by mouth or intravenously.

Bulging Soft Spot. If the anterior fontanel is tense and bulging, the brain is under pressure. Since the fontanel normally bulges with crying, assess it when your child is quiet and in an upright position.

Stiff Neck. To test for a stiff neck, lay your child down, then lift the head until the chin touches the middle of the chest. If he or she is resistant, place a toy or other object of interest on the belly so he or she will have to look down to see it. A stiff neck can be an early sign of meningitis.

Injured Neck. Discuss any injury to the neck, regardless of symptoms, with your child's physician because of the risk of damage to the spinal cord.

Purple Spots. Purple or blood-red spots on the skin can be a sign of a serious bloodstream infection, with the exception of explained bruises, of course.

Fever Over 105° F (40.6° C). All the preceding symptoms are stronger indicators of serious illness than the level of fever. All of them can occur with low fevers as well as high ones.

Fevers become strong indicators of serious infection only when the temperature rises above 105° F (40.6° C). In infants a rectal temperature less than 97.5° F (36.5° C) can also be serious.

Instructions for Pediatric Patients by Barton D. Schmitt, M.D., *Pediatrician*

DEFINITION

Average Frequencies of Infections

Some children seem to have the constant sniffles. They get one cold after another. Many a parent wonders, "Isn't my child having too many colds?" Children start to get colds after about 6 months of age. During infancy and the preschool years they average seven or eight colds each year. During the school-age years they average five or six colds each year. During adolescence they finally reach an adult level of approximately four colds per year. Colds account for more than 50% of all acute illnesses with fever.

In addition, children can have diarrheal illnesses (with or without vomiting) two or three times per year. Some children are especially worrisome to their parents because they tend to get high fevers with most of their colds or they have sensitive gastrointestinal (GI) tracts and develop diarrhea with most of their colds.

Similar Condition

If your child is over 3 years of age, sneezes a lot, has a clear nasal discharge that lasts over 1 month, doesn't have a fever, and especially if these symptoms occur during pollen season, your child probably has a nasal allergy.

Causes

The main reason your child is getting all these infections is that he or she is being exposed to new viruses. There are at least 200 cold viruses. The younger the child, the less the previous exposure and subsequent protection. Your child is exposed more if he or she attends day care, play group, a church nursery, or a preschool. Your child has more indirect exposures if he has older siblings in school. Therefore colds are more common in large families. The rate of colds triples in the winter when people spend more time crowded together indoors breathing recirculated air. In addition, smoking in the home increases your child's susceptibility to colds, coughs, ear infections, sinus infections, croup, wheezing, and asthma.

WHAT DOESN'T CAUSE FREQUENT INFECTIONS

Most parents are worried that their repeatedly ill child has some serious underlying disease. A child with immune system disease (inadequate antibody or white blood cell production) doesn't experience any more colds than the average child. Instead, the child has two or more bouts per year of pneumonia, sinus infection, draining lymph nodes, or boils and heals slowly from these infections. In addition, a child with serious disease does not gain weight adequately. Tell us if your family is worried about a particular diagnosis so we can discuss this concern with you. Also, recurrent ear infections don't mean that your child has a serious health problem. They mean only that the eustachian tubes don't drain properly.

Some parents worry that they have in some way neglected their child or done something wrong to cause frequent colds. On the contrary, having all these colds is an unavoidable part of growing up. Colds are the one infection we can't prevent yet. From a medical standpoint, colds are an educational experience for your child's immune system.

DEALING WITH FREQUENT INFECTIONS

Look at Your Child's General Health. If your child is vigorous and gaining weight, you don't have to worry about his or her health. Your child is no sicker than the average child of his or her age. Children get over colds by themselves. Although you can reduce the symptoms, you can't shorten the course of each cold. Your child will muddle through like every other child. The long-term outlook is good. The number of colds will decrease over the years as your child's body builds up a good antibody supply to the various viruses. For perspective, note the findings of a recent survey: on any given day 10% of children have colds, 8% have fevers, 5% have diarrhea, and 3% have ear infections.

Send Your Child Back to School as Soon as Possible. The main requirement for returning your child to school is that the fever is gone and the symptoms are not excessively noisy or distracting to classmates. It doesn't make sense to keep a child home until we can guarantee that he or she is no longer shedding any viruses because this could take 2 or 3 weeks. If isolation for respiratory infections were taken seriously, insufficient days would remain to educate children. Also the "germ warfare" that normally occurs in schools is fairly uncontrollable. Most children shed germs during the first days of their illness before they even look sick or have symptoms. In other words, contact with respiratory infections is unavoidable in group settings such as schools or day care.

Also, as long as your child's fever has cleared, there is no reason he or she cannot attend parties, play with friends after school, and go on scheduled trips. Gym and team sports may need to be postponed for a few days.

Try Not to Miss Work. When both parents work, these repeated colds are extremely inconvenient and costly. Since the complication rate is low and the improvement rate is slow, don't hesitate to leave your child with someone else at these times. Perhaps you have a babysitter who is willing to care for a child with a fever. Because there are so many working mothers these days, "sick child" day-care programs are starting to spring up around the United States and can be another alternative to staying home with your child.

(Continued on the reverse side)

Instructions for Pediatric Patients by Barton D. Schmitt, M.D., *Pediatrician*
Adapted from YOUR CHILD'S HEALTH, Copyright © 1991 by Barton D. Schmitt, M.D.
Reprinted by permission of Bantam Books.

FREQUENT INFECTIONS *Continued*

If your child goes to day care or preschool, he or she can go back once the fever is gone. There is no reason to prolong the recovery at home if you need to return to work. Early return of a child with a respiratory illness won't increase the complication rate for your child or the exposure rate for other children. Likewise, you don't need to cancel an important social engagement because your child has a minor acute illness. In addition, you don't need to take your child out of preschool or day care permanently because of these repeated illnesses.

WHAT DOESN'T HELP

There are no instant cures for recurrent colds and other viral illnesses. Antibiotics are not helpful unless your child develops complications such as an ear infection, sinus infection, or pneumonia. Having your child's tonsils removed is not helpful because colds are not caused by bad tonsils. Colds are not caused by poor diet or lack of vitamins. They are not caused by bad weather, air conditioners, or wet feet. Again, the best time to have these infections and develop immunity is during childhood.

Instructions for Pediatric Patients by Barton D. Schmitt, M.D., *Pediatrician*
Adapted from YOUR CHILD'S HEALTH, Copyright © 1991 by Barton D. Schmitt, M.D.
Reprinted by permission of Bantam Books.

DEFINITION

Diagnostic Findings

—Severe sore throat
—Swollen lymph nodes in the neck, armpits, and groin
—Fever for 7 to 14 days
—Enlarged spleen (in 50% of children)
—Blood smear showing many atypical (unusual) lymphocytes
—Positive blood test for mononucleosis

Cause

Mononucleosis (mono) is caused by the Epstein-Barr virus (EBV). This virus is transmitted in saliva through coughing, sneezing, and kissing. Although mononucleosis can occur at any age, it occurs more often in 15- to 25-year-olds, possibly because of more intimate contacts with others.

Expected Course

Most children have only mild symptoms for 1 week. Even those with severe symptoms usually feel completely well in 2 to 4 weeks. Complications are rare and require hospitalization when they occur. The most common complication is dehydration from not drinking enough fluids. Breathing may be obstructed by enlarged tonsils, adenoids, and other lymph tissue in the back of the throat. On rare occasions, the enlarged spleen will rupture if the abdomen is hit or strained. Because over 90% of youngsters with mononucleosis will develop a severe rash if they receive ampicillin or amoxicillin, these medications should be avoided in this condition.

Chronic Fatigue Syndrome

The symptoms of chronic fatigue syndrome include fatigue, tiredness, weakness, recurrent pains, and the need for more sleep. The symptoms must be present for at least 6 months. There is no good scientific evidence to support mononucleosis as a cause of this syndrome. Recent evidence points to a retrovirus as the cause of chronic fatigue syndrome.

• • •

In general, mononucleosis is neither lingering nor progressive. All symptoms are gone by 4 weeks after they first appeared. Persistent laboratory findings of the Epstein-Barr virus in saliva and antibodies to this virus in the blood have caused some of this confusion. However, 10% to 20% of healthy adults at any given time have the Epstein-Barr virus in their saliva because it periodically reappears without any symptoms. Second, the number of mononucleosis antibodies in the blood increases in response to new infections by other viruses. Neither of these findings means that mononucleosis has recurred.

HOME TREATMENT FOR MONONUCLEOSIS

Fever and Pain Medicines. No specific medicine will cure mononucleosis. However, symptoms can usually be reduced by medicines. The pain of swollen lymph nodes and fever over 102° F (39° C) can usually be relieved by appropriate doses of acetaminophen.

Sore Throat Treatment. Older children can gargle with warm salt water (½ teaspoon of salt per glass) or an antacid solution. Sucking on hard candies also relieves symptoms (butterscotch seems to be a soothing flavor). Since swollen tonsils can make some foods hard to swallow, provide a soft diet as long as necessary. To prevent dehydration, be sure that your youngster drinks enough fluids.

Activity. Your child does not need to stay in bed. Bed rest will not shorten the course of the illness or reduce symptoms. Your child can select how much rest he or she needs. Usually children voluntarily slow down until the fever has resolved. Most children will want to be back to full activity by 2 to 4 weeks.

Precautions for an Enlarged Spleen. A blow to the abdomen can cause rupture of an enlarged spleen and bleeding. This is a surgical emergency. Therefore all children with mononucleosis should avoid contact sports for at least 4 weeks. Athletes especially must restrict their activity until the spleen returns to normal size by physical exam. We will check your child weekly until the spleen size returns to normal. Constipation and heavy lifting should also be avoided because of the sudden pressures they can put on the spleen.

Contagiousness. Infectious mononucleosis is most contagious while your child has a fever. After the fever is gone, the virus is still carried in the saliva for up to 6 months, but in small amounts. Overall, mononucleosis is only slightly contagious from contacts. Boyfriends, girlfriends, roommates, and relatives rarely get it. (The incubation period is 4 to 10 weeks after contact.) The person with mononucleosis does not need to be isolated. However, he or she should definitely use separate glasses and utensils and avoid kissing until the fever has been gone for several days.

 ## CALL OUR OFFICE

IMMEDIATELY if
—Breathing becomes difficult.
—Croup occurs.
—Abdominal pain occurs (especially high on the left).
—Left shoulder pain occurs.
—The skin suddenly becomes pale.

(Continued on the reverse side)

INFECTIOUS MONONUCLEOSIS *Continued*

—Bleeding into the skin occurs.
—Your child starts acting very sick.

Within 24 hours if
—Your child is not drinking enough fluids.
—Swallowing becomes very difficult.
—Sleeping becomes very difficult.

—Sinus or ear pain occurs.
—You feel your child is getting worse.

During regular hours if
—The fever isn't gone within 10 days.
—Your child isn't back to school in 2 weeks.
—Any symptoms remain after 4 weeks.
—You have other questions or concerns.

 Instructions for Pediatric Patients by Barton D. Schmitt, M.D., *Pediatrician* © 1992 by W. B. Saunders Company

DEFINITION

Diagnostic Findings

—Bright red or rosy rash on both cheeks for 1 to 3 days ("slapped cheek" appearance)
—Rash on cheeks is followed by pink "lacelike" (or "net-like") rash on extremities
—"Lacey" rash mainly on thighs and upper arms; comes and goes several times over 1 to 3 weeks
—No fever or low-grade fever (less than 101° F [38.4° C])

Similar Conditions

Fifth disease was so named because it was the fifth pink-red infectious rash to be described by physicians. The other four are

1. Scarlet Fever
2. Measles
3. Rubella
4. Roseola (controversial)

Cause

Fifth disease is caused by the human parvovirus B19.

Expected Course

This is a very mild disease with either no symptoms or a slight runny nose and sore throat. The lacelike rash may come and go for 5 weeks, especially after warm baths, exercise, and sun exposure.

HOME CARE

Treatment. No treatment is necessary. This distinctive rash is harmless and causes no symptoms that need treatment.

Contagiousness. Over 50% of exposed children will come down with the rash in 10 to 14 days. Because the disease is mainly contagious during the week before the rash begins, a child who has the rash is no longer contagious and does not need to stay home from school.

Adults with Fifth Disease. Most adults who get fifth disease develop just a mild pinkness of the cheeks or no rash at all. Adults develop joint pains, especially in the knees, more often than a rash. These pains may last 1 to 3 months. Taking a nonprescription ibuprofen product usually relieves these symptoms. An arthritis workup is not necessary for joint pains that occur after exposure to fifth disease.

Pregnant Women Exposed to Fifth Disease. Recent research showed that 10% of fetuses who are infected with fifth disease before birth develop severe anemia or may even die. This virus, however, doesn't cause any birth defects. If you are pregnant and exposed to a child with fifth disease before the child develops the rash, see your obstetrician. He or she will get a sample of your blood for an antibody test to see if you already had the disease and are protected from becoming infected again. If you do not have antibodies against fifth disease, your pregnancy will need to be monitored closely.

CALL OUR OFFICE

During regular hours if
—The rash becomes itchy.
—Your child develops a fever over 101° F (38.4° C).
—You feel your child is getting worse.
—You have other concerns or questions.

Instructions for Pediatric Patients by Barton D. Schmitt, M.D., *Pediatrician*
Adapted from YOUR CHILD'S HEALTH, Copyright © 1991 by Barton D. Schmitt, M.D.
Reprinted by permission of Bantam Books.

INFLUENZA

DEFINITION

Influenza (flu) is a viral infection of the nose, throat, trachea, and bronchi that occurs in epidemics every 3 or 4 years (for example, Asian influenza). The main symptoms are a stuffy nose, sore throat, and nagging cough. There may be more muscle pain, headache, fever, and chills than with usual colds. For most people, influenza is just a "bad cold." The dangers of influenza for healthy people are overrated.

HOME CARE

The treatment of influenza depends on the child's main symptoms and is no different from the treatment for other viral respiratory infections. Bed rest is unnecessary.

Fever or Aches. Use acetaminophen every 4 to 6 hours. Aspirin should be avoided in children and adolescents with suspected influenza because of the possible link with Reye's syndrome.

Cough or Hoarseness. Give your child cough drops. If your child is 4 years old or younger, give corn syrup.

Sore Throat. Saltwater or antacid solution gargles and a soft diet will help.

Stuffy Nose. Warm-water nose drops and suction (or nose blowing) will open most blocked noses. Vasoconstrictor nose drops or spray may be added for resistant stuffiness.

CALL OUR OFFICE

During regular hours if your child develops any complications such as an earache, sinus pain or pressure, a yellow nasal discharge lasting over 24 hours, a fever lasting over 3 days, or difficulty with breathing.

INFLUENZA VACCINE AND PREVENTION

Influenza vaccine gives protection for only 1 or 2 years. In addition, the vaccine itself can cause fever in 20% of all people and a sore injection site in 10%. Therefore the vaccine is not recommended for healthy children (unless an especially severe form of influenza comes along). Only children with chronic diseases (for example, asthma) need to have yearly influenza boosters. Talk about this with your physician if you think your child should have flu shots.

Instructions for Pediatric Patients by Barton D. Schmitt, M.D., *Pediatrician*
Adapted from YOUR CHILD'S HEALTH, Copyright © 1991 by Barton D. Schmitt, M.D.
Reprinted by permission of Bantam Books.

Lyme disease is the most common disease spread by a tick bite. About 7000 cases are reported each year in the United States. Complications, however, are rare. Giving up picnics, hikes, and camping because of this pest is an overreaction to the small risk. Lyme disease has been divided into three stages. If treated with antibiotics, it does not progress from one stage to the next.

Stage 1 occurs 3 to 32 days after the tick bite. A unique rash develops in 70% to 80% of people. The rash (called erythema migrans) consists of a red ring or bull's-eye that starts where the person was bitten and expands in size. The rash is neither painful nor itchy. It lasts 2 weeks to 2 months. About 50% of children also develop smaller spots at several locations. Some also develop a flulike illness, including fever, chills, sore throat, and headache, for several days.

Stage 2 occurs 2 to 12 weeks after the tick bite. It only affects 15% of untreated patients. The main symptoms are neurologic ones such as stiff neck (aseptic meningitis), weak facial muscles (seventh nerve paralysis), and weakness or numbness of the extremities (polyneuritis). A few children develop some abnormalities of heart rhythm (myocarditis).

Stage 3 occurs 6 weeks to 2 years after the tick bite. It affects about 50% of untreated patients, often without any stage 2 symptoms. The main symptom is recurrent attacks of painful, swollen joints (arthritis), usually of the knees. The arthritis becomes chronic in 10% of children.

CAUSE

Lyme disease is caused by a corkscrew-shaped bacterium called a spirochete. It is transmitted by little deer ticks that are the size of a pinhead, dark brown, and hard to see. Lyme disease is not carried by the more common wood tick which is ¼ to ½ inch in size. In most states only 2% of deer ticks carry Lyme disease. In Wisconsin, Minnesota, and the New England states, however, up to 50% of ticks are infected. If left undisturbed, a tick will remain attached and feed for 3 to 6 days. How long a tick is attached determines the likelihood of passing on the infection. For Lyme disease to be transmitted, the tick needs to be attached for 18 to 24 hours.

TREATMENT

Antibiotics

Lyme disease usually responds to 14 days of oral antibiotics if it is diagnosed during stage 1. If diagnosis is delayed until stage 2 or 3, it may require a month of antibiotics, and these usually need to be given by needle into a muscle or vein. Antibiotics are indicated for any youngster who develops a rash characteristic of Lyme disease within 1 month of receiving a tick bite or being in a high-risk area. Some physicians also begin antibiotics in children without a rash who were definitely bitten by a deer tick, if the tick was attached for more than 18 hours *and* if they live in a highly infected area. Keep in mind that most deer tick bites do not pass on Lyme disease.

Prevention of Tick Bites

Ticks like to hide in underbrush and shrubbery. Children and adults who are hiking in tick-infested areas should wear long clothing and tuck the ends of the pants into the socks. Apply an insect repellent to shoes and socks. During the hike perform tick checks using a buddy system every 2 to 3 hours to remove ticks on the clothing or exposed skin. Immediately after the hike or at least once each day, do a bare skin check. A brisk shower at the end of a hike will also remove any tick that isn't firmly attached. Because the bite is painless and doesn't itch, the child will usually be unaware of its presence. Favorite hiding places for ticks are in the hair so carefully check the scalp, neck, armpit, and groin. Removing ticks promptly may prevent infection because transmission of Lyme disease requires 18 to 24 hours of feeding. Also the tick is easier to remove before it becomes firmly attached. To prevent the spread of Lyme disease from your dog, wash him with an antitick soap during the spring and summer months. Perform tick checks on him if he accompanies you on a hike. Pull off any that are found.

Tick Removal

The simplest and quickest way to remove a tick is to pull it off. Use a tweezers to grasp the tick as close to the skin as possible. (Try to get a grip on its head.) Apply a steady upward traction until it releases its grip. Do not twist the tick or jerk it suddenly, thus breaking off its head or mouth parts. Do not squeeze the tweezers to the point of crushing the tick, because the secretions released may spread disease. If you don't have a tweezers, pull the tick off in the same way using your fingers, a loop of thread around the tick's jaws, or a needle between the tick's jaws for traction. Some tiny ticks need to be scraped off with a knife blade or the edge of a credit card.

If the body is removed but the head is left in the skin it must be removed. Use a sterile needle (as you would to remove a sliver). Dispose of the tick by returning it to nature or flushing it down the toilet. You don't need to save the tick for positive identification by your physician; physicians have seen more than their share of ticks. If you are unsure if it's a dog or a deer tick, measure it but don't save it. Don't crush ticks with your fingers, since this practice increases your chance of getting a

(Continued on the reverse side)

disease. Wash the wound and your hands with soap and water after removal.

A recent study showed that embedded ticks do not back out when covered with petroleum jelly, fingernail polish, or rubbing alcohol. We used to think that this would block the tick's breathing pores and take its mind off eating. Unfortunately, ticks breathe only a few times per hour. The study also found that the application of a hot match to the tick failed to cause it to detach and also carried the risk of inducing the tick to vomit infected secretions into the wound.

CALL OUR OFFICE

IMMEDIATELY if
—You can't remove the tick.
—The tick's head remains embedded.

During regular hours if
—You think your child has some of the symptoms of Lyme disease.
—You think your child has been bitten by a deer tick and it was probably attached for more than 18 hours. (**NOTE**: You do not need to call us if your child was bitten by a tick and it was removed promptly.)

 Instructions for Pediatric Patients by Barton D. Schmitt, M.D., *Pediatrician*

DEFINITION

Diagnostic Findings

—3 or 4 days of red eyes, cough, runny nose, and fever before the rash begins
—Pronounced blotchy red rash starting on the face and spreading downward over the entire body in 3 days
—White specks on the lining of the mouth (Koplik's spots)
—Exposure to a child with measles 10 to 12 days earlier

Cause

The measles virus

Expected Course

Measles can be a miserable illness. The rash usually lasts 7 days. Your child will usually begin to feel a lot better by the fourth day of the rash. Ear and eye infections are common complications.

HOME CARE

Treatment

—Fever: Use acetaminophen in the usual dosage for your child's age.
—Cough: Use corn syrup for children less than 1 year old, honey for children 1 to 4 years old, or cough drops for children over 4 years old. If the cough interferes with sleep, give a cough suppressant such as dextromethorphan (DM). Also, use a humidifier.
—Red eyes: Wipe your child's eyes frequently with a clean, wet cotton ball. The eyes are usually sensitive to bright light, so your child probably won't want to go outside for several days unless he wears sunglasses.
—Rash: The rash requires no treatment.

Contagiousness. The disease is no longer contagious after the rash is gone. This usually takes 7 days.

Measles Exposure. Any child or adult who has been exposed to your child and who has not had measles or the measles vaccine should call his physician. If given early, a measles vaccine is often protective.

CALL OUR OFFICE

IMMEDIATELY if
—Breathing becomes labored *and* no better after you clear the nose.
—Your child becomes confused or delirious.
—Your child becomes hard to awaken completely.
—Your child develops a severe headache.
—Your child starts acting very sick.

Within 24 hours if
—Your child develops an earache.
—The eyes develop a yellow discharge.
—The nasal discharge becomes yellow and stays yellow for more than 24 hours.
—The fever is still present on the fourth day of the rash.
—Fever returns after the temperature has been normal for more than 24 hours.
—You have other concerns or questions.

MUMPS

DEFINITION

Diagnostic Findings

—Swollen parotid gland in front of the ear and crossing the corner of the jaw
—Both parotid glands swollen in 70% of children
—Tenderness of the swollen gland
—Pain increased with chewing
—Fever over 100° F is present
—No prior mumps vaccine
—Exposure to another child with mumps 16 to 18 days earlier (adds weight to the diagnosis)

Cause

Mumps is an acute viral infection of the parotid, a gland that produces saliva and is located in front of and below each ear.

Expected Course

The fever is usually gone in 3 to 4 days. The swelling and pain are cleared in 7 days.

HOME CARE

Pain and Fever Relief. Give acetaminophen. Cold compresses applied to the swollen area may also relieve pain.

Diet

—Avoid sour foods or citrus fruits that increase saliva production and parotid swelling.
—Avoid foods that require much chewing.
—Consider a liquid diet if chewing is very painful.

Contagiousness. The disease is contagious until the swelling is gone (usually 6 or 7 days). Your child should be kept out of school and away from other children who have not had mumps or mumps vaccine.

Mumps Exposure. Mumps exposure is important if a person has never received the mumps vaccine or had mumps, but only 10% of adults are really susceptible. Adults who as children lived in the same household with siblings who had mumps can be considered protected. Those who are not protected should call our office during office hours to see if the mumps vaccine would be helpful and should use the following guidelines:
—Children: All should receive the mumps vaccine.
—Adolescent or adult males: The mumps vaccine is optional. (The risk of testicular infection [orchitis] is 2.5%.)
—Adult females: The mumps vaccine is unnecessary. No serious complications occur.

CALL OUR OFFICE

IMMEDIATELY if
—Your child develops a stiff neck or severe headache.
—Your child vomits repeatedly.
—Your child starts acting very sick.

During regular hours if
—The swelling lasts for 8 days or more.
—The fever lasts for 5 days or more.
—The skin over the mumps gland becomes reddened.
—In adolescent males, the testicle becomes painful.
—You have other concerns or questions.

Instructions for Pediatric Patients by Barton D. Schmitt, M.D., *Pediatrician*
Adapted from YOUR CHILD'S HEALTH, Copyright © 1991 by Barton D. Schmitt, M.D.
Reprinted by permission of Bantam Books.

DEFINITION

Diagnostic Findings

—Labored breathing (respiratory distress)
—Rapid breathing
—Occasionally painful breathing
—Coughing
—Fever, sometimes with chills
—Abnormal patch on chest x-ray film

NOTE: Most rattly breathing is not pneumonia.

Causes

Pneumonia is an infection of the lung that causes fluid to collect in the air sacs (alveoli). Approximately 80% of pneumonia cases are caused by viruses and 20% by bacteria. Viral pneumonia is usually milder than bacterial pneumonia. Bacterial pneumonia tends to have a more abrupt onset, higher fevers (often over 104° F), and a larger infiltrate (greater lung involvement) visible on the chest x-ray film. Only bacterial pneumonia is helped by antibiotics. Because it's difficult to distinguish bacterial from viral pneumonia in all cases, antibiotics are prescribed for some of the children with viral pneumonia. Because pneumonia is usually a complication of a cold, it is not considered contagious.

Expected Course

Before antibiotics were available, bacterial pneumonia was dangerous. With antibiotics, it improves within 24 to 48 hours. On the other hand, viral pneumonia can continue for 2 to 4 weeks. Most children with pneumonia can be cared for at home. Admission to the hospital for oxygen or intravenous fluids is required in less than 10% of cases. Most children admitted to the hospital are young infants or children who have extensive involvement of the lungs. Recovery from viral pneumonia is gradual but complete. Recurrences of pneumonia are rare.

HOME TREATMENT FOR PNEUMONIA

Antibiotics. Children with bacterial pneumonia need an antibiotic. Your child's antibiotic is

_____. Give _____

every _____ hours. Continue the antibiotic for

a full _____ days.

Medicines for Fever. Use acetaminophen for moderate fever (over 102° F). This can be repeated every 4 to 6 hours.

Acetaminophen can also help chest pain.

Warm Fluids for Coughing Spasms. Coughing spasms are often caused by sticky secretions in the back of the throat. Warm liquids usually relax the airway and loosen the secretions. Offer your child warm lemonade or apple juice. In addition, breathing warm moist air helps to loosen the sticky mucus that may be choking your child. You can provide warm mist by placing a warm, wet, washcloth loosely over your child's nose and mouth; or you can fill a humidifier with warm water and have your child breathe in the warm mist it produces. Avoid steam vaporizers because they can cause burns. Don't give cough suppressant medicines (such as those containing dextromethorphan) to children with pneumonia. The infectious secretions need to be coughed up.

Humidity. Dry air tends to make coughs worse. Use a humidifier in your child's bedroom. The new ultrasonic humidifiers not only have the advantage of quietness, but also kill molds and most bacteria that might be in the water.

No Smoking. Tobacco smoke aggravates coughing and makes coughs last longer. Don't let anyone smoke around your child. In fact, try not to let anybody smoke inside your home. Remind a teenager with pneumonia, if he or she smokes, that the cough will last weeks longer than it normally would without smoking.

CALL OUR OFFICE

IMMEDIATELY if
—Breathing becomes more labored.
—Breathing becomes more difficult.
—Retractions (tugging between the ribs) become worse.
—The lips become bluish.
—Grunting sounds occur when your child pushes the air out.
—Your child starts acting very sick.

Within 24 hours if
—Your child is unable to sleep.
—Your child is not drinking enough fluids.
—The fever lasts over 48 hours on an antibiotic.
—You feel your child is getting worse.

During regular hours if
—The cough lasts over 3 weeks.
—You have other questions or concerns.

PREVENTION OF INFECTIONS

Public health methods have had the greatest impact in preventing the spread of infectious diseases. Proper sewage disposal and safe water supplies have largely eliminated epidemics such as typhoid fever and cholera. Immunizations and vaccinations constitute the other aspect of modern medicine that has controlled infectious diseases such as smallpox and polio.

Precautions within the home can limit the spread of gastrointestinal illnesses. Unfortunately, controlling the spread of colds, coughs, and sore throats within a family unit is impractical.

HOW INFECTIOUS DISEASES ARE SPREAD

—Nose, mouth, and eye secretions are the most common sources of respiratory infections. These secretions are usually spread by contaminated hands or occasionally by kissing. Toddlers are especially prone to spreading these infections because of their habits of touching or mouthing everything.
—Droplet spread from coughing or sneezing is a less common means of transmission of respiratory infections. Droplets can travel up to 6 feet.
—Fecal contamination of hands or other objects accounts for the spread of most diarrhea, as well as infectious hepatitis. Unlike urine, which is usually sterile, bowel movements are composed of up to 50% bacteria.
—The discharge from sores such as chickenpox and fever blisters can be contagious. However, most red rashes without a discharge are not contagious by skin contact.
—Contaminated food or water accounted for many epidemics in earlier times. Even today some foods frequently contain bacteria that cause diarrhea. (For example, 50% of raw turkey or chicken contains *Campylobacter* or *Salmonella* organisms. By contrast, only 1% of raw eggs are contaminated with *Salmonella* organisms.)
—Contaminated utensils such as bottles and dishes can occasionally be a source of respiratory or intestinal infections.
—Contaminated objects such as combs, brushes, and hats can lead to the spread of lice, ringworm, or impetigo.

PREVENTION OR REDUCTION OF SPREAD OF INFECTIOUS DISEASES

The following preventive actions can help reduce the spread of disease within your household.

Encourage Hand Washing. Hand washing helps to prevent the spread of gastrointestinal infections more than all other approaches combined. Rinsing your hands vigorously with plain water is probably as effective as using soap and water. Hand washing is especially important after using the toilet, changing diapers, and coming in contact with turtles or aquarium water. Choose a day-care center where the staff practices good hand washing after changing diapers. Young children must be supervised in their use of toilets and sinks. Recent studies have found that hand washing is also the mainstay in preventing the spread of respiratory disease. (Wash the hands after blowing or touching the nose.)

Discourage Habits of Touching the Mouth and Nose. Again, this advice is helpful in preventing the spread of respiratory infections to others. Also, touching the eyes after touching the nose is a common cause of eye infections.

Don't Smoke around Your Children. Passive smoking increases the frequency and severity of colds, coughs, croup, ear infections, and asthma.

Discourage Your Child from Kissing Pets. Pets (especially puppies) can transmit bloody diarrhea, worms, and other things. Pets are for petting.

Cook All Poultry Thoroughly. Undercooked poultry is a common cause of diarrhea. If the poultry is frozen, thaw it in the refrigerator rather than at room temperature to prevent multiplication of the bacteria. After preparation, carefully wash your hands and any object that comes in contact with raw poultry (such as the knife and cutting board) before using them with other foods. Never serve chicken that is still pink inside (a common problem with outdoor grilling). Don't place the cooked meat on the same platter that the uncooked meat was removed from.

Use a Plastic Cutting Board. Germs can't be completely removed from wooden cutting boards.

Avoid Eating Raw Eggs. Don't undercook your eggs. If you make your own eggnog or ice cream, use pasteurized eggs.

Choose a Small Day-care Home over a Day-care Center. Day care provided in private homes has a lower rate of infectious disease. Children who are cared for in their own homes by babysitters have the lowest rate of infection. Since colds have more complications during the first year of life, try to arrange for home-based day care if you child is in this age group.

Clean Contaminated Areas with Disinfectants. These products kill most bacteria, including *Staphylococcus* organisms. Disinfecting the diaper-changing area, cribs, strollers, play equipment, and food service items limits intestinal diseases at home and in day-care centers.

Contact our Office if Your Child is Exposed to Meningitis or Hepatitis. Antibiotics can prevent some types of bacterial meningitis in exposed children under 4 years of age. An injection of gamma globulin helps to prevent hepatitis in children who have had intimate contact (longer than 4 hours) with someone with this disease.

Keep Your Child's Immunizations Up-to-date

Don't Attempt to Isolate Your Child. Isolation is mentioned last because its value within a family unit is questionable. By the time a child shows symptoms, he or she has already shared the germs with the family. Also, isolation at home is impossible to enforce.

Instructions for Pediatric Patients by Barton D. Schmitt, M.D., *Pediatrician*
Adapted from YOUR CHILD'S HEALTH, Copyright © 1991 by Barton D. Schmitt, M.D.
Reprinted by permission of Bantam Books.

DEFINITION

Diagnostic Findings

—Age 6 months to 3 years
—Presence of a fine pink rash, mainly on the trunk
—High fever during the preceding 2 to 4 days that cleared within 24 hours before the rash appeared
—Child only mildly ill during the time with fever
—Child acting fine now

Cause

Roseola is caused by the human herpesvirus-6.

Expected Course

The rash lasts 1 or 2 days, followed by complete recovery. Some children have 3 days of fever without a rash.

HOME CARE

No particular treatment is necessary. Roseola is contagious until the rash is gone. Other children of this age who have been with your child may come down with roseola in about 12 days.

 ## CALL OUR OFFICE

IMMEDIATELY if
—The spots become purple or blood colored.

During regular hours if
—The rash lasts more than 3 days.
—The rash becomes itchy.
—Any new symptoms develop that concern you.

Instructions for Pediatric Patients by Barton D. Schmitt, M.D., *Pediatrician*
Adapted from YOUR CHILD'S HEALTH, Copyright © 1991 by Barton D. Schmitt, M.D.
Reprinted by permission of Bantam Books.

RUBELLA (GERMAN MEASLES)

DEFINITION

Diagnostic Findings

—Widespread pink-red spots
—Rash beginning on the face and moving rapidly downward, covering the body in 24 hours
—Lasts 3 to 4 days ("3-day measles")
—Enlarged lymph nodes at back of neck
—Mild fever
—Child never given the rubella vaccine

The rash with rubella is not distinctive. Many other viral rashes look like it. Physicians have difficulty being certain of this diagnosis even after examining the child. Don't try to make this diagnosis at home unless there is an epidemic of it in your community.

Cause

Rubella is caused by a virus. The incubation period is 14 to 21 days.

Expected Course

The disease is mild. Your child should be completely recovered in 3 or 4 days. Complications in general are very rare. However, complications to the unborn child are disastrous and include deafness, cataracts, heart defects, growth retardation, and encephalitis. Pregnant women should avoid anyone with suspected rubella.

HOME CARE

If we have determined that your child probably has rubella, the following may be helpful:

Treatment. No treatment is probably necessary. Give acetaminophen for fever over 102° F (38.9° C), sore throat, or other pains.

Avoid Pregnant Women. If your child might have rubella, keep him away from any pregnant women. He is contagious for 5 days after the start of the rash.

Exposure of Adult Women to Rubella. The nonpregnant woman exposed to rubella should avoid pregnancy during the following 3 months.

A pregnant woman exposed to rubella should see her obstetrician. If she has already received the rubella vaccine, she (and her unborn child) are probably protected. Even if she thinks she had the German measles disease as a child and the present exposure was minor or brief, she should have a blood test to determine her immunity against rubella.

Rubella Vaccine. Get your children immunized against rubella at 15 months of age so we won't have to worry about pregnant women getting exposed to rubella when a child gets a pink or red rash. It's quite safe to immunize the child who has a pregnant mother.

CALL OUR OFFICE

IMMEDIATELY if
—The rash becomes purple.
—Your child starts acting very sick.

During regular hours if
—The rash becomes itchy.
—The fever lasts more than 3 days.
—You have other concerns or questions.

Instructions for Pediatric Patients by Barton D. Schmitt, M.D., *Pediatrician*
Adapted from YOUR CHILD'S HEALTH, Copyright © 1991 by Barton D. Schmitt, M.D.
Reprinted by permission of Bantam Books.

DEFINITION

Diagnostic Findings

—Reddened, sunburned-looking skin (especially of the chest and abdomen)
—Increased redness in skin folds (especially the groin, armpits, and elbow creases)
—Full-blown rash within 24 hours
—Rough feeling of reddened skin, somewhat like sandpaper
—Flushed face with paleness around the mouth
—Sore throat and fever (usually preceding the rash by 18 to 24 hours)

Cause

Scarlet fever is a strep throat infection with a rash. The complication rate is no different than the complication rate for strep throat alone. The rash is caused by a special rash-producing toxin that is present in some strep bacteria.

Expected Course

The red rash usually clears in 4 or 5 days. Sometimes the skin peels in 1 to 2 weeks where the rash was most prominent (for example, the groin). The skin on the fingertips also commonly peels. Your child will stop having a sore throat and fever after 1 or 2 days of taking penicillin.

HOME TREATMENT

Antibiotics. Your child's antibiotic is penicillin.

Your child's dose is _____ three times daily during waking hours (that is, before breakfast, midafternoon, and at bedtime) for 10 days.

Try not to forget any doses. If your child goes to school or a babysitter, arrange for someone to give the midafternoon dose. Give the medicine until all the pills are gone or the bottle is empty. Even though your child will feel better in a few days, give the antibiotic for 10 days to keep the strep throat from flaring up again.

If the medicine is a liquid, store it in the refrigerator. Use a measuring spoon to be sure that you give the right amount.

A long-acting penicillin (Bicillin) injection can be given if your child will not take oral medicines or if it will be impossible for you to give the medicine regularly. (**NOTE:** If given correctly, the oral penicillin works just as rapidly and effectively as a shot.)

Contagiousness. Your child is no longer contagious after he or she has been on an antibiotic for 24 hours. Therefore your child can return to school after one day if he or she is feeling better. The rash itself is not contagious.

Throat Cultures for the Family. Scarlet fever and strep throat can spread to others in the family. Any child or adult who lives in your home and has a fever, sore throat, runny nose, headache, vomiting, or sores; or who doesn't want to eat; or who develops these symptoms in the next 5 days should be brought in for a throat culture. In most homes we need to culture only those who are sick. We will call you if any of the cultures are positive for strep. (**EXCEPTION:** In families where relatives have had rheumatic fever or frequent strep infections, everyone should have a throat culture.)

Follow-up Visit. Repeat throat cultures are not necessary if your child takes all of the antibiotic.

CALL OUR OFFICE

IMMEDIATELY if
—Your child develops drooling or great difficulty in swallowing.
—The urine becomes red or cola colored.
—Your child starts acting very sick.

During regular hours if
—The fever lasts over 48 hours after your child starts taking penicillin.
—You have other concerns or questions.

Instructions for Pediatric Patients by Barton D. Schmitt, M.D., *Pediatrician*
Adapted from YOUR CHILD'S HEALTH, Copyright © 1991 by Barton D. Schmitt, M.D.
Reprinted by permission of Bantam Books.

© 1992 by W. B. Saunders Company

DEFINITION

A sinus infection is a bacterial infection of one of the seven sinuses that normally drain into the nose. Sinus congestion can occur without an infection if one of the sinus openings becomes blocked from a cold or hay fever. As bacteria multiply within the sinuses, pain and pressure occur above the eyebrow, behind the eye, or over the cheekbone. Other symptoms include a yellow nasal discharge, postnasal drip, fever, and bad breath. Until recent years, we didn't recognize that a chronic cough can be caused by a sinus infection. Swallowing sinus secretions is normal and harmless but may lead to some nausea. The following treatment should reduce pain and fever within 48 hours or less.

HOME TREATMENT

Antibiotics.   Your child's antibiotic is _____ .

Your child's dose is _____ given

_____ times per day by mouth during waking hours

for _____ days.

This medicine will kill bacteria that are causing the sinus infection. Try not to forget any of the doses. If your child goes to school or to a babysitter, arrange for someone to give the afternoon dose. If the medicine is a liquid, use a measuring spoon so you give the right amount. Also, an antibiotic should not be saved from one illness to the next because it loses its strength. Even though your child will feel better in a few days, give all the medicine to prevent the infection from flaring up.

Decongestant Nose Drops or Spray.   To drain the sinuses, use a generic, long-acting vasoconstrictor nose drop or spray (such as oxymetazoline), which is nonprescription. The usual dose for adolescents is 2 drops or sprays per nostril twice daily. For younger children use 1 drop or spray each day. Use the medicine routinely for the first 3 days of treatment. Thereafter don't use the spray or nose drops unless the sinus congestion or pain recurs. Stop the drops or spray for 2 days out of every 7 days to prevent rebound swelling.

Oral Antihistamines.   If your child also has hay fever, give him or her allergy medicine. Otherwise, avoid antihistamines because they can slow down the movement of secretions out of the sinuses.

Pain Relief Medicines.   Acetaminophen can be given for a few days for sinus pain or any fever over 102° F (39° C).

Contagiousness.   Sinus infections are not contagious. Your child can return to school or day care when he or she is feeling better and the fever is gone.

CALL OUR OFFICE

IMMEDIATELY if
—Redness or swelling occurs on the cheek, eyelid, or forehead.

Within 24 hours if
—The fever or pain is not gone after your child has taken the antibiotic for 48 hours.
—The yellow nasal discharge is not gone after 5 days.
—You feel that your child is getting worse.

    Instructions for Pediatric Patients by Barton D. Schmitt, M.D., *Pediatrician*

DEFINITION

Diagnostic Findings

—The child complains of a sore throat.
—In children too young to talk, a sore throat may be suspected if they refuse to eat or begin to cry during feedings.
—When examined with a light, the throat is bright red.

Cause

Most sore throats are caused by viruses and are part of a cold. About 10% of sore throats are due to the strep bacteria. A throat culture or rapid strep test is the only way to distinguish strep pharyngitis from viral pharyngitis. Without treatment, a strep throat can have some rare but serious complications. Tonsillitis (temporary swelling and redness of the tonsils) is usually present with any throat infection, viral or bacterial. The presence of tonsillitis does not have any special meaning.

Children who sleep with their mouths open often wake in the morning with a dry mouth and sore throat. It clears within an hour of having something to drink. Use a humidifier to help prevent this problem. Children with a postnasal drip from draining sinuses often have a sore throat from frequent throat clearing.

Expected Course

Sore throats with viral illnesses usually last 3 or 4 days. Strep throat responds well to penicillin. After taking the medication for 24 hours, your child is no longer contagious and can return to day care or school if the fever is gone and he's feeling better.

CALL OUR OFFICE

IMMEDIATELY if
—The pain is severe.
—Your child is drooling, spitting, or having great difficulty in swallowing.
—Your child can't fully open his mouth.
—Breathing is difficult *and* is not due to a stuffy nose.
—Your child is acting very sick.

During regular hours
—To make an appointment for a throat culture for any other child with a sore throat.

EXCEPTION: If the sore throat is very mild *and* the main symptom is croup, hoarseness, or a cough, a throat culture is probably not needed. Throat cultures are recommended for all other sore throats because a resurgence of acute rheumatic fever began in 1987. Rheumatic fever is a complication of strep infections that can lead to permanent damage to the valves of the heart.

HOME CARE

Local Pain Relief. Children over 8 years of age can gargle with warm salt water (¼ teaspoon of salt per glass) or an antacid solution. Children over 4 years of age can suck on hard candy (butterscotch seems to be a soothing flavor) as often as necessary. Younger children can be given 1 teaspoon of corn syrup periodically to soothe the throat. Swollen tonsils can make some foods hard to swallow. Provide your child with a soft diet for a few days if he prefers it.

Fever. Acetaminophen may be given for a few days if your child has a fever over 102° F (39° C) or a great deal of throat discomfort.

Common Mistakes in Treating Sore Throat

—Avoid expensive throat sprays or throat lozenges. Not only are they no more effective than hard candy, but also many contain an ingredient (benzocaine) that may cause a drug reaction.
—Avoid using leftover antibiotics from siblings or friends. These should be thrown out because they deteriorate faster than other drugs. Unfortunately, antibiotics only help strep throats. They have no effect on viruses, and they can cause harm. They also make it difficult to find out what is wrong if your child becomes sicker.

Rapid Strep Tests. Rapid strep tests are helpful only when their results are positive. If they are negative, a throat culture should be performed to pick up the 20% of strep infections that the rapid tests miss. Avoid rapid strep tests performed in shopping malls or at home because they tend to be inaccurate.

CALL OUR OFFICE

Later if
—A sunburned-looking rash appears.
—Breathing or swallowing becomes difficult.
—A fever lasts more than 3 days.

Instructions for Pediatric Patients by Barton D. Schmitt, M.D., *Pediatrician*
Adapted from YOUR CHILD'S HEALTH, Copyright © 1991 by Barton D. Schmitt, M.D.
Reprinted by permission of Bantam Books.

STREP THROAT INFECTION

DEFINITION

Your child has a strep throat infection diagnosed by a throat culture or rapid strep slide test. The treatment of strep throats can prevent some rare but serious complications, namely, rheumatic fever (heart disease) or glomerulonephritis (kidney disease). In addition, treatment usually eliminates the fever and much of the sore throat within 24 hours.

HOME TREATMENT

Antibiotics. Your child's antibiotic is penicillin.

Your child's dose is _____ given three times each day during waking hours (that is, before breakfast, midafternoon, and at bedtime) for _____ days.

Try not to forget any doses. If your child goes to school or a babysitter, arrange for someone to give the midafternoon dose. If the medicine is a liquid, store the antibiotic in the refrigerator and use a measuring spoon to be sure that you give the right amount. Give the medicine until all the pills are gone or the bottle is empty. Even though your child will feel better in a few days, give the antibiotic for 10 days to keep the strep throat from flaring up.

A long-acting penicillin (Bicillin) injection can be given if your child refuses oral medicines or if it will be impossible for you to give the oral medicine regularly. (**NOTE:** If given correctly, the oral penicillin works just as rapidly and effectively as a shot.)

Local Pain Relief. Older children can gargle with warm saltwater (¼ teaspoon of salt per glass) or suck on hard candy (butterscotch seems to be a soothing flavor).

Younger children can be given 1 teaspoon of corn syrup periodically to soothe the throat. Since swollen tonsils can make some foods hard to swallow, provide your child with a soft diet for a few days. Acetaminophen may be given if your child has a fever over 102° F (39° C) or a great deal of throat discomfort.

Contagiousness. Your child is no longer contagious after he or she has taken the antibiotic for 24 hours. Therefore your child can return to school after one day if he or she is feeling better.

Throat Cultures for the Family. Strep throat can spread to others in the family. Any child or adult who lives in your home and has a fever, sore throat, runny nose, headache, vomiting, or sores; doesn't want to eat; or develops these symptoms in the next 5 days should be brought in for a throat culture. In most homes we need to culture only those who are sick. We will call you if any of these cultures are positive for strep. (**EXCEPTION:** In families where relatives have had rheumatic fever or frequent strep infections, everyone should come in for a throat culture.)

Follow-up Visit. Repeat cultures are unnecessary if your child receives all of the antibiotic.

 ## CALL OUR OFFICE

IMMEDIATELY if
—Your child develops drooling.
—Your child develops great difficulty with swallowing.
—The fever lasts for over 48 hours after starting penicillin.
—You feel your child is getting worse.

86   Instructions for Pediatric Patients by Barton D. Schmitt, M.D., *Pediatrician*   © 1992 by W. B. Saunders Company

DEFINITION

Diagnostic Findings

—Itchy and painful ear canals
—Currently engaged in swimming
—Pain when the earlobe is moved up and down
—Pain when the tab of the earlobe overlying the ear canal is pushed in
—A feeling that the ear is plugged up
—Slight, clear discharge initially; without treatment, it becomes yellowish

Cause

Swimmer's ear is an infection of the skin lining the ear canal. When water gets trapped in the ear canal the lining becomes swollen and prone to infection. Ear canals were meant to be dry. Children are more likely to get swimmer's ear from swimming pools than from lakes. The chlorine in pools kills all the good bacteria in the ear canal, and harmful bacteria tend to take over.

Expected Course

With treatment, symptoms should be better in 3 days.

HOME TREATMENT

Antibiotic Ear Drops. Your child's ear drops are

_____ . Put in _____ drops

_____ times each day.

Run the ear drops down the side of the ear, opening and moving the ear, so that air isn't trapped under them.

Continue the ear drops until all the symptoms are cleared up for 48 hours. Use acetaminophen for pain relief.

Generally, your child should not swim until the symptoms are gone. If he is on a swim team, he may continue but should use the ear drops as a rinse after each session.

Prevention. The key to prevention is keeping the ear canals dry when your child is not swimming. After swimming, get all water out of the ear canals by turning the head to the side and pulling the earlobe in different directions to help the water run out. Dry the opening to the ear canal carefully. If recurrences are a big problem, rinse your child's ear canals with rubbing alcohol for 1 minute each time he finishes swimming or bathing.

Common Mistakes. Don't use earplugs of any kind for prevention or treatment. They tend to jam ear wax back into the ear canal. Also, they don't keep all water out of the ear canals. Cotton swabs also shouldn't be inserted in ear canals. Wax buildup traps water behind it and increases the risk of swimmer's ear. A rubbing alcohol mixture is helpful for preventing swimmer's ear but not for treating it because it would sting too much.

 ## CALL OUR OFFICE

During regular hours if
—The symptoms are not cleared up in 3 days.
—The pain becomes worse after 24 hours of treatment.
—A fever (over 100° F [37.8° C]) occurs.
—The ear becomes severely painful.
—The lymph node behind the earlobe becomes swollen and tender.
—You have other concerns or questions.

Instructions for Pediatric Patients by Barton D. Schmitt, M.D., *Pediatrician*
Adapted from YOUR CHILD'S HEALTH, Copyright © 1991 by Barton D. Schmitt, M.D.
Reprinted by permission of Bantam Books.

© 1992 by W. B. Saunders Company

URINARY TRACT INFECTION

DEFINITION

A urinary tract infection (UTI) is an infection of the bladder (cystitis) and sometimes the kidneys (pyelonephritis). It is important to treat UTIs so that the kidneys are not damaged.

Diagnostic Findings

Various symptoms are possible:
—Painful urination
—Bladder frequency or urgency
—Daytime and nighttime wetting
—Dribbling
—Foul-smelling urine
—Fever
—Stomachaches
—Vomiting

Cause

Urinary tract infections are caused by bacteria. The bacteria enter the bladder by traveling up the urethra. In general, the urethra is protected, but if the opening of the urethra (or the vulva in girls) is irritated, bacteria can grow there. Common irritants are bubble bath, shampoo, or fecal soiling. A rare cause of UTIs (1% in girls and 5% in boys) is obstruction of the urinary tract that leads to incomplete emptying of the bladder.

HOME TREATMENT

Antibiotics.   Your child's antibiotic is _____ .

Your child's dose is _____ given _____ times per day during waking hours for _____ days. This medicine will kill the bacteria that are causing the UTI.

If the medicine is liquid, store it in the refrigerator and shake the bottle well before measuring each dose. Use a measuring spoon to be sure that you give the right amount.

Try not to forget any of the doses. If your child goes to school or a babysitter, arrange for someone to give the afternoon dose. Give the medicine until all the pills are gone or the bottle is empty. Even though your child will feel better in a few days, give the antibiotic for the full 10 days to keep the UTI from flaring up.

Extra Fluids.   Encourage your child to drink extra fluids to help clear the infection.

Fever and Pain Relief.   Acetaminophen may be given if your child develops a fever over 102° F (39° C) or if urination is quite painful.

Medical Follow-up.   Two days after your child begins antibiotics, it is important to contact us to find out the results of the urine culture and make sure that your child's symptoms are responding to the antibiotic.

Two weeks after your initial visit we will want to see your child for another urine culture. Because the chances are high that your daughter will develop a second infection (occurs in 50% of cases), we would like to recheck the urine at the following times: 1, 4, and 12 months after the first infection is cleared up.

Instructions for Collecting a Midstream, Clean-catch Urine Specimen at Home.   If you are told to bring in a urine sample, try to collect the first one in the morning. Use a sterile jar.

Wash off the genital area several times with cotton balls and warm water. Have your child then sit on the toilet seat with her legs spread widely so that the labia (skin folds of the vagina) don't touch. Have her start to urinate into the toilet, and then place the clean container directly in line with the urine stream. Remove it after you have collected a few ounces but before she stops. The first or last ounce that comes out of the bladder may be contaminated.

Keep the urine in the refrigerator until you take it to the office. Bring it in chilled (for example, put the jar in a plastic bag with some ice).

PREVENTION OF UTIs

—Wash the genital area with water, not soap.
—Don't put bubble bath, shampoo, or other soaps into the bath water. Don't let a bar of soap float around in the tub.
—Keep bath time less than 15 minutes. Have your child urinate after baths.
—Teach your daughter to wipe herself correctly from front to back, especially after a bowel movement.
—Try not to let your child become constipated.
—Encourage her to drink enough fluids each day to keep the urine light colored.
—Encourage her to urinate at least every 3 to 4 hours during the day and not "hold back."
—Have her wear loose cotton underpants. Discourage wearing underpants at night.

CALL OUR OFFICE

IMMEDIATELY if
—Fever or painful urination is not gone after your child has taken the antibiotic for 48 hours.
—Your child is able to pass only very small amounts of urine.
—The urine becomes bloody.
—Your child starts acting very sick
Within 24 hours if
—Your child refuses to take the antibiotic.
—Your child gets worse while taking the medicine.
—You have other concerns or questions.

   Instructions for Pediatric Patients by Barton D. Schmitt, M.D., *Pediatrician*

DEFINITION

Diagnostic Findings

—Discomfort with passing urine (dysuria)
—Burning or stinging with passing urine
—Urgency, frequency, and straining are occasionally present

Cause

The most common cause of mild pain or burning with urination in young girls is an irritation of the vulva (vulvitis) and the opening of the urethra (urethritis). The irritation is usually caused by bubble bath, shampoo, or soap that was left on the genital area. Occasionally, it is due to poor hygiene. This chemical urethritis occurs almost exclusively before puberty. However, since 5% of young girls get urinary tract infections (UTIs), one must always consider this diagnosis. A UTI is a bacterial infection of the bladder (cystitis) and sometimes the kidneys.

Expected Course of Bubble Bath (Chemical) Urethritis

With warm soaks, the pain and burning usually clear in 12 hours.

HOME CARE

Warm Vinegar-water Soaks. Have your daughter soak her bottom in a basin or bathtub of warm water for 20 minutes. Put ½ cup of white vinegar in the water. Be sure she spreads her legs and allows the water to cleanse the genital area. No soap should be used. Repeat this once in 2 hours and again in 12 hours. This will remove any soap, concentrated urine, or other chemicals from the genital area. Thereafter, cleanse the genital area once daily with warm water.

Prevention of Recurrences of Pain with Urination

—Wash the genital area with water. Don't wash the genitals with soap until after puberty.
—Don't use bubble bath or put any other soaps or shampoo into the bath water. Don't let a bar of soap float in the bathtub. If you are going to shampoo your child's hair, do this at the end of the bath.
—Keep bath time less than 15 minutes. Have your child urinate immediately after baths.

—Teach your daughter to wipe herself correctly from front to back, especially after a bowel movement.
—Encourage her to drink enough fluids each day to keep the urine light colored.
—Encourage her to urinate at least every 4 hours during the day.
—Sexually active young women should urinate after sexual intercourse.
—Have her wear cotton underpants. Underpants made of synthetic fibers (polyester or nylon) don't allow the skin to "breathe." Discourage wearing underpants at night.

Instructions for Collecting a Midstream, Clean-catch Urine Specimen at Home. If you are told to bring in a urine sample, try to collect the first one in the morning. Use a jar and lid that have been sterilized by boiling them for 10 minutes.

Wash off the genital area several times with cotton balls and warm water. Have your child then sit on the toilet seat with her legs spread widely so that the labia (skin folds of the vagina) don't touch. Have her start to urinate into the toilet, and then place the clean container directly in line with the urine stream. Remove it after you have collected a few ounces but before she stops urinating. The first or last ounce that comes out of the bladder may be contaminated.

Keep the urine in the refrigerator until you take it to the office. Put the jar in a plastic bag with some ice when you bring it in.

CALL OUR OFFICE

IMMEDIATELY if
—The pain with urination becomes severe.
—Your child develops a high fever (over 104° F [40° C]) or chills.
—Any abdominal or back pain occurs.
—Your child can only pass very small amounts of urine.
—The urine becomes bloody or cola colored.
—Your child starts acting very sick.

During regular hours if
—The pain and burning continue for more than 12 hours after a warm vinegar-water soak.
—Your child develops any fever (over 100° F [37.8° C]).
—Day or night wetting begins to occur.
—You have other concerns or questions.

Instructions for Pediatric Patients by Barton D. Schmitt, M.D., *Pediatrician*
Adapted from YOUR CHILD'S HEALTH, Copyright © 1991 by Barton D. Schmitt, M.D.
Reprinted by permission of Bantam Books.

DEFINITION

Diagnostic Findings

Vomiting is the forceful ejection of a large portion of the stomach's contents through the mouth. The mechanism is strong stomach contractions against a closed stomach outlet. By contrast, regurgitation is the effortless spitting up of one or two mouthfuls of stomach contents that is commonly seen in babies under 1 year of age.

Cause

Most vomiting is caused by a viral infection of the stomach or eating something that disagrees with your child. Often, the viral type is associated with diarrhea.

Expected Course

The vomiting usually stops in 6 to 24 hours. Dietary changes usually speed recovery.

HOME CARE FOR VOMITING

Special Diet for Vomiting

No Solids for 8 Hours

Clear Fluids for 8 Hours. Offer child clear fluids (not milk) in small amounts until 8 hours have passed without vomiting. For vomiting without any diarrhea, the best clear fluid at any age is water. For infants you can also use one of the new oral electrolyte solutions (such as Pedialyte, Resol, or Ricelyte). After this age, soft drinks (cola, lemon-lime, or ginger ale) are also acceptable. Stir until no fizz remains (the bubbles inflate the stomach and increase the chances of continued vomiting).

Start with 1 teaspoon to 1 tablespoon, depending on age, every 10 minutes. Double the amount each hour. If your child vomits using this treatment, rest the stomach completely for 1 hour and then start over but with smaller amounts. The one-swallow-at-a-time approach rarely fails.

Bland Foods after 8 Hours without Vomiting. After 8 hours without vomiting, your child can gradually return to a normal diet.

For older children, start with foods such as saltine crackers, honey on white bread, bland soups (for example, "chicken with stars") rice, and mashed potatoes.

For babies, start with foods such as applesauce, strained bananas, and rice cereal. If your baby only takes formula, give 1 or 2 ounces less per feeding than usual.

Usually your child can be back on a normal diet within 24 hours after recovery from vomiting.

Diet for Breast-fed Babies. The key to treatment is providing breast milk in smaller amounts than usual. If your baby has only vomited once or twice, continue breast-feeding but nurse on only one side each time for 10 minutes. After 8 hours have passed since your baby last vomited, return to both sides.

If vomiting occurs three or more times, put your baby on water or an oral electrolyte solution. As soon as 4 hours elapse without vomiting, return to nursing, but again with smaller than usual amounts for 8 hours.

Medicines. Discontinue all medicines for 8 hours. Oral medicines can irritate the stomach and make vomiting worse. If your child has a fever over 102° F (38.9° C), use acetaminophen suppositories. Call our office if your child needs to be taking a prescription medicine.

Common Mistakes in Treatment of Vomiting. A common error is to give as much clear fluid as your child wants rather than gradually increasing the amount. This almost always leads to continued vomiting. Keep in mind that there is no effective drug or suppository for vomiting and that diet therapy is the answer. Vomiting alone rarely causes dehydration unless you give drugs by mouth, milk, or too much clear fluid.

 ## CALL OUR OFFICE

IMMEDIATELY if
—Your child develops diarrhea and vomits clear fluids three or more times.
—Your child does not urinate in more than 8 hours.
—Crying produces no tears.
—Any blood appears in the vomited material *and* it's not from a recent nosebleed.
—Abdominal pain develops and lasts for more than 4 hours.
—Your child becomes difficult to awaken or confused.
—Poisoning with a plant, bad food, medicine, or other chemical becomes a possibility.
—Your child starts acting very sick.

During regular hours if
—The vomiting continues for more than: 12 hours in children under 6 months old, for more than 24 hours in children 6 months to 2 years old, or for more than 48 hours in children over 2 years old.
—You have other concerns or questions.

Instructions for Pediatric Patients by Barton D. Schmitt, M.D., *Pediatrician*
Adapted from YOUR CHILD'S HEALTH, Copyright © 1991 by Barton D. Schmitt, M.D.
Reprinted by permission of Bantam Books.

PART 5

PEDIATRIC DERMATOLOGY

DEFINITION

Diagnostic Findings

—Blackheads, whiteheads (pimples), or red bumps
—Face, neck, and shoulders involved
—Adolescent and young adult years
—Larger red lumps quite painful

Cause

Acne is due to an overactivity and plugging of the oil glands. More than 90% of teenagers have some acne. The main cause of acne is increased levels of hormones during adolescence. It is not caused by diet, and it is unnecessary to restrict fried foods, chocolate, or any other food. Acne is not caused by sexual activity of any kind, nor by dirt or not washing the face often enough. The tops of blackheads are black because of the chemical reaction of the oil plug with the air.

Expected Course

Acne usually lasts until 20 or 25 years of age. It is rare for acne to leave any scars, and people worry needlessly about this.

HOME CARE

There is no magic medicine at this time that will cure acne. However, good skin care can keep acne under control and at a mild level.

Basic Treatment for All Acne

—Soap: The skin should be washed twice each day, the most important time being at bedtime. A mild soap such as Dove should be used.
—Hair: The hair should be shampooed daily. Hair can make acne worse by friction if it is too long.
—Avoid picking. This keeps acne from healing.

Additional Treatment for Pimples.
Pimples are infected oil glands. They should be treated with the following:
—Benzoyl peroxide 5% lotion or gel. This lotion helps to open pimples and unplug blackheads, and it also kills bacteria. It is available without a prescription. Ask your pharmacist to recommend a brand. The lotion should be applied daily at bedtime. In redheads and blonds it should be applied every other day initially. An amount the size of a pea should cover most of the face. If the skin becomes red or peels, you are using too much of the medicine or applying it too often, so slow down. This lotion may be needed for several years.
—Pimple opening: In general, it is better not to "pop" pimples, but teenagers do it anyway. Therefore do

it safely. Never open a pimple before it has come to a head. Wash your face and hands first. Use a sterile needle (sterilized by alcohol or a flame). Nick the surface of the yellow pimple with the tip of the needle. The pus should run out without squeezing. Wipe away the pus and wash the area with soap and water. Scarring will not result from opening small pimples, but it can result from squeezing boils or other large, red, tender lumps.

Additional Treatment for Blackheads (Comedones).
Blackheads are the plugs found in blocked-off oil glands. They should be treated with the following:
—Benzoyl peroxide: This agent is also excellent for removing thickened skin that blocks the openings to oil glands. It should be used as described above for additional treatment for pimples.
—Blackhead extractor: Blackheads that are a cosmetic problem can sometimes be removed with a blackhead extractor. This instrument costs about one dollar and is available at any drugstore. By placing the hole in the end of the small metal spoon directly over the blackhead, uniform pressure can be applied that does not hurt normal skin. This method is much more efficient than anything you can accomplish with your fingers. Soak your face with a warm washcloth before you try to remove blackheads. If the blackhead does not come out the first time, leave it alone.

Common Mistakes in Treating Acne

—Avoid scrubbing the skin. Hard scrubbing of the skin is harmful because it irritates the openings of the oil glands and can cause them to be more tightly closed.
—Avoid applying any oily or greasy substances to the face. They make acne worse by blocking off oil glands. If you must use cover-up cosmetics, use water-based ones and wash them off at bedtime.
—Avoid hair tonics or hair creams (especially greasy ones). With sweating, these will spread to the face and aggravate the acne.

CALL OUR OFFICE

During regular hours if
—A boil develops on the face.
—Several large, tender, red lumps appear.
—Acne is not improved after treating it with benzoyl peroxide for 2 months.
—Benzoyl peroxide makes the face itchy or swollen.
—You have other concerns or questions.

Instructions for Pediatric Patients by Barton D. Schmitt, M.D., *Pediatrician*
Adapted from YOUR CHILD'S HEALTH, Copyright © 1991 by Barton D. Schmitt, M.D.
Reprinted by permission of Bantam Books.

ATHLETE'S FOOT (TINEA PEDIS)

DEFINITION

Diagnostic Findings

—A red, scaly, cracked rash between the toes
—Itchy, burning rash
—Rash raw and weepy with scratching
—Often spreads to instep
—Unpleasant foot odor
—Mainly occurs in adolescents

Cause

A fungus infection that grows best on warm, damp skin

Expected Course

With proper treatment, it usually clears in 2 to 3 weeks.

HOME CARE

Antifungal Cream. Buy Tinactin or Micatin lotion at your drugstore. You won't need a prescription. First rinse the feet in plain water or water with a little white vinegar added. Dry the feet carefully, especially between the toes. Then apply the cream to the rash area and well beyond its borders twice a day. Continue Tinactin or Micatin for several weeks or for at least 7 days after the rash seems to have cleared.

Dryness. Athlete's foot improves dramatically if the feet are kept dry. It helps to go barefoot or wear sandals or thongs as much as possible. Wear shoes that allow the feet to breathe. Cotton socks should be worn because they absorb sweat and keep the feet dry. Change the socks twice daily. Dry the feet thoroughly after baths and showers.

Foot Odor. Foot odor will often clear as the athlete's foot improves. Rinsing the feet and changing the socks twice daily are essential. If you can still smell your child coming, take off his tennis shoes and wash them in your washing machine with some soap and bleach.

Discourage Scratching. Scratching infected feet will delay a cure.

Contagiousness. The condition is not very contagious. The fungus won't grow on dry, normal skin. Your child may take physical education and continue with sports.

 ## CALL OUR OFFICE

During regular hours if
—The athlete's foot is not improved in 1 week.
—It is not completely cured after using this treatment for 4 weeks.
—Pus starts draining from the rash.
—You have other concerns or questions.

 Instructions for Pediatric Patients by Barton D. Schmitt, M.D., *Pediatrician*
Adapted from YOUR CHILD'S HEALTH, Copyright © 1991 by Barton D. Schmitt, M.D.
Reprinted by permission of Bantam Books.

DEFINITION

Diagnostic Findings

—Tender, red lump in skin
—Causes pain even when not being touched
—Usually ½ to 1 inch across

Cause

A bacterial infection of a hair root or skin pore caused by *Staphylococcus* organisms.

Expected Course

Without treatment, the body will wall off the infection. After about 1 week, the center of the boil becomes soft and mushy (filled with pus). The overlying skin then develops a pimple or becomes thin and pale. The boil is now ready for draining. Without lancing, it will drain by itself in 3 or 4 days. Until it drains, a boil is extremely painful.

HOME TREATMENT

Antibiotics. Boils heal faster and are less likely to recur if your child receives an antibiotic that kills *Staphyloccocus* bacteria. Your child's antibiotic is

_____. Your child's dosage is

_____ given _____ times each day for

_____ days.

Lancing or Draining the Boil. In general, it's better not to open a boil on your own child because it's a very painful procedure. Until the abscess comes to a head or becomes soft, apply warm compresses three times daily for 20 minutes. When the boil is ready, contact our office. If you must open it yourself, use a sterile needle (sterilized with alcohol or a flame), make a large opening, and squeeze very gently or not at all. Once opened, it will drain pus for 2 or 3 days and then heal. Since the pus is contagious, the boil must be covered by a large 4-inch × 4-inch piece of gauze and microporous tape. This bandage should be changed and the area washed with an antiseptic soap (for example, Dial or Safeguard) three times daily.

Prevention of More Boils. Boils can easily become a recurrent problem. The *Staphylococcus* bacteria on the skin can be decreased by showering and washing the hair daily with an antibacterial soap. Showers are preferred because during a bath, bacteria are just relocated to other parts of the skin.

Contagiousness. Boils are contagious. Be certain that other people in your family do not use your child's towel or washcloth. Any clothes, towels, or sheets that are contaminated with drainage from the boils should be washed with Lysol. Any bandages with pus on them should be carefully thrown away.

Common Mistakes in Treatment of Boils. Sometimes friends or relatives may advise you to squeeze a boil until you get the core out. The pus in a boil will come out easily if the opening is large enough. Vigorous squeezing is not only very painful but also entails the risk of forcing bacteria into the bloodstream or causing other boils in the same area. Again, squeezing should be done very gently or not at all (as on the face).

 ## CALL OUR OFFICE

IMMEDIATELY if
—Your child develops an unexplained fever (over 100° F [37.8° C]).
—A spreading red streak runs from the boil.
—Your child starts acting very sick.

During regular hours if
—The boil has come to a head and needs to be opened.
—Your child develops more boils.
—You have other concerns or questions.

Instructions for Pediatric Patients by Barton D. Schmitt, M.D., *Pediatrician*
Adapted from YOUR CHILD'S HEALTH, Copyright © 1991 by Barton D. Schmitt, M.D.
Reprinted by permission of Bantam Books.

© 1992 by W. B. Saunders Company

DEFINITION

Dry skin is mainly caused by removing the skin's natural oils through too much bathing and soap. Dry climates make it worse, as does winter weather ("winter itch"). The problem is less common in teenagers because their oil glands are more active. Dry, rough, bumpy skin on the back of the upper arms is called keratosis pilaris. Dry, pale spots on the face are called pityriasis alba. Both are complications of scrubbing dry skin with soap. The dry areas are often itchy, and this is the main symptom.

Cracked skin most commonly occurs on the soles of the feet, especially the heels and big toes (called juvenile plantar dermatosis). Deep cracks are painful and periodically bleed. The main cause is wearing wet shoes and socks or swimming a lot. Cracks can also develop on the hands in children who frequently wash dishes or suck their thumbs. The lips can become cracked (chapped) in children with a habit of licking their lips or from excessive exposure to sun or wind.

HOME CARE

Soap and Bathing. For children with dry skin, avoid all soaps. Have your child bathe or shower with plain water—perhaps twice weekly. Avoid soaps, detergents, and bubble baths.

Teenagers can get by with applying soap only to the armpits, genitals, and feet. Buy a special soap for dry skin (such as Dove). Rinse well. Don't let a bar of soap float in the tub. Use no soap on itchy areas. Don't lather up (the outer arms are often affected for this reason).

Lubricating Cream. Buy a large bottle of lubricating cream (special hand lotion). Apply the cream to any dry or itchy areas several times daily, especially after bathing. You will probably have to continue this throughout the winter. If the itch persists after 4 days, use ½% hydrocortisone cream (nonprescription) temporarily.

Humidifier. If your winters are dry, run a room humidifier. The presence of static electricity means your home is much too dry. During cold weather, have your child wear gloves outside to protect against the rapid evaporation of moisture from the hands.

Bath Oils. It does not make much sense to pour bath oils into the bathwater; most of the oil goes down the drain. It also makes the bathtub slippery and dangerous. If you prefer a bath oil over hand lotion, apply it immediately after baths. Baby oil (mineral oil) is inexpensive and keeps the skin moisture from evaporating.

Healing Cracked Skin. Even deep cracks of many years' duration can be healed in about 2 weeks if they are constantly covered with an ointment (such as petroleum jelly). If the crack seems mildly infected, use Bacitracin ointment (no prescription needed). Covering the ointment with a Band-Aid, socks, or gloves speeds recovery even more. For chapped lips, a lip balm can be applied frequently.

 ## CALL OUR OFFICE

During regular hours if
—No improvement occurs within 2 weeks.
—The cracks develop a yellow discharge.
—You have other concerns or questions.

 Instructions for Pediatric Patients by Barton D. Schmitt, M.D., *Pediatrician*
Adapted from YOUR CHILD'S HEALTH, Copyright © 1991 by Barton D. Schmitt, M.D.
Reprinted by permission of Bantam Books.

DEFINITION

Diagnostic Findings

—Red, extremely itchy rash
—Often starts on the cheeks at 2 to 6 months of age
—Most common on flexor surfaces (creases) of elbows, wrists, and knees
—Occasionally, neck, ankles, and feet involved
—Rash raw and weepy if scratched
—Constant dry skin
—Previous confirmation of diagnosis by physician is helpful

Cause

Eczema is an inherited type of sensitive skin. A personal history of asthma or hay fever or a family history of eczema makes it more likely that your child has eczema. Flare-ups occur when there is contact with irritating substances (for example, soap or chlorine).

In 30% of infants with eczema, certain foods cause the eczema to flare up. If you suspect a particular food item (for example, cow's milk, eggs, or peanut butter) is causing your child's flare-ups, feed that food to your child one time (a "challenge") after avoiding it for 2 weeks. If it does cause flare-ups, the eczema should become itchy or develop hives within 2 hours of ingestion. If this occurs, avoid ever giving this food to your child and talk to us about food substitutes.

Expected Course

This is a chronic condition and will usually not go away before adolescence. Therefore early treatment of any itching is the key to preventing a severe rash.

HOME TREATMENT

Steroid Creams. Steroid cream is the main treatment for eczema. Your child's cream is ———————— .

Apply this cream ———— times daily when the eczema flares up. When the rash quiets down, use it at least once daily for an additional 2 weeks. After that, use it immediately on any spot that itches. When you travel with your child, always take the steroid cream with you. If your supply starts to run out, get the prescription renewed.

Bathing and Hydrating the Skin. Your child should have one bath each day for 10 minutes. Water-soaked skin is far less itchy. Eczema is very sensitive to soaps. Young children can usually be cleaned without any soap. Teenagers need a soap to wash under the arms, the genital area, and the feet. They can use a nondrying soap such as Dove for these areas. Keep shampoo off the eczema.

Lubricating Cream. Children with eczema always have dry skin. After a 10-minute bath, the skin is hydrated and feels good. Help trap the moisture in the skin by applying an outer layer of cream to the entire skin surface while it is damp. Apply it after steroid cream has been applied to any itchy areas. Apply the lubricating cream once daily (twice daily during the winter). Some lubricating creams are Keri, Lubriderm, Nivea, and Nutraderm. Avoid applying any ointments, petroleum jelly, or vegetable shortening because they can block the sweat glands, increase itching, and worsen the rash. Also, soap is needed to wash them off. For severe eczema, ointments may be needed temporarily to heal the skin.

Itching. At the first sign of any itching, apply the steroid cream to the area that itches. Keep your child's fingernails cut short. Also, wash your child's hands with water frequently to avoid infecting the eczema.

Prevention. Wool fibers and clothes made of other scratchy, rough materials make eczema worse. Cotton clothes should be worn as much as possible. Avoid triggers that cause eczema to flare up, such as excessive heat, sweating, excessive cold, dry air (use a humidifier), chlorine, harsh chemicals, and soaps. Never use bubble bath. Also, keep your child off the grass during grass pollen season (May and June). Keep your child away from anyone with fever blisters since the herpes virus can cause a serious skin infection in children with eczema. Try to breast-feed all high-risk infants. Also avoid cow's milk products, soy, eggs, peanut butter, wheat, and fish during the first year of life.

 ## CALL OUR OFFICE

IMMEDIATELY if
—The rash appears to be infected and your child has a fever.
—The rash flares up after contact with someone with fever blisters (herpes).

Within 24 hours if
—The rash becomes raw and bleeding in several places.
—The rash becomes infected, as evidenced by pus or soft yellow scabs.

During regular hours if
—The rash hasn't greatly improved after 7 days of using this treatment.
—The itching interferes with sleep.
—You have other concerns or questions.

Instructions for Pediatric Patients by Barton D. Schmitt, M.D., *Pediatrician*
Adapted from YOUR CHILD'S HEALTH, Copyright © 1991 by Barton D. Schmitt, M.D.
Reprinted by permission of Bantam Books.

© 1992 by W. B. Saunders Company

FINGERNAIL INFECTION (PARONYCHIA)

DEFINITION

Diagnostic Findings

—A large pimple at the junction of the cuticle and the fingernail
—Redness and tenderness of this area
—Occasionally, pus draining from this area

Cause

A paronychia is usually infected with the *Staphylococcus* bacteria. The cause is usually a break in the skin resulting from pulling on or chewing on the cuticle. Thumb sucking may also contribute.

Expected Course

With proper treatment, this infection should clear up in 7 days. If not, your physician will probably prescribe an oral antibiotic.

HOME TREATMENT

Antiseptic Soaks. Soak the infected finger three times daily for 10 minutes in a warm 1:120 bleach so-lution with a little liquid soap added. This antiseptic solution is made by adding 1 tablespoon of bleach to 2 quarts of water. Do this for 4 days or longer if the wound has not healed.

Antibiotic Ointments. Apply an antibiotic ointment six times daily. Your child's ointment is _____.

Prevention. Discourage any picking or chewing of hangnails (loose pieces of cuticle). Instead, cut these off with nail clippers.

 CALL OUR OFFICE

IMMEDIATELY if
—Fever or chills develop.
—A red streak spreads beyond the cuticle.
—The finger pad becomes swollen and tender.

During regular hours if
—The infection is not improved by 48 hours on home treatment.
—The infection is not totally cleared up by 7 days.
—You have other concerns or questions.

Instructions for Pediatric Patients by Barton D. Schmitt, M.D., *Pediatrician*   © 1992 by W. B. Saunders Company
Adapted from YOUR CHILD'S HEALTH, Copyright © 1991 by Barton D. Schmitt, M.D.
Reprinted by permission of Bantam Books.

HAND, FOOT, AND MOUTH DISEASE

DEFINITION

Diagnostic Findings

—Small ulcers in the mouth
—A mildly painful mouth
—Small water blisters or red spots located on the palms and soles and between the fingers and toes
—Five or fewer blisters per extremity
—Sometimes, small blisters or red spots on the buttocks
—Low-grade fever (over 100° F [37.8° C])
—Mainly occurs in children 6 months to 4 years of age

Cause

Hand, foot, and mouth disease is always caused by a Coxsackie A virus. It has no relationship to hoof and mouth disease of cattle.

Expected Course

The fever and discomfort are usually gone by day 3 or 4. The mouth ulcers resolve in 7 days, but the rash on the hands and feet can last 10 days. The only complication seen with any frequency is dehydration from refusing fluids.

HOME CARE

Diet. Avoid giving your child citrus, salty, or spicy foods. Also avoid foods that need much chewing. Change to a soft diet for a few days and encourage plenty of clear fluids. Cold drinks, Popsicles, and sherbert are often well received. Have your child rinse the mouth with warm water after meals.

Fever. Acetaminophen may be given for a few days if the fever is above 102° F (39° C).

Contagiousness. Hand, foot, and mouth disease is quite contagious and usually some of your child's playmates will develop it at about the same time. The incubation period after contact is 3 to 6 days. Because the spread of infection is extremely difficult to prevent and the condition is harmless, these children do not need to be isolated. They can return to school when the fever returns to normal range.

CALL OUR OFFICE

IMMEDIATELY if
—Your child has not urinated for more than 8 hours.
—The neck becomes stiff.
—Your child becomes confused or delirious.
—Your child becomes hard to awaken completely.
—Your child starts acting very sick.

During regular hours if
—Your child is not drinking much.
—The fever lasts more than 3 days.
—The mouth pain becomes severe.
—The gums become red, swollen, or tender.
—You feel your child is getting worse.
—You have other concerns or questions.

HIVES (URTICARIA)

DEFINITION

Diagnostic Findings

—Very itchy rash
—Raised pink spots with pale centers (Hives look like mosquito bites.)
—Size range of ½ inch to several inches across
—Shapes quite variable
—Rapid and repeated changes of location, size, and shape

Cause

Hives are an allergic reaction to a food, drug, viral infection, insect bite, or a host of other substances. Usually the cause is not found. Hives are not contagious.

Expected Course

More than 10% of children get hives. Most children who develop hives have it only once. The hives come and go for 3 or 4 days and then mysteriously disappear.

HOME TREATMENT

Antihistamine Medicine. The best drug for hives is an antihistamine. An antihistamine won't cure the hives, but it will reduce their number and relieve itching. Benadryl, one of the most commonly used drugs for hives, has recently become available without prescription. The main side effect of this drug is drowsiness. If you have another antihistamine (for example, any drug for hay fever) at home, use it until you can get some Benadryl. Give Benadryl four times daily in the following dosages:

	CHILD'S WEIGHT (LB)					
	20	40	60	80	100	120
Benadryl liquid, 12.5 mg/5 ml	3 ml	6 ml	10 ml	13 ml	16 ml	20 ml
Benadryl tablets (25 mg)	—	—	1	1	1½	2

Your child's drug is _____.

Give _____ every _____ hours. Continue the medicine until the hives are completely gone for 24 hours.

A cool bath will also make your child feel better. In the meantime, avoid anything you think might have brought on the hives.

Common Mistakes in Treatment of Hives. Many parents wait to give the antihistamine until new hives have appeared. This means your child will become itchy again. The purpose of the medicine is to keep your child comfortable until the hives go away. Therefore give the medicine regularly until you are sure the hives are completely gone. Since hives are not contagious, your child can be with other children.

CALL OUR OFFICE

IMMEDIATELY if
—Breathing or swallowing becomes difficult.
—The tongue becomes swollen.
—Any abdominal pain occurs.
—Your child starts acting very sick.

During regular hours if
—Most of the itch is not relieved after your child has been taking the medicine for 24 hours.
—The hives last more than 1 week.
—A fever (over 100° F [37.8° C]) occurs.
—Joint swelling or pain occurs.
—You have other concerns or questions.

Instructions for Pediatric Patients by Barton D. Schmitt, M.D., *Pediatrician*
Adapted from YOUR CHILD'S HEALTH, Copyright © 1991 by Barton D. Schmitt, M.D.
Reprinted by permission of Bantam Books.

A bite involves biting with the insect's mouth parts and removing a drop of blood from the human. A sting involves injecting a poison into the human from the insect's stinger. The following three types of bites or stings are covered:
—Bee stings
—Itchy or painful bites
—Tick bites

1. BEE STINGS

DEFINITION

Your child was stung by a honeybee, bumblebee, hornet, wasp, or yellow jacket. Over 95% are from yellow jackets. These stings cause immediate painful red bumps. Although the pain is usually better in 2 hours, the swelling may increase for up to 24 hours. Multiple stings (more than 10) can cause vomiting, diarrhea, a headache, and fever. This is a toxic reaction related to the amount of venom received (that is, not an allergic reaction). A sting on the tongue can cause swelling that interferes with breathing.

CALL OUR OFFICE

IMMEDIATELY if
—Breathing or swallowing is difficult.
—Hives are present.
—There are 10 or more stings.
—A sting occurs inside the mouth.

HOME CARE

Treatment. If you see a little black dot in the bite, the stinger is still present (this only occurs with honeybee stings). Remove it by scraping it off. If only a small fragment remains, use tweezers or a sterile needle just as you would to remove a sliver. Then rub each sting for 15 minutes with a cotton ball soaked in a meat tenderizer solution. This will neutralize the venom and relieve the pain. If meat tenderizer is not available, apply an ice cube while you obtain some.

Prevention. Some bee stings can also be prevented by avoiding gardens and orchards and by not going barefoot. Insect repellents are not effective against these stinging insects.

CALL OUR OFFICE

Later if
—You can't remove the stinger.
—The swelling continues to spread after 24 hours.
—Swelling of the hand (or foot) spreads past the wrist (or ankle).
—You want a nurse or physician to look at the sting.

2. ITCHY OR PAINFUL INSECT BITES

DEFINITION

Bites of mosquitoes, chiggers, fleas, and bedbugs usually cause itchy, red bumps. The size of the swelling can vary from a dot to 1 cm (½ inch). The larger size does not mean that your child is allergic to the insect bite. Mosquito bites near the eye always cause massive swelling. The following are clues that a bite is due to a mosquito: itchiness, a central raised dot in the swelling, bites on surfaces not covered by clothing, summertime, and the age of the child (that is, he is an infant). In contrast to mosquitoes, fleas and bedbugs don't fly; therefore, they crawl under clothing to nibble. Flea bites often turn into little blisters in young children.

Bites of horseflies, deerflies, gnats, fire ants, harvester ants, blister beetles, and centipedes usually cause a painful, red bump. Within a few hours, fire ant bites change to blisters or pimples.

HOME CARE

Itchy Insect Bites. Apply calamine lotion or a baking soda solution to the area of the bite. If the itch is severe (as with chiggers), apply nonprescription ½% hydrocortisone cream. Another way to reduce the itch is to apply firm, sharp, direct, steady pressure to the bite for 10 seconds. A fingernail, pen cap, or other object can be used. Encourage your child not to pick at the bites or they will leave marks.

Painful Insect Bites. Rub the area of the bite with a cotton ball soaked in meat tenderizer solution. This will relieve the pain. If you don't have any meat tenderizer, ammonia is a fair substitute. If these substances are not available, an ice cube may help.

PREVENTION

Mosquitoes and Chiggers. Many of these bites can be prevented by applying an insect repellent sparingly

(Continued on the reverse side)

to the clothing or exposed skin before your child goes outdoors or into the woods. Repellents are essential for infants (especially those less than 1 year old) because they cannot bat the insects away.

Bedbugs. The bed and baseboards can be sprayed with 1% malathion, but young children must be kept away from the area because this substance is somewhat poisonous. You may need to call an exterminator.

Fleas. Usually you will find the fleas on your dog or cat. If the bites started after a move into a different home, fleas from the previous owner's pet are the most common cause. Fleas can often be removed by bringing a dog or cat inside the house for 2 hours to collect the fleas (they prefer the dog or cat to living in the carpet) and then applying flea powder or soap to the animal outdoors. Careful daily vacuuming will usually capture any remaining fleas.

Precautions with DEET Insect Repellents. Insect repellents containing DEET must be used with caution. DEET can be absorbed across the skin into the bloodstream and can cause seizures or coma. Young children may also have reactions to DEET from licking it off the skin. To prevent harmful reactions, take the following precautions:
—Apply repellent mainly to clothing and shoes.
—To prevent contact with the mouth or eyes, don't put any repellent on the hands.
—Don't put any repellent on areas that are sunburned or have rashes because the DEET is more easily absorbed in these areas.
—Warn older children who apply their own repellent that a total of 3 or 4 drops can protect the whole body.
—Because one application of repellent lasts 4 to 8 hours, apply it no more than twice daily.
—If repellent is put on the skin, wash it off after your child comes indoors.

 CALL OUR OFFICE

Later if
—The bites are from fire ants.
—Itching or pain interferes with sleep.
—The bites become infected.

3. TICK BITES

DEFINITION

A tick is a small brown insect that attaches to the skin and sucks blood for 3 to 6 days. The bite is usually painless and doesn't itch. The wood tick (or dog tick), which transmits Rocky Mountain spotted fever and Colorado tick fever, is up to ½ inch in size. The deer tick, which transmits Lyme disease, is the size of a pinhead.

HOME CARE

Tick Removal. The simplest and quickest way to remove a tick is to pull it off. Use tweezers to grasp the tick as close to the skin as possible (try to get a grip on its head). Apply a steady upward traction until the tick releases its grip. Do not twist the tick or jerk it suddenly because these maneuvers can break off the tick's head or mouth parts. Do not squeeze the tweezers to the point of crushing the tick; the secretions released may contain germs that cause disease.

If you have no tweezers, pull the tick off in the same way using your fingers. Some tiny ticks need to be scraped off with a knife blade or the edge of a credit card. If the body is removed but the head is left in the skin, use a sterile needle to remove the head (in the same way that you would remove a sliver).

Wash the wound and your hands with soap and water after removal. A recent study by Dr. G.R. Needham showed that embedded ticks do not back out with the application of a hot match or when covered with petroleum jelly, fingernail polish, or rubbing alcohol. We formerly thought that petroleum jelly, fingernail polish, or alcohol would block the tick's breathing pores and take its mind off eating. Unfortunately, ticks breathe only a few times per hour.

Prevention. Children and adults who are hiking in tick-infested areas should wear long clothing and tuck the end of the pants into the socks. Apply an insect repellent to shoes and socks. During the hike perform tick checks using a buddy system every 2 to 3 hours to remove ticks on the clothing or exposed skin. Immediately after the hike or at least once daily, do a bare skin check. A brisk shower at the end of a hike will also remove any tick that isn't firmly attached. Because the bite is painless and doesn't itch, the child will usually be unaware of its presence. Favorite hiding places for ticks are in the hair, so carefully check the scalp, neck, armpit, and groin. Removing ticks promptly may prevent infection because transmission of Lyme disease requires 18 to 24 hours of feeding. Also the tick is easier to remove before it becomes firmly attached.

 CALL OUR OFFICE

Later if
—You can't remove the tick.
—The tick's head remains embedded.
—A fever or rash occurs in the week following the bite.
—You think your child has some of the symptoms of Lyme disease.
—You think your child has been bitten by a deer tick and it was probably attached for more than 18 hours.

NOTE: You do not need to call if your child was bitten by a tick and it was removed promptly.

 Instructions for Pediatric Patients by Barton D. Schmitt, M.D., *Pediatrician*   © 1992 by W. B. Saunders Company
Adapted from YOUR CHILD'S HEALTH, Copyright © 1991 by Barton D. Schmitt, M.D.
Reprinted by permission of Bantam Books.

DEFINITION

Diagnostic Findings

—Sores are less than 1 inch in diameter.
—Sores begin as small red bumps that rapidly change to cloudy blisters, then pimples, and finally sores.
—Sores (any wounds that don't heal) increase in size.
—Sores are often covered by a soft, yellow-brown scab.
—Scabs may be draining pus.
—Sores increase in number.
—First sores are usually near the nose or mouth.

Cause

Impetigo is a superficial infection of the skin, caused by *Streptococcus* bacteria (60%) or by *Staphylococcus* bacteria (40%). It is more common in the summer when the skin is often broken by cuts, scrapes, and insect bites.

Expected Course

With proper treatment, the skin will be completely healed in 1 week. Some blemishes will remain for 6 to 12 months, but scars are unusual unless your child picks his sores.

HOME TREATMENT

Antibiotic (Oral or Injectable). Most children with impetigo need an antibiotic. Your child's antibiotic is

_____. Your child's dosage is

_____ given _____ each day for _____ days.

Removing the Scabs. The bacteria live underneath the soft scabs, and until these are removed, the antibiotic ointment cannot get through to the bacteria to kill them. Scabs can be soaked off using a warm 1:120 bleach solution (1 tablespoon of bleach to 2 quarts of water). The area may need to be gently rubbed, but it should not be scrubbed. A little bleeding is common if you remove all the crust.

Antibiotic Ointment. After the crust has been removed, antibiotic ointment should be applied to the raw surface three times daily. Buy Betadine ointment (or Bacitracin ointment) at your drugstore. You won't need a prescription. Apply for 7 days or longer if necessary. The area should be washed with an antibacterial soap (Dial or Safeguard) each time. Any new crust that forms should not be removed since this delays healing.

Preventing Spread of Impetigo to Other Areas of the Body. Every time your child touches the impetigo and then scratches another part of the skin with that finger, he can start a new site of impetigo. To prevent this, discourage your child from touching or picking at the sores. Keep his fingernails cut short, and wash his hands often with one of the antibacterial soaps.

Contagiousness. Impetigo is quite contagious. Be certain that other people in the family do not use your child's towel or washcloth. Your child should be kept out of school until he has taken oral antibiotics for 24 hours or until you have used the antibiotic ointment for 48 hours.

CALL OUR OFFICE

IMMEDIATELY if
—The urine becomes red or cola colored.
—The face becomes bright red *and* tender to the touch.
—Any big blisters (more than 1 inch across) develop.

Within 24 hours if
—Other people in the family develop impetigo.
—The impetigo increases in size and number of sores after 48 hours of treatment.
—A fever or a sore throat occurs.
—You have other concerns or questions.

JOCK ITCH

DEFINITION

Jock itch is also called ringworm of the crotch or tinea cruris.

Diagnostic Findings

—Pink, scaly, itchy rash
—Inner thighs, groin, and scrotum involved (**NOTE**: The penis is not involved.)
—Almost exclusively in males

HOME CARE

Antifungal Medicine. Buy Tinactin or Micatin powder or spray (nonprescription) at your drugstore. It needs to be applied twice daily to the rash and at least 1 inch beyond the borders. Make sure you get it in all the creases. Continue it for several weeks or for at least 7 days after the rash seems to have cleared.

Dryness. Jock itch will improve dramatically if the groin area is kept dry. Loose-fitting cotton shorts should be worn. Shorts and athletic supporters should be washed frequently. The rash area should be carefully cleansed daily with plain water and carefully dried. Avoid using soap on the rash.

Scratching. Scratching will delay the cure, so have your child avoid scratching the area.

Contagiousness. The condition is not very contagious. The fungus won't grow on dry, normal skin. Your child may continue to take physical education and play sports.

 ## CALL OUR OFFICE

During regular hours if
—There is no improvement in 1 week.
—The rash is not completely cured in 1 month.

Instructions for Pediatric Patients by Barton D. Schmitt, M.D., *Pediatrician*   © 1992 by W. B. Saunders Company
Adapted from YOUR CHILD'S HEALTH, Copyright © 1991 by Barton D. Schmitt, M.D.
Reprinted by permission of Bantam Books.

DEFINITION

Diagnostic Findings

—Nits (white eggs) are firmly attached to hairs.
—Unlike dandruff, nits can't be shaken off.
—Gray bugs (lice) are 1/16 inch long, move quickly, and are difficult to see.
—The scalp itches and has a rash.
—The back of the neck is the favorite area.
—The nits are easier to see than the lice because they are white and very numerous.

Cause

Head lice only live on human beings and can be spread quickly by using the hat, comb, or brush of an infected person or simply by close contact. Anyone can get lice despite good health habits and frequent hair washing. The nits (eggs) normally hatch in about 1 week. Pubic lice ("crabs") are slightly different but are treated the same way. They can be transmitted from bedding or clothing and do not signify sexual contact.

Expected Course

With treatment, all lice and nits will be killed.

HOME TREATMENT

Antilice Shampoo. Your child's antilice shampoo is

_____ . Pour about 2 ounces of the shampoo into the hair. Add a little warm water to work up a lather. Scrub the hair and scalp for 10 minutes, by the clock. Rinse the hair thoroughly and dry it with a towel. These shampoos kill both the lice and the nits. Repeat the antilice shampoo once in 7 days to prevent reinfection. (**NOTE**: A new prescription antilice shampoo called Nix only requires one application.)

Removing Nits. Remove the nits by back combing with a fine-tooth comb or pull them out individually. The nits can be loosened using a mixture of half vinegar and half rubbing alcohol. Even though the nits are dead, most schools will not allow children to return if nits are present. Obviously, the hair does not need to be shaved to cure lice.

Lice in the Eyelashes. If you see any lice or nits in the eyelashes, apply petrolatum to the eyelashes twice a day for 8 days. The lice won't survive.

Cleaning the House. Lice can't live for more than 72 hours (3 days) off the human body. Your child's room should be vacuumed. Combs and brushes should be soaked for 1 hour in a solution made from the antilice shampoo. Wash your child's sheets, blankets, and pillowcases in hot water. Items that can't be washed (hats or coats) can be set aside in plastic bags for 3 weeks (the longest that nits can survive). Antilice sprays or fumigation of the house is unnecessary.

Contagiousness. Check the heads of everyone else living in your home. If any have scalp rashes, sores, or itching, they should be treated with the antilice shampoo even if lice and nits are not seen. Your child can return to school after one treatment with the shampoo. Reemphasize to your child that he or she should not share combs and hats.

CALL OUR OFFICE

During regular hours if
—Itching interferes with sleep.
—The rash is not cleared by 1 week after treatment.
—The rash clears and then returns.
—New eggs appear in the hair.
—The sores start to spread or look infected.

Instructions for Pediatric Patients by Barton D. Schmitt, M.D., *Pediatrician*
Adapted from YOUR CHILD'S HEALTH, Copyright © 1991 by Barton D. Schmitt, M.D.
Reprinted by permission of Bantam Books.

© 1992 by W. B. Saunders Company

LYMPH NODES OR GLANDS, SWOLLEN

DEFINITION

Diagnostic Findings

—Normal nodes are less than ½ inch across (often the size of a pea or baked bean).

—Active nodes with viral infection are usually ½ to 1 inch across. Slight enlargement and mild tenderness mean the lymph node is fighting infection and succeeding.

—Nodes seriously infected with bacteria are usually more than 1 inch across and tender to the touch. If they are over 2 inches across or the overlying skin is pink, the nodes are not controlling the infection and may contain pus.

Cause

Lymph glands stop the spread of infection and protect the bloodstream from invasion (blood poisoning). They enlarge with cuts, scrapes, scratches, splinters, burns, insect bites, rashes, impetigo, or any break in the skin. Try to locate and identify the cause of the swollen gland by remembering that the groin nodes drain lymph from the legs and lower abdomen, the armpit nodes drain the arms and upper chest, the back-of-the-neck nodes drain the scalp, and the front-of-the-neck nodes drain the lower face, nose, and throat. Most enlarged neck nodes are due to colds. A disease such as chickenpox can cause all the nodes to swell.

Expected Course

With the usual viral infections or skin injuries, nodes quickly swell to a peak size in 2 or 3 days and then slowly return to normal size over 2 to 4 weeks. However, you can still see and feel nodes in most normal children, especially in the neck and groin. Don't check for lymph nodes because you can always find some normal ones.

HOME CARE

Facts about Nodes. The body contains more than 500 lymph nodes. They can always be felt in the neck and groin. Normal nodes are largest at age 10 to 12. At this age they can be twice the normal adult size. Minor skin infections and irritations can cause lymph nodes to double in size. It may take 1 month for them to return to normal size. However, they won't completely disappear. HANDS OFF: Poking and squeezing lymph nodes may keep them from shrinking back to normal size. Don't check them more than once each month, and be sure your child doesn't fidget with them.

Treatment. No treatment is necessary for the nodes, just for the underlying disease (for example, remove the sliver or treat the skin rash).

 ## CALL OUR OFFICE

IMMEDIATELY if
—The node becomes 2 or more inches across.
—The node becomes quite tender to the touch.
—Red streaks develop near the node, or the overlying skin becomes red.
—The node interferes with moving the neck, breathing, or swallowing.
—Your child starts acting very sick.

During regular hours if
—The node becomes 1 to 2 inches across.
—The node remains larger than ½ inch for more than 1 month.
—An unexplained fever (over 100° F [37.8° C]) occurs.
—You feel your child is getting worse.
—You have other concerns or questions.

Instructions for Pediatric Patients by Barton D. Schmitt, M.D., *Pediatrician*
Adapted from YOUR CHILD'S HEALTH, Copyright © 1991 by Barton D. Schmitt, M.D.
Reprinted by permission of Bantam Books.

© 1992 by W. B. Saunders Company

DEFINITION

Diagnostic Findings

—Redness and blisters
—Eruption on exposed body surfaces (for example, hands)
—Shaped like streaks or patches
—Extreme itchiness
—Onset 1 or 2 days after the patient was in a forest or field

Cause

Poison ivy, poison oak, and poison sumac cause the same type of rash and are found throughout the United States. More than 50% of people are sensitive to the oil of these plants.

Expected Course

Poison ivy usually lasts 2 weeks. Treatment reduces the symptoms but doesn't cure the disease. The best approach is prevention.

HOME TREATMENT

Cool Soaks. Soak the involved area in cold water or massage it with an ice cube for 20 minutes as often as necessary. Then let it air dry. This will reduce itching.

Steroid Creams. If applied early, a steroid cream can

reduce the itching. Your child's cream is _____.

Apply it _____ times per day for _____ days.

The sores should be dried up and no longer itchy in 10 to 14 days. In the meantime, cut your child's fingernails short and encourage him not to scratch himself.

Contagiousness. The fluid from the sores themselves is not contagious. However, anything that has poison ivy oil or sap on it is contagious for about 1 week. This includes the shoes and clothes the patient last wore into the woods, as well as any pets that may have oil on their fur. Be sure to wash them off with soap and water. The rash begins 1 to 2 days after skin contact.

Prevention. Learn to recognize these plants. Otherwise, avoid all plants with three large shiny, green leaves. Another clue is the presence of shiny black spots on damaged leaves. (The sap of the plant turns black when exposed to air.)

Wear long pants or socks when walking through woods that may contain poison ivy, oak, or sumac. If you think your child has had contact with one of these plants wash the exposed areas of skin with any available soap several times. Do this as soon as possible, because after 1 hour it is of little value in preventing absorption of the oil.

 CALL OUR OFFICE

During regular hours if
—The face, eyes, or lips become involved.
—The itching interferes with sleep.
—Any big blisters develop.
—The rash becomes open and oozing.
—Signs of infection occur, such as pus or soft yellow scabs.
—You have other concerns or questions.

Instructions for Pediatric Patients by Barton D. Schmitt, M.D., *Pediatrician*
Adapted from YOUR CHILD'S HEALTH, Copyright © 1991 by Barton D. Schmitt, M.D.
Reprinted by permission of Bantam Books.

RINGWORM OF THE BODY (TINEA CORPORIS)

DEFINITION

Diagnostic Findings

—Ring-shaped pink patch
—Scaly, raised border
—Clear center
—Usually ½ to 1 inch in size
—Mildly itchy

Cause

Ringworm is caused by a fungus infection of the skin, often transferred from puppies or kittens who have it.

Expected Course

It responds well to appropriate treatment.

HOME CARE

Antifungal Cream. Buy Tinactin or Micatin cream at your drugstore. You won't need a prescription. Apply the cream twice daily to the rash and 1 inch beyond its borders. Continue this treatment for 1 week after the ringworm patch is smooth and seems to be gone. Encourage your child to avoid scratching the area.

Contagiousness. Ringworm of the skin is not contagious enough to worry about. After 48 hours of treatment, it is not contagious at all. Your child doesn't have to miss any school (or day care).

Treatment of Pets. Kittens and puppies with ringworm usually do not itch. If ringworm patches are seen, apply Micatin or Tinactin cream as described for humans. If no patches are present, treat the animal only if ringworm recurs in your child. Use Micatin or Tinactin powder and apply it to the entire fur twice weekly for 3 weeks. Also have your child avoid close contact with the animal. Natural immunity also develops in animals after 4 months. Call your veterinarian for other questions.

CALL OUR OFFICE

During regular hours if
—The rash has not cleared up in 4 weeks.
—The ringworm continues to spread after 1 week of treatment.
—The scalp becomes involved. (Reason: an oral medicine is needed.)
—You have other concerns or questions.

Instructions for Pediatric Patients by Barton D. Schmitt, M.D., *Pediatrician*
Adapted from YOUR CHILD'S HEALTH, Copyright © 1991 by Barton D. Schmitt, M.D.
Reprinted by permission of Bantam Books.

DEFINITION

Diagnostic Findings

—Round patches of hair loss that slowly increase in size
—A black-dot, stubbled appearance of the scalp from hair shafts that are broken off at the surface
—The scalp may have scaling
—Mild itching of the scalp
—Ringworm of the face may also be present
—Usually occurs in children age 2 to 10 years
—This diagnosis requires a positive microscope test (KOH prep) or fungus culture.

Cause

A fungus infects the hairs and causes them to break. Ringworm is not caused by a worm. Over 90% of cases are due to *T. tonsurans*, which is transmitted from other children who are infected. Combs, brushes, hats, barrettes, seat backs, pillows, and bath towels can transmit the fungus. Less than 10% of the cases are caused by infected animals. The animal type causes more scalp irritation, redness, and scaling. If your child has the animal type of fungus, he is not contagious to other children.

Expected Course

Ringworm of the scalp is not dangerous. Without treatment, however, the hair loss and scaling may spread to other parts of the scalp. Some children develop a kerion, which is a boggy, tender swelling of the scalp that can drain pus. Kerions are an allergic reaction to the fungus and require additional treatment with an oral steroid. Hair regrowth is normal after treatment but will take 6 to 12 months. In the meantime, your child can wear a hat or scarf to hide the bald areas.

TREATMENT

Oral Antifungal Medicine. The main treatment for ringworm of the scalp is griseofulvin taken orally for 8 weeks. Your child's dosage is_____

taken twice a day. (The product comes in a 125 mg per 5 ml suspension and 250 mg capsules.) Griseofulvin is best absorbed if taken with fatty foods such as milk or ice cream. Antifungal creams or ointments are not effective in killing the fungus that causes ringworm of the scalp.

Antifungal Shampoo. The use of an antifungal shampoo makes your child less contagious and allows him to return to child care or school. Purchase a nonprescription shampoo containing selenium sulfide (for example, Selsun). Lather up and leave it on for 10 minutes before rinsing. Use the antifungal shampoo twice a week for the next 8 weeks. On other days, use a regular shampoo.

Contagiousness. Ringworm is mildly contagious. In the days before antifungal medications, about 5% of school contacts usually became infected. However, 25% of siblings (close contacts) developed ringworm. Once your child has been started on griseofulvin and received one washing with the special shampoo, he can return to school.

Common Mistakes. It is psychologically harmful and unnecessary to shave the hair, give a close haircut, or to force your child to wear a protective skull cap.

Follow-Up Appointment. In 6 weeks return for lab tests of your child's hair to be certain we have achieved a cure. If not, the griseofulvin will need to be given for longer than 8 weeks.

CALL OUR OFFICE

During regular hours if
—The ringworm becomes infected with pus or a yellow crust.
—The scalp becomes swollen or boggy.
—The ringworm continues to spread after 2 weeks of treatment.
—You have questions or concerns.

SCABIES

DEFINITION

Scabies are little bugs (mites) that burrow under the skin and cause severe itching and little red bumps. They are so small that they can only be seen with a microscope. They rarely attack the skin above the neck, except in infants. Usually more than one person in a family has them.

HOME CARE

Scabies Cream or Lotion.   Your child's medicine is

_____. (Kwell lotion or 5% Nix cream is usually used.) Apply the cream or lotion to every square inch of the body from the neck down. (Infants less than 1 year old also need it carefully applied to the scalp, forehead, temples, and neck. Avoid the lower face.) Don't forget the navel, between the toes, or other creases. Leave some under the fingernails. Areas that don't seem infected should still be covered.

Eight hours later give your child a bath and remove the cream or lotion. (If Kwell is used, babies under 1 year of age should have it washed off in 4 hours.) Leaving Kwell on longer than this can cause side effects. Swallowing Kwell can be quite harmful, so cover the hands with gloves or socks if your child is a thumb sucker. One treatment is usually effective. For severe rashes, repeat the treatment once in 1 week.

Pregnant Women.   Pregnant women cannot use Kwell. If you use 5% Nix cream, wash it off in 8 hours.

If you use Eurax, leave the first coat on. Apply a second coat 24 hours later. Wash the Eurax off 48 hours after the second application. The Eurax 2-day treatment needs to be repeated in 1 week.

Itching.   The itching and rash may last for 2 to 3 weeks after successful treatment with Kwell or Eurax. This itch can be helped by frequent cool baths without use of soap, followed by 0.5% hydrocortisone cream, which you can buy without a prescription.

Contagiousness.   Children can return to school after one treatment with the scabies medicine.

Family Contacts.   Scabies is highly contagious. The symptoms take 30 days to develop after exposure. Therefore everyone living in the house should be treated preventively with one application of the scabies medicine. Close contacts of the infected child (such as a friend who spent the night or a babysitter) should also be treated.

Cleaning the House.   Machine wash all your child's sheets, pillowcases, underwear, pajamas, and recently worn clothing. Blankets can be put away for 3 days. Scabies cannot live outside the human body for more than 3 days.

 CALL OUR OFFICE

During regular hours if
—You have other concerns or questions.

   Instructions for Pediatric Patients by Barton D. Schmitt, M.D., *Pediatrician*

DEFINITION

Sunburn is due to overexposure of the skin to the ultraviolet rays of the sun or a sunlamp. Most people have been sunburned many times. Vacations can quickly turn into painful experiences when the power of the sun is overlooked. Unfortunately, the symptoms of sunburn do not begin until 2 to 4 hours after the sun's damage has been done. The peak reaction of redness, pain, and swelling is not seen for 24 hours. Minor sunburn is a first-degree burn that turns the skin pink or red. Prolonged sun exposure can cause blistering and a second-degree burn. Sunburn never causes a third-degree burn or scarring.

Repeated sun exposure and suntans cause premature aging of the skin (wrinkling, sagging, and brown sunspots). Repeated sunburns increase the risk of skin cancer in the damaged area. Each blistering sunburn doubles the risk of developing malignant melanoma, which is the most serious type of skin cancer.

HOME CARE

Pain Relief. The sensation of pain and heat will probably last for 48 hours.
—Aspirin or ibuprofen products started early and continued for 2 days can reduce the discomfort.
—Nonprescription ½% hydrocortisone cream or moisturizing creams applied three times each day may also cut down on swelling and pain, but only if used early. (Avoid petrolatum or other ointments because they keep heat and sweat from escaping.)
—The symptoms can also be helped by cool baths or wet compresses several times daily.
—Showers are usually too painful.
—Peeling will usually occur in about a week. Apply a moisturizing cream.
—Offer extra water to replace the fluid lost into the swelling of sunburned skin and to prevent dehydration and dizziness.

Prevention of Sunburns. The best way to prevent skin cancer is to prevent sunburn. Although skin cancer occurs in adults, it is caused by the sun exposure and sunburns that occurred during childhood. Every time you apply sunscreen to your child, you are preventing skin cancer down the line.
—Apply sunscreen anytime your child is going to be outside for more than 30 minutes.
—Try to keep sun exposure to small amounts early in the season until a tan builds up. (**CAUTION:** Although people with a suntan can tolerate a little more sun, they can still get a serious sunburn.) Start with 15 or 20 minutes per day and increase by 5 minutes per day. Decrease daily exposure time if the skin becomes reddened. Because of the 2- to 4-hour delay before sunburn starts, don't expect

symptoms to tell you when it's time to get out of the sun.
—About 15% of white people have skin that never tans but only burns. These fair-skinned children need to be extremely careful about the sun throughout their lives. The big risk factors for sunburn are red hair, blond hair, blue eyes, green eyes, or freckles. These children are also at increased risk for skin cancer. They need to be instructed repeatedly to use a sunscreen throughout the summer and to avoid the sun whenever possible.
—The skin of infants is thinner and more sensitive to the sun. Sunscreens, longer clothing, and a hat with a brim are essential for these children. Don't apply sunscreen to areas where the infant may lick it off. Don't use a sunscreen containing PABA on infants less than 6 months old.
—Avoid the hours of 10:00 AM to 3:00 PM, when the sun's rays are most intense.
—Don't let overcast days give you a false sense of security. Over 70% of the sun's rays still get through the clouds. Over 30% of the sun's rays can also penetrate loosely woven fabrics (for instance, a T-shirt).
—Sun exposure increases by 4% for each 1000 feet of elevation. A sunburn can occur quickly when hiking above the timberline.
—Water, sand, or snow increases the sun exposure. The shade from a hat or umbrella won't protect you from reflected rays.
—Also protect your child's eyes. Years of exposure to ultraviolet light increase the risk of cataracts. Buy sunglasses with ultraviolet (UV) protection.
—Set a good example. Did you apply your sunscreen?

Sunscreens. There are good sunscreens on the market that prevent sunburn but still permit gradual tanning to occur. The sun protection factor (SPF) or filtering power of the product determines what percent of the ultraviolet rays gets through to the skin. The SPF of various products ranges from 2 to 45. An SPF of 15 allows only 1/15 (7%) of the sun's rays to get through and thereby extends safe sun exposure from 20 minutes to 5 hours without sunburning. For practical purposes, an SPF higher than 15 is rarely needed because sun exposure beyond 5 hours is unusual. Fair-skinned whites (with red or blond hair) need a sunscreen with an SPF of 15 or higher, most whites need an 8 to 10, and Mediterranean whites need a 6 to 8. The simplest approach is to use an SPF of 15 or greater on all white children.

Apply the sunscreen 30 minutes before exposure to the sun to give it time to penetrate the skin. Give special attention to the areas most likely to become sunburned, such as your child's nose, ears, cheeks, and shoulders. Most products need to be reapplied every 3 to 4 hours, as well as immediately after swimming or profuse sweating. A "waterproof" sunscreen stays on for about 30 minutes in water. Do not towel off after swimming. Most people apply too little (the average adult requires 1 ounce of sunscreen per application).

(Continued on the reverse side)

Instructions for Pediatric Patients by Barton D. Schmitt, M.D., *Pediatrician*
Adapted from YOUR CHILD'S HEALTH, Copyright © 1991 by Barton D. Schmitt, M.D.
Reprinted by permission of Bantam Books.

To prevent sunburned lips, apply a lip coating that also contains PABA. If your child's nose or some other area has been repeatedly burned during the summer, protect it completely from all the sun's rays with zinc oxide ointment.

Common Mistakes in Treatment of Sunburn. Avoid applying ointments or butter to a sunburn; they are painful to remove and not helpful. Don't buy any first aid creams or sprays for burns. They often contain benzocaine that can cause an allergic rash. Don't confuse sunscreens that block the sun's burning rays with suntan lotions or oils that mainly lubricate the skin.

CALL OUR OFFICE

IMMEDIATELY if
—Your child becomes unable to look at lights because of eye pain.
—An unexplained fever over 102° F (38.9° C) occurs.
—The sunburn becomes infected.
—Your child starts acting very sick.

During regular hours if
—The blisters start to break open.
—You have other concerns or questions.

Instructions for Pediatric Patients by Barton D. Schmitt, M.D., *Pediatrician*
Adapted from YOUR CHILD'S HEALTH, Copyright © 1991 by Barton D. Schmitt, M.D.
Reprinted by permission of Bantam Books.

DEFINITION

Symptoms and Characteristics

—There is a linear rash that follows the path of a nerve.
—The rash occurs on only one side of the body.
—The rash starts with clusters or red bumps, changes to water blisters, and finally becomes dry crusts.
—The back, chest, and abdomen are the most common sites.
—The rash usually doesn't burn or itch in children (in contrast to the adult form).
—Your child does not have a fever or feel sick.
—Your child had chickenpox in the past.

Cause

Zoster is caused by the chickenpox virus. The disease is not caught from other people with active shingles or chickenpox. The chickenpox virus lies dormant in the bodies of some people and is reactivated for unknown reasons as zoster. Children with zoster are usually over 3 years old.

Expected Course

New shingles continue to appear for several days. All the rash dries up by 7 to 10 days. Complications do not occur unless the eye is involved. Most people have shingles just once; a second attack occurs in 5% of children who get zoster.

HOME CARE

Relief of Symptoms. Most children have no symptoms. For pain, give acetaminophen as necessary. Avoid giving aspirin for zoster because of the possible link with Reye's syndrome. Discourage itching or picking the rash. The rash does not need any cream.

Contagiousness. Children with zoster can transmit chickenpox (but not zoster) to others. Although they are far less contagious than children with chickenpox, children with zoster should stay home from school for 7 days unless they can keep the rash covered until it crusts over. Children or adults who have not had chickenpox should avoid visiting the child with zoster (unless the rash is covered).

 ## CALL OUR OFFICE

During regular hours if
—The rash becomes very painful or very itchy.
—The rash lasts more than 14 days.
—The rash becomes infected with pus or soft yellow scabs.
—You feel your child is getting worse.
—You have other questions or concerns.

DEFINITION

Symptoms and Characteristics

—The name means "multicolored ringworm."
—The condition occurs in adolescents and adults.
—Numerous spots and patches appear on the neck, upperback, and shoulders.
—The spots are covered by a fine scale.
—The spots vary in size.
—In summer, the spots are light and don't tan.
—In winter, the spots are darker (often pink or brown) than normal Caucasian skin.

Cause

This superficial infection is caused by a yeastlike fungus call *Malassezia furfur*. It is more common in warm, humid climates.

Expected Course

The problem tends to wax and wane for many years. Since complications do not occur, tinea versicolor is solely a cosmetic problem. Itching is uncommon.

HOME CARE

Selsun Blue Shampoo. Selsun Blue (selenium sulfide) is a nonprescription medicated shampoo that can cure this condition. Apply this shampoo once each day for 14 days. Apply it to the affected skin areas as well as 2 or 3 inches onto the adjacent normal skin. Rub it in and let it dry. Be careful to keep it away from the eyes and genitals, since it is irritating to these tissues. After 20 minutes, take a shower. In 2 weeks the scaling should be stopped, and the rash temporarily cured. Normal skin color will not return for 6 to 12 months.

Prevention of Recurrences. Tinea versicolor tends to recur. Prevent this by applying Selsun Blue shampoo to the formerly involved areas once each month for several years. Leave it on for 1 to 2 hours. This precaution is especially important in the summer months, because this fungus thrives in warm weather.

Contagiousness. Tinea versicolor is not contagious. This fungus is a normal inhabitant of the hair follicles in many people. Only a few develop the overgrowth of the fungus and a rash.

 ## CALL OUR OFFICE

During regular hours if
—The rash is not improved with this treatment after 2 weeks.
—You feel your child is getting worse.
—You have other questions or concerns.

Instructions for Pediatric Patients by Barton D. Schmitt, M.D., *Pediatrician*
Adapted from YOUR CHILD'S HEALTH, Copyright © 1991 by Barton D. Schmitt, M.D.
Reprinted by permission of Bantam Books.

DEFINITION

If your child has tenderness, redness, and swelling of skin surrounding the corner of the toenail on one of the big toes, proceed with this guideline. Ingrown toenails are usually due to tight shoes (for example, cowboy boots) or improper cutting of the toenails. They take several weeks to clear up.

HOME CARE

Soaking.   Soak the foot twice daily in a 1:120 bleach solution for 20 minutes. Use 1 tablespoon of bleach per 2 quarts of water. This solution kills most germs. Add a little liquid soap to help penetration. While the foot is soaking, massage outward the swollen part of the cuticle.

Antibiotic Ointment.   If your child's cuticle is just red and irritated, an antibiotic ointment is probably not needed. But if the cuticle becomes swollen or oozes secretions, apply Neosporin ointment (no prescription needed) five or six times daily.

Cutting off the Corner of the Toenail.   The pain is always caused by the corner of the toenail rubbing against the raw cuticle. Therefore we have cut this corner off so that the irritated tissue can quiet down and heal. We need to do this only once. The main purpose of treatment is to help the nail grow over the nail cuticle rather than get stuck in it. Therefore during soaks try to bend the corners of the nail upward.

Shoes.   Have your child wear sandals or go barefoot as much as possible to prevent pressure on the toenail. When he must wear closed shoes, protect the ingrown toenail as follows: If the inner edge is involved, tape cotton between the first and second toes to keep them from touching. If the outer edge is involved, tape cotton to the outside of the ball of the toe to keep the toenail from touching the side of the shoe.

Prevention.   Prevent recurrences by making sure that your child's shoes are not too narrow. Get rid of any pointed or tight shoes. After the cuticle is healed, cut the toenails straight across, leaving the corners. Don't cut them too short.

 ## CALL OUR OFFICE

IMMEDIATELY if
—Fever or chills occur.
—A red streak spreads beyond the toe.

During regular hours if
—The ingrown toenail develops pus or yellow drainage.
—The problem is not much better in 1 week.
—The problem is not totally resolved in 2 weeks.
—You have other concerns or questions.

DEFINITION

Diagnostic Findings

—Raised, round, rough-surfaced growth on the skin that looks like a wart
—Most commonly on the hands
—Not painful unless located on the sole of the foot
—Brown dots within the wart (unlike a callus) and a clear boundary with the normal skin

Cause

Warts are caused by papilloma viruses.

Expected Course

Most warts disappear without treatment in 2 or 3 years. With treatment they resolve in 2 to 3 months. There are no shortcuts in treating warts.

HOME TREATMENT

Wart-removing Acids. Your child's wart-removing

acid is _____ . Apply it once per day. Keep the lid on the container closed tightly so it won't evaporate.

The acid will turn the top of the wart into dead skin. The acid will work faster if it is covered with adhesive tape. Once or twice each week, remove the dead wart material by paring it down with a razor blade. The dead wart will be easier to slice if you soak the area first in warm water for 10 minutes. If the cutting causes any pain or minor bleeding, you have cut into living wart tissue. Since you are using an acid, avoid getting any near the eyes or mouth.

Contagiousness. Encourage your child not to pick at the wart because this may cause it to spread. If your child chews or sucks the wart, cover the area with a Band-Aid and change it daily. Encourage your child to give up this habit because chewing on warts can cause warts on the lips or face. Warts are not very contagious to other people.

CALL OUR OFFICE

During regular hours if
—Warts develop on the feet, genitals, or face.
—A wart becomes open *and* looks infected.
—New warts develop after 2 weeks of treatment.
—The warts are still present after 8 weeks of treatment.
—You have other concerns or questions.

 Instructions for Pediatric Patients by Barton D. Schmitt, M.D., *Pediatrician*   © 1992 by W. B. Saunders Company
Adapted from YOUR CHILD'S HEALTH, Copyright © 1991 by Barton D. Schmitt, M.D.
Reprinted by permission of Bantam Books.

PART 6

MISCELLANEOUS PHYSICAL PROBLEMS

DEFINITION

An anal fissure is a shallow tear or crack in the skin at the opening of the anus. More than 90% of children with blood in their stools have an anal fissure.

Diagnostic Findings

—The blood is bright red.
—The blood is only a few streaks or flecks.
—The blood is on the surface of the stool or on the toilet tissue after wiping.
—Your child passed a large or hard bowel movement (BM).
—You can see a shallow tear at the opening of the anus when the buttocks are spread apart, usually at 6 or 12 o'clock. (A tear cannot always be seen).
—Touching the tear causes mild pain.

Cause

Trauma to the anal canal during constipation is the usual cause of anal fissures.

Expected Course

Bleeding from a fissure stops on its own in 5 or 10 minutes.

HOME CARE

Warm Saline Baths. Give your child warm baths for 20 minutes, three times each day. Have him sit in a basin or tub of warm water with about 2 tablespoons of table salt or baking soda added. Don't use any soap on the irritated area. Then gently dry the anal area.

Ointments. If the anus seems irritated, you can apply ½% hydrocortisone ointment (nonprescription). If the pain is severe, apply 2½% Xylocaine or 1% Nupercainal ointment (no prescription needed) four times each day for a few days to numb the area.

Diet. The most important aspect of treatment is to keep your child on a nonconstipating diet. Increase the amounts of fresh fruits and vegetables, beans, and bran products that your child eats. Reduce the amounts of milk products your child eats or drinks.

Occasionally, a stool softener (such as mineral oil) is needed temporarily.

 ## CALL OUR OFFICE

During regular hours if
—The anal fissure is not completely healed after 3 days of treatment.
—The bleeding increases in amount.
—The bleeding occurs more than two times (especially if it's painless).
—You have other concerns or questions.

Adapted from YOUR CHILD'S HEALTH, Copyright © 1991 by Barton D. Schmitt, M.D.
Reprinted by permission of Bantam Books.

DEFINITION

Anemia means that the number of red blood cells in your child's body is below normal. The red blood cells carry oxygen in the bloodstream, and iron is needed for your body to produce red blood cells. Iron deficiency anemia is caused by too little iron in the diet.

HOME TREATMENT

Iron Medicines. The iron medicine for your child

is _____. Your child's dose is

_____ ml given _____ times each day for

_____ weeks.

This medicine contains iron and will need to be taken for 2 to 3 months to get your child's red blood cells back to a normal level. It can occasionally cause an upset stomach and should be taken with food to prevent this. Mix the iron medicine with a juice containing vitamin C (orange juice, for example). This will improve iron absorption and prevent staining of the teeth. (**NOTE:** If the teeth become stained, the stain can be brushed off with baking soda.) The iron may change the color of bowel movements to greenish black, but this is harmless. Too much iron can be dangerous. Treat iron like any medicine: Keep it out of your child's reach.

Diet. If your child's diet is well balanced, he or she won't get anemia again. The following foods contain iron:
—Meats, fish, and poultry have the most iron.
—Raisins, dried fruits, sweet potatoes, lima beans, kidney beans, chili beans, pinto beans, green peas, peanut butter, enriched cereals, and breads are other iron-rich foods. Spinach and egg yolks also contain iron, but it is in a form that is not readily available to the body.

Your child should not drink more than 24 ounces of milk each day (about three glasses) so that he or she has an adequate appetite for iron-containing foods. Milk doesn't contain any iron.

Follow-up Visits. We would like to see your child in 1 week and again in 2 months to be sure the level of red cells in the blood has returned to normal.

CALL OUR OFFICE

During regular hours if
—Your child refuses the iron medicine.
—You have other concerns or questions.

Instructions for Pediatric Patients by Barton D. Schmitt, M.D., *Pediatrician*   © 1992 by W. B. Saunders Company

DEFINITION

—Wheezing: a high-pitched whistling sound produced during breathing out
—Recurrent attacks of wheezing, coughing, chest tightness, and difficulty in breathing
—Often associated with sneezing and a runny nose
—Usually no fever
—Also called reactive airway disease (RAD)

Causes

Asthma is an inherited type of "twitchy" lung. The airways go into spasm and become narrow when allergic or irritating substances enter them. Viral respiratory infections trigger most attacks, especially in younger children. If asthma is caused by pollens, the asthma only flares up during a particular season. Asthma often occurs in children who have other allergies such as eczema or hay fever. Although an emotional stress can occasionally trigger an attack, emotional problems are not the cause of asthma. Some common triggers are listed under "Prevention."

Expected Course

Although asthma attacks may be frightening, they are treatable. When medicines are taken as directed, the symptoms are reversible and there are no permanent lung changes. Although asthma can be a long-lasting disease, over half of children outgrow it during adolescence.

HOME CARE

Asthma is a chronic disease that requires close follow-up by a physician who coordinates your child's treatment program. If you have any doubt about whether your child is wheezing, start the following asthma medicines. The later medicines are begun, the longer it takes to stop the wheezing. Once medicine is begun, your child should keep taking it until he has not wheezed or coughed for 48 hours (should take medicine for 7 days minimum). If your child has one or more attacks of wheezing each month, he probably needs to be on continuous medicines.

Asthma Inhalers. Your child's metered-dose inhaler

is _____. Your child's dose is 2

puffs every _____ hours for _____ days. Your child will need careful instructions on how to use the inhaler.
1. The canister must be shaken.
2. The inhaler should be held 2 inches in front of the open mouth.

3. Your child should breathe out completely.
4. The spray should be released at the start of slowly breathing in.
5. The breath should be held for 10 seconds after the lungs are filled.
6. Wait 10 minutes before taking the second puff.

NOTE: These inhalers usually can't be coordinated by children less than 6 years old unless you also use a plastic airway spacer (or chamber).

Oral Asthma Medicines. Although inhaled medicines work best for asthma, some children also need to take medicines by mouth. Your child's asthma medicine is

_____. Give _____ every

_____ hours for _____ days.

Begin Treatment Early. Many children wheeze soon after they get coughs and colds. For some children, itching of the neck or chest means an asthma attack will soon begin. If this is the case for your child, start the asthma medicine or inhaler at the first sign of any coughing or itching. The best "cough medicine" for a child with asthma is the asthma medicine. Always keep this medicine handy; take it with you on trips. If your supply runs low, obtain a refill.

Fluid Intake. Fluids keep the normal lung mucus from becoming sticky. Encourage your child to drink one glass of some fluid every 2 hours while awake (½ glass in children under 5 years of age). Clear fluids are best. Sipping warm fluids may improve the wheezing.

Exercise-induced Asthma. Most people with asthma also get 20- to 30-minute attacks of coughing and wheezing with strenuous exercise. Running, especially in cold air, is the main trigger. This problem should not interfere with participation in most sports nor require a physical education excuse. The symptoms can be prevented by using an oral asthma medicine 90 minutes before exercise or an inhaler 10 minutes before exercise. Children with asthma usually have no problems with swimming or sports not requiring rapid breathing.

Going to School. Asthma is not contagious. Your child should go to school during mild asthma attacks but avoid physical education on these days. Arrange to have the asthma medicines available at school. If your child uses an inhaler, he should be permitted to keep it with him so he can use it readily. For continued wheezing, your child should be seeing a physician on a daily basis.

Common Mistakes. The most common mistake is delaying the start of asthma medicines or not replacing them when they run out. Nonprescription inhalers and medicines are not helpful. Another common error is keeping a cat that your child is allergic to. Also, prohibit

(Continued on the reverse side)

all smoking in your home; tobacco smoke can persist for up to a week. In addition, don't panic during asthma attacks. Fear can make tight breathing worse, so try to remain calm and reassuring to your child. Finally, don't let asthma restrict your child's activities, sports, or social life.

PREVENTION BY AVOIDING ASTHMA TRIGGERS

Try to discover and avoid the substances that trigger attacks in your child (consider strong odors such as cologne, exhaust fumes, and frying foods). Routinely avoid common triggers such as feather pillows and tobacco smoke. Try to keep pets outside or at least out of your child's room. Learn how to dust proof your child's bedroom. Change the filters on your hot air heating system or air conditioner regularly. If there has been any recent contact with grass, pollen, weeds, or animals that your child might be allergic to, the pollen remaining in the hair and clothing is probably keeping the wheezing going. Have your child shower, wash his hair, and put on clean clothes.

CALL OUR OFFICE

IMMEDIATELY if
—The wheezing is severe.
—The breathing is labored.
—Your child is unable to sleep or speak.
—The lips are bluish or dusky.
—Pain develops in the chest or neck.
—The medicines are vomited.
—The wheezing is not improved after the second dose of asthma medicine.

Within 24 hours if
—Fluid intake is poor.
—Your child has congested sinuses or a yellow nasal discharge.
—The theophylline medicine may be causing vomiting or stomach pain.
—You feel your child is getting worse.

During regular hours if
—The wheezing is not completely cleared by 5 days.
—Your child has been hospitalized within the past year for asthma.
—You have other questions or concerns.

DEFINITION

Diagnostic Findings

—Painful passage of stools: The most reliable sign of constipation is discomfort with the passage of a bowel movement.

—Inability to pass stools: These children feel a desperate urge to have a bowel movement (BM), have discomfort in the anal area, and strain, but they are unable to pass anything.

—Infrequent movements: Going 4 or more days without a BM can be considered constipation, even though this may cause no pain in some children and even be normal for a few. EXCEPTION: After the second month or so of life, many breast-fed babies pass normal, large, soft BMs at infrequent intervals (up to 7 days is not abnormal) without pain.

Common Misconceptions in Defining Constipation

Large or hard BMs unaccompanied by any of the conditions just described are usually normal variations in BMs. Some normal people have hard BMs daily without any pain. Babies less than 6 months of age commonly grunt, push, strain, draw up the legs, and become flushed in the face during passage of BMs. However, they don't cry. These behaviors are normal and should remind us that it is difficult to have a BM while lying down.

Causes

Constipation is often due to a diet that does not include enough fiber. Drinking or eating too many milk products can cause constipation. It's also caused by repeatedly waiting too long to go to the bathroom. If constipation begins during toilet training, usually the parent is applying too much psychologic pressure.

Expected Course

Changes in the diet usually relieve constipation. After your child is better, be sure to keep him on a nonconstipating diet so that it doesn't happen again.

Sometimes the trauma to the anal canal during constipation causes an anal fissure (a small tear). This is confirmed by finding small amounts of bright red blood on the toilet tissue or the stool surface.

HOME CARE

Diet Treatment for Infants (Less than 1 Year Old)

—Give fruit juices (such as grape or prune juice) twice each day to babies less than 4 months old. Switching to soy formula may also result in looser stools.

—If your baby is over 4 months old, add strained foods with a high fiber content, such as cereals, apricots, prunes, peaches, pears, plums, beans, peas, or spinach twice daily. Avoid strained carrots, squash, bananas, and apples.

Diet Treatment for Older Children (More than 1 Year Old)

—Make sure that your child eats fruits or vegetables at least three times each day (raw unpeeled fruits and vegetables are best). Some examples are prunes, figs, dates, raisins, peaches, pears, apricots, beans, celery, peas, cauliflower, broccoli, and cabbage. WARNING: Avoid any foods your child can't chew easily.

—Increase bran. Bran is an excellent natural stool softener because it has a high fiber content. Make sure that your child's daily diet includes a source of bran, such as one of the new "natural" cereals, unmilled bran, bran flakes, bran muffins, shredded wheat, graham crackers, oatmeal, high-fiber cookies, brown rice, or whole wheat bread. Popcorn is one of the best high-fiber foods.

—Decrease consumption of constipating foods, such as milk, ice cream, yogurt, cheese, and cooked carrots.

—Increase the amount of water your child drinks.

Sitting on the Toilet (Children Who Are Toilet Trained). Encourage your child to establish a regular bowel pattern by sitting on the toilet for 10 minutes after meals, especially breakfast. Some children and adults repeatedly get blocked up if they don't do this. If your child is resisting toilet training by holding back, stop the toilet training for a while and put him back in diapers or Pull-ups.

Stool Softeners. If a change in diet doesn't relieve the constipation, give your child a stool softener with dinner every night for 1 week. Stool softeners (unlike laxatives) are not habit-forming. They work 8 to 12 hours after they are taken. Examples of stool softeners that you can buy at your drugstore without a prescription are Maltsupex (2 tablets), Haley's M-O (1 tablespoon), Metamucil or Citrucel (1 tablespoon), or plain mineral oil (1 tablespoon).

Common Mistakes in Treating Constipation. Don't use any suppositories or enemas without your physician's advice. These can cause irritation or fissures (tears) of the anus, resulting in pain and stool holding. Do not give your child strong oral laxatives without asking your physician because they can cause cramps and become habit forming.

Enemas for Acute Constipation. If your child has acute rectal pain needing immediate relief and your physician has said it's OK to give an enema, one of the following will usually provide quick relief: a glycerine suppository, a gentle rectal dilation with a lubricated finger (covered with plastic wrap), or a normal saline enema. The normal saline solution is made by adding 2 teaspoons of table salt to 1 quart of lukewarm water. Enemas with soapsuds, hydrogen peroxide, or tap water are dangerous.

(Continued on the reverse side)

Instructions for Pediatric Patients by Barton D. Schmitt, M.D., *Pediatrician*
Adapted from YOUR CHILD'S HEALTH, Copyright © 1991 by Barton D. Schmitt, M.D.
Reprinted by permission of Bantam Books.

Your child should lie on his stomach with his knees pulled under him; the enema tube should be lubricated and inserted 1½ inches to 2 inches into the rectum. The enema fluid should be delivered gradually by gravity, with the enema bag no more than 2 feet above the level of the anus. Your child should hold the enema until a strong need to have a bowel movement is felt (2 to 10 minutes). If you do not have an enema apparatus, you can use a rubber bulb syringe.

The amount of normal saline that should be given to children at various ages is:

1 yr	4 oz
1-3 yr	6 oz
3-6 yr	8 oz
6-12 yr	12 oz
Adolescents and adults	16 oz

CALL OUR OFFICE

IMMEDIATELY for advice about an enema or suppository if
—Your child develops extreme pain.
—Pain becomes constant *and* persists for more than 2 hours.

During regular hours if
—Your child does not have a bowel movement after 3 days on this nonconstipating diet.
—The anal area develops any tears (fissures) that won't heal.
—Your child soils himself (leaking BMs).
—Constipation becomes a recurrent problem for your child.
—You have other concerns or questions.

 Instructions for Pediatric Patients by Barton D. Schmitt, M.D., *Pediatrician*
Adapted from YOUR CHILD'S HEALTH, Copyright © 1991 by Barton D. Schmitt, M.D.
Reprinted by permission of Bantam Books.

DEFINITION

Febrile convulsions are seizures triggered by high fever. They are the most common type of convulsion (occurring in 4% of children) and in general are harmless. The children are usually between 6 months and 4 years of age. Most first seizures occur by 2 years of age. The average temperature at which they occur is 104° F (40° C). The fever itself can be caused by an infection in any part of the body. Each febrile seizure usually lasts 1 to 10 minutes without any treatment.

Most of these children (60%) have just one febrile seizure in a lifetime. The other 40% have two or three recurrences over the years. Febrile seizures usually stop occurring by 5 or 6 years of age. They do not cause any brain damage; however, a few children (3%) will later have seizures without fever.

FIRST AID

Reduce the Fever. Bringing your child's fever down as quickly as possible will shorten the seizure. Remove your child's clothing and apply cold washcloths to the face and neck. Sponge the rest of the body with cool water. As the water evaporates, your child's temperature will fall. When the seizure is over and your child is awake, give the usual dose of acetaminophen and encourage cool fluids.

Protect Your Child's Airway. If your child has anything in the mouth, clear it with a finger to prevent choking. Place your child on the side or abdomen (face down) to help drain secretions. If the child vomits, help clear the mouth. Use a suction bulb if available. If your child's breathing becomes noisy, pull the jaw and chin forward.

Common Mistakes in First Aid of Convulsions. During the seizure, don't try to restrain your child or stop the seizure movements. Once started, the seizure will run its course no matter what you do. Don't try to force anything into your child's mouth. This is unnecessary and can cut the mouth, injure a tooth, cause vomiting, or result in a serious bite of your finger. Don't try to hold the tongue. While children may rarely bite the tongue during a convulsion, they can't "swallow the tongue."

 ## CALL OUR OFFICE

IMMEDIATELY
—After the seizure has stopped.
—If the febrile convulsion continues for more than 10 minutes.

NOTE: If you are told to drive to our office, keep the fever down during the drive. Dress your child lightly and continue sponging if necessary. (**WARNING:** Prolonged seizures caused by persistent fever have been caused by bundling up sick infants during a long drive.)

HOME CARE

If your physician decides the seizure can be treated safely at home, the following information may help you.

Oral Fever-reducing Medicines. If your physician agrees, give your child acetaminophen at the regular dosage for your child's age every 4 hours for the next 48 hours (or longer if the fever persists). Awaken him once during the night for the medicine.

Fever-reducing Suppositories. Have some acetaminophen suppositories on hand in case your child ever has another febrile seizure (same dosage as oral medicine). These suppositories may be kept in a refrigerator at the pharmacy, so you may have to ask for them.

Prevention. The only way to completely prevent future febrile convulsions is for your child to take an anticonvulsant medicine on a daily basis until 3 or 4 years of age. Since anticonvulsants have side effects and febrile seizures are generally harmless, anticonvulsants are rarely prescribed any more unless your child has other neurologic problems. Your physician will discuss this decision with you.

Try to control fever more closely than is necessary for children without febrile seizures. Begin acetaminophen at the first sign of any fever (temperature over 100° F [37.8° C]). Febrile convulsions usually occur during the first day of an illness. Because fever is common after DPT immunizations, begin acetaminophen in the physician's office when your child is immunized and continue it for at least 24 hours. If your child has a fever at bedtime, awaken him once during the night to give acetaminophen. Avoid covering your child with more than one blanket because bundling during sleep can push the temperature up 1 or 2 extra degrees.

CALL OUR OFFICE

IMMEDIATELY if
—Another seizure occurs.
—The neck becomes stiff.
—Your child becomes confused or delirious.
—Your child becomes difficult to awaken.
—You feel your child is getting worse.

HAY FEVER (ALLERGIC RHINITIS)

DEFINITION

Diagnostic Findings

—There is a clear nasal discharge with sneezing, sniffing, and nasal itching.
—Symptoms occur during pollen season.
—Similar symptoms occurred during the same month of the previous year.
—Previous confirmation of this diagnosis by a physician is helpful.
—Eye allergies are commonly associated.
—Sinus or ear congestion is sometimes associated.

Cause

Hay fever is an allergic reaction of the nose (and sinuses) to an inhaled substance. This sensitivity is often inherited. During late April and May the most common offending pollen is from trees. From late May to mid-July, the offending pollen is usually grass. From late August to the first frost, the leading cause of hay fever is ragweed pollen. Although the inhaled substance is usually a pollen, it can also be animal dander or other agents your child is allergic to. Hay fever is the most common allergy; more than 15% of the population have it.

Expected Course

This is a chronic condition that will probably recur every year, perhaps for a lifetime. Therefore it is important to learn how to control it.

HOME TREATMENT

Antihistamine Medicine. The best drug for hay fever is an antihistamine. The antihistamine for your child is _____ . Give _____ , _____ times each day. (Some effective nonprescription antihistamines are Chlor-Trimeton, Dimetane, and Teldrin.)

Symptoms clear up faster if antihistamines are given at the first sign of sneezing or sniffing. For children with occasional symptoms, antihistamines can be taken on days when symptoms are present or expected. For children with daily symptoms the best control is attained if antihistamines are taken continuously (several times each day) throughout the pollen season.

The main side effect of antihistamines is drowsiness. If your child becomes drowsy, switch to a combination product that contains an antihistamine with a decongestant (such as pseudoephedrine or phenylpropanolamine). If your child remains drowsy, continue the drug, but temporarily decrease the dosage. Tolerance of the regular dosage should occur in 1 to 2 weeks.

GOOD NEWS: Severe hay fever can now usually be controlled by new cromolyn or steroid nasal sprays rather than allergy shots. Since these sprays must be used when the nose is not dripping, antihistamines must be given first to stop the drainage.

Pollen Removal to Decrease Symptoms of Hay Fever. Pollen tends to collect on the exposed body surfaces and especially in the hair. Shower your child and wash his hair every night before going to bed. Avoid handling pets that have been outside and are probably covered with pollen.

Prevention of Hay Fever Symptoms. Your child's exposure to pollen can be reduced by not going on drives in the country, not sitting by an open car window on necessary drives, not being near someone cutting the grass during pollen season, staying indoors when it is windy or the pollen count is especially high, and closing the windows that face the prevailing winds. If your child's hay fever is especially bad and you don't have air-conditioning, you may wish to take him to an air-conditioned store or theater for a few hours. Avoid feather pillows, pets, farms, stables, and tobacco smoke if any of them seem to bring on symptoms of nasal allergy.

Eye Allergies Associated with Hay Fever. If your child also has itchy watery eyes, wash the face and eyelids to remove pollen. Then apply a cold compress to the eyelids. Also instill 2 drops of long-acting vasoconstrictor eye drops every 8 to 12 hours (a nonprescription item). Ask your pharmacist for help in choosing a reliable product.

Common Mistakes. Vasoconstrictor nose drops or nasal sprays usually do not help hay fever because they are washed out by nasal secretions as soon as they have been instilled. Also, when used for more than 5 days, they can irritate the nose and make it more congested.

 ## CALL OUR OFFICE

During regular hours if
—The treatment does not relieve most of the symptoms.
—The secretions become thick yellow for more than 24 hours.
—Your child develops sinus pain or pressure.
—Your child is missing any school, work, or social activities because of his hay fever.
—The hay fever keeps your child from playing or sleeping.
—You have other concerns or questions.

Instructions for Pediatric Patients by Barton D. Schmitt, M.D., *Pediatrician*
Adapted from YOUR CHILD'S HEALTH, Copyright © 1991 by Barton D. Schmitt, M.D.
Reprinted by permission of Bantam Books.

DEFINITION

Diagnostic Findings

—History of a blow to the head
—Scalp trauma (cut, scrape, bruise, or swelling)

Cause

Every child sooner or later strikes his head. Falls are especially common when your child is learning to walk. Most bruises occur on the forehead. Sometimes black eyes appear 3 days later because the bruising spreads downward by gravity.

Expected Course

Most head trauma simply results in a scalp injury. Big lumps can occur with minor injuries because the blood supply to the scalp is so plentiful. For the same reason small cuts here can bleed profusely. Only 1% to 2% of injured children get a skull fracture. Usually there are no associated symptoms except for a headache at the site of impact. Your child has not had a concussion unless there is temporary unconsciousness, confusion, and amnesia.

 CALL OUR OFFICE

IMMEDIATELY if
—Bleeding won't stop after 10 minutes of direct pressure.
—The skin is split open and probably needs sutures.
—The accident was a severe one involving great force (for example, a fall down a stairway).
—Your child is less than 1 year old.
—The crying lasted more than 10 minutes after the injury.
—Your child had a seizure (convulsion).
—Your child was unconscious or confused after the injury.
—Your child has amnesia regarding the accident (can't remember it).
—A severe headache is present. (Young children with severe headaches either cry or are extremely restless.)
—Vomiting occurred more than twice.
—Your child is acting confused.
—Your child is unusually sleepy and difficult to awaken.
—Speech is slurred.
—Vision is blurred or double.
—Walking or crawling is unsteady.
—The arms are weak.
—There is any neck pain.
—Blood or watery fluid is coming from the nose or ears.

—The pupils are unequal in size.
—The eyes are crossed.
—There are other symptoms that concern you.

HOME CARE

Wound Care. If there is a scrape, wash it off with soap and water. Then apply pressure with a clean cloth (sterile gauze if you have it) for 10 minutes to stop any bleeding. For swelling, apply ice for 20 minutes.

Observation. Observe during the first 2 hours after an injury. Encourage your child to lie down and rest until all symptoms have cleared. Your child can be allowed to sleep; trying to keep your child awake continuously is unnecessary. Just keep an eye on him while he's sleeping and awaken him after 2 hours to check his ability to walk and talk.

Diet. Only give clear fluids (ones you can see through) until your child has gone 6 hours without vomiting. Vomiting is common after head injuries, and there is no need to have him vomit up his dinner.

Pain Medicines. Don't give any pain medicine. If the headache is bad enough to need acetaminophen or aspirin, your child should be checked by a physician.

Special Precautions and Awakening. Although your child is probably fine, close observation for 48 hours will ensure that no serious complication is missed.
—Awakening your child twice during the night: Do this once at your bedtime and once 4 hours later. Awakening him every hour is unnecessary and next to impossible. Arouse him until he is walking and talking normally. Do this for two nights. Sleep in his room or have him sleep in your room for those two nights. If his breathing becomes abnormal or his sleep is otherwise unusual, awaken him to be sure a coma is not developing.
—Checking pupils to make sure they are equal in size and become smaller when you shine a flashlight on them is unnecessary. Unequal pupils are never seen before other symptoms such as confusion and difficult walking are present. In addition, this test is difficult to perform with uncooperative children or dark-colored irises.

 CALL OUR OFFICE

Later if
—The headache becomes severe.
—Vomiting occurs three or more times.
—The pupils become unequal in size.
—Your child becomes difficult to awaken or confused.
—Walking or talking becomes difficult.
—Your child's condition worsens in any other way.

MENSTRUAL CRAMPS (DYSMENORRHEA)

DEFINITION

Diagnostic Findings

—Cramps during the first 1 or 2 days of a period
—Pain in lower midabdomen
—Pain possibly radiating to the lower back or both thighs
—Associated symptoms of nausea, vomiting, diarrhea, or dizziness in some girls

Cause

Menstrual cramps are experienced by more than 50% of girls and women during menstrual periods. They are caused by strong contractions (even spasms) of the muscles in the womb (uterus) as it tries to expel menstrual blood. Menstrual periods usually are not painful during the first 1 to 2 years after a girl has started having periods. However, once ovulation (the release of an egg from the ovary) begins, the level of progesterone in the bloodstream increases and leads to stronger contractions and some cramps.

Expected Course

Cramps last 2 or 3 days and usually occur with each menstrual period. There are some drugs that can keep the pain to a very mild level. The cramps often disappear permanently after the first pregnancy and delivery, probably because the opening of the womb (cervical os) is stretched.

HOME CARE

Ibuprofen. Ibuprofen (Advil and Nuprin are two brand names) is an excellent drug for menstrual cramps. It not only decreases the pain but also decreases contractions of the uterus. Until the fall of 1984, it was only available by prescription (as Motrin). Because of an excellent safety record, it can now be obtained without a prescription in 200 mg tablets.

Your daughter can take one or two tablets four or fives times per day. Always give two tablets as the first dosage. The drug should be started as soon as there is any menstrual flow or the day before, if possible. Don't wait for the onset of menstrual cramps. Ibuprofen should make your daughter feel good enough not to miss anything important.

If you don't have ibuprofen, give aspirin until you can obtain ibuprofen.

Local Heat. A heating pad or warm washcloth applied to the area of pain may be helpful. A 20-minute warm bath twice daily may reduce the pain.

Aggravating Factors. Any type of pain will seem more severe in people who are tired or upset. Your daughter should try to avoid exhaustion and inadequate sleep during menstrual periods. If your daughter has troubles or worries, encourage her to share them with someone.

Full Activity During Menstrual Cramps. Your daughter should not miss any school, work, or social activities because of menstrual cramps. If the pains are limiting your daughter's activities even though she is using ibuprofen, ask your physician about stronger medication.

Common Mistakes. A common mistake is to go to bed, but people who are busy usually notice their pain less. There are absolutely no restrictions; your daughter can go to school, take physical education classes, swim, take a shower or bath, wash her hair, go outside in bad weather, date, and so on during her menstrual periods.

 CALL OUR OFFICE

IMMEDIATELY if
—The pain becomes so bad that your daughter is unable to walk normally.
—An unexplained fever (over 100° F [37.8° C]) occurs.
—Your daughter starts feeling very sick.

During regular hours if
—Ibuprofen doesn't provide adequate pain relief.
—The menstrual cramps cause your daughter to miss school or other important activities.
—A vaginal discharge occurs.
—The pain increases with urination or bowel movements.
—The pain persists beyond the last day of menstrual flow.
—You have other concerns or questions.

Instructions for Pediatric Patients by Barton D. Schmitt, M.D., *Pediatrician*
Adapted from YOUR CHILD'S HEALTH, Copyright © 1991 by Barton D. Schmitt, M.D.
Reprinted by permission of Bantam Books.

DEFINITION

Nosebleeds (epistaxis) are very common throughout childhood. They are usually caused by dryness of the nasal lining plus the normal rubbing and picking that all children do when the nose becomes blocked. Vigorous nose blowing can also cause bleeding. All of these behaviors are increased in children with nasal allergies.

HOME CARE

Lean Forward and Spit Out Any Blood. Have your child sit up and lean forward so he does not have to swallow the blood. Have a basin available so he can spit out any blood that drains into his throat. Blow his nose free of any large clots that might interfere with applying pressure.

Squeeze the Soft Part of the Nose. Tightly pinch the soft parts of the nose against the center wall for 10 minutes. Don't release the pressure until 10 minutes are up. If the bleeding continues, you may not be pressing on the right spot. During this time, your child will have to breathe through his mouth.

If Bleeding Continues, Use Vasoconstrictor Nose Drops and Squeeze Again. If the nosebleed hasn't stopped, insert a piece of gauze covered with vasoconstrictor nose drops (for example, Neo-Synephrine) or petroleum jelly into the nostril. Squeeze again for 10 minutes. Leave the gauze in for another 10 minutes before removing it. If bleeding persists, call our office but continue the pressure in the meantime.

Swallowed blood is irritating to the stomach. Don't be surprised if it is vomited up.

Prevention

—A small amount of petroleum jelly applied twice each day to the center wall (septum) inside the nose is often helpful for relieving dryness and irritation.

—Increasing the humidity in the room at night by using a humidifier may also be helpful.
—Get your child into the habit of putting 2 or 3 drops of warm water in each nostril before blowing a stuffy nose.
—Avoid aspirin. One aspirin can increase the tendency of the body to bleed easily for up to a week and can make nosebleeds last much longer.
—If your child has nasal allergies, treating them with antihistamines will help break the itching-bleeding cycle.

Common Mistakes in Treating Nosebleed

—A cold washcloth applied to the forehead, back of the neck, or under the upper lip does not help to stop a nosebleed.
—Pressing on the bony part of the nose does not stop a nosebleed.
—Avoid packing the nose with anything, because when it is removed, bleeding usually recurs.

CALL OUR OFFICE

IMMEDIATELY if
—The bleeding does not stop after 20 minutes of direct pressure.
—Your child faints or feels dizzy when he stands up.

During regular hours if
—Nosebleeds occur daily even after petroleum jelly and humidification are used.
—You have other concerns or questions.

Instructions for Pediatric Patients by Barton D. Schmitt, M.D., *Pediatrician*
Adapted from YOUR CHILD'S HEALTH, Copyright © 1991 by Barton D. Schmitt, M.D.
Reprinted by permission of Bantam Books.

DEFINITION

A pinworm is a white, very thin worm about ¼ inch long that moves. If it doesn't move it's probably lint or a thread. Pinworms usually are seen in the anal and buttock area, especially at night or early in the morning. Occasionally one is found on the surface of a bowel movement. More than 10% of children have them. They do not cause any serious health problems, but they can cause considerable itching and irritation of the anal area and buttocks.

HOME TREATMENT WHEN PINWORM IS SEEN

Antipinworm Medicine. If you have definitely seen a pinworm, your child needs to be treated. The pinworm

medicine is called _____. The

dose is _____, given _____.

Treatment of Other Family Members for Pinworm. Children are usually infected by children outside the family. If anyone else in your family has symptoms or anyone sleeps with your child, call our office during office hours for instructions. Physicians do not agree on whether to treat everyone in the family or only those with symptoms. If any of your child's friends have similar symptoms, be sure to tell their parents to get them tested. Dogs and cats do not carry pinworms.

 ## CALL OUR OFFICE

During regular hours if
—The skin around the anus becomes red or tender. (*Streptococcus* bacteria have a special affinity for this site.)
—The anal itching is not resolved within 1 week after treatment.
—You have other concerns or questions.

SUSPICIOUS SYMPTOMS BUT PINWORM NOT SEEN

Definition

If your child has itching or irritation of the anal area, he could have pinworms. Keep in mind that many children get itching in this area just from washing their anal area too frequently or vigorously with soap.

Check your child for pinworms as follows: First, look for a ¼ inch, white, threadlike worm that moves. Examine the area around the anus using a flashlight. Do this a few hours after your child goes to bed and first thing in the morning for two consecutive nights. If no adult pinworm is seen, do a cellophane tape test for pinworm eggs.

Instructions for Cellophane Tape Test

Pick up glass slides at our office (two for each child) and mark your child's name on the slides. Touch the sticky side of a piece of clear cellophane tape to the skin on both sides of the anus. Do this in the morning soon after your child has awakened and definitely before any bath or shower. Do this two mornings in a row. Apply one piece of tape to each slide. Bring the slides to our office for examination with a microscope. We will call you to give you the results. If pinworm eggs are seen, we will prescribe a medication.

PINWORM EXPOSURE OR CONTACT

If your child has had recent contact with a child who has pinworms but has no symptoms, your child probably won't get them. Pinworms are harmless and are never present very long without causing some anal itching. If you want to be sure your child doesn't have them, wait for at least 1 month. The swallowed egg will not mature into an adult pinworm for 3 to 4 weeks. Then contact our office about doing a cellophane tape test for pinworm eggs.

PREVENTION OF PINWORMS

Infection is caused by swallowing pinworm eggs. Your children can get pinworms no matter how carefully you keep them and your house clean. The following hygiene measures, however, can help to reduce the chances of reinfection of your child or new infections in other people.
—Have your child scrub hands and fingernails thoroughly before each meal and after each use of the toilet. Keep the fingernails cut short because eggs can collect here. Thumb sucking and nail biting should be discouraged.
—Vacuum or wet mop your child's entire room once every week because any eggs scattered on the floor are infectious for 1 to 2 weeks.
—Machine washing at regular temperature will kill any eggs present in clothing or bedding.

 Instructions for Pediatric Patients by Barton D. Schmitt, M.D., *Pediatrician*
Adapted from YOUR CHILD'S HEALTH, Copyright © 1991 by Barton D. Schmitt, M.D.
Reprinted by permission of Bantam Books.

The following four skin injuries are covered. Go directly to the type of injury that pertains to your child.

1. Cuts and scratches
2. Scrapes (abrasions)
3. Puncture wounds
4. Bruises

1. CUTS AND SCRATCHES

DEFINITION

Most cuts are superficial and extend only partially through the skin. They are caused by sharp objects. The cuts that need sutures are deep and leave the skin edges separated. Another rule of thumb is that cuts need sutures if they are longer than ½ inch (¼ inch if on the face).

CALL OUR OFFICE

IMMEDIATELY if
—Bleeding won't stop after 10 minutes of direct pressure.
—The skin is split open.
—The cut is deep.
—There is any dirt in the wound that you can't get out.

NOTE: Lacerations must be sutured within 8 hours of the time of injury, and the infection rate is far lower if they are closed within 2 hours.

During regular hours if
—Your child hasn't had a tetanus booster in more than 10 years (5 years for dirty cuts).

HOME CARE

Treatment. Wash your hands. Then wash the wound vigorously for at least 5 minutes with water and liquid soap. Rinse the wound well. If the area is one that will probably get dirty (such as the hands or feet), cover it with a bandage or sterile gauze and adhesive tape for several days. Change the dressing daily. Antiseptic ointments or sprays are unnecessary. Don't use alcohol or Merthiolate on open wounds. They sting and damage normal tissue.

Common Mistakes in Treating Cuts and Scratches. Teach your children that kissing an open wound is dangerous, because the wound will become contaminated by the many germs in the human mouth. Let the scab fall off by itself; picking it off may cause a scar.

CALL OUR OFFICE

Later if
—The cut looks infected (for example, there is pus).
—A red streak runs from the wound.
—Pain, redness, or swelling increases after 48 hours.
—The wound doesn't heal by 10 days.

2. SCRAPES (ABRASIONS)

DEFINITION

An abrasion is an area of superficial skin that has been scraped off during a fall (for example, a floor burn or skinned knee).

CALL OUR OFFICE

IMMEDIATELY if
—There is any dirt or grime in the wound that you can't get out.
—It was a bicycle-spoke injury.
—It was a washing machine wringer injury.
—It is quite deep.
—It involves a very large area.
—The pain is severe.

During regular hours if
—Your child hasn't had a tetanus booster in over 10 years.

HOME CARE

Cleaning the Scrape. First, wash your hands. Then wash the wound vigorously for at least 5 minutes with warm water and liquid soap. The area will probably need to be scrubbed several times with a wet piece of gauze to get all the dirt out. You may have to remove some dirt particles (for example, gravel) with a tweezers. If there is tar in the wound, it can often be removed by rubbing it with petroleum jelly, followed by soap and water again. A liquid soap cuts grease better than bar soap. Pieces of loose skin should be cut off with sterile scissors, especially if the pieces of skin are dirty. Rinse the wound well.

Dressing the Scrape. If the scrape is small, leave it exposed to the air. If it is large, cover it with a nonsticking dressing. Change this in 12 hours, and after 24 hours leave the wound exposed to the air. **EXCEPTION:** Abra-

(Continued on the reverse side)

Instructions for Pediatric Patients by Barton D. Schmitt, M.D., *Pediatrician*
Adapted from YOUR CHILD'S HEALTH, Copyright © 1991 by Barton D. Schmitt, M.D.
Reprinted by permission of Bantam Books.

sions on the hands and feet or overlying joints need daily dressing changes until healed.

Antibiotic Ointments.   Antiseptic ointments or sprays in general are unnecessary. However, abrasions overlying the elbow or knee undergo constant stretch. To prevent cracking and reopening of these, apply an antibiotic ointment to keep the crust soft. Use Bacitracin or Betadine ointment. Cleanse the area daily with warm water, and then reapply the ointment.

Pain Relief.   Because abrasions can hurt badly, use acetaminophen for the first day.

 ## CALL OUR OFFICE

Later if
—The scrape looks infected (for example, pus is present).
—The scrape doesn't heal by 2 weeks.

3. PUNCTURE WOUNDS

DEFINITION

The skin has been completely punctured by an object that is pointed and narrow, such as a nail. The wound is not wide enough to need sutures. Since puncture wounds usually seal over quickly, there is a greater chance of wound infection with this type of skin injury. Puncture wounds of the upper eyelid are especially dangerous and can lead to a brain abscess. A deep infection of the foot can begin with swelling of the top of the foot 1 to 2 weeks after the puncture. Another risk is tetanus if your child is not immunized.

 ## CALL OUR OFFICE

IMMEDIATELY if
—A dirty object caused the puncture wound.
—The skin was quite dirty at the time.
—You can see some debris in the wound after soaking.
—The tip of the object could have broken off in the wound.
—The puncture is on the head, chest, or abdomen or overlying a joint.
—Your child has never received a tetanus shot.

During regular hours if
—Your child hasn't had a tetanus booster in more than 5 years.

HOME CARE

Treatment.   Soak the wound in hot water and a liquid soap for 15 minutes. Cut off any flaps of loose skin. If you can make the wound rebleed, that will be helpful. A bandage and antibiotic ointment on the wound for 12 hours will help to keep the opening clean.

 ## CALL OUR OFFICE

Later if
—The wound looks infected (for example, pus is present).
—A red streak runs from the wound.
—Pain, redness, or swelling increases after 48 hours.

4. BRUISES

DEFINITION

Bleeding into the skin from damaged blood vessels gives a black and blue mark. Since the skin is not broken, there is no risk of infection. Bruises usually follow injury caused by blunt objects. Unexplained bruises can indicate a bleeding tendency. (**EXCEPTION:** "Unexplained" bruises overlying the shins are usually not a sign of a bleeding tendency: children often bump this area and then forget about it.)

CALL OUR OFFICE

IMMEDIATELY If
—Bruises are unexplained *and* several in number.

HOME CARE

Bruises.   Apply ice for 20 to 30 minutes. No other treatment should be necessary. Give acetaminophen for pain. Avoid aspirin because it may prolong the bleeding. Bruises clear in about 2 weeks.

Blood Blisters.   Do not open blisters; it will only increase the possibility of infection. They will dry up and peel off in 1 to 2 weeks.

Instructions for Pediatric Patients by Barton D. Schmitt, M.D., *Pediatrician*
Adapted from YOUR CHILD'S HEALTH, Copyright © 1991 by Barton D. Schmitt, M.D.
Reprinted by permission of Bantam Books.

Surgical removal of the tonsils and adenoids (known as a T&A) is the most common operation performed on children in the United States (400,000 per year). It has been described as "an American ritual." Although as many as 30% of children in some communities undergo a T&A, only 2% or 3% of children have adequate medical indications for this procedure. Although the decision to proceed is a medical one, the frequency of questionable surgery means that parents need to be armed with more facts.

The tonsils are not just some worthless pieces of tissue that block our view of the throat. They have a purpose. They produce antibodies that fight nose and throat infections. They confine the infection to the throat, rather than allowing it to spread to the neck or bloodstream. Other beneficial functions of the tonsils and adenoids are being studied.

RISKS OF A T&A

T&A procedures are not without risk. Under ideal conditions, the death rate is still 1 child per 15,000 operations. Approximately 5% of children bleed on the fifth to eighth postoperative day and require a transfusion or additional surgery. All children experience throat discomfort for several days. Some children whose speech was previously normal develop hypernasal speech because the soft palate no longer closes completely.

ERRONEOUS REASONS FOR A T&A

Many T&As are performed for unwarranted reasons. By all means, don't pressure a physician to remove your child's tonsils. A few physicians have difficulty saying no. You can always find someone to perform surgery on your child; in fact, this is the main risk of "doctor shopping."

"Large" Tonsils. Large tonsils do not mean "bad" tonsils or infected tonsils. The tonsils are normally large during childhood (called "physiologic hypertrophy"). They can't be "too large" unless they touch each other. The peak size is reached between 8 and 12 years of age. Thereafter, they spontaneously shrink in size each year, as do all of the body's lymph tissues.

Recurrent Colds and Viral Sore Throats. Several studies have shown that T&As do not decrease the frequency of viral upper respiratory infections (URIs). These URIs are unavoidable. Eventually your child develops immunity to these viruses and experiences fewer colds per year.

Recurrent Strep Throats. Recent studies have shown that a child does not have fewer streptococcal infections of the throat after the tonsils are removed unless the child experiences seven or more strep infections per year (a rare occurrence). For children with seven or more severe throat infections per year, some physicians would recommend daily penicillin for 6 months instead of a T&A, since penicillin can almost always eradicate the strep bacteria from the tonsils. The strep carrier state (which causes no symptoms and is harmless and not contagious) is not an indication for a T&A.

Recurrent Ear Infections. This reason for a T&A was formerly controversial, but more recent studies have shown that removal of the adenoids will not open the eustachian tube and decrease the frequency of ear infections or fluid in the middle ear. The exceptions are children who also have persistent nasal obstruction and mouth breathing caused by large adenoids. Recurrent ear infections usually respond to a 3-month course of antibiotics. Persistent middle-ear fluid may require the insertion of ventilation tubes in the eardrums.

School Absence. If your child misses school for vague reasons (including sore throats), removing the tonsils will not improve attendance.

Miscellaneous Conditions. A T&A will not help a poor appetite, hay fever, asthma, febrile convulsions, or bad breath. There are few medical conditions that have not at one time or another been blamed on the tonsils.

MEDICAL INDICATIONS FOR A T&A

Yes, sometimes the tonsils should come out. But the benefits must outweigh the risks. All but the first two of the following valid reasons are rare. The ear, nose, and throat physician will decide if the tonsils, adenoids, or both need removal.

Persistent Mouth Breathing. Mouth breathing during colds or hay fever is common. Continued mouth breathing is less common and deserves an evaluation to see if it is due to large adenoids. The open-mouth appearance results in teasing, and the mouth breathing itself leads to changes in the facial bone structure (including an overbite that could require orthodontics).

Abnormal Speech. The speech can be muffled by large tonsils or made hyponasal (no nasal resonance) by large adenoids. Although other causes are possible, an evaluation is in order.

Severe Snoring. Snoring can have many causes. If the adenoids are the cause, they should be removed. In severe cases, the loud snoring is associated with retractions (pulling in of the spaces between the ribs) and is interrupted by 30- to 60-second bouts of stopped breathing (sleep apnea).

Heart Failure. Rarely, large tonsils and adenoids interfere so much with breathing that blood oxygen is reduced and the right side of the heart goes into failure. Children with this condition are short of breath, have limited exercise tolerance, and have a rapid pulse.

Persistent Swallowing Difficulties. During a throat infection, the tonsils may temporarily swell enough to cause swallowing problems. If the problem is persistent and the tonsils are seen to be touching, an evaluation is in order. This problem more often occurs in children with a small mouth.

(Continued on the reverse side)

Instructions for Pediatric Patients by Barton D. Schmitt, M.D., *Pediatrician*
Adapted from YOUR CHILD'S HEALTH, Copyright © 1991 by Barton D. Schmitt, M.D.
Reprinted by permission of Bantam Books.

Recurrent Abscess (Deep Infection) of the Tonsil. Your child's physician will make this decision.

Recurrent Abscess of a Lymph Node Draining the Tonsil. Your child's physician will make this decision.

Suspected Tumor of the Tonsil. These rare tumors cause one tonsil to be much larger than the other. The tonsil is also quite firm to the touch, and usually enlarged lymph nodes are found on the same side of the neck.

CALL OUR OFFICE

During regular hours if
—You think your child has a valid indication for a T&A.
—You have other concerns or questions.

REMEMBER: Do not give permission for a T&A unless your child has one of the preceding indications.

Instructions for Pediatric Patients by Barton D. Schmitt, M.D., *Pediatrician*   © 1992 by W. B. Saunders Company
Adapted from YOUR CHILD'S HEALTH, Copyright © 1991 by Barton D. Schmitt, M.D.
Reprinted by permission of Bantam Books.

Ventilation tubes are tiny plastic tubes that are inserted through the eardrum by an ear, nose, and throat surgeon. They are also called tympanostomy tubes, because they are placed in the tympanic membrane (eardrum). At least 1 million children in the United States (most of them 1 to 3 years of age) have ventilation tubes placed each year. The operation costs about $300 if done in the office (only possible with older, cooperative children) and about $1000 if it needs to be done in the hospital with the child under brief anesthesia.

The ventilation tubes are used to drain fluid out of the middle ear space and ventilate the area with air. The eardrum normally vibrates with sound because the space behind it (the middle ear) is filled with air. If it is filled with fluid, the hearing is muffled. This happens with ear infections. Sometimes after the infection clears, the fluid remains. This occurs if the eustachian tube (which runs from the back of the nose to the middle ear) has become blocked and no longer allows air in and fluid out. Following an ear infection, approximately 30% of children still have fluid in the middle ear at 1 month, 20% at 2 months, and 5% at 4 months. The main concern about prolonged fluid in the middle ear is that the associated hearing deficit may have an impact on speech development. Fluid is especially likely to persist if the first bout of ear infection occurs before 6 months of age. By 5 years of age, the eustachian tube is wider and fluid usually doesn't persist long after ear infections are treated.

BENEFITS

Ventilation tubes allow secretions to drain out of the middle ear space and air to reenter. The risk of recurrent ear infections is greatly reduced. The hearing returns to normal with the tube in place and speech development can get back on track. Tubes also prevent the fluid from becoming thicker (a "glue ear") and damaging the middle ear. The ventilation tubes also buy time while the child matures and the eustachian tubes begin to function better.

RISKS

First, approximately 10% of children with ventilation tubes continue to have ear infections with drainage and pain. These bouts of infection, which require antibiotics, probably would have occurred anyway. Second, complications may occur around the tubes coming out. Normally the tubes come out and fall into the ear canal after about 1 year. Sometimes they come out too quickly and need to be replaced by another set. Rarely, they fall into the middle ear space and need to be removed by the surgeon. If they remain in the eardrum for over 2 years, the ear, nose, and throat specialist may need to remove them. Third, after they come out, some leave scarring of the eardrum or a small hole (perforation) that doesn't heal. These both can cause a small hearing loss. Because

of these possible complications and the requirement for an anesthetic, physicians recommend ventilation tubes only for children who definitely need them.

DEALING WITH TEMPORARY HEARING LOSS

As described earlier, most children with a hearing loss caused by fluid in their middle ear just have it on a temporary basis. During this time when you talk with your child, get close to him, get eye contact, get his full attention, and occasionally check that he understands what you have said. If not, speak in a louder voice than you normally use. A common mistake is to assume your child is ignoring you when actually he doesn't hear you. Reduce any background noise from radio or television while talking with your child. If your child goes to school, be sure he sits in front near the teacher. (Middle ear fluid interferes with the ability to hear in a crowd or classroom.) Keep in mind that most children's speech will catch up following a brief period of incomplete hearing.

MEDICAL INDICATIONS

The surgical placement of ventilation tubes is usually indicated if several of the following conditions are met:
— The fluid has been present continuously for over 4 months.
— Both ears are involved.
— The fluid has caused a documented hearing loss. (Although a loss greater than 20 decibels (db) can significantly affect speech, many children with fluid in their ears have nearly normal hearing.)
— The fluid has caused a speech delay (for example, child is not using 3 words by 18 months or 20 words by 2 years).
— Recurrent ear infections have failed to respond to treatment with continuous antibiotics for several months.

PREVENTION OF CHRONIC EAR FLUID

Chronic ear fluid and recurrent ear infections are usually due to a blocked eustachian tube. In some children, however, there are contributing factors:
— Exposure to adults who smoke can cause ear problems.
— Drinking a bottle while lying down (or bottle propping) can cause milk to enter the middle ear space.
— Children with nasal allergies have more frequent ear fluid buildup. Consider this factor if your child has associated hay fever, eczema, asthma, or food allergies.

(Continued on the reverse side)

Instructions for Pediatric Patients by Barton D. Schmitt, M.D., *Pediatrician*
Adapted from YOUR CHILD'S HEALTH, Copyright © 1991 by Barton D. Schmitt, M.D.
Reprinted by permission of Bantam Books.

VENTILATION TUBES SURGERY *Continued*

—Children with nightly snoring caused by large adenoids may also have ear problems (request the guideline: "Tonsil and Adenoid Surgery").

If any of these triggers are present with your child, treat or eliminate them before considering ventilation tubes.

CALL OUR OFFICE

During regular hours if
—You have other questions or concerns regarding ventilation tubes.

Instructions for Pediatric Patients by Barton D. Schmitt, M.D., *Pediatrician*
Adapted from YOUR CHILD'S HEALTH, Copyright © 1991 by Barton D. Schmitt, M.D.
Reprinted by permission of Bantam Books.

DEFINITION

Most contaminated wounds that are going to become infected do so 24 to 72 hours after the initial injury. Keep in mind that a 2 mm to 3 mm rim of pinkness or redness confined to the edge of a wound can be normal, especially if the wound is sutured. However, the area of redness should not spread. Pain and tenderness also occur normally, but the pain and swelling should be greatest during the second day and should thereafter diminish.

HOME CARE

Do not wash the area for 24 hours. Then begin gently washing it with warm water and liquid soap one or two times each day. Apply an antibiotic ointment afterward to keep a scab from forming over the sutures. Swimming and baths are safe after 48 hours.

SUTURE REMOVAL

Sutures are ready for removal at different times, depending on the site of the wound. The following table can serve as a guide.

AREA OF BODY	NUMBER OF DAYS
Face	3 to 4
Neck	5
Scalp	6
Anterior chest or abdomen	7
Arms and back of hands	7
Legs and top of feet	10
Back	12
Palms and soles	14

Have your child's stitches removed on the correct day. Stitches removed too late can leave unnecessary skin marks or even scarring. If any sutures come out early, call your child's physician. In the meantime, reinforce the wound with tape.

SCARS

If your child needed sutures, your child will develop a scar. All wounds heal by scarring. The scar can be kept to a minimum by taking the sutures out at the right time, preventing wound infections, and protecting the wound from being reinjured during the following month. The healing process goes on for 6 to 12 months, and only then will the scar assume its final appearance.

CALL OUR OFFICE

IMMEDIATELY if
—An unexplained fever (over 100° F [37.8° C]) occurs.
—A red streak runs from the wound.

Within 24 hours if
—Pus starts to drain from the wound.
—The wound becomes more tender than it was on the second day.
—A pimple starts to form where a stitch comes through the skin.
—A stitch comes out early.
—You have other concerns or questions.

Instructions for Pediatric Patients by Barton D. Schmitt, M.D., *Pediatrician*
Adapted from YOUR CHILD'S HEALTH, Copyright © 1991 by Barton D. Schmitt, M.D.
Reprinted by permission of Bantam Books.

PART 7

BEHAVIOR PROBLEMS

SLEEP PROBLEMS

CRYING BABY (COLIC)

SLEEP PROBLEMS, PREVENTION OF

NIGHT AWAKENING IN OLDER INFANTS

BEDTIME RESISTANCE

SLEEPING WITH THE PARENTS (BED SHARING)

NIGHTMARES

NIGHT TERRORS

SLEEPWALKING

EARLY MORNING RISER

DISCIPLINE PROBLEMS

STUBBORN TODDLERS

DISCIPLINE BASICS

DISCIPLINE: TIME-OUT TECHNIQUE

DISCIPLINE: PHYSICAL PUNISHMENT

SPOILED CHILDREN, PREVENTION OF

TEMPER TANTRUMS

BITING

HURTING ANOTHER CHILD

SIBLINGS' ARGUMENTS AND QUARRELS

INFANT, TODDLER, AND PRESCHOOLER PROBLEMS

SIBLING RIVALRY TOWARD A NEWBORN

THUMB SUCKING

PACIFIERS

BREATH-HOLDING SPELLS

APPETITE SLUMP IN TODDLERS—See Part 2, Feeding and Eating

TOILET-TRAINING BASICS

TOILET-TRAINING RESISTANCE (ENCOPRESIS AND DAYTIME WETTING)

SOILING WITH CONSTIPATION
TOILET-TRAINING PROBLEMS, PREVENTION OF
SEX EDUCATION FOR PRESCHOOLERS
TICS (TWITCHES)
STUTTERING VERSUS NORMAL DYSFLUENCY

SCHOOL AGE PROBLEMS

SCHOOL PHOBIA OR REFUSAL
ATTENTION DEFICIT DISORDER (SHORT ATTENTION SPAN)
HOMEWORK AND SCHOOLWORK PROBLEMS (SCHOOL UNDERACHIEVERS)
SCHOOLWORK RESPONSIBILITY: HOW TO INSTILL IT
VIDEO GAMES
TELEVISION: REDUCING THE NEGATIVE IMPACT
R-RATED MOVIES: PROTECTING OUR CHILDREN
DIVORCE: ITS IMPACT ON CHILDREN
ADOLESCENTS: DEALING WITH NORMAL REBELLION
BED-WETTING (ENURESIS)
BED-WETTING ALARMS

DEFINITION

—Unexplained crying
—Intermittent crying one or two times per day
—Healthy child (not sick or in pain)
—Well-fed child (not hungry)
—Bouts of crying usually last 1 to 2 hours
—Child fine between bouts of crying
—Child usually consolable when held
—Onset under 4 weeks of age
—Resolution by 3 months of age

Cause

Normally infants do some crying during the first months of life. When babies cry without being hungry, overheated, or in pain, we call it "colic." About 10% of babies have colic. Although no one is certain what causes colic, these babies seem to want to be cuddled or to go to sleep. Colic tends to occur in high-needs babies with a sensitive temperament. Colic is not the result of bad parenting, so don't blame yourself. Colic is also not due to excessive gas, so don't bother with extra burping or special nipples. Cow's milk allergy may cause crying in a few babies, but only if your baby also has diarrhea or vomiting.

Colic is not caused by abdominal pain. The reason the belly muscles feel hard is that a baby needs these muscles to cry. Drawing up the legs is also a normal posture for a crying baby, as is flexing the arms.

Expected Course

This fussy crying is harmless for your baby. The hard crying spontaneously starts to improve at 2 months and is gone by 3 months. Although the crying can't be eliminated, the minutes of crying per day can be dramatically reduced with treatment. In the long run, these children tend to remain more sensitive and alert to their surroundings.

COPING WITH COLIC

1. **Cuddle and rock your baby whenever he cries.** A soothing, rhythmic activity is the best approach to helping a baby relax, settle down, and go to sleep. You can't spoil a baby during the first 3 or 4 months of life. Consider using the following:
—Cuddling your child in a rocking chair
—Rocking your child in a cradle
—Placing your child in a baby carrier or sling (which frees your hands for housework)
—A windup swing or a vibrating chair
—A stroller (or buggy) ride outdoors or indoors
—Anything else you think may be helpful (for example, a pacifier, a warm bath, or massage)

If all else fails, Sleep Tight is a new device that attaches under the crib and simulates the motion and sound of a moving car. This gadget has lessened colicky behavior in over 90% of babies. It costs about $70. For more information call 1-800-662-6542.

2. **A last resort: Let your baby cry himself to sleep.** If none of these measures quiet your baby after 30 minutes of trying and he has been fed recently, your baby is probably trying to go to sleep. He needs you to minimize outside stimuli while he tries to find his own way into sleep. Wrap him up and place him stomach down in his crib. He will probably be somewhat restless until he falls asleep. Close the door, go into a different room, turn up the radio, and do something you want to do. Even consider earplugs or earphones. Save your strength for when your baby definitely needs you. But if he cries for over 15 minutes, pick him up and again try the soothing activities.

3. **Prevent later sleep problems.** Although babies need to be held when they are crying, they don't need to be held all the time. If you overinterpret the advice for colic and rock your baby every time he goes to sleep, you will become indispensable to your baby's sleep process. Your baby's colic won't resolve at 3 months of age. To prevent this from occurring, when your baby is drowsy but not crying, place him in the crib and let him learn to self-comfort and self-induce sleep. Don't rock or nurse him to sleep at these times. Although colic can't be prevented, secondary sleep problems can be.

4. **Promote nighttime sleep (rather than daytime sleep).** Try to keep your infant from sleeping excessively during the daytime. If your baby has napped 3 hours, gently awaken your baby, and entertain or feed him, depending on his needs. In this way the time when your infant sleeps the longest (often 5 hours) will occur during the night.

5. **Try these feeding strategies.** Don't feed your baby every time he cries. Being hungry is only one of the reasons babies cry. It takes about 2 hours for the stomach to empty, so wait that long between feedings or you may cause cramps from bloating. For breast-fed babies, however, nurse them every time they cry until your milk supply is well established and your baby is gaining weight (usually 2 weeks). Babies who feed too frequently during the day become hungry at frequent intervals during the night. If you are breast-feeding, avoid drinking coffee, tea, and colas and avoid taking other stimulants. Suspect a cow's milk allergy if your child also has diarrhea, vomiting, eczema, wheezing, or a strong family history of milk allergy. If any of these factors are present, try a soy formula for 1 week. Soy formulas are nutritionally complete and no more expensive than regular formula. If you are breast-feeding, avoid all forms of cow's milk in your diet for 1 week. If the crying dramatically improves when your child is on the soy formula, call us for additional advice about keeping him on the formula. Also, if you think your child is allergic, but he doesn't improve with soy formula, call us about the elemental formulas.

6. **Get rest and help for yourself.** Although the crying can be reduced, what's left must be endured and shared. Avoid fatigue and exhaustion. Get at least one

(Continued on the reverse side)

Instructions for Pediatric Patients by Barton D. Schmitt, M.D., *Pediatrician*
Adapted from YOUR CHILD'S HEALTH, Copyright © 1991 by Barton D. Schmitt, M.D.
Reprinted by permission of Bantam Books.

nap each day in case the night goes badly. Ask your husband, a friend, or a relative for help with other children and chores. Caring for a colicky baby is a two-person job. Hire a babysitter so you can get out of the house and clear your mind. Talk to someone every day about your mixed feelings. The screaming can drive anyone to desperation.

7. **Avoid these common mistakes.** If you are breast-feeding, don't stop. If your baby needs extra calories, talk with a lactation consultant about ways to increase your milk supply. The available medicines are ineffective and many (especially those containing phenobarbital) are dangerous for children of this age. The medicines that slow intestinal activity (the anticholinergics) can cause fever or constipation. The ones that remove gas bubbles are not helpful according to recent research, but they are harmless. Inserting a thermometer or suppository into the rectum to "release gas" does nothing except irritate the anal sphincter. Don't place your baby face down on a water bed, sheepskin rug, bead-filled pillow, or other soft pillow. While these surfaces can be soothing, they also increase the risk of suffocation and crib death. A young infant may not be able to lift the head adequately to breathe. Stay with TLC (tender loving care) for best results.

CALL OUR OFFICE

IMMEDIATELY if
—It becomes a painful cry rather than a fussy one.
—Your baby cries constantly for more than 3 hours.
—You are afraid you might hurt your baby.
—You have shaken your baby.
—You can't find a way to soothe your baby (inconsolable crying).

During regular hours if
—The colic type of crying occurs three or more times per day.
—The crying began after 1 month of age.
—The crying continues after your baby reaches 3 months of age.
—Diarrhea, vomiting, or constipation occurs with the crying.
—Your baby is not gaining and may be hungry.
—You are exhausted from all the crying.
—Your baby mainly cries when you're trying to sleep.
—You have other questions or concerns.

 Instructions for Pediatric Patients by Barton D. Schmitt, M.D., *Pediatrician*   © 1992 by W. B. Saunders Company
Adapted from YOUR CHILD'S HEALTH, Copyright © 1991 by Barton D. Schmitt, M.D.
Reprinted by permission of Bantam Books.

DEFINITION

Parents want their children to go to bed without resistance and to sleep through the night. They look forward to a time when they can again have 7 or 8 hours of uninterrupted sleep. Newborns, however, have a limit to how many hours they can sleep (usually 4 or 5 hours). By 2 months of age, some 50% of infants can sleep through the night. By 4 months, most infants have acquired this capacity. It may not develop, however, unless you have a plan. Consider the following guidelines if you want to teach your baby that nighttime is a special time for sleeping, that her crib is where she stays at night, and that she can put herself back to sleep. It is far easier to prevent sleep problems before 6 months of age than it is to treat them later.

Newborns

1. **Place your baby in the crib when he is drowsy but awake.** This step is very important. Without it, the other preventive measures will fail. Your baby's last waking memory should be of the crib, not of you or of being fed. He must learn to put himself to sleep without you. Don't expect him to go to sleep as soon as you lay him down. It often takes 20 minutes of restlessness for a baby to go to sleep. If he is crying, rock him and cuddle him; but when he settles down, try to place him in the crib before he falls asleep. Handle naps in the same way. This is how your child will learn to put himself back to sleep after normal awakenings. Don't help your infant when he doesn't need any help.

2. **Hold your baby for all fussy crying during the first 3 months.** All new babies cry some during the day and night. If your baby cries excessively, the cause is probably colic. Always respond to a crying baby. Gentle rocking and cuddling seem to help the most. Babies can't be spoiled during the first 3 or 4 months of life, but even colicky babies have a few times each day when they are drowsy and not crying. On these occasions, place the baby in his crib and let him learn to self-comfort and self-induce sleep.

3. **Carry your baby for at least 3 hours each day when he isn't crying.** This practice will reduce fussy crying.

4. **Do not let your baby sleep for more than 3 consecutive hours during the day.** Attempt to awaken him gently and entertain him. In this way, the time when your infant sleeps the longest will occur during the night. (NOTE: Many newborns can sleep 5 consecutive hours and you can teach your baby to take this longer period of sleep at night.)

5. **Keep daytime feeding intervals to at least 2 hours for newborns.** More frequent daytime feedings (such as hourly) lead to frequent awakenings for small feedings at night. Crying is the only form of communication newborns have. Crying does not always mean your baby is hungry. He may be tired, bored, lonely, or too hot. Hold your baby at these times or put him to bed. Don't let feeding become a pacifier. For every time you nurse your baby, there should be four or five times that you snuggle your baby *without* nursing. Don't let him get into the bad habit of eating every time you hold him. That's called "grazing."

6. **Make middle-of-the-night feedings brief and boring.** You want your baby to think of nighttime as a special time for sleeping. When he awakens at night for feedings, don't turn on the lights, talk to him, or rock him. Feed him quickly and quietly. Provide extra rocking and playtime during the day. This approach will lead to longer periods of sleep at night.

7. **Don't awaken your infant to change diapers during the night.** The exceptions to this rule are soiled diapers or times when you are treating a bad diaper rash. If you must change your child, use as little light as possible (for example, a flashlight), do it quietly, and don't provide any entertainment.

8. **Don't let your baby sleep in your bed.** Once your baby is used to sleeping with you, a move to his own bed will be extremely difficult. Although it's not harmful for your child to sleep with you, you probably won't get a restful night's sleep. So why not teach your child to prefer his own bed? For the first 2 or 3 months, you can keep your baby in a crib or box next to your bed.

9. **Give the last feeding at your bedtime (10 or 11 PM).** Try to keep your baby awake for the 2 hours before this last feeding. Going to bed at the same time every night helps your baby develop good sleeping habits.

Two-Month-Old Babies

1. **Move your baby's crib to a separate room.** By 3 months of age, your baby should be sleeping in a separate room. This will help parents who are light sleepers sleep better. Also, your baby may forget that her parents are available if she can't see them when she awakens. If separate rooms are impractical, at least put up a screen or cover the crib railing with a blanket so that your baby cannot see your bed.

2. **Try to delay middle-of-the-night feedings.** By now, your baby should be down to one feeding during the night. Before preparing a bottle, try holding your baby briefly to see if that will satisfy her. If you must feed her, give 1 or 2 ounces less formula than you would during the day. If you are breast-feeding, nurse for less time at night. As your baby gets close to 4 months of age, try nursing on just one side at night. Never awaken your baby at night for a feeding except at your bedtime.

Four-Month-Old Babies

1. **Try to discontinue the 2:00 AM feeding before it becomes a habit.** By 4 months of age, your bottle-fed baby does not need to be fed more than four times per day. Breast-fed babies do not need more than five nursing sessions per day. If you do not eliminate the night feeding at this time, it will become more difficult to stop as your child gets older. Remember to give the last feeding at 10 or 11 AM. If your child cries during the night, comfort him with a back rub and some soothing words instead of

(Continued on the reverse side)

Instructions for Pediatric Patients by Barton D. Schmitt, M.D., *Pediatrician*
Adapted from YOUR CHILD'S HEALTH, Copyright © 1991 by Barton D. Schmitt, M.D.
Reprinted by permission of Bantam Books.

with a feeding. NOTE: Some breast-fed babies who are not gaining well may need to have formula or cereal supplements several times during the day to help them go without nighttime nursing.

2. **Don't allow your baby to hold his bottle or take it to bed with him.** Babies should think that the bottle belongs to the parents. A bottle in bed leads to middle-of-the-night crying because your baby will inevitably reach for the bottle and find it empty or on the floor.

3. **Make any middle-of-the-night contacts brief and boring.** Comfort your child as little as possible between 10 PM and 6 AM. All children have four or five partial awakenings each night. They need to learn how to go back to sleep on their own. If your baby cries for more than 5 minutes, visit him but don't turn on the light, play with him, or take him out of his crib. Comfort him with a few soothing words and stay for less than 1 minute. This brief contact usually will not be enough to encourage your baby to keep waking you up every night. If your child is standing in the crib, don't try to make him lie down. He can do this himself. If the crying continues, you can check your baby every 15 to 20 minutes, but do not take him out of the crib nor stay in the room until he goes to sleep. (EXCEPTIONS: You feel your baby is sick or afraid.)

Six-Month-Old Children

1. **Provide a friendly soft toy for your child to hold in her crib.** At the age of 6 months, children start to be anxious about separation from their parents. A stuffed animal, doll, or blanket can be a security object that will give comfort to your child when she wakes up during the night.

2. **Leave the door open to your child's room.** Children can become frightened when they are in a closed space and are not sure that their parents are still nearby.

3. **During the day, respond to separation fears by holding and reassuring your child.** This lessens nighttime fears and is especially important for mothers who work outside the home.

4. **For middle-of-the-night fears, make contacts prompt and reassuring.** For mild nighttime fears, check on your child promptly and be reassuring, but keep the interaction as brief as possible. If your child panics when you leave or vomits with crying, stay in your child's room until she is either calm or goes to sleep. Do not take her out of the crib but provide whatever else she needs for comfort, keeping the light off and not talking too much. At most, sit next to the crib with your hand on her.

These measures will calm even a severely upset infant.

One-Year-Old Children

1. **Establish a pleasant and predictable bedtime ritual.** Bedtime rituals, which can start in the early months, become very important to a child by 1 year of age. Children need a familiar routine. Both parents can be involved at bedtime, taking turns with reading or making up stories. Both parents should kiss and hug the child "good night." Be sure that your child's security objects are nearby. Finish the bedtime ritual before your child falls asleep.

2. **Once put to bed, your child should stay there.** Some older infants have temper tantrums at bedtime. They may protest about bedtime or even refuse to lie down. You should ignore these protests and leave the room. You can ignore any ongoing questions or demands your child makes and enforce the rule that your child can't leave the bedroom. If your child comes out, return him quickly to the bedroom and avoid any conversation. If you respond to his protests in this way every time, he will learn not to try to prolong bedtime.

3. **If your child has nightmares or bedtime fears, reassure him.** Never ignore your child's fears or punish him for having fears. Everyone has four or five dreams every night. Some of these are bad dreams. If nightmares become frequent, try to determine what might be causing them, such as something your child might have seen on television.

4. **Don't worry about the amount of sleep your child is getting.** Different people need different amounts of sleep at different ages. The best way you can know that your child is getting enough sleep is that he is not tired during the day. Naps are important to young children but keep them less than 2 hours long. Children stop taking morning naps between 18 months and 2 years of age and give up their afternoon naps between 3 and 6 years of age.

DEFINITION

Approximately 10% to 15% of children between 4 months and 24 months of age have problems sleeping through the night. They wake up and cry one or more times during the night in order to be fed or entertained by their parents. These interruptions usually occur every night. In most instances the child has behaved this way since birth. If your child fits this description, the information presented here will help you understand the problem and take steps to establish a normal nighttime sleeping pattern.

All children have four or five partial awakenings each night after dreams. Most can put themselves back to sleep. Children who have not learned self-comforting and self-quieting skills cry for a parent. If your custom at naps and bedtime is to rock or feed your child until asleep, your infant will not learn how to go back to sleep without your help.

Trained Night Feeders

If your child is over 4 months of age and wants to be fed during the night, deal with this problem first. From birth to 2 months of age, most babies normally awaken twice each night for feedings. Between 2 and 3 months, most need one middle-of-the-night feeding. By 4 months of age, about 90% of infants sleep more than 8 consecutive hours without feeding. Normal children of this age do not need any calories during the night to remain healthy. The other 10% can learn to sleep through the night if you take the following steps:

1. **Lengthen the time between daytime feedings to 4 hours or more.** Nighttime feeding intervals cannot be extended if the daytime intervals are short. If a baby's stomach is conditioned to expect frequent feedings during the day, he will have hunger pangs during the night. This bad habit is called "grazing." It often happens to mothers who don't separate holding from nursing. For every time you nurse your baby, there should be four or five times that you snuggle your baby without nursing. Gradually postpone daytime feeding times until they are more normal for your child's age. If you currently feed your baby hourly, go to 1½ hours. When this is accepted, go to 2 hours. When he cries, provide cuddling or a pacifier. Your goal for formula-fed babies is four meals each day by 4 months of age. (Breast-fed babies often need five feedings each day until 6 months of age when baby foods are introduced.)

2. **Place your baby in the crib drowsy but awake.** When your baby starts to act drowsy, stop feeding him and place him in the crib. His last waking memory needs to be of the crib, not of the breast or bottle. He needs to learn to put himself to sleep. He will need this self-quieting skill to cope with normal awakenings at night. This change will require some crying. For crying, go to your child every 15 minutes, but don't feed him or lift him out of the crib. Give him a hug and leave. Stay for less than 1 minute. Help him learn to self-initiate sleep at naps and bedtime when you can better tolerate the

crying. For middle-of-the-night crying, you can rock him to sleep for now.

3. **Discontinue any bottle in bed immediately.** If you feed your child at bedtime, don't let her hold the bottle. Also feed her in a different room than the bedroom. Try to separate mealtime and nap times. If your baby needs to suck on something to help her go to sleep, offer a pacifier or help her find a thumb. Also, encourage attachment to a favorite stuffed animal or blanket.

4. **Phase out night feedings.** For now, after the 10 or 11 PM last feeding of the day, only feed your baby once during the night and make it brief and boring. If it takes more than 20 minutes, handling or burping is excessive. For other awakenings at night, rock your child to sleep.

After the daytime feeding intervals are normal, start to gradually reduce the amount you feed your baby at night. For bottle-fed babies, the amount of formula you give can be decreased by 1 ounce every few nights until your infant no longer has a craving for food at night. Nurse breast-fed babies on just one side and for fewer minutes.

Trained Night Criers

If your baby is over 4 months of age, cries during the night, calms down when you hold her, and doesn't need to be fed, you have a trained night crier. If you usually rock, cuddle, or walk your baby at the moment of sleep, he becomes unable to return himself to sleep during normal awakenings at night.

1. **Place your baby in the crib drowsy but awake at naps and bedtime.** It's good to hold babies. But when your baby starts to look drowsy, place him in the crib. His last waking memory needs to be of the crib, not of you. He needs to learn to put himself to sleep. If your baby is very fussy, rock him until he settles down or is almost asleep, but stop before he's fully asleep.

2. **For crying, make brief contact every 15 minutes.** Infants cannot learn to self-comfort without some crying. This crying is not harmful. If the crying continues, visit your baby in the crib every 15 minutes. Don't stay longer than 1 minute. Act sleepy. Whisper, "Shhh, be quiet, everyone's sleeping." Add a few reassuring comments and give some gentle pats. Do not turn on the lights or remove your child from the crib. Do not rock or play with the baby, bring her to your bed, or stay in the room for more than 1 minute. Most young infants will cry for 30 to 90 minutes and then fall asleep. If the crying persists, you may recheck your baby every 15 minutes, for 1 minute or less each visit. This brief contact will not reward your baby sufficiently to perpetuate the behavior.

3. **For middle-of-the-night crying, rock your baby to sleep temporarily.** Until your child learns how to put himself to sleep at naps and bedtime, make the middle of the night as easy as possible. Take your crying child out of the crib and rock him to sleep. However, don't talk to him, leave the room, or turn on the lights. After he has learned to quiet himself for naps and bedtime, you can place the same demands on him for middle-

(Continued on the reverse side)

Instructions for Pediatric Patients by Barton D. Schmitt, M.D., *Pediatrician*
Adapted from YOUR CHILD'S HEALTH, Copyright © 1991 by Barton D. Schmitt, M.D.
Reprinted by permission of Bantam Books.

of-the-night crying. Namely, go to him every 15 minutes—but make your contact brief and boring. By then, this problem can be turned around in a few nights.

Fearful Night Criers

After 6 months of age, the normal separation fears of many infants are greater at bedtime and during the night. When you try to leave your child's bedroom, he becomes hysterical, cries nonstop for hours, or cries until he vomits. If your child is between 6 and 18 months of age and has major daytime fears when you leave him, treat his sleep problem as follows:

1. **Stay with your child if he is fearful.** At bedtime and naptime, put your child in the crib drowsy but awake. Stay as long as it takes to calm him, but don't lift him out of the crib. At the most, sit in a chair next to the crib with your hand on his body. A headphone with some good music may help you pass the time. Make a few reassuring comments initially, and then don't talk to him. If it's the middle of the night, consider going to sleep in your child's room in a sleeping bag.

2. **Leave briefly every 15 minutes.** Leave for 1 or 2 minutes every now and then to teach your child that separation is tolerable because you do come back. Leave the door open and a night-light on if your child has separation fears.

3. **Provide lots of holding during the day.** During the day, respond to your child's fears with lots of hugs and comforting. Young babies may need more time being carried about in a front sling or backpack. Children of mothers working outside the home need extra attention and cuddling in the evenings. Also, play separation games such as peekaboo, hide-and-seek, or chase me. Fears and insecurities can be completely treated during the day.

Steps To Take for All Types of Sleep Problems

Whether your baby's problem is trained night feeding, trained night crying, or fearful night crying, the following measures should be helpful:

1. **Move the crib to another room.** If the crib is in your bedroom, move it to a separate room. If this is impossible, cover one of the side rails with a blanket so your baby can't see you when he awakens.

2. **Eliminate long daytime naps.** If your baby has napped for more than 2 hours, awaken her. If she is in the habit of taking three naps during the day, try to change her habit to two naps each day.

3. **Don't change wet diapers during the night.** Change the diaper if it is soiled or if you are treating a bad diaper rash. If you must change your child, use as little light as possible (for example, a flashlight), do it quietly, and don't provide any entertainment.

4. **If he's standing up in the crib, leave him in that position.** Don't try to get him to lie down every time you go in. He will just spring back up as you start toward the door. He can lie down without your help. Encouraging him to lie down soon becomes a game.

CALL OUR OFFICE

During regular hours if
—Your child acts sick.
—Someone in your family cannot tolerate the crying.
—The steps outlined here do not improve your child's sleeping habits within 2 weeks.
—You have other questions or concerns.

Instructions for Pediatric Patients by Barton D. Schmitt, M.D., *Pediatrician*
Adapted from YOUR CHILD'S HEALTH, Copyright © 1991 by Barton D. Schmitt, M.D.
Reprinted by permission of Bantam Books.

DEFINITION

—These children are over 2 years old and refuse to go to bed or stay in the bedroom.

—These children can come out of the bedroom because they no longer sleep in a crib.

—In the usual form, the child goes to sleep while watching television with the parent or sleeps in the parents' bed.

—In a milder form, the child stays in his bedroom but prolongs the bedtime interaction with ongoing questions, unreasonable requests, protests, crying, or temper tantrums.

—In the morning, these children sleep late or have to be awakened.

Cause

These are attempts to test the limits, not fear. Your child has found a good way to postpone bedtime and receive extra entertainment. Your child is stalling and taking advantage of your good nature. If given a choice, over 90% of children would stay up until their parents' bedtime. These children also often try to share the parents' bed at bedtime or sneak into their parents' bed during the middle of the night. By contrast, the child who comes to the parents' bed if he is frightened or not feeling well should be supported at these times.

DEALING WITH BEDTIME RESISTANCE

These recommendations apply to children who are manipulative at bedtime, not fearful.

1. **Start the night with a pleasant bedtime ritual.** Provide a bedtime routine that is pleasant and predictable. Most prebedtime rituals last about 30 minutes and include taking a bath, brushing teeth, reading stories, talking about the day, saying prayers, and other interactions that relax your child. Try to keep the same sequence each night because familiarity is comforting for children. Try to have both parents take turns in creating this special experience. Never cancel this ritual because of misbehavior earlier in the day. Before you give your last hug and kiss and leave your child's bedroom, ask, "Do you need anything else?"

2. **Establish a rule that your child can't leave the bedroom at night.** Enforce the rule that once the bedtime ritual is over and your child is placed in the bedroom, he cannot leave that room. Your child needs to learn to put himself to sleep for naps and at bedtime in his own bed. Do not stay in the room until he lies down or falls asleep. Establish a set bedtime and stick to it. Make it clear that your child is not allowed to leave the bedroom between 8:00 at night and 7:00 in the morning (or whatever sleep time you decide on). Obviously, this change won't be accomplished without some crying or screaming for a few nights.

If your child has been sleeping with you, tell him "Starting tonight, we sleep in separate beds. You have your room, we have our room. You have your bed, we have our bed. You are too old to sleep with us anymore."

3. **Ignore verbal requests.** For ongoing questions or demands from the bedroom, ignore them and do not engage in any conversation with your child. All of these requests should have been dealt with during your prebedtime ritual. Don't return or talk with your child unless you think he is sick. SOME EXCEPTIONS: If your child says he needs to use the toilet, tell him to take care of it himself. If your child says his covers have fallen off and he is cold, promise him you will cover him up after he goes to sleep. You will usually find him well covered.

4. **Close the bedroom door for screaming.** For screaming from the bedroom, tell your child, "I'm sorry I have to close your door. I'll open it as soon as you're quiet." If he pounds on the door, you can open it after 1 or 2 minutes and suggest that he go back to bed. If he does, you can leave the door open. If he doesn't, close the door again. For continued screaming or pounding on the door, reopen it approximately every 15 minutes, telling your child that if he quiets down, the door can stay open. Never spend more that 30 seconds reassuring him.

5. **Close the bedroom door for coming out.** If your child comes out of the bedroom, return him immediately to his bed. During this process, avoid any lectures and skip the hug and kiss. Get good eye contact and remind him again that he cannot leave his bedroom during the night. Warn him that if he comes out again, you're sorry but you will need to close the door. If he comes out, close the door. Tell him, "I'll be happy to open your door as soon as you're in your bed." If your child says he's in his bed, open the door. If he says nothing, every 10 to 15 minutes, open the door just enough to ask your child if he's in his bed now.

6. **Barricade or lock the bedroom door for repeated coming out.** If your child is very determined and continues to come out of the bedroom, consider putting a barricade in front of his door, such as a strong gate. A half-door or plywood plank may also serve this purpose. If your child makes a ruckus at night, you can go to him without taking him out of his bedroom and say, "Everyone is sleeping, I'll see you in the morning."

If your child learns to climb over the barricade, a full door may need to be kept closed until morning with a hook, piece of rope, or chain lock. While you may consider this step extreme, it can be critical for protecting children less than 5 years old who wander through the house at night without an understanding of dangers (such as the stove, hot water, electricity, knives, and going outdoors).

If your child does not get into trouble at night, you can open the door as soon as he falls asleep. Reassure him that you will do this. Also, each night give him a fresh chance to stay in the bedroom with the door open. (CAUTION: If your child has bedtime fears, don't close his door. Get him some counseling.)

(Continued on the reverse side)

Instructions for Pediatric Patients by Barton D. Schmitt, M.D., *Pediatrician*
Adapted from YOUR CHILD'S HEALTH, Copyright © 1991 by Barton D. Schmitt, M.D.
Reprinted by permission of Bantam Books.

7. **Return him if he comes into your bed at night.** For middle-of-the-night attempts to crawl into your bed, unless your child is fearful, sternly order your child back to his own bed. If he doesn't move, escort him back immediately without any physical contact or pleasant conversation. If you are asleep when your child crawls into your bed, return him as soon as you discover his presence. If he attempts to come out again, temporarily close his door. If you are a deep sleeper, consider using some signaling device that will awaken you if your child enters your bedroom (such as a chair placed against your door or a loud bell attached to your doorknob). Some parents simply lock their bedroom door. Remind your child that it is not polite to interrupt other people's sleep. Tell him that if he awakens at night and can't go back to sleep, he can read or play quietly in his room, but he is not to bother his parents.

8. **Help the roommate.** If the bedtime screaming wakes up a roommate, have the well-behaved sibling sleep in a separate room until the nighttime behavior has improved. Tell your child with the sleep problem that his roommate cannot return until he stays in his room quietly for three consecutive nights. If you have a small home, have the sibling sleep in your room temporarily and this will be an added incentive for your other child to improve.

9. **Praise appropriate sleeping behavior.** Praise your child in the morning if he stayed in his bedroom all night. Tell him that people are happier when they get a good night's sleep. If he fought bedtime and fell asleep late, wake him up at the regular time so he will be tired earlier the next evening.

10. **Start bedtime later if you want to minimize bedtime crying.** The later the bedtime, the more tired your child will be and the less resistance he will offer. For most children, you can pick the bedtime hour. For children who are very stubborn and cry a lot, you may want to start the bedtime at 10 PM (or whenever your child naturally falls asleep). If the bedtime is at 10 PM, start the bedtime ritual at 9:30 PM. After your child learns to fall asleep without fussing at 10 PM, move the bedtime back by 15 minutes every week. In children who can't tell time, you can gradually (over 8 weeks or so) achieve an 8 PM bedtime in this way with many fewer tantrums (this technique was described by Adams and Rickert in 1989). However, don't let your child sleep late in the morning or you won't be able to advance the bedtime.

CALL OUR OFFICE

During regular hours if
—Your child is not sleeping well after trying this program for 2 weeks.
—Your child needs to be locked in the bedroom for more than 7 nights.
—Your child is frightened at bedtime (he probably needs some counseling).
—Your child has lots of nightmares.
—Your child also has several discipline problems during the day.
—You have other questions or concerns.

Instructions for Pediatric Patients by Barton D. Schmitt, M.D., *Pediatrician*
Adapted from YOUR CHILD'S HEALTH, Copyright © 1991 by Barton D. Schmitt, M.D.
Reprinted by permission of Bantam Books.

In general, bed sharing is not recommended. Although it's not harmful for your children to sleep with you, it's unnecessary and it may cause problems for you. Once begun, it's a rather hard habit to undo; so don't start until you have all the facts.

1.   Your child doesn't need this arrangement to be secure and happy. Children's fears and insecurities can be dealt with during the day. The majority of children in the United States sleep happily in their own bed. In poor countries, families sleep together by necessity.

2.   Bed sharing is not quality time. If your child is asleep in your bed, it is neutral time. If your child is crying and keeping you awake, it is aggravating time. So there is really no quality time here.

3.   Several studies have shown that over 50% of children who sleep with parents resist going to bed and awaken several times at night. Most parents who bed share have to lie down with their child for 30 minutes to get them to sleep. Most of these parents also do not get a good night's sleep.

4.   Bed sharing is never a long-term solution to sleep problems. Your child will not learn to sleep well in your bed and then decide on his own to start sleeping in his bed. With every passing month, the habit becomes harder to change.

PREVENTION OF BED SHARING

—During infancy, place your child in the crib drowsy but awake. In this way he will learn to put himself back to sleep following normal awakenings.
—Make middle-of-the-night feedings brief and boring. This is hard to do if you are sleeping with your child.

—Put your child in his own room by 3 or 4 months of age. Have a rule that he does not leave the crib at night, and after 2 years old, that he does not leave the bedroom. Most children in the United States follow these guidelines and do just fine.

PUTTING AN END TO BED SHARING

If you are sleeping with your child and want to stop it, here are some suggestions:
—Tell your child the new rule. "You are too old to sleep with us anymore. You have your bed, and we have our bed. Starting tonight, we want you to stay in your bed during the night."
—If your child leaves the bedroom, return him immediately. If he does it again, close the door until he's in his bed.
—If he crawls into your bed during the night, order him back to his own bed using a stern voice. If he doesn't move, escort him back immediately without any conversation.
—If you are asleep when he crawls into your bed, return him as soon as you discover him. If he attempts to come out again, temporarily close his door. If you are a deep sleeper, consider using some signaling device that will awaken you if your child enters your bedroom (such as a chair placed against your door or a loud bell attached to your doorknob). Some parents simply lock their bedroom door. Remind your child that "it is not polite to interrupt people who are sleeping."
—Expect some crying. Young children normally cry when they don't get their way. But continue to be firm and you will win back the privacy of your bed.

Instructions for Pediatric Patients by Barton D. Schmitt, M.D., *Pediatrician*
Adapted from YOUR CHILD'S HEALTH, Copyright © 1991 by Barton D. Schmitt, M.D.
Reprinted by permission of Bantam Books.

DEFINITION

Nightmares are scary dreams that awaken a child. Occasional bad dreams are normal at all ages after about 6 months of age. When infants have a nightmare, they cry and scream until someone comes to them. When preschoolers have a nightmare, they usually cry and run into their parents' bedroom. Older children begin to understand what a nightmare is and put themselves back to sleep without waking their parents.

Cause

Everyone dreams four or five times each night. Some dreams are good, and some are bad. Dreams help the mind process complicated events or information. The content of nightmares usually relates to developmental challenges: toddlers have nightmares about separation from their parents; preschoolers, about monsters or the dark; and school-age children, about death or real dangers. Frequent nightmares may be caused by violent television shows or movies.

DEALING WITH NIGHTMARES

1.   **Reassure and cuddle your child.** Explain to your child that she was having a bad dream. Sit on the bed until your child is calm. Offer to leave the bedroom door open (never close the door on a fearful child). Provide a night-light, especially if your child has fears of the dark. Most children return to sleep fairly quickly.

2.   **Help your child talk about the bad dreams during the day.** Your child may not remember what the dream was about unless you can remind him of something he said about it when he woke up. If your child was dreaming about falling or being chased, reassure him that lots of children dream about that. If your child has the same bad dream over and over again, help him imagine a good ending to the bad dream. Encourage your child to use a strong person or a magic weapon to help him overcome the bad person or event in the dream. You may want to help your child draw pictures or write stories about the new happier ending for the dream. Working through a bad fear often takes several conversations about it.

3.   **Protect your child against frightening movies and television shows.** For many children, violent or horror movies cause bedtime fears and nightmares. These fears can persist for months or years. Absolutely forbid these movies before 13 years of age. Between 13 and 17 years, the maturity and sensitivity of your child must be considered carefully in deciding when he is ready to deal with the uncut versions of R-rated movies. Be vigilant about slumber parties or Halloween parties. Tell your child to call you if the family he is visiting is showing scary movies.

CALL OUR OFFICE

During regular hours if
—The nightmares become worse.
—The nightmares are not minimal after using this approach for 2 weeks.
—The fear interferes with daytime activities.
—Your child has several fears.
—You have other concerns or questions.

Instructions for Pediatric Patients by Barton D. Schmitt, M.D., *Pediatrician*
Adapted from YOUR CHILD'S HEALTH, Copyright © 1991 by Barton D. Schmitt, M.D.
Reprinted by permission of Bantam Books.

DEFINITION

—Your child is frightened but cannot be awakened or comforted.

—Your child is agitated and may sit up or run helplessly about, possibly screaming or talking wildly.

—Your child doesn't appear to realize that you are there. Although the eyes are wide open and staring, your child looks right through you.

—Your child may mistake objects or persons in the room for dangers.

—The episode lasts from 10 to 30 minutes.

—Your child cannot remember the episode in the morning (amnesia).

—The child is usually 1 to 8 years old.

Cause

Night terrors are an inherited disorder in which a child tends to have dreams during deep sleep from which it is difficult to awaken. They occur in 2% of children and usually are not caused by psychologic stress. Being overtired can trigger night terrors, so be sure your child goes to bed at a reasonable time. For younger children, consider having them return to a daily nap.

Expected Course

Night terrors usually occur within 2 hours of bedtime. Night terrors are harmless and each episode will end of its own accord in deep sleep. The problem usually disappears by 12 years of age or sooner.

DEALING WITH NIGHT TERRORS

1. **Try to help your child return to normal sleep.** Your goal is to help your child go from agitated sleep to a calm sleep. You won't be able to awaken your child, so don't try to. Turn on the lights so that your child is less confused by shadows. Make soothing comments such as "You are all right. You are home in your own bed. You can rest now." Speak slowly and repetitively. Such comments are usually better than silence. Some children like to have their hand held during this time, but most will pull away. Hold your child only if it seems to help your child feel better. There is no way to abruptly shorten the episode. Shaking your child or shouting at him will just cause the child to become more agitated and will prolong the attack.

2. **Protect your child against injury.** During a night terror, a child can fall down a stairway, run into a wall, or break a window. Try to gently direct your child back to bed.

3. **Prepare babysitters or overnight leaders for these episodes.** Explain to people who care for your child what a night terror is and what to do if one happens. Understanding this will prevent them from overreacting if your child has a night terror.

4. **Try to prevent night terrors with prompted awakenings.** If your child has frequent night terrors, Dr. B. Lask of London has found a new way to eliminate this distressing sleep pattern in 90% of children. For several nights, note how many minutes elapse from falling asleep to the onset of the night terror. Then awaken your child 15 minutes before the expected time. Keep your child fully awake and out of bed for 5 minutes. Carry out these prompted awakenings for seven consecutive nights. If the night terrors return, repeat this seven-night program.

 ## CALL OUR OFFICE

During regular hours if

—Any drooling, jerking, or stiffening occurs.

—The episodes occur two or more times per week after doing the seven prompted awakenings.

—Episodes last longer than 30 minutes.

—Your child does something dangerous during an episode.

—Episodes occur during the second half of the night.

—Your child has several daytime fears.

—You feel family stress may be a factor.

—You have other questions or concerns.

Instructions for Pediatric Patients by Barton D. Schmitt, M.D., *Pediatrician*
Adapted from YOUR CHILD'S HEALTH, Copyright © 1991 by Barton D. Schmitt, M.D.
Reprinted by permission of Bantam Books.

DEFINITION

—Your child walks while asleep.
—Your child's eyes are open but blank.
—Your child is not as well coordinated as when awake.
—Your child may perform semipurposeful acts such as dressing and undressing, opening and closing doors, or turning lights on and off.
—The episode may last 5 to 20 minutes.
—During this time your child cannot be awakened no matter what the parent does.
—The child is usually 4 to 15 years old.

Cause

Sleepwalking is an inherited tendency to wander during deep sleep. About 15% of normal children sleepwalk.

Expected Course

Sleepwalking usually occurs within 2 hours of bedtime. Children stop sleepwalking during adolescence.

DEALING WITH SLEEPWALKING

1. **Gently lead your child back to bed.** First, steer your child into the bathroom because he may be looking for a place to urinate. Then guide him to his bedroom. The episode may end once he's in bed. Don't expect to awaken him, however, before he returns to normal sleep.

2. **Protect your child from accidents.** Although accidents are rare, they do happen, especially if the child wanders outside. Sleepwalkers can be hit by a car or bitten by a dog, or they may become lost. Put gates on your stairways and special locks on your outside doors (above your child's reach). Do not let your child sleep in a bunk bed.

3. **Help your child avoid exhaustion.** Fatigue and a lack of sleep can lead to more frequent sleepwalking. So be sure your child goes to bed at a reasonable hour, especially when ill or exhausted.

4. **Try prompted awakenings to prevent sleepwalking.** If your child has frequent sleepwalking, try to eliminate this distressing sleep pattern. For several nights, note how many minutes elapse from falling asleep to the onset of the sleepwalking. Then awaken your child 15 minutes before the expected time. Keep your child fully awake for 5 minutes. Carry out these prompted awakenings for 7 consecutive nights. If the sleepwalking returns, repeat this seven-night program.

Instructions for Pediatric Patients by Barton D. Schmitt, M.D., *Pediatrician*
Adapted from YOUR CHILD'S HEALTH, Copyright © 1991 by Barton D. Schmitt, M.D.
Reprinted by permission of Bantam Books.

Some children awaken before their parents do, usually between 5 and 6 AM. These 1 to 3 year olds are well rested and raring to go. They come out of their room or call out from the crib and want everyone to wake up. They are excited about the new day and want to share it with you. If people don't respond, they make a racket. Such a child is a morning person.

Causes

Most of these children have received plenty of sleep. They are no longer tired. They are not awakening early on purpose. Most of them were put to bed too early the night before, had too many naps, or had naps that were too long. (NOTE: early morning naps that begin within 2 hours after breakfast also contribute to early morning awakening.) Some of them have a reduced sleep requirement—one that is below the average of 10 to 12 hours per night that most children 1 to 10 years old need—this is a genetic trait. Such children often have a parent who only needs 6 hours or so of sleep at night. Other children may begin awakening early in the springtime because of sunlight streaming through their window. (This scenario is easily remedied with dark shades or curtains.) Finally, those children who are given a bottle in their crib, fed an early breakfast, or allowed to come into their parents' bed early in the morning may develop a bad habit that persists after the original cause (for example, too much nap time) is removed.

HELPING YOUR CHILD SLEEP LATER

1. **Reduce naps.** Assume your child is getting too much sleep during the day. Many children over 1 year of age and most over 18 months of age need only one nap (unless they are sick). If your child needs two naps, be sure the first nap doesn't begin before 9 AM. If cutting back to one 2-hour nap after lunch doesn't help, shorten the nap to 1½ hours maximum. Also make sure your child gets plenty of exercise after his nap, so he'll be tired at night.

2. **Delay bedtime until 8 or 9 PM.** These two steps should cure your child unless he has a below-average sleep requirement. In that case, proceed with the following limit-setting suggestions.

3. **Establish a rule**: "You can't leave your bedroom until your parents are up. You can play quietly in your bedroom until breakfast." Also, tell your child, "It's not polite to wake up someone who is sleeping. Your parents need their sleep."

4. **If your child is in a crib, leave him there until 6 AM.** Put some toys in a bag in his crib the night before (but not ones he can stand on). If you put them in before he goes to sleep, he may play with them for awhile, fall asleep later, and sleep longer. If he cries, go in once to reassure him and remind him of the toys. Don't include any surprises or treats in his toy bag or he'll awaken early as children do on holiday mornings. If he makes loud noises with the toys, remove those particular toys. If he cries, ignore it. If crying continues, visit him briefly every 15 minutes to reassure him that all is well and most people are sleeping. Don't turn on the lights, talk much, give him a bottle, remove him from the crib, or stay more than 1 minute.

5. **If your child is in a floor-level bed, keep him in his bedroom until 6 AM.** Get him a clock radio and set it for 6 AM. Tell him he can't leave his bedroom until the music comes on. Tell him he can play quietly until then. Help him put out special toys or books the night before. If he comes out of his room, put up a gate or close the door. Tell him that you'll be happy to open the door as soon as he is back in his bed. If this is a chronic problem, put up the gate the night before.

6. **If you meet strong resistance, change the wake-up time gradually.** Some children protest a great deal about the new rule, especially if they have been coming into your bed in the morning. In that case, move ahead a little more gradually. If he's been awakening at 5 AM, help him to wait until 5:15 for 3 days. Set the clock radio for that time. After your child has adjusted to 5:15, change the clock radio to 5:30. Move the wake-up time forward every 3 or 4 days.

7. **Praise your child for not waking other people in the morning.** A star chart or special treat at breakfast may help your child wait more cooperatively.

8. **Change your tactics for weekends.** Many parents want their child to sleep in on Saturday and Sunday mornings. If this is your preference, keep your early morning riser up an hour later the night before. If you are using a clock radio with your program, turn it off or reset the times for an hour later. As a last resort, put a breakfast together for your child the night before and allow him to watch a preselected videotape.

CALL OUR OFFICE

During regular hours if
—Your child's sleep doesn't improve after trying this approach for 4 weeks.
—Your child has several other behavior problems.
—You have other questions or concerns.

Instructions for Pediatric Patients by Barton D. Schmitt, M.D., *Pediatrician*
Adapted from YOUR CHILD'S HEALTH, Copyright © 1991 by Barton D. Schmitt, M.D.
Reprinted by permission of Bantam Books.

STUBBORN TODDLERS

DEFINITION

Negativism is a normal phase most children go through between 18 months and 3 years of age. It begins when children discover they have the power to refuse other people's requests. They respond negatively to many requests, including pleasant ones. In general, they are stubborn rather than cooperative. They delight in refusing a suggestion, whether it's about getting dressed or taking off their clothes, taking a bath or getting out of the bathtub, going to bed or getting up. Unless understood, this behavior can become extremely frustrating for parents. Handled appropriately, it lasts about 1 year.

DEALING WITH A NEGATIVE, STUBBORN TODDLER

Consider the following guidelines for helping you and your child through this phase.

1. **Don't take this normal phase too personally.** By "no" your child means "Do I have to?" or "Do you mean it?" A negative response should not be confused with disrespect. Also, it is not meant to annoy you. This phase is critical to the development of independence and identity. Try to look at it with a sense of humor and amazement.

2. **Don't punish your child for saying "no."** Punish your child for what he does, not what he says. Since saying "no" is not something you control, ignore it. If you argue with your child about saying "no," you will probably prolong this behavior.

3. **Give your child plenty of choices.** This is the best way to increase your child's sense of freedom and control, so that she will become more cooperative. Examples of choices are letting your child choose between a shower or a bath; which book to read; which toys to take into the tub; which fruit to eat for a snack; which clothes or shoes to wear; which breakfast cereal to eat; and which game to play, whether inside or outside, in the park or in the yard. For tasks your child doesn't like, give her a say in the matter by asking, "Do you want to do it slowly or fast?" or "Do you want me to do it, or you?" The more quickly your child gains a feeling that she is a decision maker, the sooner she will become cooperative.

4. **Don't give your child a choice when there is none.** Safety rules, such as sitting in the car seat, are not open to discussion, although you can explain why the rule must be followed. Going to bed or to day care also is not negotiable. Don't ask a question when there's only one acceptable answer, but direct your child in as kind a way as possible (for example, "I'm sorry, but now you have to go to bed."). Commands such as "do this or else" should be avoided.

5. **Give transition time when changing activities.** If your child is having fun and must change to another activity, he probably needs a transition time. For example, if your child is playing with trucks as dinnertime approaches, give him a 5-minute warning. A kitchen timer sometimes helps a child accept the change better.

6. **Eliminate excessive rules.** The more rules you have, the less likely it is that your child will be agreeable about following them. Eliminate unnecessary expectations and arguments about wearing socks or cleaning her plate. Help your child feel less controlled by having more positive interactions than negative contacts each day.

7. **Avoid responding to your child's requests with excessive "no's."** Be for your child a model of agreeableness. When your child asks for something and you are unsure, try to say "yes" or postpone your decision by saying "Let me think about it." If you are going to grant a request, do so right away, before your child whines or begs for it. When you must say "no," tell your child that you're sorry and give your child a reason.

CALL OUR OFFICE

During regular hours if
—You or your spouse can't accept your child's need to say "no."
—You or your spouse have trouble controlling your temper.
—Your child has several other discipline problems.
—This approach doesn't bring improvement within 1 month.
—You have other questions or concerns.

Instructions for Pediatric Patients by Barton D. Schmitt, M.D., *Pediatrician*   © 1992 by W. B. Saunders Company
Adapted from YOUR CHILD'S HEALTH, Copyright © 1991 by Barton D. Schmitt, M.D.
Reprinted by permission of Bantam Books.

The first goal of discipline is to protect your child from danger. Another important goal is to teach your child an understanding of right from wrong. Reasonable limit setting keeps us from raising a "spoiled" child. To teach respect for the rights of others, first teach your child to respect your rights. Begin *external* controls by 6 months of age. Children don't start to develop *internal* controls (self-control) until 3 or 4 years of age. They continue to need external controls, in gradually decreasing amounts, through adolescence.

GUIDELINES FOR SETTING RULES

1. **Begin discipline after 6 months of age.** Young infants don't need any discipline. By the time they crawl, all children need rules for their safety.

2. **Express each misbehavior as a clear and concrete rule.** Examples of clear rules are "Don't push your brother" and "Don't interrupt me on the telephone."

3. **Also state the acceptable or appropriate behavior.** Your child needs to know what is expected of him or her. Examples are "Play with your brother," "Look at books when I'm on the telephone," or "Walk, don't run."

4. **Ignore unimportant or irrelevant misbehavior.** Avoid constant criticism. Behavior such as swinging the legs, poor table manners, or normal negativism is unimportant during the early years.

5. **Use rules that are fair and attainable.** A child should not be punished for behavior that is part of normal emotional development, such as thumb sucking, fears of being separated from the parents, and toilet-training accidents.

6. **Concentrate on two or three rules initially.** Give highest priority to issues of safety, such as not running into the street, and to the prevention of harm to others. Of next importance is behavior that damages property. Then come all the annoying behavior traits that wear you down (such as tantrums or whining).

7. **Avoid trying to change "no-win" behavior through punishment.** Examples are wetting pants, pulling their own hair, thumb sucking, body rocking, masturbation, not eating enough, not going to sleep, and refusal to complete schoolwork. The first step in resolving such a power struggle is to withdraw from the conflict and stop punishing your child for the misbehavior. Then give your child positive feedback when he or she behaves as you'd like.

8. **Apply the rules consistently.** After the parents agree on the rules, it may be helpful to write them down and post them.

DISCIPLINE TECHNIQUES (INCLUDING CONSEQUENCES)

1. **Techniques to use for different ages are summarized here.** The techniques mentioned here are further described after this list.
—From birth to 6 months: no discipline necessary

—From 6 months to 3 years: structuring the home environment, distracting, ignoring, verbal and nonverbal disapproval, physically moving or escorting, and temporary time-out
—From 3 years to 5 years: the preceding techniques (especially temporary time-out) plus natural consequences, restricting places where the child can misbehave, and logical consequences
—From 5 years to adolescence: the preceding techniques plus delay of a privilege, "I" messages, and negotiation via family conferences
—Adolescence: logical consequences, "I" messages, and family conferences about house rules; time-out and manual guidance can be discontinued

2. **Structure the home environment.** You can change your child's surroundings so that an object or situation that could cause a problem is eliminated. Examples are gates, locks, and fences.

3. **Distracting your child from misbehavior.** Distracting a young child from temptation by attracting his or her attention to something else is especially helpful when the child is in someone else's house or a store (for example, distract with toys, food, or games).

4. **Ignore the misbehavior.** Ignoring helps to stop unacceptable behavior that is harmless—such as tantrums, sulking, whining, quarreling, or interrupting.

5. **Use verbal and nonverbal disapproval.** Mild disapproval is often all that is required to stop a young child's misbehavior. Get close to your child, get eye contact, look stern, and give a brief "no" or "stop."

6. **Physically move or escort ("manual guidance").** "Manual guidance" means that you move a child from one place to another (for example, to bed, bath, car, or time-out chair) against his will and help him as much as needed (for example, carrying).

7. **Use temporary time-out or social isolation.** Time-out is the most effective discipline technique available to parents. Time-out is used to interrupt unacceptable behavior by removing the child from the scene to a boring place, such as a playpen, corner of a room, chair, or bedroom. Time-outs should last about 1 minute per year of age and not more than 5 minutes.

8. **Restrict places where a child can misbehave.** This technique is especially helpful for behavior problems that can't be eliminated. Allowing nose picking and masturbation in your child's room prevents an unnecessary power struggle.

9. **Use natural consequences.** Your child can learn good behavior from the natural laws of the physical world; for example, not dressing properly for the weather means your child will be cold or wet, or breaking a toy means it isn't fun to play with anymore.

10. **Use logical consequences.** These should be logically related to the misbehavior, making your child accountable for his or her problems and decisions. Many logical consequences are simply the temporary removal of a possession or privilege if your child has misused the object or right.

11. **Delay a privilege.** Examples of work before play are "After you clean your room, you can go out and play"

(Continued on the reverse side)

Instructions for Pediatric Patients by Barton D. Schmitt, M.D., *Pediatrician*
Adapted from YOUR CHILD'S HEALTH, Copyright © 1991 by Barton D. Schmitt, M.D.
Reprinted by permission of Bantam Books.

or "When you finish your homework, you can watch television."

12. **Use "I" messages.** When your child misbehaves, tell your child how you feel. Say, "I am upset when you do such and such." Your child is more likely to listen to this than a message that starts with "you." "You" messages usually trigger a defensive reaction.

13. **Negotiate and hold family conferences.** As children become older they need more communication and discussion with their parents about problems. A parent can begin such a conversation by saying, "We need to change these things. What are some ways we could handle this? What do you think would be fair?"

14. **Temporarily discontinue any physical punishment.** Most out-of-control children are already too aggressive. Physical punishment teaches them that it's acceptable to be aggressive (for example, hit or hurt someone else) to solve problems.

15. **Discontinue any yelling.** Yelling and screaming teach your child to yell back; you are thereby legitimizing shouting matches. Your child will respond better in the long run to a pleasant tone of voice and words of diplomacy.

16. **Don't forget to reward acceptable (desired) behaviors.** Don't take good behavior for granted. Watch for behavior you like, and then praise your child. At these times, move close to your child, look at him or her, smile, and be affectionate. A parent's attention is the favorite reward of most children.

GUIDELINES FOR GIVING CONSEQUENCES (PUNISHMENTS)

1. **Be unambivalent.** Mean what you say and follow through.

2. **Correct with love.** Talk to your child the way you want people to talk to you. Avoid yelling or using a disrespectful tone of voice. Correct your child in a kind way. Sometimes begin your correction with "I'm sorry I can't let you . . . ."

3. **Apply the consequence immediately.** Delayed punishments are less effective because young children forget why they are being punished. Punishment should occur very soon after the misbehavior and be administered by the adult who witnessed the misdeed.

4. **Make a one-sentence comment about the rule when you punish your child.** Also restate the preferred behavior, but avoid making a long speech.

5. **Ignore your child's arguments while you are correcting him or her.** This is the child's way of delaying punishment. Have a discussion with your child at a later more pleasant time.

6. **Make the punishment brief.** Take toys out of circulation for no more than 1 or 2 days. Time-outs should last no longer than 1 minute per year of the child's age and 5 minutes maximum.

7. **Follow the consequence with love and trust.** Welcome your child back into the family circle and do not comment upon the previous misbehavior or require an apology for it.

8. **Direct the punishment against the misbehavior, not the person.** Avoid degrading comments such as "You never do anything right."

 ## CALL OUR OFFICE

During regular hours if
—Your child's misbehavior is dangerous.
—The instances of misbehavior seem too numerous to count.
—Your child is also having behavior problems at school.
—Your child doesn't seem to have many good points.
—Your child seems depressed.
—The parents can't agree on discipline.
—You can't give up physical punishment. (**NOTE:** Call immediately if you are afraid you might hurt your child.)
—The misbehavior does not improve after 1 month of using this approach.

RECOMMENDED READING

1. Edward R. Christophersen: Little People. Westport Publishers, Kansas City, Mo., 1988.
2. Don Dinkmeyer and Gary D. McKay: Parenting Young Children. American Guidance Service, Circle Pines, Minn., 1989.
3. Michael Popkin: Active Parenting. Harper and Row Publishers, San Francisco, 1987.
4. Jerry Wyckoff and Barbara C. Unell: Discipline Without Spanking or Shouting. Meadowbrook, Deephaven, Minn., 1984.

Instructions for Pediatric Patients by Barton D. Schmitt, M.D., *Pediatrician*   © 1992 by W. B. Saunders Company

DEFINITION

Time-out is a form of discipline used to interrupt unacceptable behavior by isolating a child in a chair or room for a brief period of time. Time-out has the advantage of providing a cooling-off period for both the child and the parent. It gives a child over 2 or 3 years old a chance to think about his misbehavior and feel a little guilty about it. When a child is less than 2 years old, time-out mainly establishes who is in charge.

Misbehaviors that respond best to time-out are aggressive, harmful, or disruptive behaviors that cannot be ignored. Time-out is much more effective than spanking, threatening, or shouting at your child. Time-out is the best form of discipline for many of the irrational behaviors of toddlers. As a child grows older, use of time-outs can gradually be replaced with logical consequences.

CHOOSING A PLACE FOR TIME-OUT

1. **Playpens or cribs.** Playpens or cribs are a convenient place for time-out for older infants. A playpen near a parent is preferable to isolation in another room because most infants are frightened if they are not in the same room as their parent.

2. **Chairs or corners.** An older child can be told to sit in a chair. The chair can be placed facing a corner. Some parents prefer to have their child stand facing the corner.

3. **Rooms with the door open.** Many parents prefer a room for time-out because it offers more confinement than a chair. The most convenient and safest room for time-out is the child's bedroom. Until 2 years of age, most children become frightened if they are put in a room with a closed door. Other ways to confine your child in a room without completely closing him off are a gate, a heavy dresser that blocks the lower part of the door frame, or a piece of plywood that covers the bottom half of the door.

4. **Rooms with the door closed.** Some children will come out of the bedroom just as soon as they are put in. If you cannot devise a barricade, then the door must be closed. You can hold the door closed for the 3 to 5 minutes it takes to complete the time-out period. If you don't want to hold the door, you can put a latch on the door that allows it to be temporarily locked. Be sure not to forget your child. The time-out should not last longer than a few minutes.

HOW TO ADMINISTER TIME-OUT

1. **Deciding the length of time-out.** The time-out should be long enough for your child to think about his misbehavior and learn the acceptable behavior. A good rule of thumb is 1 minute per year of the child's age, with a maximum of 5 minutes. A kitchen timer can be set for the required number of minutes. If your child leaves time-out early ("escapes"), he should be returned to time-out and the timer should be reset. By the age of 6 years, most children can be sent to their room and asked to stay there until they feel ready to behave.

2. **Putting your child in time-out.** If your child misbehaves, briefly explain the rule she has broken and send her to the time-out chair or room. If your child doesn't go immediately, lead or carry her there. Expect your child to cry, protest, or have a tantrum on the way to time-out. Don't lecture or spank her on the way.

3. **Keeping your child in time-out.** Once children understand time-out, most of them will stay in their chair, corner, or room until the time is up. However, you will have to keep an eye on your child. If he gets up from a chair, put him back gently but quickly without spanking him and reset the timer. If your child comes out of the room, direct him back into the room and reset the timer. Threaten to close the door if he comes out a second time. If your child is a strong-willed 2- or 3-year-old and you are just beginning to use time-outs, you may initially need to hold him in the chair with one hand on his shoulder for the entire 2 minutes. Don't be discouraged; this does teach him that you mean what you say. If your child yells or cries during time-out, ignore it. The important thing is that he remain in time-out for a certain amount of time. Your child will not be able to understand the need for quietness during time-out until at least 3 years of age, so don't expect this of him before then.

4. **Ending the time-out.** Make it clear that you are in charge of when time-out ends. When the time is up, go to your child and state, "Time-out is over. You can get up (or come out) now." Then treat your child normally. Don't review the rule your child broke. Try to notice when your child does something that pleases you and praise her for it as soon as possible.

5. **Practicing time-out with your child.** If you have not used time-out before, explain it to your child in advance. Tell him it will replace spanking, yelling, and other such forms of discipline. Talk to him about the misbehaviors that will lead to time-outs. Also discuss with him the good behavior that you would prefer to see. Then pretend with your child that he has broken one of the rules. Take him through the steps of time-out so that he will understand your directions when you send him to time-out in the future. Also teach your babysitter about time-outs.

Instructions for Pediatric Patients by Barton D. Schmitt, M.D., *Pediatrician*
Adapted from YOUR CHILD'S HEALTH, Copyright © 1991 by Barton D. Schmitt, M.D.
Reprinted by permission of Bantam Books.

DISCIPLINE: PHYSICAL PUNISHMENT

The place of physical punishment in discipline is controversial. There are several good arguments for not using corporal punishment at all. We can raise children to be agreeable, responsible, productive adults without ever spanking them. All children need discipline on hundreds of occasions, but there are alternatives to spanking, such as sending a child to his or her room. Spanking carries the risk of triggering the unrelated pent-up anger that many adults carry inside them. This anger could find an outlet in the spanking and end in child abuse. Parents who turn to spanking as a last resort for "breaking their child's will" may find that they have underestimated their child's determination. In addition, physical punishment worsens aggressive behavior because it teaches a child to lash out when he or she is angry. Other forms of discipline can be more constructive, leaving a child with some sense of guilt and contributing to the formation of a conscience.

If you feel the need occasionally to spank your child, follow these guidelines for safe physical punishment:

—Hit only with an open hand. Hit through clothing. It is difficult to judge how hard you are hitting your child if you hit him or her with an object other than your hand. Paddles and belts commonly cause bruises.

—Hit only on the buttocks, legs, or hands. Hitting a child on the face is demeaning as well as dangerous; in fact, slapping the face is inappropriate at any age.

—Give only one swat; that is enough to change behavior. Hitting your child more than once may relieve your anger but will probably not teach your child anything additional.

—Don't spank children less than 1 year of age. Spanking is inappropriate before your child has learned to walk and should be unnecessary after the age of 5 to 6 years. Use negotiation and discussion to resolve most differences with school-age children.

—Avoid shaking children, because of the serious risk of causing blood clots on the brain (subdural hematomas).

—Don't use physical punishment more than once each day. The more your child is spanked, the less effect it will have.

—Learn alternatives to physical discipline. Isolating a child in a corner or bedroom for a time-out is much more civilized and effective. Learn how to use such forms of discipline.

—Never spank your child when you are out of control, scared, or drinking. A few parents can't stop hitting their child once they start. They can't control their rage and need help for themselves, such as from Parents Anonymous groups. They must learn to walk away from their children and never use physical punishment.

—Don't use physical punishment for aggressive misbehavior, such as biting, hitting, or kicking. Physical punishment under such circumstances teaches a child that it is all right for a bigger person to strike a smaller person. Aggressive children need to be taught restraint and self-control. They respond best to time-outs, which give them an opportunity to think about the pain they have caused.

—Don't allow baby-sitters and teachers to spank your children.

Instructions for Pediatric Patients by Barton D. Schmitt, M.D., *Pediatrician*
Adapted from YOUR CHILD'S HEALTH, Copyright © 1991 by Barton D. Schmitt, M.D.
Reprinted by permission of Bantam Books.

DEFINITION

A spoiled child is undisciplined, manipulative, and unpleasant to be with much of the time. He has many of the following behaviors by age 2 or 3:
—Doesn't follow rules or cooperate with suggestions
—Doesn't respond to "no," "stop," or other commands
—Protests everything
—Doesn't know difference between his needs and wants
—Insists on having his own way
—Makes unfair or excessive demands on others
—Doesn't respect other people's rights
—Tries to control other people
—Has a low frustration tolerance
—Frequently whines or throws tantrums
—Constantly complains about being bored

Causes

The main cause of spoiled children is a lenient, permissive parent who doesn't set limits and gives in to tantrums and whining. If the parent gives the child too much power, he will become more self-centered. Such parents also rescue the child from normal frustrations (such as waiting and sharing). Occasionally, the child of working parents is left with a nanny or baby-sitter who spoils the child by providing constant entertainment and giving in to unrealistic demands.

The reason some parents are overly lenient is that they confuse the child's needs (for example, for demand feeding) with the child's wants or whims (for example, for demand play). They do not want to hurt their child's feelings or to cause any crying. In the process, they may take the short-term solution of doing whatever prevents crying, which in the long run causes more crying. The child's ability to deliberately cry and fuss to get something usually doesn't begin before 5 or 6 months of age. There may be a small epidemic of spoiling in the United States because some working parents come home feeling guilty about not having enough total time for their children and so spend their free time together trying to avoid any friction or limit setting.

Confusion exists about the differences between giving attention to children and spoiling children. In general, attention is good for children. Indeed, it is essential for normal development. Attention can become harmful if it is excessive, given at the wrong time, or always given immediately. Attention from you is excessive if it interferes with your child's learning to do things for himself and deal with life's frustrations. An example of giving attention at the wrong time is when you are busy and your child is demanding attention. Another wrong time is when a child has just misbehaved and needs to be ignored. If attention is always given immediately, your child won't learn to wait.

Holding is a form of attention that some parents unnecessarily worry about. Holding babies is equivalent to loving them. People in many cultures hold their babies much more than we do. Lots of holding by the mother and father does not cause a spoiled infant or child.

Expected Outcome

Without changes in child rearing, spoiled children run into trouble by school age. Other children do not like them because they are too bossy and selfish. Adults do not like them because they are rude and make excessive demands on them. Eventually they become hard for even the parent to love because of their behaviors. As a reaction to not getting along well with other children and adults, spoiled children eventually become unhappy. Spoiled children may show reduced motivation and perseverance in schoolwork. Because of poor self-control they may become involved with adolescent risk-taking behaviors, such as drug abuse. Overall, spoiling a child prepares that child poorly for life in the real world.

HOW TO PREVENT A SPOILED CHILD

1. **Provide age-appropriate limits or rules for your child**. Parents have the right and responsibility to take charge and make rules. Adults must keep their child's environment safe. Age-appropriate discipline must begin by the age of crawling. Saying "no" occasionally is good for children. Children need external controls until they develop self-control and self-discipline. Your child will still love you after you say "no." If your children like you all the time, you are not being a good parent.

2. **Require cooperation with your important rules**. It is important that your child be in the habit of responding properly to your directions long before entering school. Important rules include staying in the car seat, not hitting other children, being ready to leave on time in the morning, going to bed, and so forth. These adult decisions are not open to negotiation. Do not give your child a choice when there is none.

Child decisions, however, involve such things as which cereal to eat, book to read, toys to take into the tub, and clothes to wear. Make sure that your child understands the difference between areas in which he has choices (control) and your rules. Try to keep your important rules to no more than 10 or 12 items and be willing to go to the mat about these. Also, be sure that all adult caretakers consistently enforce these rules.

3. **Expect your child to cry**. Distinguish between needs and wants. Needs include crying from pain, hunger, or fear. In these cases, respond immediately. Other crying is harmless. Crying usually relates to your child's wants or whims. Crying is a normal response to change or frustration. When the crying is part of a tantrum, ignore it. Don't punish him for crying, tell him he's a crybaby, or tell him he shouldn't cry. Although not denying your child his feelings, don't be moved by his crying. To compensate for the extra crying your child does during a time when you are tightening up on the rules, provide extra cuddling and enjoyable activities at a time when he is not crying or having a tantrum. There are times when it is necessary to temporarily withhold attention and comforting to help your child learn some-

(Continued on the reverse side)

Instructions for Pediatric Patients by Barton D. Schmitt, M.D., *Pediatrician*
Adapted from YOUR CHILD'S HEALTH, Copyright © 1991 by Barton D. Schmitt, M.D.
Reprinted by permission of Bantam Books.

thing that is important (such as he can't pull on your earrings).

4. **Do not allow tantrums to work**. Children throw temper tantrums to get your attention, to wear you down, to change your mind, and to get their way. The crying is to change your "no" vote to a "yes" vote. Tantrums may include whining, complaining, crying, breath holding, pounding the floor, shouting, or slamming a door. As long as your child stays in one place and is not too disruptive or in a position to harm himself, you can leave him alone at these times. By all means, don't give in to tantrums.

5. **Don't overlook discipline during quality time**. If you are working parents, you will want to spend part of each evening with your child. This special time spent with your child needs to be enjoyable but also reality based. Don't ease up on the rules. If your child misbehaves, remind him of the existing limits. Even during fun activities, you occasionally need to be the parent.

6. **Don't start democratic child rearing until your child is 4 or 5 years old**. Don't give away your power as a parent. At 2 years of age, be careful not to talk too much with your toddler about the rules. Toddlers don't play by the rules. By 4 or 5 years of age, you can begin to reason with your child about discipline issues, but he still lacks the judgment necessary to make the rules. During the elementary school years, show a willingness to discuss the rules. By 14 to 16 years old, an adolescent can be negotiated with as an adult. At that time you can ask for his input about what rules or consequences would be fair (that is, rules become joint decisions).

The more democratic the parents are during the first 2 or 3 years, the more demanding the children tend to become. Generally, young children do not know what to do with power. Left to their own devices, they usually spoil themselves. If they are testing everything at age 3, it is abnormal. If you have given away your power, take it back (that is, set new limits and enforce them). You don't have to explain the reason for every rule. Sometimes it is just because "I said so."

7. **Teach your child to get himself unbored**. Your job is to provide toys, books, and art supplies. Your child's job is playing with them. Assuming you talk and play with your child several hours each day, you do not need to become your child's constant playmate, nor do you need to constantly provide him with an outside friend. When you're busy, expect your child to amuse himself. Even 1-year-olds can keep themselves occupied for 15-minute blocks of time. By 3 years, most children can entertain themselves half the time. Sending your child outside to "find something to do" is doing him a favor. Much good creative play, thinking, and daydreaming come out of solving boredom. If you can't seem to resign as social director, enroll your child in a preschool.

8. **Teach your child to wait**. Waiting helps children better deal with frustration. All jobs in the adult world carry some degree of frustration. Delaying immediate gratification is a trait your child must gradually learn and it takes practice. Don't feel guilty if you have to make your child wait a few minutes now and then (for example, don't allow your child to interrupt your conversations with others in person or on the telephone). Waiting doesn't hurt him as long as he doesn't become overwhelmed or unglued by waiting. His perseverance and emotional fitness will be enhanced.

9. **Don't rescue your child from normal life challenges**. Changes such as moving and starting school are normal life stressors. These are opportunities for learning and problem solving. Always be available and supportive, but don't help your child if he can handle it for himself. Overall, make your child's life as realistic as he can tolerate for his age, rather than going out of your way to make it as pleasant as possible. His coping skills and self-confidence will benefit from this practice.

10. **Don't overpraise your child**. Children need praise, but it can be overdone. Praise your child for good behavior and following the rules. Encourage him to try new things and work on difficult tasks, but teach him to do things for his own reasons too. Self-confidence and a sense of accomplishment come from doing and completing things that he is proud of. Praising your child while he is in the process of doing something may make him stop at each step and want more praise. Giving your child constant attention can make him "praise dependent" and demanding. Avoid the tendency (so common with the first born) to overpraise your child's normal development.

11. **Teach your child to respect parents' rights and time together**. The needs of your children for love, food, clothing, safety, and security obviously come first. However, your needs should come next. Your children's wants (for example, for play) and whims (for example, for an extra bedtime story) should come after your needs are met and as time is available on that day. This is especially important for working parents where family time is limited. It is both the quality and quantity of time that you spend with your children that are important. Quality time is time that is enjoyable, interactive, and focused on your child. Children need some quality time with their parents every day. Spending every free moment of every evening and weekend with your child is not good for your child or your marriage. You need a balance to preserve your mental health. Scheduled nights out with your mate will not only nurture your marriage but also help you to return to parenting with more to give. Your child needs to learn to trust other adults and that he can survive separations from you. If your child isn't taught to respect your rights, he may not respect the rights of other adults.

CALL OUR OFFICE

During regular hours if
—You feel your child is becoming spoiled.
—You and your spouse often disagree on discipline.
—Your child doesn't improve after 2 months of tightening up on limit setting.
—You have other questions or concerns.

Instructions for Pediatric Patients by Barton D. Schmitt, M.D., *Pediatrician*   © 1992 by W. B. Saunders Company
Adapted from YOUR CHILD'S HEALTH, Copyright © 1991 by Barton D. Schmitt, M.D.
Reprinted by permission of Bantam Books.

DEFINITION

A temper tantrum is an immature way of expressing anger. No matter how calm and gentle a parent you are, your child will probably throw some tantrums. Try to teach your child that temper tantrums don't work and that you don't change your mind because of them. By 3 years of age, you can begin to teach your child to verbalize his feelings ("You feel angry because . . . ."). We need to teach children that anger is normal but that it must be channeled appropriately. By school age, temper tantrums should be rare. During adolescence, tantrums reappear, but your teenager can be reminded that blowing up creates a bad impression and that counting to 10 can help him regain control.

RESPONSES TO TEMPER TANTRUMS

Overall, praise your child when he controls his temper, verbally expresses his anger, and is cooperative. Be a good model by staying calm and not screaming or having adult tantrums. Avoid spanking for tantrums because it conveys to your child that you are out of control. Try using the following responses to the different types of temper tantrums.

1. **Support and help children having frustration- or fatigue-related tantrums.** Children often have temper tantrums when they are frustrated with themselves. They may be frustrated because they can't put something together. Young children may be frustrated because their parents don't understand their speech. Older children may be frustrated with their inability to do their homework.

At these times your child needs encouragement and a parent who listens. Put an arm around him and say something brief that shows understanding such as "I know it's hard, but you'll get better at it. Is there something I can do to help you?" Also give praise for not giving up. Some of these tantrums can be prevented by steering your child away from tasks that he can't do well.

Children tend to have more temper tantrums when they are tired (for example, when they've missed a nap) because they are less able to cope with frustrating situations. At these times put your child to bed. Hunger can contribute to temper tantrums. If you suspect this, give your child a snack. Temper tantrums also increase during sickness.

2. **Ignore attention-seeking or demanding-type tantrums.** Young children may throw temper tantrums to get their way. They may want to go with you rather than be left with the baby-sitter, want candy, want to empty a desk drawer, or want to go outside in bad weather. They don't accept rules for their safety. Tantrums for attention may include whining, crying, pounding the floor or wall, slamming a door, or breath holding. As long as your child stays in one place and is not too disruptive, you can leave him alone.

If you recognize that a certain event is going to push your child over the edge, try to shift his attention to something else. However, don't give in to your child's demands. During the temper tantrum, if his behavior is harmless, ignore it completely. Once a tantrum has started, it rarely can be stopped.

Move away, even to a different room; then your child no longer has an audience. Don't try to reason with your child—it will only make the tantrum worse. Simply state, "I can see you're very angry. I'll leave you alone until you cool off. Let me know if you want to talk." Let your child regain control. After the tantrum, be friendly and try to return things to normal. You can prevent some of these tantrums by saying "no" less often.

3. **Physically move children having refusal-type tantrums.** If your child refuses something unimportant (such as a snack or lying down in bed), let it go before a tantrum begins. However, if your child must do something important, such as go to bed or to day care, he should not be able to avoid it by having a tantrum. Some of these tantrums can be prevented by giving your child a 5-minute warning instead of asking him suddenly to stop what he is doing. Once a tantrum has begun, let your child have the tantrum for 2 or 3 minutes. Try to put his displeasure into words: "You want to play some more, but it's bedtime." Then take him to the intended destination (for example, the bed), helping him as much as is needed (including carrying).

4. **Use time-outs for disruptive-type tantrums.** Some temper tantrums are too disruptive for parents to ignore. On such occasions send or take your child to his room for 2 to 5 minutes. Examples of disruptive behavior include
—Clinging to you or following you around during the tantrum
—Hitting you
—Screaming or yelling for such a long time that it gets on your nerves
—Having a temper tantrum in a public place such as a restaurant or church (Move your child to another place for his time-out. The rights of other people need to be protected.)
—Throwing something or damaging property during a temper tantrum

5. **Hold children having harmful or rage-type tantrums.** If your child is totally out of control and screaming wildly, consider holding him. His loss of control probably scares him. Also hold your child when he is having tantrums that carry a danger of self-injury (such as if he is violently throwing himself backward).

Take your child in your arms, tell him you know he is angry, and offer him your sense of control. Hold him until you feel his body start to relax. This usually takes 1 to 3 minutes. Then let him go. This comforting response is rarely needed after 3 years of age.

Some children won't want you to comfort them. Hold your child only if it helps. If your child says "Go away," do so. After the tantrum subsides, your child will often want to be held briefly. This is a good way to get him back into the family activities.

(Continued on the reverse side)

Instructions for Pediatric Patients by Barton D. Schmitt, M.D., *Pediatrician*
Adapted from YOUR CHILD'S HEALTH, Copyright © 1991 by Barton D. Schmitt, M.D.
Reprinted by permission of Bantam Books.

TEMPER TANTRUMS *Continued*

CALL OUR OFFICE

—The tantrums also occur in school.
—Your child has several other behavior problems.
—One of the parents has tantrums or screaming bouts and can't give them up.
—This approach does not bring improvement within 2 weeks.
—You have other questions or concerns.

During regular hours if
—Your child has hurt himself or others during tantrums.
—The tantrums occur five or more times per day.

Instructions for Pediatric Patients by Barton D. Schmitt, M.D., *Pediatrician*
Adapted from YOUR CHILD'S HEALTH, Copyright © 1991 by Barton D. Schmitt, M.D.
Reprinted by permission of Bantam Books.

Biting another child is one of the more unacceptable aggressive behaviors in Western society. The parent of the child who has been bitten is usually very upset and worried about the risk of infection. If it happens in a child-care setting, the other parents want the biter to be expelled. If it happens in another's home, the child is often told never to return. Most children first learn to bite by doing it to their parents in a playful manner. It is very important to interrupt this primitive behavior at this early stage.

CAUSES

Biting is usually a chance discovery around 1 year of age, at a time when teething and mouthing are normal behaviors. It often continues because the parents initially think it is cute and the child considers it a type of game to get attention. Later, children may use it when they are frustrated and want something from another child. At this age when children have minimal verbal skills, biting becomes a primitive form of communication. Only after 2 or 3 years of age can it become a deliberate way to express anger and intimidate others.

RECOMMENDATIONS FOR BITING

1. **Establish a rule.** "We never bite people." Give your child a reason for the rule, namely, that biting hurts. Other reasons (that won't interest him at his age) are that bites can lead to infection or scarring.

2. **Suggest a safe alternative behavior.** Tell your child if he wants something he should come to you and ask for help or point to it, rather than biting the person who has it. If he bites when he is angry, tell him "If you are mad, come to me and tell me." If your child is at the chewing everything stage (usually less than 18 months), help him choose a toy that he can bite rather than telling him that he cannot bite anything. A firm toy or teething ring will do. Encourage him to carry his "chewy" with him for a few days.

3. **Interrupt biting with a sharp "no."** Be sure to use an unfriendly voice and look him straight in the eye. Try to interrupt him when he looks like he might bite somebody, before he actually does it, leaving the victim hurt and screaming. Extra close supervision may be necessary until the biting has stopped.

4. **Give your child a time-out for biting others.** Send him to a boring place for approximately 1 minute per year of age. If he attempts to bite you while you are holding him, say "no," always put him down immediately, and walk away (a form of time-out). If time-out does not work, take away a favorite toy for the remainder of the day.

5. **Never bite your child for biting someone else.** Biting back will make your child upset that you hurt him and may teach him that it is okay to bite if you are bigger. Also do not wash the mouth out with soap, pinch the cheek, or slap the mouth. In fact, if your child tends to be aggressive, avoid physical punishment in general (for example, spanking). Also eliminate "love bites," since your child will be unable to distinguish them from painful biting.

6. **Praise your child for not biting.** The most important time to praise him is when he is in situations or with particular children where he used to frequently bite. Initially give him a kind reminder just before these high-risk visits. Then praise him afterward for good behavior.

7. **Prevention.** The best time to stop a biting behavior from becoming a habit is when it first starts. Be sure that no one laughs when he bites and that no one treats it like a game. (This includes older siblings.) Also never "give in" to your child's demands because of biting. Since biting commonly occurs in child-care settings, be sure the providers understand your approach and are willing to apply it.

CALL OUR OFFICE

IMMEDIATELY if
—Biting causes a puncture or a cut that completely breaks the skin.

During regular hours if
—Biting behavior lasts for more than 4 weeks with this approach.
—Your child bites or hurts himself.
—Your child has several other behavior problems.
—You have other questions or concerns.

Instructions for Pediatric Patients by Barton D. Schmitt, M.D., *Pediatrician*
Adapted from YOUR CHILD'S HEALTH, Copyright © 1991 by Barton D. Schmitt, M.D.
Reprinted by permission of Bantam Books.

HURTING ANOTHER CHILD

Some aggressive behaviors that children experiment with are hitting, slapping, pinching, scratching, poking, hair pulling, biting, kicking, shoving, and knocking down. Since these behaviors are unacceptable in the adult world and potentially harmful, they should not be allowed between children.

CAUSES

Many children fight when they are angry. They do not like something another child did and they retaliate. They want something another child has and see force as the easiest way to get it. Most children try aggressive behaviors because they see this behavior in playmates or on television. If children get their way through hitting, it will only become more frequent. Occasionally children become excessively aggressive because they receive lots of spankings at home or witness spouse or sibling abuse.

RECOMMENDATIONS

1. **Establish a rule**. "Do not hit because it hurts. We do not hurt people."

2. **For aggressive behavior give your child a brief time-out in a boring place.** Being in time-out helps a child learn to cool down (rather than blow up) when he is angry. When it looks as if your child might hurt someone, intervene immediately. Stop the behavior at the early threatening or shoving stage. Do not wait until the victim is hurt or screams. If a time-out does not seem to be effective, also take away your child's favorite toy or television time for the remainder of the day.

3. **Suggest acceptable ways to express anger.** In the long run you want your child to be able to verbalize his anger in a calm but assertive way. Encourage your child to come to you when he's angry and talk about it until he feels better. A second option is to teach your child to stop and count to 10 before doing anything about his anger. A third option is to help him learn to walk away from a bad situation. Giving your child a time-out is one way of teaching him to walk away from anger.

Younger children with limited expressive language (less than 3 or 4 years old) need time to develop these skills. When they are in time-out, don't be surprised if they pout, mutter to themselves, yell in their room, or pound on their door. If these physical outlets for anger are blocked, a more aggressive outburst may occur. As long as the behavior is not destructive, ignore it. Teaching your child how to control anger provides him with a valuable resource.

4. **Verbalize your child's feelings for him.** If your child can't talk about his anger, put it into words for him: "I know that you feel angry." It is unrealistic to expect your child not to feel anger. You may need to make an understanding statement such as "You wish you could punch your brother, but we cannot hurt other people."

5. **Teach your child acceptable ways to get what he wants.** Teach him how to negotiate (ask for) what he wants, rather than taking it. Teach him how to take turns or how to trade one of his toys to gain use of another child's toy.

6. **Give special attention to the victim.** After putting your child in time-out, pick up the child who has been injured and give him extra sympathy and attention. It is especially helpful if you can rescue the victim before he is hurt. In your child's mind the attention he wanted is now being given to the other person and that should give him some "food for thought." If fighting is a pattern with certain playmates or siblings, be sure the "victim" isn't "setting up" the "perpetrator" to gain attention.

7. **Never hit your child for hitting someone else.** Hitting your child only teaches that it is fine to hit if you are bigger. If your child tends to be aggressive it's critical to eliminate all physical punishment (such as spanking). You can use many other consequences (such as time-out) to teach your child right from wrong.

8. **Praise your child for friendly behavior.** Praise him for being nice to people, playing with age mates in a friendly way, sharing things, and helping other children. Remind your child that people like to be treated kindly, not hurt. Some children respond to a system of receiving a treat or a star on a chart for each day they go without any "hitting" type of behavior.

9. **Prevention.** Set a good example. Show self-control and verbal problem solving. Avoid playmates who often tease or other situations where your child frequently gets into fights. And when your child becomes tired or hungry, leave the play setting until these needs are met.

CALL OUR OFFICE

During regular hours if
—The aggressive behavior is very frequent.
—Your child has seriously hurt another child.
—Your child can't keep friends.
—Your child seems very angry.
—The misbehavior lasts more than 4 weeks with this approach.
—You have other questions or concerns.

Instructions for Pediatric Patients by Barton D. Schmitt, M.D., *Pediatrician*
Adapted from YOUR CHILD'S HEALTH, Copyright © 1991 by Barton D. Schmitt, M.D.
Reprinted by permission of Bantam Books.

Most siblings argue and bicker occasionally. They fight over possessions, space on the sofa, time in the bathroom, the last donut, and so on. Quarrelling is an inevitable part of sibling relationships. On some days, brothers and sisters are rivals and competitors, but on most days they are friends and companions. This ambivalence between love and hate is a part of all close relationships, and it becomes more intense in siblings because both of them want to gain their parents' attention and be their parents' favorite. The positive side of this sibling rivalry is that it gives children a chance to learn to give and take, share, and stand up for their rights.

COPING WITH SIBLING QUARRELS

1. **Encourage children to settle their own disagreements.** Have a rule: "Settle your own arguments but no hitting, property damage, or name calling." The more you intervene, the more you will be called on to intervene. When possible, stay out of disagreements as long as they remain verbal. Children can't go through life having a referee to resolve their differences. They need to learn how to negotiate with people and find the common ground. Arguing with siblings and peers provides this experience. The only exception is if they are both under 2 or 3 years of age and one of them is aggressive. At this age they do not understand the potential dangers of fighting and they need to be supervised more closely.

2. **If they come to you, try to stay out of the middle.** Try to keep your children from bringing their argument to you for an opinion. Remind them again to settle it themselves. If you do become involved, help them clarify what they are arguing about. To achieve this, try to teach them to listen better. Encourage each child to describe the problem for 1 or 2 minutes without being interrupted by the other. If they still don't understand the issue, reframe it for them. Unless there's an obvious culprit, do not try to decide who is to blame, who started it, or who is right. Interrogation in this area can be counterproductive because it may cause them to exaggerate or lie. Also do not impose a solution. Since it's their problem, let them find their own solution whenever possible.

3. **If an argument becomes too loud, do something about it.** If the arguing becomes annoying or interferes with your ability to think, go to your children and tell them "I do not want to hear your arguing. Please settle your differences quietly or find another place to argue." If they do not change at that point, send them to the basement, outdoors, or to time-out in separate rooms. If they are arguing over an object such as the television, take it away. If they are arguing over who gets to sit in the front seat of the car, have them both sit in the back seat. If they are arguing about going somewhere, cancel the trip for both.

4. **Do not permit hitting, breaking things, or name calling.** Under these circumstances punish both of your children. If they are hurting each other, send them both to time-out in separate places no matter who you see doing the hitting when you come on the scene. That may

not be the person who took the first swing or provoked it. Name calling or teasing hurts people's feelings and should never be allowed (for example, calling a child who is not good in school "dummy"; one who is not athletic "clumsy"; or one who has a bed-wetting problem "smelly"). Derogatory comments such as these can be harmful to self-esteem and should not be permitted.

5. **Stop any arguing that occurs in public places.** If you are in a shopping mall, restaurant, or movie theater and your children begin arguing, you need to stop them because it is annoying to other people. If the arguing continues after a warning, separate them (for example, by sitting between them). If that doesn't work, give them a brief (2- to 5-minute) time-out outside or at an out-of-the-way spot. If they are over 4 or 5 years old, you can sometimes tell them to stop or they will get a 30-minute time out (or 30-minute loss of television time) on arrival at home. Sometimes you will have to leave the public setting and take them home.

6. **Protect each child's personal possessions, privacy, and friendships.** When children argue over toys, if the toy belongs to one of the children, return it to that child. Although children don't have to share their possessions, warn them that sharing works both ways. For family "toys" (such as video games or board games) teach taking turns. Also teach sharing toys when friends come over. Sharing is a skill they will need in order to have friends and get along in school. Younger siblings often intrude on older siblings' friendships and play. It is helpful if the younger sibling is provided with a playmate or special activity when your older child has a friend over. Your child's study time also deserves protection from interruption. Designating a study room often helps.

7. **Avoid showing favoritism.** It is critical that all punishment for arguing or fighting be "group punishment." Parents must avoid the myth that fighting is always started by the brother rather than the sister, by the older child rather than the younger one, or by one child who is the "troublemaker." Rivalry will be intense if the parent shows favoritism. Try to treat your children as unique and special individuals. Do not take sides. Do not compare them and do not polarize them into good ones and bad ones. Do not listen to tattle taling. And if one of your children complains about you not being fair, either ignore this comment or restate the rule that has been broken. If you're feeling guilty, remind yourself that "it all balances out."

8. **Praise cooperative behavior.** Catch your children "being good," namely, playing together in a friendly way. Give "group praise" whenever possible. Compliment them for helping each other and settling disagreements politely.

9. **Prevention of fighting or name calling.** First, help your children acknowledge their feelings. Let them know it is acceptable to be angry toward a sibling but they should not vent their anger by fighting or name calling. Give them useful alternatives to hurtful arguing such as talking to you about it. Second, provide access to outside friends and different settings, rather than expecting your children to constantly play with each other. Third, avoid

(Continued on the reverse side)

Instructions for Pediatric Patients by Barton D. Schmitt, M.D., *Pediatrician*
Adapted from YOUR CHILD'S HEALTH, Copyright © 1991 by Barton D. Schmitt, M.D.
Reprinted by permission of Bantam Books.

CALL OUR OFFICE

showing favoritism toward one child over another. Try to talk with each child every day and to schedule a special individualized activity once or twice each week. Most importantly, show your child how to settle disagreements peacefully and in a calm voice. Try not to act disrespectful, disagreeable, or ill tempered to your children or other people.

During regular hours if
—Sibling interactions have not improved after using this approach for 6 weeks.
—Your children constantly fight with each other.
—Your children have several other behavior problems.
—One of your children constantly teases the other.
—One of your children has physically harmed the other.
—You have other questions or concerns.

Instructions for Pediatric Patients by Barton D. Schmitt, M.D., *Pediatrician*   © 1992 by W. B. Saunders Company
Adapted from YOUR CHILD'S HEALTH, Copyright © 1991 by Barton D. Schmitt, M.D.
Reprinted by permission of Bantam Books.

DEFINITION

Sibling rivalry refers here to the natural jealousy of children toward a new brother or sister. Older siblings can feel jealous when a new baby arrives until they are 4 or 5 years old. Not surprisingly, most children prefer to be the only child at this age. Basically, they don't want to share your time and affection. The arrival of a new baby is especially stressful for the first born and for those less than 3 years old. The jealousy arises because the older sibling sees the new comer receiving all the attention, visitors, gifts, and special handling.

The most common symptom of sibling rivalry is lots of demands for attention: the older child wants to be held and carried about, especially when mother is busy with the newborn. Other symptoms include acting like a baby again (regressive behavior), such as thumb sucking, wetting, or soiling. Aggressive behavior—for example, handling the baby roughly—can also occur. All of these symptoms are normal. Although some can be prevented, the remainder can be improved within a few months.

PREVENTION OF SIBLING RIVALRY

During Pregnancy

—Prepare the older sibling for the newcomer. Talk about the pregnancy. Have her feel your baby's movements.
—Try to find a hospital that provides sibling classes where children can learn about babies and sharing parents. Try to give your older child a chance to be around a new baby so that he has a better idea of what to expect.
—Encourage your older child to help you prepare the baby's room.
—Move your older child to a different room or new bed several months before the baby's birth so she won't feel pushed out by the new baby. If she will be enrolling in a play group or nursery school, start it well in advance of the delivery.
—Praise your older child for mature behavior, such as talking, using the toilet, feeding or dressing himself, and playing games.
—Don't make any demands for new skills (such as toilet training) during the months just preceding the delivery. Even if your child appears ready, postpone these changes until your child has made a good adjustment to the new baby.
—Tell your child where she'll go and who will care for her when you go to the hospital, if she won't be home with her father.
—Read books together about what happens during pregnancy as well as after the baby is born.
—Look through family photographs and talk about your older child's first year of life.

In the Hospital

—Call your older child daily from the hospital.
—Try to have your older child visit you and the baby in the hospital. Many hospitals will allow this.
—If your older child can't visit you, send her a picture of the new baby.
—Encourage Dad to take your youngster on some special outings at this time (for example, to the park, zoo, museum, or fire station).

Coming Home

—When you enter your home, spend your first moments with the older sibling. Have someone else carry the new baby into the house.
—Give the sibling a gift "from the new baby."
—Ask visitors to give extra notice to the older child. Have your older child unwrap the baby's gifts.
—From the beginning, refer to your newborn as "our baby."

The First Months at Home

—Give your older child the extra attention he needs. Help him feel more important. Try to give him at least 30 minutes every day of exclusive, uninterrupted time. Hire a baby-sitter and take your older child outside or look through his baby album with him. Make sure that the father and relatives spend extra time with him during the first month. Give him lots of physical affection throughout the day. If he demands to be held while you are feeding or rocking the baby, try to include him. At least talk with him when you are busy taking care of the baby.
—Encourage your older child to touch and play with the new baby in your presence. Allow him to hold the baby while sitting in a chair with arms. Avoid such warnings as "Don't touch the baby." Newborns are not fragile, and it is important to show your trust. However, you can't allow the sibling to carry the baby until he reaches school age.
—Enlist your older child as a helper. Encourage him to help with baths, dry the baby, get a clean diaper, or find toys or a pacifier. At other times encourage him to feed or bathe a doll when you are feeding or bathing the baby. Emphasize how much the baby "likes" the older sibling. Make comments such as "Look how happy she gets when you play with her" or "You can always make her laugh."
—Don't ask the older siblings to "be quiet for the baby." Newborns can sleep fine without the house being perfectly quiet. This request can lead to unnecessary resentment.
—Accept regressive behavior, such as thumb sucking or clinging, as something your child needs to do temporarily. Do not criticize him.
—Intervene promptly for any aggressive behavior. Tell him that "we never hurt babies." Send your child to time-out for a few minutes. Don't spank your child or slap his hand at these times. If you hit him,

(Continued on the reverse side)

Instructions for Pediatric Patients by Barton D. Schmitt, M.D., *Pediatrician*
Adapted from YOUR CHILD'S HEALTH, Copyright © 1991 by Barton D. Schmitt, M.D.
Reprinted by permission of Bantam Books.

he will eventually try to do the same to the baby as revenge. For the next few weeks don't leave the two of them alone.

— If your child is old enough, encourage him to talk about his mixed feelings about the new arrival. Give him an alternative behavior: "When you're upset with the baby, come to me for a big hug."

CALL OUR OFFICE

During regular hours if
—Your older child tries to hurt the baby.
—Regressive behavior doesn't improve by 1 month.
—You have other questions or concerns.

Instructions for Pediatric Patients by Barton D. Schmitt, M.D., *Pediatrician*   © 1992 by W. B. Saunders Company
Adapted from YOUR CHILD'S HEALTH, Copyright © 1991 by Barton D. Schmitt, M.D.
Reprinted by permission of Bantam Books.

DEFINITION

—A child sucks on the thumb or fingers when not hungry.
—A security object, such as a blanket, may become part of the ritual.
—Thumb sucking begins before birth or by 3 months of age at the latest.

Causes

An infant's desire to suck on the breast or bottle is a drive that is essential for survival. More than 80% of babies also do some extra sucking when they are not hungry (nonnutritive sucking). Thumb sucking also appears to help a child comfort herself and often increases when breast or bottle feedings decrease. It does not mean that a child is insecure or has emotional problems.

Expected Course

The sucking need is strongest during the first 6 months of a child's life. By 4 years of age, only 15% of children still suck their thumbs. Those children who continue sucking their thumbs after 4 years of age often have become involved in a power struggle with a parent who tried to stop their thumb sucking at too young an age. Occasionally the thumb sucking simply persists as a bad habit. Thumb sucking must be stopped before a child's permanent teeth erupt (6 or 7 years of age), because it can lead to an overbite ("buck teeth").

HOW TO OVERCOME THUMB SUCKING

1. **Before 4 years of age, distract or ignore**. Thumb sucking should be considered normal before the age of 4 years, especially when your child is tired. However, if the thumb sucking occurs when your child is bored and he is over 1 year old, try to distract him. Give him something to do with his hands without mentioning your concern about the thumb sucking. Occasionally praise your child for not thumb sucking. Until your child is old enough for you to reason with him, any pressure you apply to stop thumb sucking will only lead to refusal and lack of cooperation.

2. **Daytime control**. After 4 years of age, help your child give up thumb sucking during the day. First get your child's commitment to giving up thumb sucking by showing her what thumb sucking is doing to her body. Show her the gap between her teeth with a mirror. Have her look at the wrinkled rough skin (callus) on her thumb. Appeal to her sense of pride. At this point most children will agree that they would like to stop thumb sucking.

Ask your child if it will be all right if you remind her when she forgets. Do this gently with comments such as "Guess what?" and put an arm around your child as she remembers that she has been sucking on her thumb again. Encourage your child to remind herself by painting a star on her thumb with a Magic Marker, putting a

Band-Aid on the thumb, or applying fingernail polish. Your child should put these reminders on herself. Praise your child whenever you notice she is not sucking her thumb in situations where she previously did. Also, give her a reward (such as a dime, a snack, or an extra story) at the end of any day during which she did not suck her thumb at all.

3. **Nighttime control**. After daytime control is established, help your child give up thumb sucking during sleep. Thumb sucking during naps and night is usually an involuntary process. Your child can be told that although the night-time thumb sucking is not his fault, he can learn not to suck his thumb during sleep by putting something on his thumb to remind him. A glove, sock, splint (thumb guard), or piece of adhesive tape that runs up one side and down the other can be used. Your child should be in charge of putting on whatever material is used to prevent thumb sucking or asking you for assistance. Help your child look on this method as a clever idea rather than any kind of penalty.

4. **Bitter-tasting medicines**. Consider using bitter-tasting medicines if your child is over 4 years of age. A recent study by Dr. P.C. Friman demonstrated a high success rate in 1 to 3 nights using a bitter-tasting solution called Stop-zit (no prescription necessary) in combination with a reward system. Use Stop-zit only if your child is over 4 years old and agrees to use it. Don't use it as a punishment. Present it as a reminder that "other kids like to use also." Help your child apply Stop-zit only to the thumbnail at the following times: (1) before breakfast, (2) before bedtime, and (3) whenever thumb sucking is observed day or night.

Look to see whether your child is thumb sucking every 30 minutes after her bedtime until you retire. After 5 nights without thumb sucking, discontinue the morning Stop-zit. After 5 more nights without any thumb sucking, stop using Stop-zit at bedtime. If the thumb sucking recurs, repeat this program.

5. **Dental help**. Bring thumb sucking to the attention of your child's dentist at least by the time your child is 6 years old. Dentists have a variety of approaches to thumb sucking. By the time a child is 7 or 8 years old, dentists can place a reminder bar in the upper part of the mouth that interferes with the ability to suck. This helpful appliance does not cause any pain to your child but may spare you the later economic pain of $2500 orthodontic treatment.

PREVENTION OF PROLONGED THUMB SUCKING

Thumb sucking lasting beyond a child's fourth year can usually be prevented if you avoid pulling your child's thumb out of his mouth at any age. Also, don't comment in your child's presence about your dissatisfaction with the habit. Scolding, slapping the hand, or other punishments will only make your child dig in his heels about thumb sucking. If you can wait, your child will usually

(Continued on the reverse side)

Instructions for Pediatric Patients by Barton D. Schmitt, M.D., *Pediatrician*
Adapted from YOUR CHILD'S HEALTH, Copyright © 1991 by Barton D. Schmitt, M.D.
Reprinted by permission of Bantam Books.

give up the thumb sucking naturally. If you turn the issue into a showdown, you will lose, since the thumb belongs to your child. The best prevention is to get your newborn to take up the pacifier instead of the thumb.

 ## CALL OUR OFFICE

During regular hours if
—Your child is over 3 years old and sucks her thumb constantly.

—Your child is over 5 years old and doesn't stop when peers tease her.
—Your child is over 6 years old and sucks her thumb at any time.
—Your child also has emotional problems.
—The thumb sucking does not improve after trying this approach.
—You have other concerns or questions.

 Instructions for Pediatric Patients by Barton D. Schmitt, M.D., *Pediatrician*
Adapted from YOUR CHILD'S HEALTH, Copyright © 1991 by Barton D. Schmitt, M.D.
Reprinted by permission of Bantam Books.

Babies vary in how much extra sucking they do when they are not feeding. This extra sucking is a beneficial self-comforting behavior. Some babies almost constantly suck on their thumb or fingers. If you have a baby like this, you may want to try to interest him or her in a pacifier. The pacifier has to be introduced during the first month or two of life for it to substitute for the thumb. Although the orthodontic type of pacifier is preferred because it prevents tongue thrusting during sucking, the regular type usually causes no problems. By trial and error, let your baby find the shape she prefers.

ADVANTAGES OF A PACIFIER OVER THUMB SUCKING

The main advantage of a pacifier is that if you can get your child to use one, he usually won't be a thumb sucker. Thumb sucking can cause a severe overbite if it is continued after the permanent teeth come in. The pacifier exerts less pressure on the teeth and causes much less overbite than the thumb. In addition, the pacifier's use can be controlled as your child grows older. You can decide when it's reasonable to discontinue it. By contrast, thumb sucking can't be stopped when you want it to, because the thumb belongs to your child.

WHEN TO OFFER THE PACIFIER

The peak age for sucking is 2 to 4 months. During the following months, the sucking drive normally decreases. A good age to make it less available is when your child starts to crawl. A pacifier can interfere with normal babbling and speech development. This is especially important after 12 months of age when speech should take off. It's hard to talk with a pacifier in your mouth. To prevent problems with pacifiers, make sure your child doesn't become overly attached to one (for example, walks around with one in his mouth.) Consider the following recommendations for preventing excessive use and a "pacifier habit":
— During the first 6 months of life, give it to your baby whenever she wants to suck, but don't offer it whenever your baby cries. Crying has a number of causes besides hunger and sucking.
— When your older infant is stressed, first try to hold and cuddle her more rather than using the pacifier for this purpose. Some infants like massage. Try not to overuse the pacifier while you are comforting her.
— After 6 months of age (or when your infant starts crawling), keep it in your child's crib. She can use it for nap time and bedtime. After your infant falls asleep, remove it from her mouth if it doesn't fall out. If you allow her to use it all the time, her interest in it will increase rather than decrease. If your child seems to want a security object while awake, offer her alternatives such as a stuffed animal.

— REMINDER: If your baby likes the pacifier, don't forget to take it with you when you travel. Keeping a spare pacifier in the car is helpful. For air travel, sucking or swallowing fluids during descent can prevent ear pain.

PACIFIER SAFETY

Some cautions regarding the pacifier should be observed.
— Use a one-piece commercial pacifier, not a homemade one. Don't try making one yourself by taping a nipple to a plastic bottle cap, A homemade pacifier can be pulled apart, become caught in your baby's throat, and cause choking.
— Don't put the pacifier on a string around your baby's neck. The string could strangle your baby. The new "catch-it-clips" that attach the pacifier to your child's clothing on a short ribbon are practical and safe.
— Don't use pacifiers with a liquid center. (Some have been found to be contaminated with germs.)
— Don't coat it with any sweets, which may cause dental cavities if teeth have erupted.
— Don't coat it with honey, which may cause a serious disease called botulism in children less than 1 year of age.
— Rinse off the pacifier each time your baby finishes using it or if it drops to the floor.
— Replace the pacifier if it becomes damaged.

STOPPING THE PACIFIER

If the pacifier's use has been restricted to nap time and bedtime, many toddlers lose interest in it between 12 and 18 months of age. If your child continues to need the pacifier, you can introduce the idea of giving it up completely by 3 or 4 years of age. Pick a time when your child is not coping with new stresses or fears. Sometimes giving it up on a birthday, holiday, or other celebration makes it easier.

Make the transition as pleasant as possible. Sometimes incentives are needed. If your child seems especially attached to it, help her give it up at nap time first. Use a star chart to mark her progress. When that goal is accomplished, offer to replace the nighttime pacifier with a new stuffed animal or encourage her to trade it for something else she wants. Never force her to give up the pacifier through punishment or humiliation. Abruptly removing the pacifier without preparation can be psychologically harmful.

Give your child a choice such as throwing it away or leaving it out for Santa Claus or the "pacifier fairy." Saving it somewhere in the house is usually not a good idea, because your child will be more likely to ask for it during periods of stress. At such times, offer to cuddle your child instead. Help your child talk about how she misses the pacifier. Praise your child for this sign of growing up.

Instructions for Pediatric Patients by Barton D. Schmitt, M.D., *Pediatrician*
Adapted from YOUR CHILD'S HEALTH, Copyright © 1991 by Barton D. Schmitt, M.D.
Reprinted by permission of Bantam Books.

BREATH-HOLDING SPELLS

DEFINITION

—Breath holding is preceded by an upsetting event, such as falling down, being frustrated or angry, or being frightened.
—Your child gives out one or two long cries and then holds his breath in expiration until the lips become bluish.
—Your child then passes out. (One third of children occasionally progress to having a few twitches or muscle jerks.)
—Your child then resumes normal breathing and becomes fully alert in less than 1 minute.
—Onset is between 6 months and 2 years old. They occur only while the child is awake.

Cause

Breath-holding spells are caused by an abnormal reflex that allows 5% of children to hold their breath long enough to actually pass out. It's not deliberate in most children. Holding the breath (when angry) and becoming bluish *without* passing out are common and not considered abnormal.

Expected Course

Breath-holding spells usually occur from one or two times daily to one or two times per month and are gone by 4 or 5 years of age. They are not dangerous, and they don't lead to epilepsy or brain damage.

HOME CARE

Treatment During Attacks of Breath Holding. These attacks are harmless and always stop by themselves. Since it's difficult to accurately estimate the length of an attack, time a few using a watch with a second hand. Have your child lie flat (rather than being held upright) to increase blood flow to the brain (this position may prevent some of the muscle jerking). Apply a cold, wet washcloth to your child's forehead until he starts breathing again. Don't start resuscitation or call 911—it's unnecessary. Also don't put anything in your child's mouth; it could cause your child to choke or vomit.

Treatment After Attacks of Breath Holding. Give your child a brief hug and go about your business. A relaxed attitude is best. If you are frightened, don't let your child know it. If your child had a temper tantrum because he wanted his way, don't give in to him after the attack.

Prevention of Breath Holding Spells. Most attacks from falling down or a sudden fright can't be prevented; neither can most attacks that are triggered by anger. However, if your child is having daily attacks, he probably has learned to trigger the attacks himself. This happens when parents run to the child and pick him up every time he starts to cry or when they give him his way as soon as the attack is over. Avoid these responses, and your child won't have an undue number of attacks.

CALL OUR OFFICE

During regular hours if
—Your child is unconscious for more than 1 minute (by the clock).
—Any muscle jerks occur during the attack.
—More than one spell occurs per week (so we can prevent them from becoming more frequent).
—You have other questions about breath holding.

CAUTION: Call a rescue squad (911) if your child has a different kind of attack where he stops breathing for more than 1 minute or turns white (not blue).

Instructions for Pediatric Patients by Barton D. Schmitt, M.D., *Pediatrician*   © 1992 by W. B. Saunders Company
Adapted from YOUR CHILD'S HEALTH, Copyright © 1991 by Barton D. Schmitt, M.D.
Reprinted by permission of Bantam Books.

DEFINITION

Your child is toilet trained when, without any reminders, your child walks to the potty, undresses, urinates or has a bowel movement, and pulls up his pants. Some children will learn to control their bladders first; others will start with bowel control. Both kinds of control can be worked on simultaneously. Bladder control through the night normally happens several years later than daytime control. The gradual type of toilet training discussed here can usually be completed in 2 weeks to 2 months.

TOILET-TRAINING READINESS

Don't begin training until your child is clearly ready. Readiness doesn't just happen; it involves concepts and skills you can begin teaching your child at 12 months of age. Reading some of the special toilet-learning books to your child can help. Most children can be made ready for toilet training by 24 months of age and many by 18 months. By the time your child is 3 years old, she will probably have trained herself. The following signs indicate that your child is ready:

— Your child understands what "pee," "poop," "dry," "wet," "clean," "messy," and "potty" mean. (Teach him these words.)
— Your child understands what the potty is for. (Teach this by having your child watch parents, older siblings, and children near his age use the toilet correctly.)
— Your child prefers dry, clean diapers. (Change your child frequently to encourage this preference.)
— Your child likes to be changed. (As soon as she is able to walk, teach her to come to you immediately whenever she is wet or dirty. Praise her for coming to you for a change.)
— Your child understands the connection between dry pants and using the potty.
— Your child can recognize the feeling of a full bladder and the urge to have a bowel movement; that is, he paces, jumps up and down, holds his genitals, pulls at his pants, squats down, or tells you. (Clarify for him: "The poop [or pee] wants to come out. It needs your help.")
— Your child has the ability to briefly postpone urinating or having a bowel movement. She may go off by herself and come back wet or soiled, or she may wake up from naps dry.

METHOD FOR TOILET TRAINING

The way to train your child is to offer encouragement and praise, be patient, and make the process fun. Avoid any pressure or punishment. Your child must feel in control of the process.

1. **Buy supplies.**
— Potty chair (floor-level type). If your child's feet can reach the floor while he sits on the potty, he has leverage for pushing and a sense of security. He also can get on and off whenever he wants to.
— Favorite treats (such as fruit slices, raisins, animal crackers, and cookies) for rewards.
— Stickers or stars for rewards.

2. **Make the potty chair one of your child's favorite possessions.** Several weeks before you plan to begin toilet training, take your child with you to buy a potty chair. Make it clear that this is your child's own special chair. Have your child help you put her name on it. Allow your child to decorate it or even paint it a different color. Then have your child sit on it fully clothed until she is comfortable with using it as a chair. Have your child use it while watching TV, eating snacks, playing games, or looking at books. Keep it in the room in which your child usually plays. Only after your child clearly has good feelings toward the potty chair (after at least 1 week), proceed to actual toilet training.

3. **Encourage practice runs on the potty.** Do a practice run whenever your child gives a signal that looks promising, such as a certain facial expression, grunting, holding the genital area, pulling at his pants, pacing, squatting, squirming, or passing gas. Other good times are after naps or 20 minutes after meals. Say encouragingly, "The poop [or pee] wants to come out. Let's use the potty." Encourage your child to walk to the potty and sit there with his diapers or pants off. Your child can then be told, "Try to go pee-pee in the potty." If your child is reluctant to cooperate, he can be encouraged to sit on the potty by doing something fun; for example, you might read a story. If your child wants to get up after 1 minute of encouragement, let him get up. Never force your child to sit there. Never physically hold your child there or strap him in. Even if your child seems to be enjoying it, end each session after 5 minutes unless something is happening.

4. **Praise or reward your child for cooperation or any success.** All cooperation with these practice sessions should be praised. For example, you might say, "You are sitting on the potty just like Mommy," or "You're trying real hard to put the pee-pee in the potty." If your child urinates into the potty, she can be rewarded with treats or stickers, as well as praise and hugs. Although a sense of accomplishment is enough for some children, others need treats to stay focused. Big rewards (such as going to the ice cream store) should be reserved for when your child walks over to the potty on her own and uses it or asks to go there with you and then uses it. Once your child uses the potty by herself two or more times, you can stop the practice runs. For the following week, continue to praise your child frequently for dryness and using the potty. (NOTE: Practice runs and reminders should not be necessary for more than 1 or 2 months.)

5. **Change your child after accidents.** Change your child as soon as it's convenient, but respond sympathetically. Say something like, "You wanted to go pee-pee in the potty, but you went pee-pee in your pants. I know that makes you sad. You like to be dry. You'll get better at this." If you feel a need to be critical, keep it to mild verbal disapproval and use it rarely (for example,

(Continued on the reverse side)

Instructions for Pediatric Patients by Barton D. Schmitt, M.D., *Pediatrician*
Adapted from YOUR CHILD'S HEALTH, Copyright © 1991 by Barton D. Schmitt, M.D.
Reprinted by permission of Bantam Books.

"Big boys don't go pee-pee in their pants," or mention the name of another child whom he likes and who is trained); then change your child into a dry diaper or training pants in as pleasant and nonangry a way as possible. Avoid physical punishment, yelling, or scolding. Pressure or force can make a 2-year-old child completely uncooperative. Do not keep your child in wet or messy pants for punishment.

6. **Introduce training pants after your child starts using the potty.** Switch from diapers to training pants after your child is cooperative about sitting on the potty chair and passes about half of her urine and bowel movements there. She definitely needs training pants if she comes to you to help her take off her diaper so she can use the potty. Take your child with you to buy the underwear and make it a reward for her success. Buy loose-fitting ones that she can easily lower and pull up by herself. Once you start using training pants, use diapers only for naps and nighttime.

Request the Guideline on Toilet Training Resistance if

—Your child won't sit on the potty or toilet.
—Your 2½-year-old child is negative about toilet training.
—You begin to use force or punishment.
—Your child is over 3 years old and not daytime toilet trained.
—The approach described here isn't working after 2 months.

RECOMMENDED READING

Joanna Cole: The Parents' Book of Toilet Teaching. Ballantine Books, N.Y., 1983.
Vicki Lansky: Koko Bear's New Potty. Bantam Books, N.Y., 1986.
Alison Mack: Toilet Learning. Little, Brown, Boston, 1978.
Katie Van Pelt: Potty Training Your Baby. Avery, N.Y., 1988.

Instructions for Pediatric Patients by Barton D. Schmitt, M.D., *Pediatrician*   © 1992 by W. B. Saunders Company
Adapted from YOUR CHILD'S HEALTH, Copyright © 1991 by Barton D. Schmitt, M.D.
Reprinted by permission of Bantam Books.

DEFINITION

Children who refuse to be toilet trained either wet themselves, soil themselves, or try to hold back their bowel movements (thus becoming constipated). Many of these children also refuse to sit on the toilet or will use the toilet only if the parent brings up the subject and marches them into the bathroom. Any child who is over 2½ years old, healthy, and not toilet trained after several months of trying can be assumed to be resistant to the process, rather than untrained. Consider how capable your child is at delaying a BM until she is off the toilet or you are on the telephone. More practice runs (as you used in toilet training) will not help. Instead your child now needs full responsibility and some incentives to respark her motivation.

The most common cause of resistance to toilet training is that a child has been reminded or lectured too much. Some children have been forced to sit on the toilet against their will, occasionally for long periods of time. A few have been spanked or punished in other ways for not cooperating. Many parents make these mistakes, especially if they have a strong-willed child.

Most children younger than 5 or 6 years of age with soiling (encopresis) or daytime wetting (without any other symptoms) are simply engaged with you in a power struggle. These children can be helped with the following suggestions. If your child holds back BMs and becomes constipated, medicines will also be needed.

HELPING YOUR CHILD WITH DAYTIME WETTING OR SOILING

1. **Transfer all responsibility to your child.** Your child will decide to use the toilet only after he realizes that he has nothing left to resist. Have one last talk with him about the subject. Tell your child that his body makes "pee" and "poop" every day and it belongs to him. Explain that his "poop" wants to go in the toilet and his job is to help the "poop" get out. Tell your child you're sorry you punished him, forced him to sit on the toilet, or reminded him so much. Tell him from now on he doesn't need any help. Then stop all talk about this subject. When your child stops receiving conversation for nonperformance (not going), he will eventually decide to perform for attention.

2. **Stop all reminders about using the toilet.** Let your child decide when he needs to go to the bathroom. He should not be reminded to go to the bathroom nor asked if he needs to go. He knows what it feels like when he has to "poop" or "pee" and where the bathroom is. Reminders are a form of pressure, and pressure doesn't work. He should not be made to sit on the toilet against his will because this will foster a negative attitude about the whole process. Don't accompany your child into the bathroom or stand with him by the potty chair.

He needs to get the feeling of success that comes from doing it on his own and then finding you to tell you what he did.

3. **Give incentives for using the toilet.** If your child stays clean and dry, he needs plenty of positive feedback, such as praise, smiles, and hugs. This positive response should occur every time your child uses the toilet. If a child soils or wets himself on some days and not others, this recognition should occur whenever he is clean for a complete day. On successful days consider taking 20 extra minutes to play a special game with your child or take him for a walk to the playground. Sometimes special incentives, such as favorite sweets or video time, can be invaluable. For using the toilet, err on the side of giving him too much (for example, a handful of sweets each time). If you want a breakthrough, make your child an offer he can't refuse.

4. **Give stars for using the toilet.** Get a calendar for your child and post it in a conspicuous location. Place a star on it every time he uses the toilet. Keep this record of progress until your child has gone 2 weeks without any accidents.

5. **If your child has never sat on the toilet, try to change his attitude.** First, give him choices by asking if he wants to use the big toilet or the potty chair. If he chooses the potty chair, be sure to keep it in the room he usually plays in. For wetting, the presence of the chair and the promise of treats will usually bring about a change in behavior. For soiling, your child may need a pleasant reminder once each day when he is clearly holding back. You can say, "The poop is trying to get out and go in the toilet. The poop needs your help." A few children temporarily may need treats for simply sitting on the toilet and trying. However, don't accompany your child into the bathroom or stand with him by the potty chair. He needs to do it on his own.

6. **Remind your child to change his clothes if he wets or soils himself.** As soon as you notice that your child has wet or messy pants, ask him to clean himself up immediately. The main role you have in this program is to enforce this rule. If your child is wet, he can probably change into dry clothes by himself. If your child is soiled, he will probably need your help with cleanup but keep him involved. Have him rinse the soiled underwear in the toilet. He may think this is "yucky" and be motivated to keep his pants clean.

7. **Don't punish or criticize your child for accidents.** Respond gently to accidents, and do not allow siblings to tease the child. Do not put your child back into diapers unless he needs to be on laxatives. Pressure will only delay successful training, and it could cause secondary emotional problems.

8. **Ask the preschool or day-care staff to use the same strategy.** Ask your child's teacher or day-care provider for unlimited privileges to go to the bathroom any time your child wants to. Keep an extra set of clean underwear at the school or with the day-care provider.

(Continued on the reverse side)

Instructions for Pediatric Patients by Barton D. Schmitt, M.D., *Pediatrician*
Adapted from YOUR CHILD'S HEALTH, Copyright © 1991 by Barton D. Schmitt, M.D.
Reprinted by permission of Bantam Books.

TOILET-TRAINING RESISTANCE (ENCOPRESIS AND DAYTIME WETTING) *Continued*

CALL OUR OFFICE

—Pain or burning occurs when he urinates.
—The resistance is not improved after 1 month on this program.
—The resistance has not stopped completely after 3 months.

During regular hours if
—Your child holds back his bowel movements or becomes constipated.

 Instructions for Pediatric Patients by Barton D. Schmitt, M.D., *Pediatrician*
Adapted from YOUR CHILD'S HEALTH, Copyright © 1991 by Barton D. Schmitt, M.D.
Reprinted by permission of Bantam Books.

DEFINITION

Children who soil their underwear with small amounts of loose bowel movement several times each day are said to have "soiling" or "encopresis." These children are severely constipated or blocked up (the medical term is "impacted"). The soiling occurs because pieces of the large mass of hard stool in the rectum break loose at unexpected times. This leakage cannot be controlled by a child until the large bowel movement ("impaction") is removed. Children can become constipated for many reasons, including diet, genetic differences, or pain with bowel movements. Occasionally, the problem is caused because a child is holding back bowel movements as a way to resist toilet training. Because the cause may be physical instead of behavioral, your child needs a complete examination by his physician.

TREATMENT

First Use Enemas to Remove the Impaction. Start with a Fleet's hyperphosphate enema. The dose is 1 ounce for every 20 pounds of your child's weight (for example, a 30-pound child should receive 1½ ounces). Give a second hyperphosphate enema 1 hour after the first enema. Give a third hyperphosphate enema in 12 to 24 hours if you think your child is still impacted because he continues to soil or a mass can still be felt in the lower abdomen. Before these enemas, give your child plenty to drink because the enemas tend to cause some dehydration. If you want to make your own enemas, make up a solution of salt and water (2 teaspoons of table salt per quart of warm water). Give 2 ounces per year of your child's age (to a maximum of 16 ounces). Once an impaction is cleared, enemas are no longer necessary and your child's constipation can be treated with oral medicines as described in the guidelines below. Do not continue to use enemas; they can irritate the rectum.

Use Stool Softeners to Keep the Bowel Movements Soft. Stool softeners make the stool softer and easier to pass. Unlike laxatives, they do not cause any bowel contractions or pressure. Some commonly prescribed stool softeners are mineral oil, Petrogalar, Kondremul, Citrucel, Metamucil, Mitrolan, Maltsupex, and fiber wafers. Your child must take stool softeners for 3 months or longer to prevent another impaction. After about 3 months, your child's intestines will be able to contract normally again.

If you use mineral oil, keep it in the refrigerator because it tastes best cold. Have your child take it with fruit juice to disguise the flavor or follow it with something tasty. Give your child a vitamin pill each day at about noon while he is taking the mineral oil.

Your child's stool softener is _____.

The dose is _____ tablespoons each morning and

_____ tablespoons each evening. Increase the dose

gradually until your child is having two or three soft bowel movements each day.

Use Laxatives to Keep the Rectum Empty if Stool Softeners Aren't Effective. Laxatives (or bowel stimulants) cause the large intestine to contract, squeezing the stool toward the rectum. Commonly used laxatives are Senokot, Fletcher's Castoria, milk of magnesia (MOM), Haley's M-O, and Dulcolax. Do not use laxatives for more than 2 or 3 months; otherwise, your child might become "laxative dependent," which means the bowels won't move without a laxative.

Your child's laxative is _____.

The dose is _____ given with dinner or

_____.

Encourage a Nonconstipating Diet. Have your child eat plenty of fruits and vegetables every day (raw ones are best). Some examples are figs, dates, raisins, peaches, pears, apricots, celery, and cabbage. Bran is an excellent natural laxative because it has a high fiber content. Have your child eat bran daily by including such foods as the new "natural" cereals, bran flakes, bran muffins, or whole wheat bread in his diet. Popcorn, nuts, shredded wheat, oatmeal, brown rice, lima beans, navy beans, chili beans, and peas are also good sources of fiber. Your child should eat constipating foods such as milk products and cooked carrots in only moderate amounts. However, don't pressure your child about diet; instead, offer choices and include your child in the decisions about what foods to eat.

Encourage Your Child to Sit on the Toilet for 10 Minutes Two Times Each Day. Your child should sit on the toilet until a bowel movement is passed or at least 10 minutes. (Use a kitchen timer if your child is restless.) Unless your child does this, the medicines will not work. Normally, children and adults know when their rectum is full because it is uncomfortable and causes some bowel contractions (the "defecation urge"). Children who have been impacted for a long time lose this sensation and need 4 to 8 weeks to get it back. During this time, your child must sit on the toilet even when he doesn't feel the need to go. The best time seems to be 20 or 30 minutes after a meal. We will try to get your child to promise to do this on his own, but he may need some help from you. Try a reminder sign. By all means, don't remind him more than two times each day or in a stern way because this will foster a negative attitude about the whole process. Never insist that he sit on the toilet if he is busy doing something else. Try to pick good times for gentle reminders and mention that "your doctor asked me to help you remember."

Other toileting tips for your child that are essential for success are

—Push while sitting on the toilet. The bowel movement won't just fall out.

—Bend forward so the chest touches the upper legs. This position opens up the rectum. Flexing and unflexing the hips may also help move stool downward.

(Continued on the reverse side)

Instructions for Pediatric Patients by Barton D. Schmitt, M.D., *Pediatrician*
Adapted from YOUR CHILD'S HEALTH, Copyright © 1991 by Barton D. Schmitt, M.D.
Reprinted by permission of Bantam Books.

—If your child's feet can't easily reach the floor, use a footstool to provide pushing leverage.

Your child should sit on the toilet 10 minutes out of every hour until he has a large bowel movement if
—Any soiling occurs (soiling always means the rectum is very full).
—Your child feels blocked up.
—Your child has a stomachache or cramps.

Praise Your Child for Staying Clean. Some children need more praise and encouragement than others, and this kind of support is never harmful. Rewards are usually unnecessary unless your child is uncooperative or less than 5 years old. Your child will probably be overjoyed to be relieved of his constipation and soiling.

Respond Gently to Accidents. If your child is on the correct medicines and sitting on the toilet, there shouldn't be any accidents. However, determining the correct treatment program may take several weeks. Also, some children will have recurrences. In such cases, handle accidents in the following way:

1. **Recognize soiling.** Don't ignore soiling. As soon as you notice soiling by odor or behavior, remind your child to immediately clean himself up. Encourage your child to come to you before anyone else notices the accident. However, don't expect your child to confess to being soiled.

2. **Have your child sit on the toilet.** After soiling, have your child sit on the toilet until a large bowel movement is passed or at least 20 minutes. If stool is leaking out, the rectum is clearly full and should be emptied.

3. **Clean the skin.** After your child sits on the toilet, suggest a 5-minute soak in the bathtub. At the least, your child's bottom needs cleaning off with a wet washcloth. Your child should be able to do most of this on his own.

4. **Clean soiled clothes.** First, scrape the underwear partially clean with a butter knife or spatula. Then rinse it out in the toilet. Finally, store the soiled underwear until the next wash day in a conveniently located bucket of water with some bleach in it and a lid. You can encourage your child to help with this, but you will need to do most of it until he is 7 or 8 years old.

5. **Avoid punishment.** Do not blame, criticize, or punish your child. In addition, do not allow siblings to tease him. Never put your child back into diapers. If anyone in your family wants to "crack down" on the child, have that person talk to us because this kind of pressure will only delay a cure and it could cause secondary emotional problems.

Ask the School Staff for Their Help. These children need ready access to the bathroom at school, especially if they are shy. Encourage your child not to be embarrassed about leaving the classroom to go to the bathroom. We will send the school a note requesting unlimited privileges to go to the school bathroom any time your child wants to and without having to raise his hand. He should also be allowed to come in from outside recess. If the problem is significant, you might also temporarily supply the school with an extra set of clean underwear.

Help Your Child Keep a Record of Progress. We will give your child a calendar to keep. Bring this to all visits. This record of soiling accidents should be kept until your child has gone 1 month without any accidents after stopping the stool softener.

Keep Follow-up Appointments. Knowing that he will return to us to report his progress will often increase your child's motivation. After 8 years of age, the treatment program should involve just your child and his physician. The more involved and responsible your child feels, the better the results will be. The first follow-up visit is especially important so that we can be sure that the impaction is completely cleaned out.

 ## CALL OUR OFFICE

During regular hours if
—Your child soils two or more times.
—Your child goes 72 hours without a bowel movement.
—You feel your child is getting worse.
—Your child won't take the medicines.
—Your child won't sit on the toilet.
—You have other questions or concerns.

 Instructions for Pediatric Patients by Barton D. Schmitt, M.D., *Pediatrician*   © 1992 by W. B. Saunders Company
Adapted from YOUR CHILD'S HEALTH, Copyright © 1991 by Barton D. Schmitt, M.D.
Reprinted by permission of Bantam Books.

Some Dos

—Change your child frequently.

—Teach your child to come to you when he needs to be changed.

—Help your child spend time with children who are trained and watch them use the toilet or potty chair.

—Read toilet-learning books to your child.

—Initially, keep the potty chair in the room your child usually plays in. This easy access markedly increases the chances he will use it without your asking him to. Consider owning two potty chairs.

—Teach him how the toilet works.

—Mention using the toilet or potty chair only if your child gives a cue that he needs to go.

—Give suggestions, not demands.

—Give your child an active role and let him do it his way.

—Be supportive.

—Keep a sense of humor.

—Keep the process fun and upbeat. Be positive about any interest your child shows.

Some Don'ts

—Don't start when your child is in a stubborn or negative phase.

—Don't use any punishment or pressure.

—Don't force your child to sit on a potty chair.

—Don't keep your child sitting on a potty chair against his will.

—Don't flush the toilet while your child is sitting on it.

—Don't lecture or remind your child.

—Avoid any friction.

—Avoid battles or showdowns.

—Don't try to control what you can't control.

—Never escalate your response, you will always lose.

—Don't act overconcerned about this normal body function. Try to appear casual and relaxed during the training.

—After your child uses the toilet, don't expect a perfect performance. Some accidents occur for months.

Instructions for Pediatric Patients by Barton D. Schmitt, M.D., *Pediatrician*
Adapted from YOUR CHILD'S HEALTH, Copyright © 1991 by Barton D. Schmitt, M.D.
Reprinted by permission of Bantam Books.

SEX EDUCATION FOR PRESCHOOLERS

By 4 years of age, most children develop a healthy sexual curiosity. They ask a variety of questions and need honest, brief answers. If they don't ask sexual questions by 5 years of age, it is your job to bring up this subject. If you don't they may acquire a lot of misinformation from their schoolmates.

PROMOTING GOOD SEX EDUCATION

—Teach the differences in anatomy and the proper names for body parts. This is easy to do during baths with siblings or friends.
—Teach about pregnancy and where babies come from. The easiest way is to get a pregnant friend to volunteer and have your child feel her baby moving about.
—Explain the birth process. Tell your child that the baby comes out through a special passage called the vagina. Help him understand the process by seeing the birth of some puppies or kittens.
—Also, explain sexual intercourse. Many parents who discuss everything else keep postponing this topic. Get past this hurdle by reading your child some picture books on sex education. If you cover these topics by 5 years of age, your child will find it easy to ask you more about them as he grows older.

NORMAL SEXUAL PLAY

A common part of normal sexual development between 3 and 5 years of age is for children to get undressed together and look at each other's genitals. This is their attempt to learn about sexual differences. There's no reason why you can't turn this discovery into a positive one.

—After your child's friends have gone home, read him a book about sex education. Help him talk about how boys' and girls' bodies differ.
—Tell your child that genitals are private. That's why we wear clothes. Clarify some basic rules: It's acceptable to see other people's genitals but not to touch them or stare at them. It's not acceptable to deliberately show someone your genitals.
—In the future, supervise the play a little more closely. If the children occasionally expose their bodies to each other, just ignore it. But if it seems to be coming more frequent, tell the children it's not po-

lite and has to stop. If this doesn't get your message across, give them a 5-minute time-out in separate rooms or send them home for the day, but don't give any major punishment or act horrified.
—It's up to parents to put the brakes on undressing games. If you don't, they usually escalate into touching and poking, but keep your response low-key.

NUDITY AND YOUR CHILD

Feelings about nudity vary from family to family. Exposure to nudity with siblings or the parent of the same sex is fine and continues indefinitely (for example, in locker rooms), but nudity with the parent or sibling of the opposite sex probably should be phased out between 4 and 5 years of age. Some reasons for this are the following:
—Your child will soon be entering school, and nudity is clearly not accepted there.
—Most families in our society practice modesty, so a child who is interested in looking at other people's bodies can get into trouble.
—It is more comfortable for children to learn genital anatomy from siblings and age-mates than from seeing their parents nude.

If you are in agreement with these comments, then between 4 and 5 years of age begin to teach a respect for privacy.
—Stop any showering and bathing with your children (especially of the opposite sex).
—Close the bathroom door when you use the toilet.
—Close the bedroom door when you get dressed and suggest they do the same.

Wasn't that easy?

 ## CALL OUR OFFICE

During regular hours if
—Your child won't stop touching other children's genitals.
—Your child won't stop exposing his or her genitals.
—Your child has an excessive interest in sex or nudity.
—You have other questions or concerns.

Instructions for Pediatric Patients by Barton D. Schmitt, M.D., *Pediatrician*
Adapted from YOUR CHILD'S HEALTH, Copyright © 1991 by Barton D. Schmitt, M.D.
Reprinted by permission of Bantam Books.

DEFINITION

Masturbation is self-stimulation of the genitals for pleasure and self-comfort. Children may rub themselves with a hand or other object. Masturbation is more than the normal inspection of the genitals commonly observed in 2-year-olds during baths. During masturbation, a child usually appears dazed, flushed, and preoccupied. A child may masturbate as often as several times each day or just once per week. Masturbation occurs more commonly when a child is sleepy, bored, watching television, or under stress.

Cause

Occasional masturbation is a normal behavior of many toddlers and preschoolers. Up to one third of children in this age group discover masturbation while exploring their bodies. Often they continue to masturbate simply because it feels good. Some children masturbate frequently because they are unhappy about something, such as having their pacifier taken away. Others are reacting to punishment or pressure to stop masturbation completely.

Masturbation has no medical causes. Irritation in the genital area causes pain or itching; it does not cause masturbation.

Expected Course

Once your child discovers masturbation, he or she will seldom stop doing it completely. Your child may not do it as often if any associated power struggles or unhappiness is remedied. By 5 or 6 years of age most children can learn some discretion and will masturbate only in private. Masturbation becomes almost universal at puberty in response to the normal surges in hormones and sexual drive.

Common Misconceptions

Masturbation does not cause any physical injury or harm to the body. It is not abnormal or excessive unless it is deliberately done in public places after 5 or 6 years of age. It does not mean your child will be oversexed, promiscuous, or sexually deviant. Only if adults overreact to a child's masturbation and make it seem dirty or wicked will it cause emotional harm, such as guilt and sexual hang-ups.

COMING TO TERMS WITH MASTURBATION IN PRESCHOOLERS

1. **Set realistic goals**. It is impossible to eliminate masturbation. Accept the fact that your child has learned about it and enjoys it. All that you can control is where he or she does it. A reasonable goal is to permit it only in the bedroom and bathroom. You might say to your child, "It's okay to do that in your bedroom when you're tired." If you completely ignore the masturbation, no matter where it's done, your child will think he or she can do it freely in any setting.

2. **Ignore masturbation at nap time and bedtime**. Leave your child alone at these times and do not keep checking on him or her. Do not forbid your child from lying on the abdomen and do not ask if his or her hands are between the legs.

3. **Distract or discipline your child for masturbation at other times**. First, try to distract your child with a toy or activity. If this fails, explain to your child: "I know that rubbing your body feels good, but you can't do that around other people. It's okay to do it in your room or the bathroom but not in the rest of the house." By the time children are 4 or 5 years old, they become sensitive to other people's feelings and understand that they should masturbate only when they are alone. Younger children may have to be sent to their rooms to masturbate.

4. **Discuss this approach with your child's day-care or preschool staff**. Ask your child's care giver or teacher to respond to your child's masturbation by first trying to distract the child. If this doesn't work, they should catch the child's attention with comments such as "We need to have you join us now." Masturbation should be tolerated at school only at nap time.

5. **Increase physical contact with your child**. Some children will masturbate less if they receive extra hugging and cuddling throughout the day. Try to be sure that your child receives at least 1 hour every day of special time together and physical affection from you.

6. **Avoid these common mistakes**. The most common mistake that parents make is to try to eliminate masturbation completely. This leads to a power struggle that the parents inevitably lose. Children should not be physically punished for masturbation, nor yelled at or lectured about it. Do not label masturbation as bad, dirty, evil, or sinful, and do not tie your child's hands or use any kind of restraints. All of these approaches lead only to resistance and possibly later to sexual inhibitions.

 ## CALL OUR OFFICE

During regular hours if
— Your child continues to masturbate when other people are around.
— You suspect that your child has been taught to masturbate by someone.
— You child tries to masturbate others.
— You feel your child is unhappy.
— You cannot accept any masturbation by your child.
— This approach does not bring improvement within 1 month.
— You have other questions or concerns.

TICS (TWITCHES)

DEFINITION

—Rapid, repeated muscle twitches (also called habit spasms), such as eye blinking, facial grimacing, forehead wrinkling, head jerking, or shoulder shrugging
—Increase with stress
—Decrease with relaxation and disappear during sleep
—Occur in 20% of children and are three times more frequent in boys than in girls
—Occur most often in children 6 to 10 years old

Causes

Tics reflect the spilling over of emotional tension. They mean your child is under pressure. They are involuntary, not deliberate. Children who have tics are usually normal, bright, and sensitive. Tics are more severe in children who are shy or overly self-conscious. Tics can be worsened by critical parents who nag, press a child for achievement beyond his ability, or draw negative comparisons with siblings.

Expected Course

If tics are ignored, they usually disappear in 2 months to 1 year. If extra effort is made to help your child relax, they usually improve more quickly. Even if the tics are not ignored and a child continues to feel stress or pressure, the tics usually improve or clear spontaneously during adolescence. Approximately 3% of children with tics develop incapacitating tics if they are not handled appropriately.

HOW TO HELP YOUR CHILD WITH TICS

Help Your Child to Relax in General. Tics are a barometer of inner tension. Make sure your child has free time and fun time every day. If your child is overscheduled with activities, try to lighten the commitments. If your child is unduly self-critical, praise him more and remind him to be a good friend to himself.

Identify and Remove Specific Environmental Stresses. Whenever your child has a flurry of tics, write in a diary the date, time, and preceding event. From this diary, you should be able to identify when your child feels pressure. (NOTE: Your child should not know that you are keeping this diary.) In general, criticize your child less about grades, music lessons, sports, keeping his room clean, table manners, and so forth. Avoid stimulant medications (such as decongestants), which can lower the threshold for tics.

Ignore Tics When They Occur. When your child is having tics, don't call his attention to them. Reminders imply that they are bothering you. If your child becomes worried about the tics, then every time they occur, the child will react with tension rather than acceptance. The tension in turn will trigger more tics. Don't allow siblings or others to tease your child about the tics. Be sure that relatives, friends, and teachers also ignore the tics. When tics occur, people should say nothing and reduce any pressure they may be giving your child.

Don't Talk about Tics When They Are Not Occurring. Stop all family conversation about tics. The less said about them, the less your child will be apprehensive of them. If your child brings up the subject, reassure him that he will eventually regain control over his facial muscles and the tics will go away.

Avoid Any Punishment for Tics. Some parents have the mistaken idea that tics are a bad habit that can be broken. This idea is absolutely false. If a child is made to practice "controlling tics" in front of a mirror, he will just realize he cannot control them. Any facial exercises or massage should be discontinued because it only draws undue attention to the problem.

 ## CALL OUR OFFICE

During regular hours if
—The tics interfere with friendships or studies at school.
—The tics involve sounds, words, or profanity.
—The tics involve coughing.
—The tics involve parts of the body other than the head, face, or shoulders.
—The tics become frequent (more than 10 each day).
—The tics have lasted for more than a year.
—The tics are not better after trying this program for 1 month.
—You have other questions or concerns.

Instructions for Pediatric Patients by Barton D. Schmitt, M.D., *Pediatrician*
Adapted from YOUR CHILD'S HEALTH, Copyright © 1991 by Barton D. Schmitt, M.D.
Reprinted by permission of Bantam Books.

DEFINITIONS

Characteristics of Normal Dysfluency and Dysarthria

"Normal dysfluency" and "pseudostuttering" are the terms used to describe the normal repetition of words or phrases children make when they are learning to speak between 18 months and 5 years of age. "Normal dysarthria" and "mispronunciation" are the terms used to describe the incorrect pronunciation of many children as they learn to speak; sounds are substituted or left out, so that some words become hard to identify.

Characteristics of True Stuttering

—Repetitions of sounds, syllables, words, or phrases
—Hesitations and pauses in speech
—Absence of smooth speech flow
—More frequent when child is tired, excited, or stressed
—Fear of talking
—Four times more likely in boys than in girls

Causes of Dysfluency, Dysarthria, and True Stuttering

Normal dysfluency occurs because the mind is able to form words faster than the tongue can produce them. The cause of normal dysarthria is usually genetic. In most cases, true stuttering develops when a child with normal dysfluency or dysarthria is pressured to improve and in the process becomes sensitive to his inadequacies. Soon thereafter the child begins to anticipate speaking poorly and struggles to correct it. The child becomes tense when he speaks, and the more he attempts to control his speech, the worse it becomes (a vicious cycle). The repetitions become multiple, rather than single. Temporary stuttering can occur at any age if a person becomes overly critical and fearful of his own speech. Although it is normal for us to be aware of what we are saying, how we are saying it is normally subconscious. Genetic factors also play a role in stuttering.

Incidence

Normal dysfluency occurs in 90% of children, in contrast to true stuttering, which occurs in only 1% of children. Approximately 70% of children pronounce words clearly from the onset of speech; however, the other 30% of children between the ages of 1 and 4 years have normal dysarthria and say many words that are unintelligible to their parents and others.

Expected Course of Dysfluency, Dysarthria, and True Stuttering

Normal dysfluency lasts for approximately 2 or 3 months if handled correctly. Unlike normal dysfluency, normal dysarthria is not a brief phase but instead shows very gradual improvement over several years as development unfolds. The speech of 90% of the children who have dysarthria becomes completely understandable by 4 years of age, and the speech of 96% is understandable by 5 or 6 years of age. Without treatment, true stuttering will become worse and persist in adulthood.

HELPING YOUR CHILD COPE WITH NORMAL DYSFLUENCY AND DYSARTHRIA

These recommendations should prevent progression to true stuttering in these children.

Encourage Conversation.   Sit down and talk with your child at least once each day. Keep the subject matter pleasant and enjoyable. Avoid asking for verbal performance or reciting. Make speaking fun.

Don't Correct Your Child's Speech.   Avoid expressing any disapproval, such as by saying, "Stop that stuttering" or "Think before you speak." Remember that this is your child's normal speech for his age and is not controllable. Do not try to improve your child's grammar or pronunciation. Also, avoid praise for good speech because it implies that your child's previous speech wasn't up to standard.

Don't Interrupt Your Child's Speech.   Give your child ample time to finish what he is saying. Don't complete sentences for him. Try to pause 2 seconds between the end of your child's sentence and the start of yours. Don't allow siblings to interrupt one another.

Don't Ask Your Child to Repeat Himself or Start Over.   If possible, guess at the message. Listen very closely when your child is speaking. Only if you don't understand a comment that appears to be important should you ask your child to restate it.

Don't Ask Your Child to Practice a Certain Word or Sound.   This just makes the child more self-conscious about his speech.

Don't Ask Your Child to Slow Down When He Speaks.   Try to convey to your child that you have plenty of time and are not in a hurry. Model a relaxed rate of speech. A rushed type of speech is a temporary phase that can't be changed by orders from the parent.

Don't Label Your Child a Stutterer.   Labels tend to become self-fulfilling prophecies. Don't discuss your child's speech problems in his presence.

Ask Other Adults not to Correct Your Child's Speech.   Share these guidelines with baby-sitters, teachers, relatives, neighbors, and visitors. Don't allow siblings to tease or imitate your child's stuttering.

Help Your Child to Relax and Feel Accepted in General.   Try to increase the hours of fun and play your child has each day. Try to slow down the pace of your family life. Avoid situations that seem to bring on stut-

(Continued on the reverse side)

© 1992 by W. B. Saunders Company

STUTTERING VERSUS NORMAL DYSFLUENCY
Continued

tering. If there are any areas in which you have been applying strict discipline, back off.

CALL OUR OFFICE

During regular hours if
—Your child is over 5 years of age.
—Your child has true stuttering.

—Your child has associated facial grimacing or tics.
—Your child has become self-conscious or fearful about his speech.
—Your family has a history of stuttering in adulthood.
—Speech is also delayed (no words by 18 months or no sentences by 2½ years).
—Speech is totally unintelligible to others, and your child is over 2 years old.
—Speech is more than 50% unintelligible to others, and your child is over 3 years old.
—Speech is 10% unintelligible to others, and your child is over 4 years old.
—The dysfluency doesn't improve after trying this program for 2 months.
—You have other questions or concerns.

Instructions for Pediatric Patients by Barton D. Schmitt, M.D., *Pediatrician*
Adapted from YOUR CHILD'S HEALTH, Copyright © 1991 by Barton D. Schmitt, M.D.
Reprinted by permission of Bantam Books.

DEFINITION

A child with school phobia is a child who misses considerable school because of vague physical symptoms. When he is not in school, he is at home; that is, he is not a truant. The symptoms are usually the type that people get when they are upset or worried, such as stomachaches, headaches, nausea, vomiting, diarrhea, tiredness, or dizziness. These physical symptoms mainly occur in the morning, and they worsen at the time of departure for school. Your child otherwise seems healthy and vigorous. School phobia is very common and affects at least 5% of elementary-school children and 2% of middle-school children. Often the symptoms begin in September or October.

Causes

A school-phobic child is usually afraid of leaving home in general, rather than afraid of anything in particular at school. For example, he may experience homesickness when staying at a friend's house. Often the first test of a child's independence comes when he must attend school daily. Aside from poor attendance, these children usually are good students and well behaved at school. The parents are typically good parents who are conscientious and loving. Such parents are sometimes overly protective and close, and the child finds it difficult to separate from them (separation anxiety). He may lack the self-confidence that comes from handling life's normal stresses without his parents' help.

Sometimes a change of schools, a strict teacher, hard tests, a learning problem, or a bully may be seen as causes of the child's fear of going to school. However, such factors may be only part of the problem, and your child should still go to school while these problems are being resolved.

Expected Course

If daily school attendance is enforced, the problem of school phobia will improve dramatically in 1 or 2 weeks. On the other hand, if you do not require your child to attend school every day, the physical symptoms and the desire to stay home will become more frequent. The longer your child stays home, the harder it will be for him to return. Your child's future social life and education may be at stake.

HELPING YOUR CHILD OVERCOME SCHOOL PHOBIA

1. **Insist on an immediate return to school.** The best therapy for school phobia is to be in school every day. Fears are overcome by facing them as soon as possible. Daily school attendance will cause most of your child's physical symptoms to magically improve. They will become less severe and occur less often, and your child will eventually enjoy school again. At first, however, your child will test your determination to send her every day. You must make school attendance a nonnegotiable, ironclad rule. Be optimistic with your child and reassure him that he will feel better after he gets to school.

2. **Be extra firm on school mornings.** In the beginning, mornings may be a difficult time. You should never ask your child how he feels because it will encourage him to complain. If he is well enough to be up and around the house, he is well enough to go to school. If your child complains of physical symptoms, but they are his usual ones, he should be sent to school promptly with minimal discussion. If you are uncertain about your child's health, try to err on the side of sending him to school; if later the symptoms worsen, the school nurse can reevaluate your child's health.

If your child is late, he should go to school anyway. When he misses the school bus, you should have a prearranged alternative plan of transportation. If your child wanders home on his own during lunch or recess, he should be sent back promptly. Sometimes a child may cry and scream, absolutely refusing to go to school. In that case, after talking with him about his worries, he has to be taken there. One parent may be better at enforcing this than the other. Sometimes a relative can take charge of the matter for a few days.

3. **Have your child see her physician on any morning she stays home.** If your child has a new physical symptom or seems quite sick, you will probably want her to stay home. If you are puzzled, your physician will usually be able to determine the cause of her sickness. Call the office as soon as it opens, and try to have your child seen that morning. If the symptom is caused by a disease, appropriate treatment can be started. If the symptom results from anxiety, your child should be back in school before noon. Working closely with your child's physician in this way can solve even the most difficult of school phobia problems. You should probably keep your child at home when she has any of the following symptoms:
—Fever (over 100° F orally)
—Vomiting (more than once)
—Frequent diarrhea
—Frequent cough
—Widespread rash
—Earache
—Toothache

On the other hand, children with a sore throat, moderate cough, runny nose, or other cold symptoms but no fever can be sent to class. Children should not be kept home for "looking sick," "poor color," "circles under the eyes," or "tiredness."

4. **Ask the school staff for assistance.** Schools are usually very understanding about school phobia, once they are informed of the diagnosis, because this problem is such a common one. Ask the school nurse to let your child lie down for 5 to 15 minutes in her office and regroup, rather than being sent home if his symptoms occur in school. It is often helpful if you talk to your child's teacher about the situation.

(Continued on the reverse side)

Instructions for Pediatric Patients by Barton D. Schmitt, M.D., *Pediatrician*
Adapted from YOUR CHILD'S HEALTH, Copyright © 1991 by Barton D. Schmitt, M.D.
Reprinted by permission of Bantam Books.

If your child has special fears, such as reciting in class, the teacher will usually make special allowances.

5. **Talk with your child about school fears.** At a time other than a school morning, talk with your child about her problems. Encourage her to tell you exactly what upsets her. Ask her what is the worst possible thing that could happen to her at school or on the way to school. If there's a situation you can change, tell her you will work on it. If she's worried about the physical symptoms becoming worse at school, reassure her that she can lie down for a few minutes in the nurse's office as needed. After listening carefully, tell her you can appreciate how she feels, but it's still necessary to attend school while she's getting better.

6. **Help your child spend more time with his age-mates.** Outside of school, school-phobic children tend to prefer to be with their parents, play indoors, be alone in their rooms, and watch a lot of television. Many of them cannot stay overnight at a friend's home without developing overwhelming homesickness. They need encouragement to play more with their peers. This can be difficult for a parent who enjoys the child's company, but it is the best course of action in the long run. Encourage your child to join clubs and athletic teams (noncontact sports are usually preferred). Send her outside more or to other children's homes. Ask her friends to join your family for outings or for overnight stays. Help your child learn to stay overnight with relatives and friends. Send your child to a summer camp—it can be a turning point.

CALL OUR OFFICE

During regular hours if
—The school phobia is not resolved in 2 weeks using this approach.
—The school phobia recurs.
—You think the cause of the symptoms may be physical rather than emotional.
—Your child continues to have other fears or separation problems.
—Your child is withdrawn in general or seems depressed.
—You have other questions or concerns.

Instructions for Pediatric Patients by Barton D. Schmitt, M.D., *Pediatrician*
Adapted from YOUR CHILD'S HEALTH, Copyright © 1991 by Barton D. Schmitt, M.D.
Reprinted by permission of Bantam Books.

DEFINITION

Attention deficit disorder (ADD) occurs in 3% to 5% of children, most of them boys. A normal attention span is 3 to 5 minutes per year of a child's age. A child in kindergarten needs a 15-minute attention span. First and second graders need a 20-minute span to do the work. (NOTE: The attention span while watching television doesn't count.) If you suspect that your child has a short attention span, ask another adult (a teacher or day-care provider, for example) if she has observed this also. The following characteristics are common:

— A child hasn't learned to listen when someone talks, wait his turn, complete a task, or return to a task if interrupted. (CAUTION: These can be normal characteristics of children less than 3 or 4 years old.)

— Some children (80% of boys and 50% of girls) also have associated hyperactivity (increased motor activity) with symptoms of being restless, impulsive, and in a hurry. This is called ADHD.

— Some children (50%) also have an associated learning disability. The most common one is an auditory processing deficit (that is, they have difficulty remembering complex verbal directions). However, the intelligence of most children with ADD is usually normal.

Similar Conditions

Disruptive children, children who don't mind, and aggressive children are sometimes included under the broad category of hyperactivity. Many problem 2-year-olds are considered "hyperactive." These children should be looked on as children with behavior problems and approached with appropriate discipline techniques.

Causes

ADD is the most common developmental disability. "Developmental" means that the disability is caused by delayed brain development (immaturity). This delay results in poor self-control, requiring external controls by the parents for a longer period of time. Often this type of temperament and short attention span are hereditary. A small percentage of children with ADD are reacting to chaotic home environments, but in most cases the parents' style of child rearing has not caused the disability. Minor brain damage has not been proven to cause ADD.

Expected Course

Children with developmental ADD can improve significantly if parents and teachers provide understanding and direction and preserve the children's self-esteem. When these children become adults, many of them have good attention spans but remain restless, have to keep busy, and, in a sense, have not entirely outgrown the problem. However, not only does society learn to tolerate such traits in adults, but in some settings the person with endless energy is prized. Children with severe ADD may need vocational counseling as adults.

GUIDELINES FOR LIVING WITH A CHILD HAVING A SHORT ATTENTION SPAN AND HYPERACTIVITY

ADD is a chronic condition that needs special parenting and school intervention. If your child seems to have a poor attention span and is over 3 years of age, these recommendations may assist you. Your main obligations involve organizing your child's home life and improving discipline. Only after your child's behavior has improved will you know for certain if your child also has a short attention span. If he does, specific interventions to help him learn to listen and complete tasks ("stretch" his attention span) can be initiated. Even though you can't be sure about poor attention span until your child is 3 or 4 years of age, you can detect and improve behavior problems after 8 months of age.

1. **Accept your child's limitations.** Accept the fact that your child is intrinsically active and energetic and possibly always will be. The hyperactivity is not intentional. Don't expect to eliminate the hyperactivity but merely to bring it under reasonable control. Any criticism or other attempt to change an energetic child into a quiet or model child will cause more harm than good. Nothing helps a hyperactive child more than having a tolerant, patient, low-keyed parent.

2. **Provide an outlet for the release of excess energy.** This energy can't be bottled up and stored. Daily outdoor activities such as running, sports, and long walks are good outlets. A fenced yard helps. In bad weather your child needs a recreational area where he can play as he pleases with minimal restrictions and supervision. A garage will suffice. Too many toys can cause him to be more easily distracted from playing with any one toy. The toys should be safe and relatively unbreakable. Encourage your child to play with one toy at a time.

Although the expression of hyperactivity is allowed in these ways, it should not be needlessly encouraged. Don't initiate roughhousing with your child. Forbid siblings to say, "Chase me, chase me" or to instigate other noisy play. Encouraging hyperactive behavior can lead to its becoming your child's main style of interacting.

3. **Keep your home well organized.** Household routines help the hyperactive child to accept order. Keep the times for wake-up, meals, chores, naps, and bed regular. Keep your environment relatively quiet to encourage thinking and listening. In general, leave the radio and television off. Predictable daily events help your child's responses become more predictable.

4. **Try not to let your child become fatigued.** When a hyperactive child becomes exhausted, his self-control often breaks down and the hyperactivity becomes worse. Try to have your child sleep or rest when he is fatigued. If he can't seem to "turn off his motor," hold and rock him in a rocking chair.

5. **Avoid taking your child to formal gatherings.** Except for special occasions, avoid places where hyperactivity would be extremely inappropriate and embarrassing (such as churches or restaurants). You also may

(Continued on the reverse side)

Instructions for Pediatric Patients by Barton D. Schmitt, M.D., *Pediatrician*
Adapted from YOUR CHILD'S HEALTH, Copyright © 1991 by Barton D. Schmitt, M.D.
Reprinted by permission of Bantam Books.

wish to reduce the number of times your child goes with you to stores and supermarkets. After your child develops adequate self-control at home, he can gradually be introduced to these situations.

6. **Maintain firm discipline.** These children are unquestionably difficult to manage. They need more carefully planned discipline than the average child. Rules should be formulated mainly to prevent harm to your child and to others. Aggressive behavior, such as biting, hitting, and pushing, should be no more accepted in the hyperactive child than in the normal child. Try to eliminate such aggressive behaviors, but avoid unnecessary or unattainable rules; that is, don't expect your child to keep his hands and feet still. Hyperactive children tolerate fewer rules than the normal child. Enforce a few clear, consistent, important rules and add other rules at your child's pace. Avoid constant negative comments like "Don't do this" and "Stop that."

7. **Enforce rules with nonphysical punishment.** Physical punishment suggests to your child that physically aggressive behavior is acceptable. We want to teach hyperactive children to be less aggressive. Your child needs adult models of control and calmness. Use a friendly, matter-of-fact tone of voice to discipline your child. If you yell, your child will be quick to imitate you.

Punish your child for misbehavior immediately. When your child breaks a rule, isolate him in a chair or time-out room if a show of disapproval doesn't work. The time-out should last about 1 minute per year of your child's age. Without a time-out system, success is unlikely.

8. **Stretch your child's attention span.** Encouraging attentive (nonhyperactive) behavior is the key to preparing your child for school. Increased attention span and persistence with tasks can be taught at home. Don't wait until your child is of school age and expect the teacher to change him. By 5 years of age he needs at least a 15-minute attention span to perform adequately.

Set aside several brief periods each day to teach your child listening skills by reading to him. Start with picture books, and gradually progress to reading stories. Coloring pictures can be encouraged and praised. Teach games to your child, gradually increasing the difficulty by starting with building blocks and progressing to puzzles, dominoes, card games, and dice games. Matching pictures is an excellent way to build your child's memory and concentration span. Later, consequence games such as checkers or tic-tac-toe can be introduced. When your child becomes restless, stop and return to it later. Praise your child for attentive behavior. This process is invaluable in preparing your child for school.

Be sure to praise your child when he plays independently rather than interrupting you when you are talking to guests or are on the telephone.

9. **Buffer your child against any overreaction by neighbors.** Ask neighbors with whom your child has contact to be helpers. If your child is labeled by some adults as a "bad" kid, it is important that this image of your child doesn't carry over into your home life. At home the attitude that must prevail is that your child is a good child with excess energy. It is extremely important that you not give up on him. Your child must always feel loved and accepted within the family. As long as a child has this acceptance, his self-esteem will survive. If your child has trouble doing well in school, help him gain a sense of success through a hobby in an area of strength.

10. **From time to time, get away from it all.** Periodic breaks help parents to tolerate hyperactive behavior. If just the father works outside the home, he should try to look after the child when he comes home, not only to give his wife a deserved break but also to understand better what she must contend with during the day. A baby-sitter one afternoon each week and an occasional evening out can provide much-needed breaks for an exhausted mother. Preschool is another helpful option. Parents need time to rejuvenate themselves so they can continue to meet their child's extra needs.

11. **Use special programs at school.** Try to start your child in preschool by 3 years of age to help him learn to organize his thoughts and develop his ability to focus. However, consider enrolling your child in kindergarten a year late (that is, at 6 years old rather than 5) because the added maturity may help him fit in better with his classmates.

Once your child enters grade school, the school is responsible for providing appropriate programs for your child's ADD and any learning disability he might have. Some standard approaches used to help children with ADD are smaller class size, isolated study space, spaced learning techniques, and inclusion of the child in tasks such as erasing the blackboard (as outlets for excessive energy). Many of these children spend part of their day with a teacher specializing in learning disabilities who helps to improve their skills and confidence.

If you think your child has ADD and he has not been tested by the school's special education team, you can request an evaluation. Usually you can obtain the help your child needs with schoolwork by working with the school through parent-teacher conferences and special meetings. Your main job is to continue to help your child improve his attention span, self-discipline, and friendships at home.

12. **Medications are sometimes helpful.** Some stimulant drugs can improve a child's ability to concentrate. You may want to discuss the use of drugs with your child's physician. In general, medications should not be prescribed before school age. They should also not be prescribed until after your child has been evaluated by a doctor and a school psychologist or special education teacher, an individualized educational plan (IEP) is in effect at school, and you have followed the suggestions we have given you. Medications without special education and home management programs have no long-term benefit. They need to be part of a broader program.

 CALL OUR OFFICE

For referral to a child psychiatrist or psychologist if
—Your child shows unprovoked aggression and destructiveness.
—Your child has repeated accidents.
—Your child has been suspended from school.
—Your child can't make or keep any friends.
—You have "given up" hope of improving your child.
—You can't stop using physical punishment.
—You are at your wit's end.

Instructions for Pediatric Patients by Barton D. Schmitt, M.D., *Pediatrician*   © 1992 by W. B. Saunders Company
Adapted from YOUR CHILD'S HEALTH, Copyright © 1991 by Barton D. Schmitt, M.D.
Reprinted by permission of Bantam Books.

DEFINITION

—Performs below his or her potential at school
—Has average or better intelligence, with no learning disabilities
—Doesn't finish schoolwork or homework
—"Forgets" to bring homework home
—"Forgets," loses, or doesn't turn in finished homework
—"Doesn't remember" what parents have taught
—Gets poor report card
—Doesn't want any help

Causes

Some children get into bad habits with their homework because they become preoccupied with television programs or video games. Some middle-school children become sidetracked by their hormones or by sports. Other children who find schoolwork difficult would simply rather play. If parents help these children cut back other activities to reasonable amounts and count on the teacher to grade the child's efforts on schoolwork and homework, most of these children will improve. Motivation for good grades eventually comes from a desire to please the teacher and be admired by peers, enjoyment in knowing things, ability to see studying as a pathway to a future career, knowledge that the student needs a 3-point average to get into college, and the student's own self-reproach when she falls short of her goals.

When parents overrespond to this behavior and exert pressure for better performance, they can start a power struggle around schoolwork. "Forgetfulness" becomes a game. The child sees the parents' pressure as a threat to his independence. More pressure brings more resistance. Poor grades become the child's best way to prove that he is independent of his parents and that he can't be pushed. Good evidence for this is the child who does worse in the areas where he receives the most help. If parental interference with a child's schoolwork continues for several years, the child becomes a school "underachiever."

HELPING YOUR CHILD REGAIN RESPONSIBILITY FOR SCHOOLWORK

Get Out of the Middle Regarding Homework. Clarify that completing and turning in homework is between your child and the teacher. Remember that the purpose of homework is to teach your child to work on his own. Don't ask your child if he has any. Don't help with homework except at your child's request. Allow the school to apply natural consequences for poor performance. Walk away from any power struggles. Your child can learn the lesson of schoolwork accountability only through personal experience. If possible, apologize to your youngster, saying, for example, "After thinking about it, we have decided you are old enough to manage your own

affairs. Schoolwork is your business and we will try to stay out of it. We are confident you will do what's best for you."

The result of this "sink or swim" approach is that arguments will stop, but your child's schoolwork may temporarily worsen. Your child may throw caution to the winds to see if you really mean what you have said. This period of doing nothing but waiting for your child to find her own reason for doing well in school may be very agonizing. However, children need to learn from their mistakes. If you can avoid "rescuing" your child, her grades will show a dramatic upsurge in anywhere from 2 to 9 months. This planned withdrawal of parental pressure is best done in the early grades, when marks are of minimal importance but the development of the child's own personal reason for learning is critical.

Avoid Reminders About Schoolwork. Repeatedly reminding your child about schoolwork promotes rebellion. So do criticizing, lecturing, and threatening your child. Pressure is different from parental interest and encouragement. If it works at all, it works only temporarily.

We can never force children to learn or to be productive. Learning is a process of self-fulfillment. It is an area that belongs to the child and one that we as parents should try to stay out of, despite our yearnings for our children's success.

Coordinate Your Plan with Your Child's Teacher. Schedule a parent-teacher conference. Discuss your views on schoolwork and homework responsibility. Tell your child's teacher that you want your child to be responsible to the teacher for homework. Clarify that you would prefer not to check or correct the work, because this has not been helpful in the past. Tell the teacher that you want to be supportive of the school and could do this best if she sent home a brief, weekly progress report. If the teacher thinks your youngster needs extra help, encourage her to suggest a tutoring program. In middle school, peer tutoring is often a powerful motivator.

Limit Television Until Schoolwork Improves. Although you can't make your child study, you can increase the potential study time. Eliminate all television and video game time on school nights. Explain to your child that these privileges will be reinstated after the teacher's weekly report confirms that all homework was handed in and the grades or overall quality of work is improving. Explain that you are doing this to help him better structure his time.

Consider Adding Incentives for Improved Schoolwork. Most children respond better to incentives than disincentives. Ask your youngster what he thinks would help. Some good incentives are taking your child to a favorite restaurant, amusement park, video arcade, sports event, or the movies. Sometimes earning "spending money" by working hard on studies will interest your child. The payments can be made weekly based on the

(Continued on the reverse side)

Instructions for Pediatric Patients by Barton D. Schmitt, M.D., *Pediatrician*
Adapted from YOUR CHILD'S HEALTH, Copyright © 1991 by Barton D. Schmitt, M.D.
Reprinted by permission of Bantam Books.

teacher's progress reports. As, Bs, and Cs can receive a different cash value. What your child buys with this money should be his business (for example, music or toys). Rewarding hard work is how the adult marketplace works.

Consider Removing Other Privileges for a Falloff in Schoolwork. You have already eliminated school-night television viewing because it obviously interferes with studying. If the school reports continue to be poor, you may need to eliminate all television and video games. Other privileges that may need to be temporarily limited should be those that matter to your child (for example, telephone, bike, outside play, or visiting friends). If your teenager drives a car, this privilege may need to be curtailed until his grades are at least a 3-point (B) average. For youngsters who have fallen behind in their work, grounding (that is, no peer contact) for 1 to 2 weeks may be required until they "catch up." Avoid severe punishment, however, because it will leave your youngster angry and resentful. Canceling something important (such as membership in Scouts or an athletic team) or taking away something they care about (such as a pet) because of poor marks is unfair and ineffective. Being part of a team is also good for motivation.

CALL YOUR CHILD'S TEACHER

For a conference if
—Your child's schoolwork and grades do not improve within 2 months.
—Homework is still an issue between you and your child after 2 months.
—You think your child has a learning problem that makes school difficult.

CALL OUR OFFICE

—If you think your child is preoccupied with some stresses in his life.
—If you think your child is depressed.
—If you have other questions or concerns.

NOTE: If these attempts to motivate your child fail, he may need an evaluation by a child psychologist or psychiatrist.

DEFINITION

Taking responsibility for schoolwork helps children grow up to be responsible adults who keep their promises, meet deadlines, and succeed at their jobs. Responsible children finish schoolwork, homework, and long-term projects on time. They remember their assignments and turn in papers. They occasionally ask for help (for example, with a spelling list) but usually like to think through their work by themselves.

HOW TO ENCOURAGE SCHOOLWORK RESPONSIBILITY

The following suggestions should help you cultivate the trait of responsibility in your child and avoid problems with schoolwork that may be difficult to correct later on.

Encourage Learning and Responsibility in the Preschool Years. Listen attentively to your child's conversation. Encourage him to think for himself. Take your child to the library and read to him regularly. Watch educational programs together and talk about them. Be a role model of someone who reads, finds learning exciting, enjoys problem solving, and likes to try new things. Ask your preschool child to help you with chores (for example, clearing the table or putting away clean clothes).

Show Your Child You Are Interested in His School Performance. Ask your child about his school day. Look at and comment positively on the graded papers your child brings home. Praise your child's strong points on his report card. Show interest in the books your child is reading. Help your child attend school regularly; don't keep him home for minor illnesses. Go to regular parent-teacher conferences and tell him about them. If you feel discouraged, rather than conveying this to your child, schedule an extra conference with his teacher.

Support the School Staff's Recommendations. Show respect for both the school system and the teacher, at least in your child's presence. Verbal attacks on the school may pit your child against the school and give him an excuse for not working. Even when you disagree with a school's policy, you should encourage your child to conform to school rules, just as he will need to conform to the broader rules of society.

Make It Clear That Schoolwork Is Between Your Child and the Teacher. When your child begins school she should understand that homework, schoolwork, and marks are strictly between her and her teacher. The teacher should set goals for better school performance, not the parents. Your child must feel responsible for successes and failures in school. People take more pride in accomplishments if they feel fully responsible for them. Parents who feel responsible for their child's school performance open the door for the child to turn his responsibilities over to them. Occasionally, elementary-school teachers may ask you to review basic facts with your child or see that your child completes work that was put off at school. When your child's teacher makes such requests, it's fine for you to help, but only as a temporary measure.

Stay Out of Homework. Asking if your child has homework, helping nightly, checking the finished homework, or drilling your child in areas of concern all convey to your child that you don't trust him. If you do your child's homework, your child will have less confidence that he can do it himself. If your child asks for help with homework, help with the particular problem only. Your help should focus on explaining the question, not on giving the answer. A good example of useful help is reading your child's spelling list to him while he writes the words, but then letting him check his own answers. A chief purpose of homework is to teach your child to work on his own.

Avoid Dictating a Study Time. Assigning a set time for your child to do homework is unnecessary and looked upon as pressure. The main thing parents can do is to provide a quiet setting with a desk, a comfortable chair, and good lighting. If any, the only rule should be "No television until homework is done." Accept your child's word that the work is done without checking. For long-term assignments, help your child organize his work the first few times if he seems overwhelmed. Help him estimate how many hours he thinks the project will take. Then help him write up a list of the days at home he will work on the project.

Provide Home Tutoring for Special Circumstances. Occasionally, a teacher will request parental assistance when a child has lots of makeup work following a prolonged absence or transfer to a new school. If your child's teacher makes such a request, ask her to send home notes about what he or she wants you to help your child with (for instance, multiplication for 2 weeks). By using this approach you are still not taking primary responsibility for your child's schoolwork because the assignments and request for help come from the teacher. Provide this home instruction in a positive, helping way. As soon as your child has met the teacher's goal for improvement, remove yourself from the role of tutor. In this way you have provided temporary tutoring to help your child over an obstacle that the school staff does not have time or resources to deal with fully.

Request Special Help for Children with Learning Problems. Some children have learning problems that interfere with learning some of the basic skills (for example, reading). The comments so far have assumed that your child has no learning limitations. If a child with a reading disability slips too far behind in class, the child may lose confidence in his ability to do schoolwork. If you have concerns about your child's ability to learn, set up a conference with your child's teacher. At that time, inquire about an evaluation by your school's special education team. With extra help, children with learning disabilities can preserve their self-esteem and sense of competency.

Instructions for Pediatric Patients by Barton D. Schmitt, M.D., *Pediatrician*
Adapted from YOUR CHILD'S HEALTH, Copyright © 1991 by Barton D. Schmitt, M.D.
Reprinted by permission of Bantam Books.

VIDEO GAMES

Home video games have swept the United States. Over 30% of American homes have a computerized game system hooked up to the television set. Over 500 different game cartridges are available. Video games are currently the most popular toy in the United States. Portable video games are the latest option. Every day more 6- to 16-year-olds become part of Nintendo mania.

VIDEO GAMES VERSUS TELEVISION

Compared to watching television, video games are a better form of entertainment. Video games are interactive. Your child's mind has to be turned on and working. The following are some potential benefits of the better games:
— Promote paying attention to details (for example, to clues), memory, sequencing, and planning strategies
— Promote eye-hand (visual motor) coordination
— Improve visual perception (spatial awareness)
— Encourage use of imagination

DISADVANTAGES OF VIDEO GAMES

The drawbacks of video games are similar to the ones we see with television:
— Video games can dominate your child's leisure and study time. Video games can eliminate time needed to develop competence in sports, music, or art. If reading and homework are displaced, school performance can be affected.
— Video games can be a solitary activity, reducing social interactions with family and friends. Your youngster can become a junior hermit, interacting with friends only to pump them for pieces of information about hidden passages or secret trapdoors. Encourage playing video games with other children.
— Violent video games can teach an acceptance of violent behavior in real life.
— Overall, realize that your child is overdosing on video games if his grades have fallen, he doesn't finish his homework, he gets inadequate sleep, he doesn't play outdoors, he has become a loner, or he is preoccupied with karate chops or other aggressive behavior that is part of one of his video games.

TAKE A STAND ON VIDEO GAMES

Don't expect your youngster to limit the time allocated to this mesmerizing form of entertainment. Given his own way, he might play Nintendo every waking moment. You are responsible for protecting your child from harm.

You must decide on rules that are appropriate for your child. If the rules are broken, the game (or control panel) needs to be put away for 1 or more days.

1. **Allow video games only after homework and chores are completed.** Access to video game time can even be presented as an incentive for finishing these tasks properly.

2. **Limit video game time.** Two hours each day or less is a reasonable goal. An alternative is to limit it to 1 hour on school nights and 2 or 3 hours per day on weekends. Some parents allow the system to be used only on weekends. If your child is doing poorly in school, temporarily eliminate video game time on school nights. Some parents have their children earn video game time by putting in equivalent time reading.

3. **Don't allow your child to postpone bedtime because he wants to finish a video game.** Remember that children who are allowed to stay up late are usually too tired the next day to remember what they are taught in school. Don't allow your child to have a video game set in her bedroom because this eliminates your control over the hours of play. When bedtime is drawing near, give your child a 10-minute warning.

4. **Encourage your children to settle their own disputes over using the video game.** When possible, stay out of disagreements, as long as they remain verbal. Children can't go through life having a referee to resolve their differences. If the agreement becomes too loud, remove the control panel until your children work out a schedule.

5. **Help your child buy video games that are not excessively violent.** Encourage him to buy or rent sports, puzzle, maze, or adventure games. Avoid games that contain lots of murder, combat, and destruction. Since your child is an active participant in the mayhem on video games, research suggests they have a greater impact on his aggressive behavior than violent televison shows, in which he is strictly an observer. If your child borrows a video cartridge from a friend, have a rule that you have to approve its contents before he uses it.

6. **If you own a computer, take advantage of some of the educational games.** These tap the motivational power of the arcade games to help your child learn. They combine academics and entertainment. They also teach computer skills. If you have a choice, buy computer games rather than video games.

7. **Try to channel your child's leisure time into a variety of activities.** Video games are not bad for children. They can teach skills. They are more educational than television. And, if you try to forbid video games, your child will play them at another child's home. So help your child learn to use them in moderation after the first weeks of normal infatuation have passed. Encourage more reading, music, hobbies, sports, and playing with friends.

Instructions for Pediatric Patients by Barton D. Schmitt, M.D., *Pediatrician*
Adapted from YOUR CHILD'S HEALTH, Copyright © 1991 by Barton D. Schmitt, M.D.
Reprinted by permission of Bantam Books.

Television has a tremendous influence on how children view our world. Many youngsters spend more hours watching television from birth to 18 years of age than they spend in the classroom. The positive aspects of television viewing include seeing different life-styles and cultures. Children today are entering school more knowledgeable than children before the era of television. In addition, television has great entertainment value. Although television can be a good teacher, many children watch it excessively and therefore experience some of the negative consequences described below.

HARMFUL ASPECTS OF TELEVISION

1. **Television displaces active types of recreation.** It decreases time spent playing with peers. A child has less time for self-directed daydreaming and thinking. It takes away time for participating in sports, music, art, or other activities that require practice to achieve competence.

2. **Television interferes with conversation and discussion time.** It reduces social interactions with family and friends.

3. **Television discourages reading.** Reading requires much more thinking than television. Reading improves a youngster's vocabulary. A decrease in reading scores may be related to too much time in front of the television.

4. **Heavy television viewing (more than 4 hours per day) definitely reduces school performance.** This much television interferes with study, reading, and thinking time. If children do not get enough sleep because they are watching television, they will not be alert enough to learn well on the following day.

5. **Television discourages exercise.** An inactive lifestyle leads to poor physical fitness. If accompanied by frequent snacking, watching television may contribute to weight problems.

6. **Television advertising encourages a demand for material possessions.** Young children will pressure their parents to buy the toys they see advertised. Television portrays materialism as the "American way."

7. **Television violence can affect how a child feels toward life and other people.** Viewing excessive violence may cause a child to be overly fearful about personal safety and the future. Television violence may numb the sympathy a child normally feels toward victims of human suffering. Young children may be more aggressive in their play after seeing violent television shows. Although television violence does not increase aggressive behavior toward people in most children, it may do so in disturbed or impulsive children.

PREVENTION OF TELEVISION ADDICTION

1. **Encourage active recreation.** Help your child become interested in sports, games, hobbies, and music. Occasionally turn off the television and take a walk or play a game with your child.

2. **Read to your children.** Begin reading to your child by 1 year of age and encourage him to read on his own as he becomes older. Some parents help children earn television or video game time by spending an equivalent time reading. Help your child improve his conversational skills by spending more of your time talking with him.

3. **Limit television time to 2 hours per day or less.** An alternative is to limit television to 1 hour on school nights and 2 or 3 hours per day on weekends. You occasionally may want to allow extra viewing time for special educational programs.

4. **Don't use television as a distraction or a babysitter for preschool children.** Preschoolers' viewing should be limited to special television shows and videotapes that are produced for young children. Because the difference between fantasy and reality is not clear for this age group, regular television shows may cause fears.

5. **If your child is doing poorly in school, limit television time to ½ hour each day.** Make a rule that homework and chores must be finished before television is watched. If your child's favorite show is on before he can watch, try to record it for later viewing.

6. **Set a bedtime for your child that is not altered by television shows that interest your child.** Children who are allowed to stay up late to watch television are usually too tired the following day to remember what they are taught in school. By all means, don't permit your child to have a television set in her bedroom because this eliminates your control over television viewing.

7. **Turn off the television set during meals.** Family time is too precious to be squandered on television shows. In addition, don't have the television always on as a background sound in your house. If you don't like a quiet house, try to listen to music without lyrics.

8. **Teach critical viewing.** Turn the television on only for specific programs. Don't turn it on at random and scan for something interesting. Teach your child to look first in the program guide.

9. **Teach your child to turn off the television set at the end of a show.** If the television stays on, your child will probably become interested in the following show and then it will be more difficult for your child to stop watching.

10. **Encourage your child to watch some shows that are educational or teach human values.** Encourage watching documentaries or real-life dramas. Use programs about love, sex, family disputes, drinking, and drugs as a way to begin family discussions on these difficult topics.

11. **Forbid violent television shows.** This means you have to know what your child is watching and turn off the television set when you don't approve of the program. Develop separate lists of programs that are acceptable for older and younger kids to watch. Make your older children responsible for keeping the younger ones out of the television room at these times. If not, the show is turned off. The availability of cable television and video-

(Continued on the reverse side)

Instructions for Pediatric Patients by Barton D. Schmitt, M.D., *Pediatrician*
Adapted from YOUR CHILD'S HEALTH, Copyright © 1991 by Barton D. Schmitt, M.D.
Reprinted by permission of Bantam Books.

TELEVISION: REDUCING THE NEGATIVE IMPACT

Continued

cassette recorders means that any child of any age has access to the uncut versions of R-rated films. Many children under 13 years of age develop daytime fears and nightmares because they have been allowed to watch such vicious movies.

12.   **Discuss the consequences of violence if you allow your older child to watch violent shows.** Point out how violence hurts both the victim and the victim's family. Be sure to discuss any program that upsets your child.

13.   **Discuss commercials with your children.** Help them identify high-pressure selling and exaggerated claims. If your child wants a toy that is a look-alike version of a television character, ask how he or she would use the toy at home. The response will probably convince you that the toy will be added to a collection rather than become a catalyst for active play.

14.   **Discuss the differences between reality and make-believe.** This type of clarification can help your child enjoy a show and yet realize that what is happening may not happen in real life.

15.   **Set a good example.** If you watch a lot of television, you can be sure your child will also. The types of programs you watch also send a clear message to your child.

Instructions for Pediatric Patients by Barton D. Schmitt, M.D., *Pediatrician*   © 1992 by W. B. Saunders Company
Adapted from YOUR CHILD'S HEALTH, Copyright © 1991 by Barton D. Schmitt, M.D.
Reprinted by permission of Bantam Books.

The following symptoms have all been reported in children after watching violent R-rated movies:
—Bedtime fears
—Recurrent nightmares
—Daytime flashbacks of something frightening
—Disruption of concentration and study
—A fearful view of the world

Since these movies were made to frighten teenagers and adults, this information should come as no surprise to you. Frequent exposures to violent material can also cause a child to become insensitive to human suffering. The impact of these movies on disturbed children may go a step further; some of them try to imitate the movies.

Causes

Most bad reactions are to R-rated movies containing horror, graphic violence, or sexual violence. The content of violent movies has changed over the last 10 years. Mutilation is the message. Thanks to improved special effects, we can now see the details of torture or brutality in slow, agonizing close-up. Recent movies show a head being chopped off, a brain being blown up, the disfigurement of a face with a knife, a neck being slashed, or a hypodermic needle being plunged into an eyeball.

The 12 year and under age group is most at risk for severe reactions. Most elementary-school children don't have the adult defense mechanisms needed to cope with these movies. They are most threatened by movie villains who seem real and play on their deepest fears (for example, surprise attack, kidnapping, torture, or death). They are especially vulnerable if they identify with the victim in the movie. Some of these mad slashers (unlike real people) are portrayed as indestructible and leave the young viewer feeling helpless. Children younger than 7 or 8 years old also think concretely. If it can happen on the screen, it could happen to them tonight.

Access to these violent movies has also changed. The uncut versions of violent movies are now readily available through cable television and video rentals. Parents say, "I didn't know she was watching that. I can't keep track of everything she sees." A popular party game in middle school involves renting a horror movie and seeing how much of it your friends can watch before becoming ill.

Most of the research done on the impact of violence on children has used television violence. This research shows that television affects children's behavior. No research review committee will ever approve a study in which children are exposed to R-rated movies. You don't have to be a psychiatrist to know that viewing graphic violence in movies (which is much more powerful than anything on television) is harmful to children. Yet some parents allow it.

Expected Course

Without treatment, these fears and preoccupations can last 1 to 6 months. With treatment, they usually improve over a few weeks.

PROTECTING YOUR CHILD FROM MOVIE VIOLENCE

Understand the Movie Rating System. Don't lump all R-rated movies together. The R rating means that children under 17 years old are not admitted without a parent. It is given for nudity, profanity, violence, *or* a combination of the above. Nudity, depending on the context, may be harmless. Profanity in the movies has contributed to the common use of profanity on elementary-school playgrounds, and this trend is probably irreversible. It is the violence in the movie that has the disturbing impact on children. In fact, if one reads the ratings carefully, the degree of violence is also often listed (for example, "graphic" violence or rape).

Forbid All R-rated Movies Before 13 Years of Age. Never allow a child who is younger than 13 years of age to see any R-rated film, no matter how liberal you may be about nudity and profanity. Between 13 and 17 years the maturity and sensitivity of your child must be carefully considered in deciding when he is ready to deal with some of these movies. Don't allow your child to see movies with personal or sexual violence (graphic violence) before 17 years of age. These movies are not a required part of life experiences at any age.

Select Your Child's Movies. Don't let your child see a movie unless you know the rating and have read a review. Don't give in to their pressure to see something that is potentially harmful (that's an adult decision). Keep a list of movies of which you approve. Look at the reviews of Colleen Harty, who is a PTA-sanctioned movie reviewer. She reviews films through the eyes of a parent and has a unique rating system that describes various aspects of the content of the movie, including cruelty to animals.

Monitor What Your Child Is Watching on Cable and Network Television. Don't allow him to turn on the cable movie channel unless he has your permission to view a specific program. Even some of the edited versions of movies on network television can be too frightening for young children. Don't let your younger children watch the programs that you have approved only for your older children (including the evening news). Young children who have viewed fires, tornadoes, earthquakes, warfare, or terrorism on the news have become worried about their personal safety.

Warn Your Child About Violent Movies Outside the Home. Protect your youngster from being unintentionally victimized by film violence. Be especially vigilant about slumber parties or Halloween parties. Tell your child to call you if the family he is visiting or a babysitter is showing any scary movies. Teach him to walk out of movies that make him scared or upset. Warn him to obey theater policies and not to sneak into R-rated movies.

(Continued on the reverse side)

Instructions for Pediatric Patients by Barton D. Schmitt, M.D., *Pediatrician*
Adapted from YOUR CHILD'S HEALTH, Copyright © 1991 by Barton D. Schmitt, M.D.
Reprinted by permission of Bantam Books.

R-RATED MOVIES: PROTECTING OUR CHILDREN
Continued

Discuss Any Movie That Upsets Your Child. Respect your child's fears. Don't make fun of them. Help him talk about what scared him. Help him gradually come to grips with the situation.

Practice Prevention. Protect your child's mental health from unnecessary fears. R-rated movies are never harmless for children in elementary school. Use the movie ratings and your common sense to choose age-appropriate movies for your child. Never let your child see anything that frightens you.

Instructions for Pediatric Patients by Barton D. Schmitt, M.D., *Pediatrician*
Adapted from YOUR CHILD'S HEALTH, Copyright © 1991 by Barton D. Schmitt, M.D.
Reprinted by permission of Bantam Books.

HELPING YOUR CHILD COPE WITH DIVORCE

More than 1 million children are affected by divorce each year. Our primary goal should be to minimize the emotional harm to these children. The main way to achieve this is to help the children maintain a close and secure relationship with both parents. The following recommendations may be helpful.

1. **Reassure your children that both parents love them.** Make it clear that, although you are unhappy with each other and disagree about many things, the one subject you both completely agree on is how much you love your children. Demonstrate this love by spending time with your children. Preschoolers especially need lots of cuddling from both parents, but don't start bad habits like letting your child sleep with you.

2. **Keep constant as many aspects of your child's world as you can.** Try to keep your child in the same home or neighborhood. The fewer the changes, the better your child will cope with the stress of divorce. If this is impossible, at least try to keep your child in the same school with the same teachers, friends, and teams, even if only temporarily. Reassure your child that although your standard of living will decrease somewhat, you will continue to have the basic necessities of living (that is, food, clothing, and shelter).

3. **Reassure your child that the noncustodial parent will visit.** Your child needs both parents. Young children are confused by divorce and fear that one parent may abandon them. Children need to know that they will have ongoing contact with both their father and their mother. Have a scheduled, predictable time for visiting. The custodial parent should strongly support the visiting schedule. One full day every 1 or 2 weeks is usually preferable to more frequent, brief (and rushed) visits. Try not to do too much in one day. If there is more than one child, all should spend equal time or the same time with the noncustodial parent to prevent feelings of favoritism. Your child will eagerly look forward to the visits, so the visiting parent must keep promises, be punctual, and remember birthdays and other special events. Both parents should work to make these visits pleasant. Allow your child to tell you he had a good time during the visit with your exspouse.

Provide your children with the telephone number of the noncustodial parent and encourage them to call at regular intervals. If the noncustodial parent has moved to a distant city, telephone calls and letters become essential to the ongoing relationship.

4. **If the noncustodial parent becomes uninvolved, find substitutes.** Ask relatives or Big Brother or Big Sister volunteers to spend time with your son or daughter. Explain to your child, "Your dad [or mom] is not capable right now of being available for you. He [she] is sorting out his [her] own problems. There's not much we can do to change that." Help your child talk about disap-

pointment and the sense of loss. If your child is a teenager, writing and calling the absent parent may eventually reengage him or her.

5. **Help your child talk about painful feelings.** At the time of separation and divorce, many children become anxious, depressed, and angry. They are frequently on the brink of tears, sleep poorly, have stomachaches, or don't do as well in school. To help your children get over these painful feelings, encourage them to talk about their feelings and respond with understanding and support. A divorce discussion group at school can help children feel less isolated and ashamed.

When anger turns into disruptive behavior, limits must be imposed while you help your child put the anger into words. Books about other children of divorce who deal with feelings of loss but ultimately emerge stronger can provide reassurance.

6. **Make sure that your children understand that they are not responsible for the divorce.** Children often feel guilty, believing that they somehow caused the divorce. Your children need reassurance that they did not in any way cause the divorce.

7. **Clarify that the divorce is final.** Some children hold on to the hope that they can somehow reunite the parents, and they pretend that the separation is temporary. Making it clear to children that the divorce is final can help them mourn their loss and move on to a more realistic adjustment to the divorce.

8. **Try to protect your child's positive feelings about both parents.** Try to mention the good points about the other parent. Don't be overly honest about negative feelings you have toward your exspouse. (You need to unload these feelings with another adult, not your children.) Devaluing or discrediting the other parent in your child's presence can reduce your child's personal self-esteem and create greater stress.

Don't ask your child to take sides. A child does not need to have a single loyalty to one parent. Your child should be able to love both of you, even though you don't love each other.

9. **Maintain normal discipline in both households.** Children need consistent child-rearing practices. Overindulgence or too much leniency by either parent can make it more difficult for the other parent to get the child to behave. Constant competition for a child's love through special privileges or gifts leads to a spoiled child. The general ground rules regarding discipline should be set by the custodial parent.

10. **Don't argue with your ex-spouse about your child in the child's presence.** Children are quite upset by seeing their parents fight. Most important, avoid any arguments regarding visiting, custody, or child support in your child's presence.

11. **Try to avoid custody disputes.** Your child badly needs a sense of stability. Challenge custody only if the custodial parent is causing obvious harm or repeated distress to your child. False accusations of physical or sexual abuse cause great emotional anguish for the child.

(Continued on the reverse side)

Instructions for Pediatric Patients by Barton D. Schmitt, M.D., *Pediatrician*
Adapted from YOUR CHILD'S HEALTH, Copyright © 1991 by Barton D. Schmitt, M.D.
Reprinted by permission of Bantam Books.

© 1992 by W. B. Saunders Company

DIVORCE: ITS IMPACT ON CHILDREN *Continued*

If possible, don't split siblings unless they are adolescents and state a clear preference for living in a different setting.

 CALL OUR OFFICE

During regular hours if
—Your child has symptoms that interfere with school-work, eating, or sleeping for more than 2 weeks.

—You feel your child is depressed.
—Your child has any physical symptoms from the divorce that last for more than 6 months.
—Your child continues to believe that the parents will come back together again, even though over a year has passed since the divorce.
—You feel the other parent is harming your child.
—Your child refuses visits with the noncustodial parent.

Instructions for Pediatric Patients by Barton D. Schmitt, M.D., *Pediatrician*
Adapted from YOUR CHILD'S HEALTH, Copyright © 1991 by Barton D. Schmitt, M.D.
Reprinted by permission of Bantam Books.

DEFINITION

The main task of adolescents in our culture is to become psychologically emancipated from their parents. The teenager must cast aside the dependent relationship of childhood. Before he can develop a new adult relationship with his parents, the adolescent must first distance himself from the way he related to them in the past. This process is characterized by a certain amount of intermittent normal rebellion, defiance, discontent, turmoil, restlessness, and ambivalence. Emotions usually run high. Mood swings are common. Under the best of circumstances, this adolescent rebellion continues for approximately 2 years; not uncommonly it lasts for 4 to 6 years.

DEALING WITH NORMAL ADOLESCENT REBELLION

The following guidelines may help you and your teenager through this difficult period.

Treat Your Teenager as an Adult Friend. By the time your child is 12 years old, start working on developing the kind of relationship you would like to have with your child when she is an adult. Treat your child the way you would like her to treat you when she is an adult. Your goal is mutual respect, support, and the ability to have fun together. Strive for relaxed, casual conversations during bicycling, hiking, shopping, playing catch, driving, cooking, and working and especially at mealtimes. Use praise and trust to help build her self-esteem. Recognize and validate your child's feelings by listening carefully and making nonjudgmental comments. Remember that listening doesn't mean you have to solve your teen's problems. The friendship model is the best basis for family functioning.

Avoid Criticism About "No-win" Topics. Most negative parent-adolescent relationships develop because the parents criticize their teenager too much. Much of the teen's objectionable behavior merely reflects conformity with the current tastes of his peer group. Peer-group immersion is one of the essential stages of adolescent development. Dressing, talking, and acting differently than adults help your child to feel independent from you.

Try to avoid any criticism of your child's clothing, hairstyle, makeup, music, dance steps, friends (unless they're in trouble with the law), recreational interests, room decorations, use of free time, career choices, use of money, speech, posture, religion, and philosophy. Allowing your teen to rebel in these minor areas often prevents testing in major areas, such as experimentation with drugs, truancy, or stealing. Intervene and try to make a change only if your teenager's behavior is harmful or infringes on your rights (see section on house rules). Another common error is to criticize your teen's mood or attitude. A negative or lazy attitude can only be changed through good example and praise. The more you talk about these nontraditional behaviors, the longer they will last.

Let Society's Rules and Consequences Teach Responsibility Outside the Home. Your teenager must learn from trial and error. As she experiments, she will learn to take responsibility for her decisions and actions. The parent should speak up only if the adolescent is going to do something dangerous or illegal. Otherwise, the parent must rely on the teen's own self-discipline, pressure from her peers to behave responsibly, and the lessons learned from the consequences of her actions.

City curfew laws will help control late hours. A school's requirement for punctual school attendance will influence when your teen goes to bed at night. If he has trouble getting up in the morning, buy him an alarm clock. School grades will usually hold your teenager accountable for homework and other aspects of school performance. (It's not your job to check the homework.) If your teen has bad work habits, she will lose her job. If your teenager makes a poor choice of friends, she may find her confidences broken or that she gets into trouble. If she doesn't practice hard for a sport, she will be pressured by the team and coach to do better. If she misspends her allowance or earnings, she will run out of money before the end of the month. If her mood or attitude is negative, she will lose friends.

If by chance your teenager asks you for advice about outside activities, try to describe the pros and cons in a brief, impartial way. Ask some questions to help her think about the main risks. Then wrap up your remarks with a comment such as, "Do what you think is best." Teenagers need plenty of opportunities to learn from their own mistakes before they leave home and have to solve problems without an ever-present support system.

Clarify the House Rules and Consequences. You have the right and the responsibility to make rules regarding your house and other possessions. Written rules cut down on misunderstandings. A teenager's preferences can be tolerated within his own room but they need not be imposed on the rest of the house. You can forbid loud music or incoming telephone calls after 10:00 PM that interfere with other people's concentration or sleep. You can forbid a television set in his room. While you should make your teen's friends feel welcome in your home, clarify the ground rules about parties or where snacks can be eaten. Your teen can be placed in charge of cleaning his room, washing his clothes, and ironing his clothes. You can insist on clean clothes and enough showers to prevent or overcome body odor. You must decide whether you will loan him your car, bicycle, camera, radio, television, clothes, and other possessions.

Reasonable consequences for breaking house rules include loss of telephone, television, stereo, and car privileges. (Time-out is rarely useful in this age group, and physical punishment can escalate to a serious breakdown in your relationship.) If your teenager breaks something, he should repair it, pay for its repair or replacement, or work for you until the debt is paid off. If he makes a

(Continued on the reverse side)

Instructions for Pediatric Patients by Barton D. Schmitt, M.D., *Pediatrician*
Adapted from YOUR CHILD'S HEALTH, Copyright © 1991 by Barton D. Schmitt, M.D.
Reprinted by permission of Bantam Books.

mess, he should clean it up. If your teen is doing poorly in school, you can restrict television time. You can also put a limit on telephone privileges and weeknights out. If your teen stays out too late or doesn't call you when he's delayed, you can ground him for a day or a weekend. In general, grounding for more than a few days is looked on as unfair and is hard to enforce.

Use Family Conferences for Negotiating House Rules. Some families find it helpful to have a brief meeting after dinner once each week. At this time your teenager can ask for changes in the house rules or bring up family issues that are causing problems. You can also bring up issues (such as your teen's demand to drive her too many places and your need for her help in arranging carpools). The family unit often functions better if the decision making is democratic. The objective of negotiation should be that both parties win. The atmosphere can be one of: "Nobody is at fault, but we have a problem. How can we solve it?"

Give Space to a Teenager Who Is in a Bad Mood. Generally when your teenager is in a bad mood, he won't want to talk about it with you. If teenagers want to discuss a problem with anybody, it is usually with a close friend. In general, it is advisable at such times to give your teen lots of space and privacy. This is a poor time to talk to your teenager about anything, pleasant or otherwise.

Use "I" Messages for Rudeness. Some talking back is normal. We want our teenagers to express their anger through talking and to challenge our opinions in a logical way. We need to listen. Expect your teenager to present his case passionately, even unreasonably. Let the small stuff go, it's only words. But don't accept disrespectful remarks, such as calling you a "jerk." Unlike a negative attitude, these mean remarks should not be ignored. You can respond with a comment like, "It really hurts me when you put me down or don't answer my question." Make your statement in as nonangry a way as possible. If your adolescent continues to make angry, unpleasant remarks, leave the room. Don't get into a shouting match with your teenager because this is not a type of behavior that is acceptable in outside relationships. What you are trying to teach is that everyone has the right to disagree and even to express anger but that screaming and rude conversation are not allowed in your house. You can prevent some rude behavior by being a role model of politeness, constructive disagreement, and the ability to apologize.

CALL OUR OFFICE

During regular hours if
— You think your teenager is depressed, suicidal, drinking, using illegal drugs, or going to run away.
— Your teenager is taking undue risks (for example, reckless driving or unsafe sex).
— Your teenager has no close friends.
— Your teenager's school performance is declining markedly.
— Your teenager is skipping school frequently.
— Your teenager's outbursts of temper are destructive or violent.
— You feel your teenager's rebellion is excessive.
— Your family life is seriously disrupted by your teenager.
— You find yourself escalating the criticism and punishment.
— Your relationship with your teenager does not improve within 3 months after you begin using these approaches.
— You have other questions or concerns.

RECOMMENDED READING

Peter H. Buntman and E. M. Saris: How to Live with Your Teenager. Ballantine Books, N.Y., 1982.
Lois Davitz and Joel Davitz: How to Live (Almost) Happily with a Teenager. Signet, N.Y., 1983.
Don Dinkmeyer and Gary D. McKay: Parenting Teenagers. American Guidance Service, Circle Pines, Minn., 1990.
Kathleen McCoy and Charles Wibbelsman: Crisis-proof Your Teenager. Bantam Books, New York, 1991.

Instructions for Pediatric Patients by Barton D. Schmitt, M.D., *Pediatrician*   © 1992 by W. B. Saunders Company
Adapted from YOUR CHILD'S HEALTH, Copyright © 1991 by Barton D. Schmitt, M.D.
Reprinted by permission of Bantam Books.

DEFINITION

"Enuresis" is the term used for the involuntary passage of urine during sleep. It is a very common problem affecting 40% of 3-year-olds, 10% of 6-year-olds, and 3% of 12-year-olds. We consider it normal until at least 6 years of age.

Causes

Most of these children have inherited small bladders, which cannot hold all the urine produced in a night. In addition, they don't awaken to the signal of a full bladder. The kidneys are normal. Physical causes are very rare, and your physician can easily detect them. Emotional problems do not cause enuresis, but they can occur if it is mishandled.

Expected Course

Most children who wet the bed overcome the problem between 6 and 10 years of age. Even without treatment, all children eventually get over it. Therefore, treatments that might have harmful complications should not be used. On the other hand, treatments without side effects can be started as soon as your child has achieved complete daytime bladder control for 6 to 12 months.

HOME CARE FOR A CHILD OF ANY AGE WHO IS WETTING THE BED

Encourage Your Child to Get Up to Urinate During the Night. This advice is more important than any other. Tell your child at bedtime, "Try to get up when you have to pee." Leaving a light on in the bathroom may help. Some preschoolers prefer to use a potty chair left next to the bed.

Encourage Postponing Urination. Encourage your child to urinate infrequently during the daytime. If your child urinates often, sometimes encourage him to wait, but don't make an issue of it. Don't remind him to use the bathroom except at bedtime.

Encourage Daytime Fluids. Encourage fluid during the morning and early afternoon. The more fluids your child drinks, the more urine your child will produce, and more urine leads to larger bladders.

Discourage Evening Fluids. Discourage your child from drinking more than 2 ounces during the 2 hours before bedtime. Give gentle reminders about this, but don't worry about a few extra swallows of water.

Protect the Bed from Urine. Your child should wear extra thick underwear in addition to his pajamas. This keeps much of the urine from getting through to the sheets. Diapers or plastic pants should no longer be used by 4 years of age. Odor becomes a problem if urine soaks into the mattress or blankets. Protect the mattress with a plastic mattress cover.

Establish a Morning Routine for Wet Pajamas and Wet Bedding. On wet mornings your child can rinse his pajamas and underwear in the sink until the odor is gone. If your child smells of urine, he will need to take a quick rinse in the shower so he won't be teased at school. You can cut down on the laundry by placing a dry towel under your child's bottom each night. This can be rinsed each morning and saved until you do your wash. If a wet bed is left open to the air, the wet sheets will usually be dry by noon. Because of odor, the sheets may need to be washed a few extra times each week.

Respond Positively to Dry Nights. Praise your child on mornings when he wakes up dry. A calendar with gold stars or "happy faces" for dry nights may also help.

Respond Gently to Wet Nights. Your child does not like being wet. Most bed-wetters feel quite guilty and embarrassed about this problem. They need sympathy, not blame or punishment. Siblings should not be allowed to tease bed-wetters. Punishment or pressure will delay a cure and cause secondary emotional problems.

ADDITIONAL HOME CARE WHEN YOUR CHILD REACHES 6 YEARS OF AGE

Follow the previous recommendations in addition to the guidelines given below:

Self-awakening Program for Children with Small Bladders. Children with small bladders cannot stay dry unless they get up to urinate one or more times every night. Make sure your child understands this. His goal should be getting up, not holding his urine until morning. Getting up can keep a person dry regardless of how small the bladder is or how much fluid he drinks. To help your child learn to awaken himself at night, encourage him to practice the following pep talk at bedtime.
—Lie on your bed with your eyes closed.
—Pretend it's the middle of the night.
—Pretend your bladder is full.
—Pretend it's starting to hurt.
—Pretend it's trying to wake you up.
—Pretend it's saying: "Get up before it's too late."
—Then run to the bathroom and empty your bladder.
—Remind yourself to get up like this during the night.

Encourage Changing Wet Clothes During the Night. If your child wets at night, he should try to get up and change himself. First, if your child feels any urine leaking out, he should try to stop the flow of urine. Second, he should hurry to the toilet to see if he has any urine left in his bladder. Third, he should change himself and put a dry towel over the wet part of the bed. This step can be made easier if dry pajamas and towels are always kept on a chair near the bed. The child who shows the motivation to carry out these steps is close to being able to awaken from the sensation of a full bladder.

Determine the Capacity (Size) of Your Child's Bladder. Do this by having your child hold his urine as long as possible on at least three occasions. Each time have

(Continued on the reverse side)

Instructions for Pediatric Patients by Barton D. Schmitt, M.D., *Pediatrician*
Adapted from YOUR CHILD'S HEALTH, Copyright © 1991 by Barton D. Schmitt, M.D.
Reprinted by permission of Bantam Books.

your child urinate into a container. Measure the amount of urine in ounces. The largest of the three measurements can be considered your child's bladder capacity. The normal capacity is 1 or more ounces per year of age. In a 6-year-old, a capacity of 5 ounces or less is small; a capacity of 6 to 8 ounces is normal and means that the bladder can hold a night's urine production until morning. Normal adult bladder size is 14 to 16 ounces.

Encourage Bladder-stretching Exercises. These can gradually enlarge the size of the bladder so that it can hold more urine at night. Just as importantly, waiting 10 to 15 minutes during the day can help the bladder wait at night until your child can get out of deep sleep and wake up. To stretch the bladder, encourage your child to hold his urine as long as possible during the daytime. Whenever your child feels the urge to go, he can try to distract himself for the 10 seconds or so it takes for the bladder spasms to stop. Learning to resist the first urge to urinate is especially important. At least once each day, have your child urinate into a measuring cup to see if he has maintained or even beaten his previous record (in ounces). Mark the highest volume achieved with a piece of masking tape on the cup. These exercises should be introduced only if your child wants to try them; for some children this won't occur before 8 years of age.

Help Your Child Assume Responsibility. Your child should feel responsible for solving this problem. The bladder exercises, self-awakening program, control of fluid intake, and record keeping need your child's involvement and commitment. By all means, don't try to awaken your child at night. As long as you are doing it, your child is less likely to do it for himself. Your child should look on his parents and physician as people who can provide suggestions and support but who do not take responsibility for the bed-wetting.

ADDITIONAL INTERVENTION WHEN YOUR CHILD REACHES 8 YEARS OF AGE

Follow the previous recommendations. Talk with us about possibly using alarms or drugs as well, as described below:

Bed-wetting Alarms

Alarms are used to teach a child to awaken when he needs to urinate during the night. They have the highest cure rate (about 70%) of any available approach. They are the treatment of choice for any bed-wetter with a small bladder who can't otherwise train himself to awaken at night. The new transistorized alarms are small,

lightweight, sensitive to a few drops of urine, not too expensive (about $50), and easy for a child to set up by himself. Children using alarms still need to work on the self-awakening program. Request the special instruction sheet on bed-wetting alarms.

Alarm Clock

If your child is unable to awaken himself at night and you can't afford a bed-wetting alarm, teach him to use an alarm clock or clock radio. Set it for 3 or 4 hours after your child goes to bed. Put it beyond arm's reach. Encourage your child to practice responding to the alarm during the day while lying on the bed with eyes closed. Have your child set the alarm each night. Praise your child for getting up at night, even if he isn't dry in the morning.

Drugs

Most bed-wetters need extra help with staying dry during slumber parties, camping trips, vacations, or other overnight stays. Some take an alarm clock with them and stay dry by awakening once at night. Some are helped by temporarily taking a drug at bedtime. One drug (given by nasal spray) decreases urine production at night and is quite safe. Another older drug (taken as a pill) temporarily increases bladder capacity. It is safe at the correct dosage but dangerous if too much is taken or a younger sibling gets into it. If you do use a drug, be careful about the amount you use and where you store the drug, and be sure to keep the safety cap on the bottle. The drawback of these medicines is that when they are stopped, the bed-wetting usually returns. They do not cure bed-wetting. Therefore children on drugs for enuresis should also be using an alarm and learning to get up at night.

 ## CALL OUR OFFICE

During regular hours if
—Urination causes pain or burning.
—The urine stream is weak or dribbly.
—Your child also has daytime wetting.
—Your child also drinks excessive fluids.
—Bed-wetting is a new problem (your child used to be dry).
—Your child is over 12 years old.
—Your child is over 6 years of age and is not better after 3 months using this treatment program.

 Instructions for Pediatric Patients by Barton D. Schmitt, M.D., *Pediatrician*
Adapted from YOUR CHILD'S HEALTH, Copyright © 1991 by Barton D. Schmitt, M.D.
Reprinted by permission of Bantam Books.

DIRECTIONS FOR YOUR YOUNGSTER ON USING A BED-WETTING ALARM

1. This is your alarm. It can help you cure your bed-wetting only if you use it correctly. Remember, the main purpose of the alarm is to help you get up during the night and use the toilet. The alarm won't work unless you listen for it carefully and respond to it quickly. Better yet, get up *before* the alarm goes off.

2. Hook up the alarm system by yourself. Trigger the buzzer a few times by touching the moisture sensors with a wet finger and practice going to the bathroom as you will do if it goes off during the night.

3. Have a night-light or flashlight near your bed so it will be easy to see what you are doing when the alarm sounds. Turn on the night-light.

4. Go through your self-awakening pep talk at bedtime. Try to "beat the buzzer." Wake up when your bladder feels full but before any urine leaks out. If the buzzer does go off, try to wake up and stop urinating at the first moment that you think you hear the alarm (even if you think you are hearing it in a dream).

5. As soon as you hear the alarm, jump out of bed and stand up. After you are standing and awake, turn off the buzzer by removing the metal strip from the little pocket in your underwear (if you have a Wet-Stop) or disconnect the clips (if you have a Nytone) and dry them off.

6. Hurry to the bathroom. Empty your bladder to see how much urine you were able to hold back.

7. Put on dry underwear and pajamas, and reconnect the alarm. Put a dry towel over the wet spot on your bed. Remind yourself to get up before the alarm buzzes next time and review your plan.

8. In the morning, write on your calendar "dry" (no alarm), "wet spot" (you got up after the alarm went off), or "wet" (you didn't get up).

9. Use the alarm every night until you go 3 or 4 weeks without bed-wetting. This usually takes 2 to 3 months, so try to be persistent.

A SELF-AWAKENING PROGRAM FOR YOUR YOUNGSTER

While using the alarm, it's very important that you also practice the following self-awakening program at bedtime. You are trying to teach yourself to awaken during the night and use the toilet when your bladder feels full. Until you learn how to do this, you won't be dry.

—Lie on your bed with your eyes closed.
—Pretend it's the middle of the night.
—Pretend your bladder is full.
—Pretend it's starting to hurt.
—Pretend it's trying to wake you up.
—Pretend it's saying: "Get up before it's too late."
—Then run to the bathroom and empty your bladder.
—Remind yourself to get up like this during the night.

PARENTS' ROLE WITH BED-WETTING ALARMS

If your child doesn't awaken immediately to the sound of the buzzer, he needs your help. You may need to be involved every night for the first 2 to 3 weeks.

1. Go to your child's room as quickly as you can. Turn on the light and say loudly, "Get out of bed and stand up."

2. If that doesn't work, get your child to a sitting position and run a cold washcloth over his face to bring him out of his deep sleep.

3. Only after your child is standing, remind him to turn off the alarm. By all means, don't turn off the buzzer for him. Your child has to learn to carry out this step for himself.

4. Make sure your child is wide awake and walks into the bathroom before you leave him. If necessary, ask him questions to help awaken him.

5. Your goal is to help your child awaken immediately and get out of bed when the buzzer goes off. Phase out of your child's alarm program as soon as possible. Going to bed with the radio *off*, going to bed at a reasonable hour, and using a night-light can help your child respond faster to the alarm.

HOW TO ORDER ENURESIS ALARMS

Alarms and information can be ordered from

Nytone Alarm: Nytone Medical Products, 2424 South 900 West, Salt Lake City, UT 84119 or call 801-973-4090

Nite Train'r Alarm: Koregon Enterprises, 9735 S.W. Sunshine Court, Beaverton, OR 97005 or call 800-544-4240

Wet-Stop Alarm: Palco Laboratories, 8030 Soquel Ave., Santa Cruz, CA 95062 or call 800-346-4488

These alarms may be covered by health insurance if your physician has written a prescription for one.

Instructions for Pediatric Patients by Barton D. Schmitt, M.D., *Pediatrician*
Adapted from YOUR CHILD'S HEALTH, Copyright © 1991 by Barton D. Schmitt, M.D.
Reprinted by permission of Bantam Books.

INDEX

Another book by the same author that might interest you. . .

YOUR CHILD'S HEALTH

Revised Edition, Bantam Books, 1991

by Barton D. Schmitt, M.D., F.A.A.P.

Director of Consultative Services, The Children's Hospital of Denver
Professor of Pediatrics, University of Colorado School of Medicine

An Accurate, Peer-Reviewed Child Care Reference

- Over 300 major topics
- Newborn and Infant Care
- Common Illnesses and Injuries
- Guidelines for Calling the Physician

- 672 pages
- First Aid for Emergencies
- Behavior and School Problems
- Preventive Pediatrics

Advantages of Recommending this Book to Parents in Your Practice

- Supplements your counseling and teaching
- Reduces unnecessary telephone calls that are "for information only"
- Clarifies for each topic when to call the physician
- Helps in training new office staff to provide safe pediatric advice
- It's still working, when you go home

Available in paperback at bookstores everywhere